## Praise for *Hitlerland*

One of Tina Brown's "Must-Reads"

—*NPR*

"I have never felt quite so horribly intimate with the Führer as I did when reading *Hitlerland* . . . history as vivid as it comes."

—Christopher Dickey, *Newsweek*

"Filled with fresh insight and riveting stories, this is an important addition to the recorded history of Hitler and the Third Reich. This is first rate reporting that captures and engages readers until the very last page."

—*Tucson Citizen*

"A compelling work for World War II history buffs or anyone who wants to understand how such devastating evil emerged while the world seemingly watched."

—*Library Journal*

"Andrew Nagorski, a deft storyteller, has plumbed the dispatches, diaries, letters, and interviews of American journalists, diplomats, and others who were present in Berlin to write a fascinating account of a fateful era."

—Henry Kissinger

"An engrossing study of the times made more fascinating and incredible in retrospect . . . contextually rich . . . [a] well marshaled study."

—*Kirkus Reviews*

"A distinguished correspondent, [Nagorski] makes these journalists the heroes of his book. . . . The eyewitnesses . . . were an impressively prolific group. . . . Most of them very quickly recognized the vicious character of Nazism."

—*The New York Review of Books*

"At times deliciously gossipy, at times thoroughly chilling, *Hitlerland* offers countless novel insights into Germany's evolution from struggling democracy in the 1920s to totalitarian dictatorship in the 1930s. The intimate portraits from Hitler down add an almost tangible sense of the foibles, ambitions, insecurities, and perversities of the relatively small top Nazi elite whose actions plunged our world into a catastrophe from which we are yet fully to recover. The Americans themselves come alive as a group of intense, enterprising journalists and diplomats faced with the greatest challenge of their lives."

—Misha Glenny, author of *The Balkans 1804–1999*

"Compulsively readable and deeply researched"

—*The Weekly Standard*

"*Hitlerland* conveys, often vividly, the difficulty Americans had coming to terms with Nazi terror. . . . Informative and interesting."

—*Minneapolis Star-Tribune*

"*Hitlerland* is a bit of a guilty pleasure. Reading about the Nazis is not supposed to be fun, but Nagorski manages to make it so. Readers new to this story will find [it] fascinating."

—*The Washington Post*

"A multidimensional view of the Austrian-born tyrant. The invaluable element of this character study of the enigmatic führer is the accumulative clout of the comments of famed American outsiders. . . . Nagorski's account is rich in anecdotal detail about how a man dismissed by many could hypnotize a nation and terrorize the world."

—*Publishers Weekly*

"The book contributes to our understanding of Germany and usefully augments our historical perspectives."

—*Jerusalem Post*

"Nagorski . . . has ingeniously stitched together the story of the diplomats, journalists, and other expatriates who worked in Germany during the two decades that ended with America's entry into World War II."

—*Columbia Journalism Review*

"A deft storyteller, Nagorski brings that history to life. . . . Nagorski opens up a window into an era that we thought we already knew and allows these Americans to tell their stories without passing judgment on their perceptiveness or the rectitude of their moral compasses clouded by the benefits of historical hindsight."

—*Jewish Book World*

"A clever way to tell a familiar story. . . . A well conceived, crafted, and executed story. Casual as well as informed World War II buffs will savor it."

—*History News Network*

"Andrew Nagorski's *Hitlerland* is a fresh, compelling portrait of Nazi Germany, as seen through the eyes of a fascinating array of Americans who lived and worked there during Hitler's rise to power. The extraordinary saga of Putzi Hanfstaengl, a Harvard graduate who became Hitler's court jester, is just one of the many page-turning stories that makes *Hitlerland* a book not to be missed."

—Lynne Olson, author of *Citizens of London*

"The rise of Hitler and the Nazi state, one of the most consequential and profound narratives in all of world politics, receives compelling new treatment in Andrew Nagorski's outstanding *Hitlerland*. By illuminating the disparate experiences of the era's preeminent American diplomats, journalists, intellectuals, and others, Nagorski has created an engrossing, harrowing, and vividly drawn mosaic of eyewitness accounts to one of history's most phenomenal catastrophes."

—Gordon M. Goldstein, author of *Lessons in Disaster: McGeorge Bundy and the Path to War in Vietnam*

# Hitler

ANDREW NAGORSKI

Simon & Schuster Paperbacks · New York  London  Toronto  Sydney  New Delhi

# land

*American Eyewitnesses
to the Nazi Rise to Power*

Simon & Schuster Paperbacks
A Division of Simon & Schuster, Inc.
1230 Avenue of the Americas
New York, NY 10020

First Simon & Schuster paperback edition March 2013

SIMON & SCHUSTER PAPERBACKS and colophon are registered trademarks
of Simon & Schuster, Inc.

For information about special discounts for bulk purchases,
please contact Simon & Schuster Special Sales at
1-866-506-1949 or business@simonandschuster.com.

The Simon & Schuster Speakers Bureau can bring authors
to your live event. For more information or to book an event,
contact the Simon & Schuster Speakers Bureau at
1-866-248-3049 or visit our website at www.simonspeakers.com.

Designed by Jill Putorti

Manufactured in the United States of America

10  9  8  7  6  5  4  3  2  1

The Library of Congress has cataloged the hardcover edition as follows:

Nagorski, Andrew.
    Hitlerland : American eyewitnesses to the Nazi rise to power / by Andrew Nagorski.—1st
Simon & Schuster hardcover ed.
        p.        cm.
    Includes bibliographical references and index.
1. Germany—Politics and government—1918–1933. 2. Germany—Politics and government—1933–1945. 3. Hitler, Adolf, 1889–1945. 4. Nazis—History. 5. Americans—Germany—Biography. 6. World War, 1939–1945—Personal narratives, American. 7. World War,
1939–1945—Social aspects—Germany. 8. Germany—Social conditions—1918–1933.
9. Germany—Social conditions—1933–1945. I. Title.
    DD253.N225 2011
    940.54'213—dc23                       2011017360
ISBN 978-1-4391-9100-2
ISBN 978-1-4391-9101-9 (pbk)
ISBN 978-1-4391-9102-6 (ebook)

Photo credits are on page 334.

*For the youngest generation,*
*Christina, Kaia, Maia, Charles, Sydney, Caye, and Stella,*
*And, as always,*
*For Krysia*

# Contents

# Introduction

Of all the Americans who reported from Germany between World War I and World War II, no one was quite as well prepared for the assignment as Sigrid Schultz. Born in Chicago in 1893 to parents who had come from Norway, she spent most of her youth, starting at age eight, in Europe. Her father was a successful portrait painter who made Paris his base, which meant Sigrid attended French schools. When he received an assignment to paint the portrait of the king and queen of Württemberg, she also attended German schools for several months, equipping her not only with the language but also with early insights into local attitudes.

"Few foreign painters were invited to German courts in those days and the other little girls tried to be nice," she recalled. "But it was clear that to be non-German was a deficiency. Any foreigner who failed to be dazzled and humbled by German Kultur or efficiency was, at best, an object of pity."

Schultz studied international law at the Sorbonne and then moved to Berlin with her parents. There, she witnessed World War I from the losing side. Once the United States entered the war in 1917, she and her parents had to report every day to the police as "enemy aliens," but she was able to continue her studies, taking courses at Berlin University. In the aftermath of that conflict, the *Chicago Tribune* hired her to work with its Berlin correspondent Richard Henry Little, who was impressed with her language skills. But from the moment she started her new job in early 1919, she demonstrated her reporting skills as well, teaming up with Little on assignments.

Together, Schultz and Little interviewed dozens of German officers to get a sense of their mood in the wake of Germany's defeat. Most were bitter, but none more so than "a sour, disagreeable little man in navy blue, whose name was Raeder," Schultz wrote. The German officer told the two reporters: "You Americans need not feel proud of yourselves. Within twenty-five years at the latest, your country and my country will be at war again. And this time we shall win, because we will be better prepared than you will be."

The Americans didn't take offense—quite the contrary. "I well remember how, on that day in 1919, we felt sorry for vengeful little Raeder," Schultz noted. "He was taking defeat so hard. He was, we felt, simply consuming himself with hatred."

Schultz became the *Chicago Tribune*'s chief correspondent for Central Europe in 1926, and she remained based in Berlin until 1941, impressing successive waves of the otherwise almost all-male American press corps with her knowledge of Germany and her tenaciousness in chasing down stories. Looking back at her experiences in her book *Germany Will Try It Again*, written and published during World War II, she argued that Raeder's bitterness was widely shared by his countrymen, along with his eagerness to avenge their defeat in the previous global conflagration.

By that point, of course, she knew where this bitterness had led, and the question arises whether some of her descriptions were colored by hindsight. But in the case of her recollection of the interview with Raeder, it appears that she only added a final flourish to emphasize the accuracy of his prediction: "When, almost twenty-two years later, Adolf Hitler declared war on the United States, the man commanding the German Navy was Grand Admiral Dr. Erich Raeder."

Much has been written about Americans in France and Great Britain during the interwar period, and even a fair amount about Americans in the Soviet Union. But, for a variety of reasons, the Americans who lived, worked or traveled in Germany at the time when Hitler was coming to power and then forged the Third Reich haven't attracted anything like that level of attention—including Schultz and many of her colleagues. In fact, they are often forgotten. Or, like diplomat George Kennan, they may be remembered, but not for their German experiences; the German chapter in their lives was eclipsed by other parts of their biographies that made them famous—in Kennan's case, as the architect of the containment policy that successive postwar presidents pursued in dealing with the Soviet Union.

As a result, Americans often have the impression that the collapse of the Weimar Republic and the subsequent rush to terror and war took place in a strange, isolated country. Few of them pause to ask who were the Americans there who witnessed these events firsthand, how they perceived and reported them either as part of their jobs or simply as curious visitors, and what kind of impact their accounts had on their countrymen's views of Germany at the time.

Today, it's conventional wisdom that Hitler's intentions were perfectly clear from the outset and that his policies could only result in World War II and the Holocaust. Most people find it hard to imagine that in the 1920s and right through the 1930s, American reporters, diplomats, entertainers, sociologists, students and others living in or passing through Germany wouldn't have all instantly seen and understood what was happening before their eyes. After all, they had ringside seats, providing them with an unparalleled view of the most dramatic story of the twentieth century. Several of them not only observed Hitler from afar, but met and spoke to him, both when he was still a local agitator in Munich and then the all-powerful dictator in Berlin. To them, he wasn't some abstract embodiment of evil but a real-life politician. Some Americans tried to take his measure very early, while others did so once he was in power. And even those who didn't have those opportunities witnessed the consequences of his actions.

Yet their readings of what was happening in Germany, and what Hitler represented, varied greatly. There were those who met Hitler and recognized he represented almost a primeval force and possessed an uncanny ability to tap into the emotions and anger of the German people, and those who dismissed him as a clownish figure who would vanish from the political scene as quickly as he had appeared. There were those who, at least initially, viewed him and his movement sympathetically or even embraced it, and those whose instinctive misgivings quickly gave way to full-scale alarm, recognizing that he was a threat not only to Germany but also to the world.

It wasn't just Americans who didn't know what to make of Hitler or who hadn't really examined what passed for his worldview. Otto Strasser, an early follower of Hitler who later broke with him and escaped from Germany, recalled a dinner with several top Nazi officials at the 1927 Party Congress in Nuremberg. When it became apparent no one had read Hitler's autobiographical screed *Mein Kampf* in its entirety, they agreed that they would ask anyone who joined them if he had done so— and stick that person with the bill. "Nobody had read *Mein Kampf*, so everyone had to pay his own bill," Strasser reported.

The unfolding of history only looks inevitable in retrospect, and the judgments of the Americans who were witnessing these events unfold were based on a variety of factors: their predispositions, the different slices of reality that they observed and whether at times they saw only what they wanted to see, whatever the signals to the contrary. Schultz chose to highlight Raeder's comments in 1919 to bolster her thesis later, once the United States and Germany were at war again, that Hitler's movement was the logical outcome of the hate fomented by the country's defeat in the previous war. But other Americans dwelled on their warm reception in the aftermath of World War I, and wanted to believe that the toll of that conflict had been so high that it had served as a decisive object lesson. Edgar Ansel Mowrer, the Berlin correspondent for the rival Chicago paper, the *Daily News*, recalled that in the 1920s "most Americans in Germany nourished a legitimate hope that Germany's defeat, humiliation, inflation and internal disorders had brought home to most citizens the folly of again seeking European hegemony."

While correspondents like Schultz and Mowrer, and diplomats like Kennan and several of his colleagues, were hardly innocents abroad— they had studied and worked elsewhere in Europe—many of the Americans who were in Germany in this period were both very young and very inexperienced. This, of course, colored their perceptions and influenced their reactions. They were alternately charmed, shocked and mesmerized by Germany's combination of old world rigidity and new, postwar world extremism, whether in political or sexual behavior.

As a result of their country's peculiar role, Americans in Germany were in a special position. Although the United States had joined in the fighting in World War I, it was only in its later stages. Most Americans were far from eager to be dragged into a new European conflict, which accounted for the strength of isolationist sentiments back home. Americans in Germany were put in a different category than the other winners of World War I: they were seen as almost neutral, far less vengeful than the French, in particular, and, in general, more willing to give the defeated Germans the benefit of the doubt. As observers, they could stand a bit outside and above the continental rivalries.

Like Americans everywhere, they also tended to live a privileged existence, observing the material deprivations and growing violence but usually sheltered from them personally. They socialized extensively with each other, celebrated Thanksgiving and other holidays, and enjoyed the trappings of the expat lifestyle while monitoring the bigger events that swirled all around them. Louis Lochner, who reported for the Associated Press throughout this period, made casual mention of life in "the American colony," and the "enviable camaraderie" among the American correspondents, "even among those who are one anothers' [sic] fiercest competitors."

To be sure, tensions erupted between those who came to radically differing views of Hitler and the Nazis, and what their military buildup signified. Then, too, there were the personal jealousies and resentments. The American Embassy in Berlin was a much leaner outpost than embassies are nowadays, and the small, overworked staffs and their spouses were often feuding about both their political views and petty grievances. There also were fissures between the politically appointed ambassadors and the professional foreign service staffers and military attachés. Throw in the perceived scandalous behavior of an ambassador's daughter and you have a recipe for real drama. All of this could happen in any diplomatic outpost, but in Berlin it was magnified by the unrelenting tensions that accompanied Hitler's reign.

The American correspondents, by contrast, were far more numerous than they are today—reaching a peak of about fifty in Berlin in the mid-1930s. Those were the days when wire services, newspaper chains and dailies from a wide array of American cities across the country, not just from New York and Washington, fielded correspondents overseas, giving them remarkable free rein to pursue their stories. And radio broadcasters soon joined that mix.

As a *Newsweek* foreign correspondent in the 1980s and 1990s, I felt I was living in what, especially from the perspective of today's cutbacks in the media business, looks like the golden era of journalism. But my predecessors in Berlin lived far more largely. Mowrer, for instance, set up a new office for the *Chicago Daily News* right above the "Kranzler Corner," a famous café at the prestigious downtown intersection of Friedrichstrasse and Unter den Linden. It boasted a second-floor reception center for American visitors, who could come by to chat, read American newspapers and even dictate to the office secretary on occasion. This was more than a news bureau; it was almost a small diplomatic mission.

There were plenty of Americans, including several who bore household names, who dropped in to see what this new Germany was all about—the likes of writers Thomas Wolfe and Sinclair Lewis, architect Philip Johnson, broadcaster Edward R. Murrow, former President Herbert Hoover, the black sociologist and historian W. E. B. DuBois and, of course, aviator Charles Lindbergh. Somewhat surprisingly, it was no great feat for Americans and other foreigners to enter and explore this curious, darkening world. "One thing one forgets is how easy it was to travel around Germany then," recalls historian Robert Conquest, who traveled all over Europe in 1938 with some fellow Oxford University students and dropped in on Germany as well. "It was far easier than in postwar communist countries."

I always have been drawn to this period of history, seeking to understand how Hitler and his followers could have gained total control of Germany as quickly as they did, with all the ensuing devastating consequences. This had a direct impact on my family's history as it did on millions of others'. My parents grew up in Poland, and my father fought in the Polish Army before escaping to the West to join up with Polish forces under British command. After the war, I was born in Edinburgh. My parents then sailed for the United States, where they started a new life as political refugees. That's why I grew up as an American instead of a Pole.

As a foreign correspondent who did two tours in Germany—the first one in Bonn during the last years of the Cold War, and the second in Berlin in the late 1990s—I often wrote about how Germans dealt with the legacy of the Nazi past. But I have to admit I knew very little about the Americans who worked in Berlin in those dramatic times. There were exceptions, of course. My colleagues and I all knew about William Shirer, the author of *The Rise and Fall of the Third Reich*, and that the Adlon Hotel, which was rebuilt and reopened after German unification, had been the hangout for Shirer, Dorothy Thompson and other star journalists of the time. But I can't say I had delved much into their personal histories.

When I began to do so for this book, I realized there was a rich vein of stories that not only provided insights into what it was like to work or travel in Germany in the midst of these seismic events but also offered a unique perspective on them. Through their experiences, I felt I was reliving this heavily dissected era with an intensity and immediacy that is often lacking elsewhere. Whenever possible, I drew on firsthand accounts—whether in memoirs, notes, correspondence or interviews with the occasional still living witness—to share that perspective with readers.

Some of these tales were published but long forgotten, while I found others in unpublished manuscripts and letters in various archives and libraries, or sometimes provided by the children of the authors. In the case of the young diplomat Jacob Beam, for example, who served in the U.S. Embassy in Berlin in the second half of the 1930s, his son Alex—a good friend from my Moscow days, when we both were stationed there as correspondents—provided me with a copy of his unpublished manuscript. Some of the most colorful details about life in Germany came from the unpublished writings of Katharine (Kay) Smith, the wife of Captain Truman Smith, who was still a junior military attaché when he became the first American official to meet Hitler.

It's important to keep in mind that this is history as seen by eyewitnesses without the benefit of knowing where these events would lead. The Wannsee Conference that formalized elaborate plans for the Holocaust was still off in the future—January 20, 1942, to be exact. The German Army was only beginning to encounter its first serious setbacks on the Eastern Front as the remaining Americans in Germany were on their way out, following Pearl Harbor and Hitler's declaration of war against the United States. To be sure, the Americans had ample opportunity to witness or hear about the widespread persecution of the Jews and anyone else deemed an enemy of the new regime, along with Hitler's string of first conquests and the early reports of mass killings. Some of these Americans demonstrated remarkable courage and prescience, while others stood back and averted their gaze, or, in a few cases, collaborated outright with the new regime.

But most of this book focuses on the perspectives and experiences of this special group of Americans during the run-up to the war and the Holocaust. As someone who has been privileged to report on more recent major events such as the collapse of the Soviet empire and the liberation of Central Europe, I understand how difficult it can be to sort out what is happening during a period of historic upheaval, and to make the right moral calls on how to behave in those circumstances. When you're in the center of a whirlwind, daily life can continue with deceptive normality at times, even when the abnormalities, absurdities and injustices are all too apparent.

Instead of rushing to pass judgment on the Americans who found themselves in Hitler's Germany, I have focused on telling their stories— and, wherever possible, letting those stories speak for themselves. The assessments of the Americans, where they were right or wrong, and where their moral compasses were on target or completely missing, should flow from their experiences, not from our knowledge based on the luxury of hindsight.

# 1

## "Nervous Breakdown"

Even today, people treat Berlin in the 1920s like a Rorschach test. There are those who immediately think of political paralysis and chaos, with revolutionaries and counterrevolutionaries battling each other in the streets. Others talk about hyperinflation wiping out lifetime savings, plunging millions of once solidly middle-class families into abject poverty. There are those who see an era of dizzying sexual freedoms—or, depending on who is doing the talking, a period of shameful degeneracy and perversion. And, finally, there are those who remember this era for its astonishing cultural renaissance, marked by an explosion of creativity in the arts and sciences, all made possible by a genuinely democratic system.

Oddly enough, all of those associations are right—all reflect a fairly accurate version of reality.

In the aftermath of World War I, Berlin was the primary political battlefield in the country—all too often, in the literal sense of that term. While unrest swept across other German cities, nowhere were the battles more intense than in Berlin. In February 1919, the newly elected National Assembly convened in Weimar to draft a new constitution precisely because they needed a less violent setting than Berlin. But the birth of the Weimar Republic quickly spawned violent revolts by both rightists and leftists, who shared a death wish for the country's new rulers and their experiment in parliamentary democracy. Demagogues of every stripe found willing recruits among a people who were still reeling from their humiliating defeat, the staggering human toll of the war, and the punitive peace terms of the Versailles Treaty.

The political chaos fed off the mounting economic desperation. As the German mark plunged in value, living standards for those on fixed incomes plunged with it. Routine purchases—a loaf of bread, for example—required thousands, then millions, then billions and, finally, trillions of marks. The worthlessness of the currency was vividly captured by a sign at the box office of one of the city's theaters: "Orchestra stalls: the same price as half a pound of butter. Rear stalls: two eggs." Amid the general poverty, there were also, as always, those who made their fortunes and lived extravagantly.

The extravagance was particularly evident when it came to sexual mores. At one of the myriad parties in the city playwright Carl Zuckmayer attended, he reported that the young women serving drinks were dressed only in "transparent panties embroidered with a silver fig leaf"— and, unlike "bunnies" in American clubs, they "could be freely handled"; their pay for the evening covered those amusements as well. A sign on the wall proclaimed: "Love is the foolish overestimation of the minimal difference between one sexual object and another."

Such sexual free-for-alls were one reason why curious foreigners were drawn to the German capital, but the biggest draw was Berlin's reputation as the most vibrant cultural hub. A city that boasted the likes of Bertolt Brecht, Albert Einstein, Marlene Dietrich and George Grosz quickly became a magnet for those who were talented and creative, adventurous and opportunistic, including a growing number of Americans.

"People have forgotten that, after World War One, the greatest concentration of intellectuals and cultural innovators was not in Paris, and certainly not in London or New York—but in Berlin," recalled Michael Danzi, a versatile American musician who played the banjo, every kind of guitar and the mandolin, and who spent most of the interwar years in the

German capital. "Berlin was truly the capital of Europe—all the railroad tracks from any European city ended up in Berlin."

From the beginning, many of the Americans were also drawn to the political and economic chaos, trying to understand the forces unleashed all over postwar Germany, particularly in Berlin, as they pondered the future of the new Weimar Republic. But just as in Christopher Isherwood's stories and the resulting musical and film *Cabaret*, the recollections of Americans about this extraordinary era are often freighted with premonitions about the sinister forces that would eventually engulf Germany and almost all of Europe.

From their earliest days as a small radical movement based in Munich, the Nazis viewed Berlin as an evil, decadent city, especially as compared to the Bavarian capital, where they enjoyed far more support. "The contrast [of Munich] with Berlin was marked," noted Kurt Ludecke, who joined the party in the 1920s and became an ardent fund-raiser and activist, including on trips to the United States. "One was the Mecca of Marxists and Jews, the other the citadel of their enemies." Even after Hitler took power and ruled from Berlin, he remained distrustful of the German capital and its inhabitants.

As far as the earliest American arrivals in postwar Germany were concerned, much of what was happening was endlessly intriguing—and totally mystifying. Ben Hecht, the future Broadway and Hollywood star writer, director and producer, came to Germany in 1918 as a twenty-four-year-old reporter for the *Chicago Daily News*. During his two years in the German capital, he described "political zanies, quibblers and adventurers—mindless and paranoid" performing as if in street theaters, and how "all was politics, revolution, antirevolution." In a letter to his managing editor Henry Justin Smith back in Chicago, he concluded: "Germany is having a nervous breakdown. There is nothing sane to report."

While most of their countrymen back home were only too happy to put World War I behind them and return to their domestic preoccupations, a new crop of American diplomats and military attachés were deploying to Germany to resume the official ties between the two countries.

They were anxious to assess the mood of the German people and to see whether their new rulers had a chance of riding out the chronic political unrest and the deepening economic crisis, allowing their democratic experiment to succeed.

For a young diplomat like Hugh Wilson, Berlin during and after the war provided confirmation that his future should be in the foreign service, not in a return to the family business he had left behind in Chicago. Shortly before the war, he had decided to try to see what "a few years of experience and diversion" as a diplomat would be like. He had taken the foreign service exam, assuming that he could always return to his old life whenever he tired of his new one. But then the whole world changed.

After his first postings in Latin America, Wilson was assigned to the Berlin embassy in 1916. He only served a few months in that city, which appeared "to be in a state of siege with the whole world," before the United States entered the war and the embassy staff was evacuated by special train to Switzerland. By the time he was reassigned to a defeated Germany, Wilson had made the decision to "call into play every atom of energy and intelligence I might possess" in what he now regarded as his life's work. It would prove to be the second of three postings for him to Berlin. The third time, in the late 1930s, he would become the last U.S. ambassador to serve in Nazi Germany.

Wilson and his wife Kate arrived in Berlin in March 1920, just as the right-wing Kapp Putsch was taking place in full view of the small contingent of Americans at what was then the U.S. Embassy building at 7 Wilhelmplatz. Wolfgang Kapp, the German nationalist who was the nominal leader of the rebel forces, had set up his headquarters at the Leopold Palace on the other side of the square, which was strewn with wire and machine-gun placements. This particular revolt fizzled out quickly, but Wilson had plenty of chances to observe other outbreaks of violence that had peculiarly German attributes. "Rioting seemed to be strictly circumscribed and there appeared to be rules of the game which the rioters themselves respected," he noted.

Wilson added: "I myself have seen fighting on one street with machine guns and rifles blazing at the other" while a few hundred yards away crowds went about their business in orderly fashion. On another occasion, he watched from his embassy window as thousands of Spartacists, as the Communists were then called, staged a protest in Wilhelmplatz in front of the Chancellery building. Although the demonstrators were "vituperative and angry," he noted, no one stepped over the low railings marking off plots of grass and flowers. That would have violated their sense of order.

For Wilson and other Americans who had been to Germany before, the most striking feature of Berlin was how dilapidated and impoverished it looked. "The shabbiness of Berlin in that period had to be seen to be believed . . . Everything needed a coat of paint, everything needed to be cleaned out," he recalled. "It was the only time that I ever saw this capital of a scrupulously clean people littered with newspapers and dirt." Even the embassy building, where many staffers lived, was in dismal shape: the roof leaked profusely whenever there was heavy rain or melting snow. Because Washington had routinely denied requests for funds to make the necessary repairs, Wilson and his colleagues used to pray for rain when senators or congressmen arrived on visits so that they would see how bad things were.

This was nothing compared to the desperate plight of the local residents, including the wounded veterans begging in the streets. The wartime blockade of Germany had continued for several months after the end of the fighting, only making things worse. Wilson pointed out that "traces of undernourishment and children's diseases, especially rickets, were found on every hand."

Katharine Smith, or Kay as she was generally known, took notice of the poverty all around her right from the moment she and her husband, Captain Truman Smith, arrived in Berlin in June 1920 to take up his post as an assistant military attaché. Like many Americans, the young, physically incongruous couple—she was twenty and only 5 feet tall, while he was twenty-six and an imposing 6 feet 4 inches—first moved into the famed Adlon Hotel. The hotel's façade was pockmarked by bullets, and even the lobby bore a few similar telling holes, but overall, Kay reported, "the interior was quite luxurious, the desk clerks very polite, the crowded lobby full of foreigners." Nonetheless, Kay only had to step outside on her first day there to see how insulated that world was.

Deciding to go for a walk, she made sure she was fashionably decked out first. "I put on a beige and blue figured voile dress, a beige coat with beige fox collar and wore, as had been the custom at home, beige suede pumps, beige stockings and a dark blue hat," she scrupulously recorded. She left the hotel and walked down Unter den Linden, pausing to admire a china display in a shop window. Suddenly, she heard murmuring behind her and turned around to see a group of shabbily dressed people, two rows deep, staring at her and whispering to each other. "I must have looked to them as if I had come from Mars!" she recalled.

One of the people asked her something she didn't quite understand, and she replied that she was an American. "Ah!" came the response. When she stepped forward, the crowd quickly made way for her and she rushed back to the hotel, where she changed from her "most inappropriate" outfit into plain dark clothes. "It had been a strange and instructive experience," she concluded.

So was the experience of moving into an apartment. First, there was the battle with fleas, which were still common all over the city. Then, when she hired a housemaid, she was taken aback by one of their early conversations. The maid was holding a plate with the remains of an egg that Truman had not finished, and she asked Kay whether she could eat it. "Eat that cold smeared egg!" Kay replied in astonishment. "Why?" The maid explained that she hadn't tasted an egg since the war began. When Kay told her to eat as many eggs as she wanted, it was the maid's turn to be shocked. In other households, servants weren't supposed to eat the same food as their employers—and food was often kept under lock and key.

As keen a social observer as Kay quickly proved to be, Truman focused just as intensely in those early days on Germany's political prospects, not just the military part of his job. That was hardly surprising given his impressive credentials. He was a 1915 Yale graduate (two noted classmates were Dean Acheson and Archibald MacLeish), a World War I infantry veteran decorated with a Silver Star for bravery, and an avid student of the German language and German politics and history. Like Wilson, he had served in Germany already—as a political advisor to the U.S. Army in Coblenz from March 1919 until his transfer to Berlin in June 1920—and he would return to Germany in the 1930s when Hitler was in power. His daughter Kätchen is convinced that he would have become a history professor if his graduate studies at Columbia University hadn't been cut short by what turned into a thirty-year military career.

For those early postwar arrivals like the Wilsons and the Smiths, the plunging German mark meant that everything was increasingly cheap—as long as the foreigners spent their money quickly right after exchanging it. "With the end of the war in victory for them everything was hilarious and life in leisure times was a mad scramble for amusement," Wilson wrote. And there were plenty of foreigners who could revel in each other's company, even if the American diplomatic presence was small by today's standards. "All of the embassies had big staffs, all entertained lavishly, and the Allied Governments maintained commissions of control comprising hundreds of foreign officers and their wives," Wilson added. "Allied uniforms were common on the streets of Berlin."

Kay Smith's letters to her mother and her unpublished memoirs describe an endless whirl of those diplomatic parties and social events. For a masked ball in 1921 hosted by Wilson and his wife Kate along with another American colleague, the invitation read in part:

> *On the nineteenth of March you are urged*
> *To come to this house fully purged*
> *Of all thoughts of dignity,*
> *Rank or insignity,*
> *But in costume on which you have splurged.*

> *At nine-thirty the jazz will begin,*
> *And when you have danced yourself thin,*
> *There'll be lots of Schinken*
> *Zu essen, and trinken,*
> *Such as rot wein and also blanc vin.*

The Americans weren't enjoying their special status in Berlin just because they were foreigners with access to what stable currencies could buy. They also recognized quickly that their enemies in the last war were affording them an unexpectedly warm welcome. "The Germans, then, in 1920, wanted to be friends with the world, but particularly they wanted to make friends with the Americans," Wilson wrote. "Curiously enough, the warrior instinct showed in this respect. One of the sources of this almost pathetic friendship was their desire to express the admiration they felt for the stupendous effort of the United States in 1917 and 1918, for the magnificent spirit and dash of our soldiers . . ."

Wilson may have overstated the admiration for American troops, but he was right about the overall pro-American mood. As Kay Smith put it, "People are laying themselves out to be nice to Americans." Truman bought a Borsalino felt hat with a large brim. This made him tower above most people on Unter den Linden and other streets he frequented, where he was instantly recognizable. "He became famous as 'The American,'" Kay proudly recalled. "Germans greatly admired a tall fine physique."

Americans, it seemed, were the good victors.

In part, the reason why the Americans emerged as the good victors was because they often reciprocated the Germans' positive feelings about them. They also shared their exasperation with the French—the bad victors, in their eyes. In the immediate aftermath of World War I, Washington and Paris were frequently at odds over how to handle a defeated Germany. The United States and Britain were inclined to give the new government in Berlin enough leeway in terms of troop deployments to suppress uprisings from the left or the right, and the Americans, in particular, disapproved of what they perceived as France's insistence on extracting exorbitant reparations. But the French protested any perceived violations of the Versailles Treaty—and quickly used them as an excuse to occupy more German territory, as they did by pushing across the Rhine after the Kapp Putsch, and then by occupying the industrialized Ruhr in 1923 as punishment for Germany's failure to pay reparations.

"The French are the most militaristic nation in Europe . . . they have learned nothing by this war," Kay Smith complained in a letter to her mother on March 12, 1920. "The next war Germany will not provoke. She wants England and America especially with her and she is making every effort to remodel herself to do so." In another letter, she wrote,

"France is terrified of another attack by Germany and her policy has been to crucify Germany as much as possible."

As Wilson pointed out, the French only made things worse by following up their push across the Rhine that year with the stationing of Senegalese and other black troops in the Rhineland, triggering immediate reports of rapes and other violence. "A flame of resentment against France arose throughout Germany," he wrote.

Those alarming allegations prompted the State Department to ask for an investigation by U.S. military officials. After looking into the charges, Major General Henry T. Allen, the commander of American troops in Germany, reported to Washington that the German press had deliberately distorted the record to play to racial prejudices and stir antipathy to France abroad, "especially in America, where the negro question is always capable of arousing feeling." In his report to the State Department that was then relayed to Congress, he acknowledged that 66 sexual crimes had been reported to the French authorities, but he also pointed out that this had resulted in 28 convictions and 11 acquittals by French military courts—suggesting a serious effort to maintain discipline.

"The wholesale atrocities by French negro Colonial troops alleged in the German press, such as the alleged abductions, followed by rape, mutilation, murder and concealment of the bodies of the victims, are false and intended for political propaganda," he concluded.

Such exaggerations, Allen added, were in part due to "the attitude of certain classes of German women toward the colored troops." Noting that the postwar economic crisis had spawned widespread prostitution, he explained that "many German women of loose character have openly made advances to the colored soldiers." Numerous love letters and photographs attested to that fact, he pointed out. In Ludwigshafen, he reported, patrols had to be sent "to drive away the German women from the barracks, where they were kissing the colored troops through the window gratings."

Even more tellingly, Allen noted that there were several interracial marriages, including one with the daughter of a prominent Rhineland official. "The color line is not regarded either by the French or the Germans as we regard it in America: to keep the white race pure." While he wasn't denying that there were many documented cases of sexual assaults, Allen was convinced that it was the behavior of German women that had been the spark to "incite trouble."

But many Americans in Germany had already made up their minds that it was France's vindictive policies that were to blame for everything, not anything the Germans were doing. They saw Germany as the victimized party, which was in keeping with much of the local political rhetoric. "I am afraid that many of us who were on duty in Germany after World War I were taken in," *Chicago Tribune* correspondent Sigrid Schultz wrote much later. "Inadvertently we supported the Germans in their sympathy drive."

On January 29, 1921, Karl Henry von Wiegand, a star reporter for the Hearst publications, wrote to C. F. Bertelli, his Hearst colleague in Paris, venting his exasperation with the French. "Your French friends appear to be as insane as they have ever been since the close of the war." Mentioning new demands by the French for reparations, he added, "Are the French never going to come to their senses, and see Europe as it actually is?" He concluded that many Americans and other Europeans "are getting rather weary of hearing France's yowl about what France suffered in the war."

Wiegand was a correspondent who already felt very much at home in Germany and the rest of Europe. Born in 1874 in Hesse, he came to the United States as a young boy, growing up on farms in Iowa where his German immigrant father struggled to make ends meet, losing two farms in the process. When his father was "a fair way to losing a third," Karl, barely fourteen at the time, decided to make his own way in the world, never telling his siblings or his parents that he wasn't coming back. "A cruel thing to do to a good father and the kindest of mothers," he would write much later in notes for an autobiography that he never completed.

He claimed to have then worked on a ranch for Buffalo Bill—who at close range was less than the romantic hero of the frontier that he had imagined from reading dime novels. He made his way further west, eventually finding work at the Associated Press in San Francisco. There, he seized the opportunity to use his German and cover World War I for the rival United Press, happily leaving behind his desk job. Three months into that conflict, he scored an exclusive interview with Crown Prince Friedrich Wilhelm, the son of the Kaiser, who famously told the American that he had warned his father the war was already lost. The subsequent headlines offered a huge boost to Wiegand's early career. He ended up jumping again—this time to Hearst.

Like any good reporter, Wiegand recognized he had to offer his editors and readers a broad range of stories about the new Germany. While dutifully reporting on every political crisis, the continuing street battles and the economic shortages ("Food Shortage Alarms All Germany," warned the headline of his May 23, 1922, story), he was also alert to other subjects that would titillate his readers—or, when it came to the racier ones that his editors might not allow, at least his colleagues.

That was particularly true when it came to postwar Germany's growing reputation for sexual licentiousness. Wiegand kept up a running private correspondence with Bertelli in Paris on the subject. In one letter from 1921, Bertelli urged Wiegand to write more about cocaine and "the alleged degeneracy of the old burg." Good stories on that subject, he added, will "get the whole of the American continent afire with indignation . . . and greedy longing!" Then, there was the usual banter about how Wiegand should research this story. "Incidentally you might discover in your night investigations (all for the good of the future generation, of course) some novel Venus . . . Be careful about taking the necessary measurements . . ."

Back home, one of Wiegand's readers concluded that the correspondent might be able to help him with a personal matter. "I am looking for a wife," R. C. Bruchman wrote him on January 14, 1921, from Danville, Illinois. "I imagine there must be an awful lot of handsome good girls in Berlin who would make a fellow a mighty fine wife." He enclosed $1.50, asking Wiegand to place an ad in a Berlin newspaper, saying that a thirty-five-year-old German-American gentleman "wants to marry girl 18 to 25 yrs. old."

An amused Wiegand agreed to the request, noting this was the first time he had been asked to act as a matrimonial agent. "As there are at least a million more women in Germany than men, you ought to have quite a lot to pick from, and I have no doubt you will get many answers," he wrote back. "It is indeed all too true that many refined and educated German girls of formerly well to do families are today facing want."

Wiegand also participated in the diplomatic party scene in Berlin, occasionally writing features about it, especially when Americans played starring roles. "Houghton Girls Make Berlin Debut" proclaimed his *Washington Times* story datelined December 30, 1922. The subheadline explained: "Brilliant Assemblage Gives Daughters of U.S. Envoy Welcome to Society." Alanson B. Houghton, an industrialist-turned-Republican-congressman-turned-diplomat, was Washington's first postwar envoy to Berlin. He was deeply troubled by the overall situation he found there, repeatedly warning Washington that Germany's economic plight and political unrest could prove to be highly dangerous for the whole continent. But this didn't prevent him from putting on some of Berlin's most lavish parties, which Wiegand wrote up enthusiastically.

At a ball in honor of their daughter and a niece, the Houghtons welcomed "four hundred members of the diplomatic set and high German officialdom, and many representative Americans," Wiegand reported. This "brilliant fete," he added, was a huge boost to American prestige. Presumably, the outfits of the daughter ("a gown of silver brocade cloth") and niece ("a gold-banded net over a novel gold cloth") all contributed to the success of the evening—as did the fact that the two young women also carried "enormous rose-colored feather fans." So, too, did an American jazz band that supplied the music, while "a moving picture machine added color by flashing alternate shades on the dancing throng." All this a half a century before the disco era.

While Wiegand enjoyed such stories, he knew that his editors wanted him to keep explaining Germany's turbulent political scene as well—a charge he took very seriously. So seriously, in fact, that he became the first American correspondent to interview a local agitator in Munich who was beginning to make his name as a fiery orator. That agitator's name was Adolf Hitler.

Wiegand declared that he had first met Hitler in 1921, but he only began taking him seriously enough to feature him prominently in his reports a year later. Given the proliferation of extremists in Bavaria at the time, that was hardly surprising. Every encounter with a radical of the right or the left hardly merited a separate story or even a mention in print. But by November 1922, following Benito Mussolini's power grab in Italy, there was a growing sense that the right was on the rise throughout Europe, providing the perfect peg for a feature about the leader of the German "Fascisti."

"Hitler Styled Mussolini of Teuton Crisis," proclaimed the headline of Wiegand's story datelined November 12, 1922, in the *New York American*, one of the Hearst papers. "The shadow of the Fascisti is arising in Germany," Wiegand wrote. Explaining that Hitler—"leader of the movement which is causing no less uneasiness in Communist and Socialist circles than in Government quarters in Berlin and Munich"—had spelled out his program to him that day, the writer offered a summary that would leave the average reader confused about the true nature of this new political movement.

While denouncing the terms of the Versailles Treaty, Hitler insisted that he wanted reconciliation with France. The idea of war, he told Wiegand, "would be suicidal, if it were not idiocy." As for domestic policy, he called on Germans to work two extra hours a day to pay off reparations and free them of their debts. He denied any intention to restore the monarchy or push separatism for Bavaria, and he attacked the Marxists head-on. "True socialism is the welfare of all the people, and not of one class at the expense of others. Therefore we oppose class warfare," he declared.

But for American readers who hadn't heard of this new politician, what probably registered the most in Wiegand's article was his personal description of Hitler. Calling him "a man of the people" who had served in the trenches of World War I and afterward worked as a carpenter-turned-master builder (almost certainly an exaggerated description of Hitler's early days as a handyman), Wiegand described him as "a magnetic speaker having also exceptional organizing genius." He then spelled out the key characteristics of "the German Mussolini," as he promptly dubbed him:

"Aged thirty-four, medium tall, wiry, slender, dark hair, cropped toothbrush mustache, eyes that seem at times to spurt fire, straight nose, finely chiseled features with a complexion so remarkably delicate that many a woman would be proud to possess it, and possessing a bearing that creates an impression of dynamic energy well under control . . .

"That is Hitler—one of the most interesting characters I have met in many months.

"With apostolic fervor and gifted with convincing oratory and a magnetism which is drawing him followers even out of the inner communistic and socialistic circles, Hitler has the earmarks of a leader. Whether it be merely a band or a great movement, only the future will tell.

"He believes firmly that his mission is to arouse and save Germany from its internal foes . . ."

Wiegand concluded his article by reporting: "The Bavarian Fascisti, like the Italians, are working secretly in the Reichswehr and the police, and there is fear that Hitler may one day proclaim himself dictator of Bavaria."

Even before he filed that story, Wiegand had been telling Ambassador Houghton in Berlin about the disarray in the southern part of the country, and warning that General Erich Ludendorff might be planning to topple the government and impose a right-wing dictatorship. Ludendorff had led the German war effort in its latter stages and, after a brief exile, had returned to Germany and taken up with Hitler and other agitators in Munich. Instead of accepting responsibility for Germany's military defeat, he blamed Socialists, leftists and Jews, laying the groundwork for what would become known as the "stab-in-the-back" theory.

Houghton decided that he needed more information about what was happening in the south. "Something is brewing in Bavaria and no one seems to know exactly what it is," he wrote in his diary. "Probably it will result in nothing definite, but too much is at stake to permit us to run any danger." To check out the situation, he turned to his young assistant military attaché, Captain Smith. At the same time that Wiegand was filing his first story about Hitler, Smith was preparing to follow in his footsteps—and to become the first American official to meet the future leader of Nazi Germany.

Smith would later point out that most foreign diplomats in Berlin at the time had written off the National Socialists as "being without significance and its leader, Adolf Hitler, as an uneducated madman." Houghton, by contrast, "seems to have had, even at this early date, a premonition that the movement and its leader might play an important role in the disturbed Germany of the early twenties." The ambassador and the embassy's military attaché Lieutenant Colonel Edward Davis, Smith's immediate superior, urged the captain to "try to make personal contact with Hitler himself and form an estimate of his character, personality, abilities, and weaknesses."

Arriving in Munich on November 15, Smith had a clear-cut set of questions to address based on the hot topics of conversation among diplomats in Berlin. First, in light of the open hostility of "the reactionary government in Munich" to "the moderately leftist Reich government in Berlin," was there a danger that Bavaria would declare itself independent? Second, was there a danger of another Communist revolt in Bavaria (a "Bavarian Soviet Republic" was briefly proclaimed in 1919)? And, third, "Did the possibility exist that Hitler's National Socialists were strong enough to seize power in Bavaria?" He was also supposed to check on the loyalty of the 7th Division of the Reichswehr, as the Army was called, and on the significance of the sporadic incidents between the Bavarians and the Allied Military Control commissions, which were still operating in Germany following that country's defeat.

Smith set out to fulfill his assignment by meeting as many people as possible, recording his discussions and impressions in his notebooks. In typical military style, he referred to himself in the third person in these notes.

Upon his arrival, he first went to the U.S. Consulate, where he met with Robert Murphy, the acting consul. Since the consulate had reopened in 1921, the four consular officers assigned there had been overwhelmed with paperwork, issuing on average about four hundred visas a day. "It seemed to us that the whole of Bavaria wanted to emigrate," Murphy recalled. But the consular officers also attempted to monitor the turbulent local politics, trying to get a fix on Hitler and other radicals. "It was a welcome relief from those chores to transform ourselves into political reporters for the benefit of the State Department," Murphy noted.

Murphy told Smith that the new Bavarian Minister President Eugen von Knilling was weak and easily manipulated by right-wing politicians.

Then their conversation turned to Hitler and the Nazis. Smith summarized Murphy's views: "The National Socialists are increasing their strength rapidly. Hitler, their leader, is of Austrian origin and a pure and simple adventurer. Nevertheless, he is a real character and is exploiting all latent discontent to increase his party's strength."

Murphy also passed along a rumor that Hitler had "a shady past" and may have misappropriated government funds in Austria. In Germany, he now commanded 40,000 men—"largely roughnecks but devoted to their leader." While some reports had suggested he might have up to 200,000 men, Murphy pointed out that even his smaller force could prove effective if well led. "Hitler thoroughly understands the Bavarian psychology. Whether he is big enough to take the lead in a German national movement is another question; probably not." Noting that the National Socialists were not working together with "the other monarchist groups," he added that the Bavarian government was permitting the Nazis "to do what they want." Still, Murphy confessed that it was difficult to assess all the competing groups. "All these nationalist societies are so mixed up among themselves that it is hard to keep them distinct."

That was only the beginning of Smith's rounds, where he asked everyone he met about Hitler. General Kress von Kressenstein, the artillery commander of the 7th Division, hadn't met Hitler, but he called his nationalist movement a "healthy drift away from socialism." The general had the impression that the man was "an oratorical genius," but he felt that "Hitler was not as radical as his speeches made him out." He was anti-Semitic in "a healthy sense," Kressenstein continued, since he wanted to keep Jews out of government positions. Barring some mistake, he predicted to Smith, his movement had "a great future before it." He added that the National Socialists favored "an evolutionary development, not a revolutionary one."

Friedrich Trefz, the chief editor of the *Münchner Neueste Nachrichten*, concurred that the National Socialists were a growing force. "Hitler was a marvelous speaker. None better," Smith recorded him as saying. Trefz told Smith he had gone to a Nazi meeting and sat between a general and a Communist; both had come out of simple curiosity—and, afterward, both signed up as party members. Trefz's conclusion: "The National Socialists present no immediate danger to the government. The ground is fertile, however, and the party will grow."

Finally, Smith made it to the informal headquarters of the Nazis at Georgenstrasse 42. There, he first met with Max Erwin von Scheubner-Richter, an early confidant of Hitler. He claimed that the party had 35,000 members in Munich, 200,000 sympathizers and a "militarily organized" underground, armed with clubs and pistols. As for the party's anti-Semitism, he assured his American visitor that it was "purely for propaganda."

In the midst of the conversation, there was a sudden flurry of activity. The National Socialists had been planning to hold a meeting in Regensburg that evening, but the Reich Ministry of Railroads had just denied them permission for a special train to transport Hitler's men. Scheubner-Richter explained that the Regensburg event had been postponed but that Hitler would be reviewing his troops, the Brownshirts, nearby. Smith was invited to watch this in the company of party ideologist Alfred Rosenberg.

"A remarkable sight indeed," Smith noted. "Twelve hundred of the toughest roughnecks I have ever seen in my life pass in review before Hitler at the goosestep under the old Reichflag wearing red armbands with *Hakenkreuzen* (swastikas)."

Addressing his followers, Hitler explained that while the German government had stopped them from getting to Regensburg that day, the National Socialists would "clean up the town" the following week. In his notebook, Smith added: "He then shouts, 'Death to the Jews' etc. and etc. There was frantic cheering. I never saw such a sight in my life." Afterward, Smith was briefly introduced to Hitler, who promised to talk with him two days later.

While waiting, Smith visited General Ludendorff at home. The famed commander had a blunt message: "The Allies *must* support a strong German government capable of combating Marxism," he insisted. As for the Fascist movement, he described it approvingly as "the beginning of a reactionary awakening in Europe." His conclusion: "America must understand that only a strong nationalist government can preserve the country from chaos and insure reparations being paid to the Allies."

Returning to the Nazi headquarters on Monday, November 21,

Smith met Hitler at 4 P.M. The American was startled by his quarters, which reminded him of a dreary back room of a New York tenement house. Later, Smith would express regret that he focused so much on the substance of Hitler's political message rather than on more observations about his personality. But his impressions that day, which he recorded in his notebook once he had returned to his room in the Hotel Marienbad, were right to the point. "A marvelous demagogue," he wrote. "I have rarely listened to such a logical and fanatical man. His power over the mob must be immense." Hitler's message was unequivocal: "Parliament and parliamentarianism must go. No one can govern with it in Germany today. Only a dictatorship can bring Germany to its feet."

In a report he filed after returning to Berlin, Smith echoed those points and added this assessment:

> The question whether Hitler's National Socialists can play a role in Germany equivalent to the role of the Fascisti in Italy can still not be answered with any degree of certainty. In the limited area of Bavaria, south of the Danube, Hitler's success cannot be gainsaid. Important gains have been registered by the National Socialists from the extreme socialist parties. It is believed that not only in Munich but in all Germany, there is a fertile field even among the factory workers for a national movement, provided the idea of a monarch, which has dominated all preceding national movements, be entirely left aside. It seems hardly probable, furthermore, that with the results already achieved, there will be any lack of money for the propagation of the idea of a national dictatorship. These facts, coupled with the magnetism and oratorical ability of the National Socialist leader, speak for a rapid and consistent development of the German "Fascisti."

Long after World War II, Smith would write *The Facts of Life*, an autobiographical manuscript that he tried but failed to publish. There, he recalled his meeting with Hitler in 1922. "The diary I kept in Munich indicates that I was deeply impressed with his personality and thought it likely he would play an important role in German politics," he wrote. "I must confess, however, that I did not see him as the future ruler of most of Europe."

\*　　　\*　　　\*

On November 17, just as Smith was making his rounds in Munich, Wiegand came to see Ambassador Houghton in the Berlin embassy again. He told the envoy about his meeting with Hitler, how the Nazi leader claimed to be seeking "some arrangement" with France, and indicated that he might try to stage a coup and install a dictatorship.

Finding this report about Hitler "disquieting," Houghton decided to write a confidential letter to Secretary of State Charles Evans Hughes on November 21, not waiting for Smith's report from his meeting with Hitler that was taking place on the same day. While Houghton mistakenly lumped Hitler together with the monarchists, much of his letter would prove to be surprisingly accurate.

"The most active of the Monarchist groups is headed by a young Austrian named Hitler who is in control, it is estimated, of thirty thousand armed men, and, who, by his vehemence and fanaticism and by his dominating and attractive personality, is rapidly becoming the leader of the whole movement," Houghton reported, mentioning that he had dispatched a military attaché to learn more about him.

Modeled after its Italian counterparts, the ambassador continued, "This Fascisti movement is unquestionably spreading throughout Germany . . . It offers a method and means by which conservative people of all shades of political opinion can get together and organize to meet and repel Socialist aggression . . . it is not unlikely to bring within its ranks a large share of the population."

Murphy, the acting consul in Munich, wasn't nearly as early in spotting the danger Hitler represented. He would admit later that he was initially misled about the Nazi leader by Paul Drey, a German employee of the consulate who was a member of a distinguished Jewish family with deep Bavarian roots. The two men attended some of Hitler's early meetings, and, at the end of the first one, Drey indignantly told Murphy: "How does this Austrian upstart dare to tell us Germans what to do?"

After witnessing some other appearances by Hitler, Murphy asked Drey, "Do you think these agitators will ever get far?"

"Of course not!" Drey replied. "The German people are too intelligent to be taken in by such scamps."

The German staffer was very much old-school—and he responded to the growing Nazi presence in an old-school way. Once when he and Murphy stopped at a tailor shop to order a suit, the tailor was openly rude. Guessing what was going on, Murphy asked if the man was a member of the Nazi Party. "Yes, I am a follower of Herr Hitler," he responded proudly. When they were out of the shop, Drey asked Murphy if he had noticed what he had done to show his contempt for the Nazi tailor. The American confessed he hadn't. "I did not tip my hat to him when we left!" Drey explained, as if that nongesture must have devastated its target.

Murphy only met Hitler for a direct conversation once, in early 1923. He was probably still influenced by Drey at that point, since he clearly did not attach much importance to it at the time. In a report back to Washington titled "Bavaria's Political Situation," dated March 17, 1923, Murphy wrote at length about a monarchist conspiracy there, adding a short section at the very end labeled "Interview with Adolf Hitler." The American's reason for requesting the meeting with Hitler was to see whether there was any truth to the rumors that Henry Ford, who was well known for his anti-Semitic views, had provided support to his movement.

"Mr. Hitler was cordial and stated to the main inquiry that unfortunately Mr. Ford's organization has so far made no money contributions to the party," Murphy reported. "He stated that his funds were principally contributed by patriotic Germans living abroad."

The two men then discussed the tensions surrounding the decision by France and Belgium to occupy the industrial Ruhr Valley in January of that year as punishment for Germany's failure to pay reparations. Murphy reported that Hitler considered this occupation "a question involving the economic and political life or death of Germany and cannot be compromised." The Nazi leader clearly backed the campaign of passive resistance that had already started, and suggested that if the French military pushed across the Rhine into Bavaria "an active campaign would certainly ensue." Murphy related those sentiments without comment, suggesting that he wasn't particularly worried by them.

As for Murphy's superiors in the State Department, they weren't nec-

essarily appreciative of his efforts to learn more about the volatile politics of the region. In a letter to Murphy dated April 8, 1924, Wilbur J.
Carr, writing on behalf of the secretary of state, complained that "a large
proportion of the reports received from Munich dealt with political and
politico-economic subjects" during the previous year. While acknowledging that "the disturbed political conditions have perhaps over-shadowed
commercial development," he urged the consular officials to focus more
on "the promotion of American commerce."

Murphy took the message to heart, at least to the extent that he
worked harder on his reporting on commercial issues. But he also began
taking Hitler seriously, while Drey persisted in dismissing him and the
Nazis as aberrations—even after they took power. As late as 1938, Murphy—alarmed by the news that a Munich synagogue had been burned—
flew back to that city to persuade his former employee to flee the country.
He also assured him that he would arrange for him to find a job with the
State Department elsewhere. Drey said he appreciated his concern, but
he wasn't going. "No, this is a temporary madness. Self-respecting Germans will not tolerate these louts much longer," he insisted.

Paul Drey would die in Dachau.

When Captain Smith was preparing for his trip to Munich, Warren Robbins, a colleague at the U.S. Embassy in Berlin, placed a phone call to
Ernst Hanfstaengl in the Bavarian capital. Explaining that Smith would
be going south, he asked a favor: "Look after him and introduce him to
a few people, will you?" It was a minor request that would prove to have
major consequences.

Robbins knew that Hanfstaengl would be happy to oblige. He and
Hanfstaengl had been classmates at Harvard and performed in a production of the Hasty Pudding Club together. The show was called *Fate
Fakirs*, and Hanfstaengl—who, just like Smith, was 6 feet 4 inches tall—
played the role of a Dutch girl called Gretchen Spootsfeiffer, decked out
in feminine garb. "I was the leading soprano there—the falsetto voice,"
he recalled. This was a towering, husky young man who always loved an
audience.

Born in Bavaria in 1887, Hanfstaengl was "half American," as he put it, the son of a German father and American mother with equally impressive lineage. "Putzi," which means "little fellow" in Bavarian and stuck as his nickname from an early age, proudly offered this description of the paternal side of his family: "The Hanfstaengls were substantial folk. For three generations they were privy councillors to the Dukes of Saxe-Coburg-Gotha and well-known as connoisseurs and patrons of the arts." Putzi's grandfather had been famous for his art reproduction work, and then his early use of photography. His father kept the family arts business going and expanded it by opening galleries in London and New York.

Putzi's mother Katharine, whose maiden name was Sedgwick, came from one of New England's truly eminent families. Her maternal uncle was General John Sedgwick, a Civil War hero. Her father was William Heine, an architect by training who had fled Dresden after the revolution of 1848, worked on the decorations of the Paris Opera, and then emigrated to the United States. There, he joined Admiral Perry as his official illustrator on his expedition to Japan. He, too, became a Civil War general, and he helped carry Abraham Lincoln's coffin at his funeral. Thus, it was hardly surprising that Putzi was dispatched to Harvard in 1905, both to learn more about his American heritage and to prepare him to take over the family art gallery on New York's Fifth Avenue.

When discussing his Harvard days, Putzi always dwelled on his prominence and connections there. "I hate to say it myself: I was popular in my class," he eagerly pointed out. Monumentally vain, Hanfstaengl was right on that score: whether he was playing Wagner or banging out marching songs on the piano for the football team, he ingratiated himself with the Harvard crowd, mingling easily with the likes of T. S. Eliot, Walter Lippmann, Robert Benchley and John Reed.

But it was an off-campus exploit that catapulted him to wider fame. On a cold morning in the spring of 1906, he was waiting for practice try-outs for the crew team on the Charles River. As Putzi recalled, "Some fool of a canoeist got into difficulties in the swift current and tipped himself out." Without hesitating, Putzi grabbed a boat and rowed out to the canoeist who was floundering badly. Fully clothed, he jumped into the cold water and managed to push the man up into the boat. The next day, the headline in the *Boston Herald* proclaimed, "Hanfstaengl, Harvard's Hero."

Putzi maintained that this episode was responsible for his getting to know another famous Harvard student: Theodore Roosevelt, Jr., the eldest son of the president. In the winter of 1908, the father—"a fellow extrovert," as Putzi described him—invited him to Washington. His strongest recollection of that first of several meetings with TR was a stag party in the White House basement and "of breaking seven bass strings on his magnificent Steinway Grand."

After Harvard, Hanfstaengl returned to Germany for a year of military service in the Royal Bavarian Foot Guards, standing guard at the royal palace and generally feeling that he was trapped in an anachronistic world. He spent another year studying in Grenoble, Vienna and Rome before returning to the United States and taking charge of the family gallery on Fifth Avenue. Eating often at the Harvard Club, he met another Roosevelt—FDR, who was then a young New York state senator. He also reconnected with the elder Theodore Roosevelt. The former president told him his military service must have been good for him. "I saw something of your army at Doeberitz as the Kaiser's guest, and discipline like that never hurt anybody," he said. "No nation can degenerate which maintains those standards."

Later, their conversation turned to both art and politics. "Hanfstaengl, your business is to pick the best pictures, but remember that in politics the choice is that of the lesser evil," the former president told him. With no sense of irony, Putzi—who would later work assiduously to help Hitler as he rose to power—noted that it was a phrase "which has stuck with me ever since."

During World War I, Hanfstaengl felt the pull of allegiance to the country of his birth. Before the United States entered the war, he tried to help the bands on German ships blockaded in New York harbor by inviting them to perform in the family gallery. Once the Americans joined the fighting, Putzi had to get a lawyer, former Senator Elihu Root, who had been TR's secretary of state, and pledge not to engage in any anti-American activities to avoid internment.

A Department of Justice report in February 1917 offered this assessment of Hanfstaengl, whom investigators had been clearly observing: "He is not a man of criminal instinct, but if war was declared between Germany and America it probably would be best that he be interned because he has the ability of an officer to lead men either here or in Mexico." Nicholas Roosevelt, another member of the famous clan, wrote to the authorities to say that Putzi was "violently anti-American," that he had been in close touch with the German Embassy until it was closed down and that he was "almost a fanatical supporter of his fatherland" and "a most dangerous man to have about."

Whatever the accuracy of that reporting, Hanfstaengl—who had recently married and had his first child—decided to return to Germany in 1921. There, he found a country "riven by faction and near destitution." Echoing Ben Hecht's comment about a country undergoing a nervous breakdown, he added: "It became evident to me that Germany, politically speaking, was a madhouse ..." It was while he was still trying to get his bearings in his transformed homeland that Putzi took the call from his former Harvard classmate who now worked at the American Embassy in Berlin.

When Smith arrived in Munich, Putzi did what he could for him, providing a few largely social introductions. He wrote in his memoirs that Smith was "a very pleasant young officer of about thirty, a Yale man, but in spite of that I was nice to him." He was also nice to Kay, who accompanied her husband to Munich. Putzi, who would soon become notorious for his womanizing, was the perfect gentleman with her. He showed her the sights as a light snow fell, ducking inside the Frauenkirche, whose medieval art charmed his American visitor. When they stopped at his family's art store, he gave her an engraving of the interior of the church. "A lovely way to be introduced to Munich," she would write later. "Perhaps this day is the reason why I have always been so fond of this place."

As it turned out, her husband didn't need all that much help from Putzi, who was impressed with how Truman "worked like a beaver" and met almost everyone who mattered politically. "He soon knew much more about Bavarian politics than I did," he admitted.

On Smith's final day in Munich, the two met for lunch. "I met the most remarkable fellow I've ever come across this morning," Smith volunteered.

Putzi asked who he was talking about. "Adolf Hitler," Smith replied.

"You must have the name wrong," Putzi said. "Don't you mean Hilpert, the German nationalist fellow, although I can't say I see anything particularly remarkable in him."

Realizing Putzi had never heard of Hitler, Smith set him straight. "There are quite a lot of placards up announcing a meeting this evening," he pointed out. "They say he puts up signs saying 'No entry for Jews,' but he has a most persuasive line about German honor and rights for the workers and a new society . . . I have the impression he's going to play a big part, and whether you like him or not he certainly knows what he wants."

Smith had been given a press pass for Hitler's appearance that evening in the Kindlkeller, a popular Munich beer hall. Since he had to take the night train back to Berlin, he asked Putzi if he could attend for him. "Could you possibly have a look at him and let me know your impressions?" he added.

Not knowing what to expect but his curiosity aroused, Hanfstaengl agreed to do so. "It is a far cry from Harvard to Hitler, but in my case the connexion is direct," he would write years later. Or as he put it to one interviewer in recalling the chain of events that would lead him to Hitler: "All that is just by some artistry of fate."

## 2

✦━━━✦━━━✦

# Up in the Air

When Putzi Hanfstaengl arrived at the Kindlkeller on the evening of November 22, 1922, the hall was already packed with people who looked like shopkeepers, civil servants, young people and artisans, many dressed in traditional Bavarian costume. Once he worked his way through the crowd to the press table, Putzi asked a reporter to point Hitler out. Looking at the future leader of Germany, Hanfstaengl was distinctly underwhelmed. "In his heavy boots, dark suit and leather waistcoat, semi-stiff white collar and odd little mustache, he really did not look very impressive—like a waiter in a railway-station restaurant," he recalled.

But after he was introduced to loud applause, Hitler straightened up and walked past the press table "with a swift, controlled step, the unmistakable soldier in mufti," noted Putzi, who was seated only about 8 feet away from the platform that Hitler now occupied. Since Hitler had recently spent a short stint in prison for incitement and he knew police agents were in the crowd, he had to be careful in choosing his words. Still, the atmosphere was "electric," as Putzi described it, and he found the orator a master of "innuendo and irony." Looking back at the first performance that he witnessed, Putzi reflected: "In his early years he had a command of voice, phrase and effect which has never been equaled, and on that evening he was at his best."

After starting in an almost light conversational tone, Hitler warmed to his subject and sharpened his rhetoric. He attacked the Jews for profiteering and contributing to the misery all around them—"a charge which it was only too easy to make stick," Hanfstaengl claimed. He denounced the Communists and Socialists, whom he accused of undermining German traditions. And he warned that anyone who was an enemy of the people would be eliminated.

Putzi saw that the audience was enjoying his speech immensely— "especially the ladies." As Hitler talked about everyday life, Putzi observed a young woman who could not tear her eyes away from the speaker. "Transfixed as if in some devotional ecstasy, she had ceased to be herself and was completely under the spell of Hitler's despotic faith in Germany's future greatness." When Hitler took a swig from a mug of beer that was passed up to him, the crowd burst into new applause and it was clear he had mesmerized them.

"Impressed beyond measure," Putzi later claimed he was already calculating how best he could guide and educate this skillful orator who "was clearly going to go far." Observing Hitler's entourage, Putzi saw no one who could "bring home to him the picture of the outside world he manifestly lacked, and in this I felt I might be able to help." In particular, he saw that Hitler had no idea how critical America's entry into World War I had been and how Europeans had to take into account the United States as a rising power. As a "half American," he viewed this as his mission.

Putzi made his way to the platform, where Hitler stood, drenched with sweat but relishing his triumph. The newcomer introduced himself and conveyed Smith's best wishes. "Ah, you are the friend of that big captain who called this morning," Hitler replied, dabbing his wet forehead with a handkerchief.

Declaring his admiration, Putzi added: "I agree with 95 per cent of what you said and would very much like to talk to you about the rest some time." In an interview long after the war, he would claim that the 5 percent he was referring to was "of course the Jews and all that," but he wanted to be careful not to hurt Hitler's feelings by spelling that out.

"Why, yes, of course," Hitler replied. "I am sure we shall not have to quarrel about the odd five per cent."

Putzi shook hands with him, feeling that here was someone who was "modest and friendly." After he went home, he couldn't fall asleep for a long time as he kept thinking about the evening and what it represented. He saw Hitler as a self-made man who could reach ordinary Germans with a non-communist program. But he hadn't liked the look of some of his followers, including "dubious types" like party ideologist Alfred Rosenberg—"a sallow, untidy fellow, who looked half-Jewish in an unpleasant sort of way."

Nonetheless, Putzi found reassurance in a quote from Nietzsche that he remembered: "The first followers of a movement do not prove anything against it."

Putzi's wife, Helen, or Helene as she was known in Germany, would play a role unlike any other in Hitler's rise to power. In her fragmentary, unpublished notes about her dealings with the Nazi leader, she wrote that her husband had returned that evening from his first encounter with him full of enthusiasm, talking about "the earnest, magnetic young man." While Putzi maintained that the second time he heard Hitler speak he was "less impressed," he quickly threw his lot in with this agitator who he felt could go very far. He started to play the role of his propagandist and press advisor, but his initial involvement was as much social as it was political. And it was very much tied to Hitler's evident attraction to Helen—an attraction that would not be hurt in the least by the fact that she was an American.

Putzi claimed that he first introduced Helen to Hitler when he took her to see him speak, striking up a conversation afterward. The future dictator, according to Putzi, "was delighted with my wife, who was blonde and beautiful and American." In her notes, Helen offered a different recollection, asserting that she met Hitler on a tram. She and Putzi were going downtown when Hitler got on and her husband introduced them. After a brief conversation, she invited him for lunch or dinner whenever he had the time. Whichever version is correct, both Putzi and Helen's stories agree that the first encounter ended with Helen extending an open invitation for him to come to their home. Hitler soon became a frequent guest in their apartment in Gentzstrasse, where they lived with their young son Egon; the Hanfstaengls jokingly referred to it as the Café Gentz.

"From that day he was a constant visitor, enjoying the quiet, cozy home atmosphere, playing with my son at intervals, and talking over for hours his plans and hopes for the renaissance of the German Reich," Helen recalled. With more than a trace of pride, she added in her postwar notes, "It seems he enjoyed our home above all others to which he was invited."

According to Helen, Hitler was dressed in a cheap white shirt, black tie, a worn dark blue suit and an "incongruous" brown leather vest, topped off by a beige trench coat "much the worse for wear," cheap shoes and an old, soft grey hat. "His appearance was really quite pathetic," she wrote. But she found the person in those clothes to be quite appealing: "He was at that time, a slim, shy young man, with a far-away look in his very blue eyes."

She maintained that she was able to see Hitler from an "absolutely different" side than others would in later years. "He was a warm person," she insisted in an interview in 1971. "One thing was really quite touching: he evidently liked children or he made a good act of it. He was wonderful with Egon." One afternoon as the little boy ran to meet Hitler, he slipped and bumped his head against a chair. With a dramatic gesture, Hitler then beat the chair, berating it for hurting "good little Egon." Helen remembered this as "a surprise and a delight," which prompted the boy to ask the visitor to go through the same act each time he came over. "Please, Uncle Dolf, spank the naughty chair," Egon would plead.

Helen was fascinated by Hitler's inclination "to talk and talk and talk," as she put it. "Nobody else had the chance to say anything. I remember, too, that he couldn't stand anyone who wanted to talk. He was the one who talked; the others listened. That was why he couldn't stand some people: because he talked too much." Whether it was in her home or at rallies in this early period, she continued, "his voice had an unusually vibrant, expressive quality, which it later lost, probably through overexertion . . . It has often been said that his voice had a mesmeric quality, and this I can verify, from my own observation."

Her fascination was in no way diminished by the main subject that Hitler focused on. "The one thing he always raved against was the Jews," she admitted. He went on about how Jews had prevented him from getting jobs when he was living in Vienna. Helen believed these experiences generated his anti-Semitism. "It began as personal but he built it up politically," she said.

Who was this American who began hosting Hitler in her home on a regular basis, offering him meals or his favorite duo of black coffee and chocolate—seemingly unconcerned about his dark side? Born in 1893 in New York City, Helen Niemeyer was the daughter of German immigrants, who made sure she spoke German and was aware of her German heritage. But her American identity is on full display in family photos of her dressed as "Liberty"—decked out like the model for the Statue of Liberty and holding a large American flag on the steps of Hoboken's City Hall. Dated 1912–1913, the photos show her as a young woman of nearly twenty, accompanied by little girls in white dresses and sashes bearing the names of different states.

Soon after they began to see each other socially, Hitler asked Helen: "How do you manage here as an American?" Helen explained about her family roots, noting that she spoke German as fluently as she did English and that she also considered herself "really half and half" in terms of her nationality, despite her U.S. passport.

Putzi told Kay Smith that Helen had walked into his family's Fifth Avenue shop one day and he had been immediately smitten. "He had been so struck with her beauty he had followed her home," she recalled. Helen wasn't film-star beautiful: she was five feet nine inches tall, big-boned, and somewhat matronly looking at an early age. But she had an expressive face with lively blue eyes, kept her hair stylishly back, and wore conservative but chic clothes. Helen and Putzi married on February 11, 1920, their marriage certificate issued by the city clerk in Queens. A year later, after Egon was born, they moved to Munich.

Their marriage wasn't easy from the beginning. When the Hanfstaengls came to Berlin for a visit and stayed with the Smiths, Kay found Putzi boisterous to the point where she had to keep him in check. At a dinner party the two couples attended, he played the piano magnificently, she noted. "He might have been a concert pianist had he wished to concentrate on that but . . . he did not work very hard at anything." When they returned to the Smiths' apartment on Olivaer Platz, he swung back into action. With a bottle of cognac at his side, he banged out "Harvard, Fair Harvard," at the same time declaring, "Ah, there's nothing like Wagner."

Both Truman and Helen slipped off to their respective bedrooms to go to sleep, but Kay only managed to stop Putzi after four in the morning. Kay recalled that it felt like she had barely fallen asleep when she heard the piano again. Throwing on some clothes, she got him to stop, since Truman and Helen were still sleeping. To keep him from returning to the piano, she convinced Putzi to accompany her on a walk through the nearly empty Tiergarten in the cold early morning hours, telling him that he had to give his wife and her husband some time to rest.

"Ah, the little Helene is always exhausted," he told her.

"I don't wonder. You are an exhausting person," Kay responded. Once Helen finally left Putzi more than a decade later, Kay observed that she had found him "too exhausting."

But when Helen was new to Germany, she shared many of the same feelings as her husband. She was struck by the economic misery of the postwar period and the political turmoil. "What wonder that in all this chaos a man like A.H. should successfully attract the attention of desperate Germany," she wrote in her precise handwriting. "His plans for the renaissance of the country sounded ideal for most citizens . . ."

Among the new American reporters in Germany at that time, there was far from universal agreement that Hitler was a force to be reckoned with. One of the best known was Hubert Renfro Knickerbocker, a red-haired, hard-charging Texan who had already worked in Moscow before moving to Berlin in 1923, although he was only twenty-five when he arrived in the German capital. During the ten years that he was based there, H. R. Knickerbocker, as his byline usually read, published six books in German, wrote regular columns for German newspapers, while still attending to his primary duties initially as a reporter for the International News Service and then for the *Philadelphia Public Ledger* and the *New York Evening Post*. As John Gunther, another famous itinerant correspondent and author of that era, recalled, he became "a definite public character in German political life."

When Knickerbocker first saw Hitler in August 1923, rallying his supporters at the Cirkus Krone in Munich, his reaction was one of comic disbelief. "The first impression he makes on any non-German is that he looks silly . . . I broke out laughing," Knickerbocker recalled. "Even if you had never heard of him you would be bound to say, 'He looks like a caricature of himself.'" He noted not just the mustache and the lock of hair, but also "the expression of his face, and especially the blank stare of his eyes, and the foolish set of his mouth in repose . . . Other times he clamps his lips together so tightly and juts out his jaw with such determination that again he looks silly, as though he were putting on an act."

There was something else that also gave Knickerbocker and many of his colleagues pause. "He is softly fat about the hips and this gives his figure a curiously female appearance," he wrote. "It is possible that the strongly feminine element in Hitler's character is one of the reasons for his violence."

By contrast, Putzi Hanfstaengl was in full agreement with his wife about Hitler's appeal, taking him very seriously. He quickly joined Hitler's entourage and began regularly playing the piano for him, especially after the Nazi leader's frequent run-ins with the police, who were increasingly monitoring his activities. The first time Putzi played, he tried out a Bach fugue, but Hitler didn't show any interest. Then, he launched into the prelude of Richard Wagner's *Meistersinger* and he suddenly had Hitler's full attention. "He knew the thing absolutely by heart and could whistle every note of it in a curious penetrating vibrato, but completely in tune," Putzi recalled. Hitler started marching up and down, waving his arms as if he were conducting. "This music affected him physically and by the time I had crashed through the finale he was in splendid spirits, all his worries gone, and raring to get to grips with the public prosecutor."

Hanfstaengl also introduced Hitler to Harvard marching songs, explaining how the music and the cheerleaders were used to whip up the crowds to the point of "hysterical enthusiasm." He played Sousa marches, and then some of his own improvisations that added the marching beat of American tunes to German ones. "That is it, Hanfstaengl, that is what we need for the movement, marvelous," Hitler exclaimed, prancing about the room like a drum majorette. Putzi would later write several marches that were used by the Brownshirts, including the one they played when they marched through the Brandenburg Gate on the day Hitler took power in 1933. "Rah, rah, rah! became *Sieg Heil, Sieg Heil!* but that is the origin of it and I suppose I must take my share of the blame," Putzi wrote in his autobiography. In fact, this sounded like a case of scarcely concealed pride of authorship.

Putzi contributed to Hitler's movement in other ways, too. After selling his share of the family art gallery in New York to a partner, he put up $1,000 to turn the four-page Nazi propaganda weekly *Völkischer Beobachter* into a daily. Hitler complained that regular newspapers ignored him and believed that such a transformation could help overcome that problem. Aside from providing the funding, Putzi hired a cartoonist to design a new masthead. He also claimed credit for thinking up its slogan *Arbeit und Brot,* work and bread. Although Putzi told Hitler that the $1,000 was a no-interest loan, he would never get it back.

As part of Hitler's circle of advisors, Putzi tried to act on his initial impulse to explain more of the world to this young firebrand—particularly the growing importance of the United States. Pointing out that it was America's entry into World War I that determined the final outcome, he told Hitler, "If there is another war it must be inevitably won by the side which America joins." All this, he continued, made it vital for Hitler to advocate a policy of friendship with the United States. While Hitler conceded his point, he didn't really seem to register it. Putzi concluded that his ideas about America were "wildly superficial." The only American who interested him then was Henry Ford, since he saw him as a fellow anti-Semite who might be tapped for funds. He was equally interested in the Ku Klux Klan. "He seemed to think it was a political movement similar to his own," Putzi noted.

By the fall of 1923, Hitler was openly calling for a revolt against the government. Inflation had turned into hyperinflation, and Putzi recalled that when he pushed his way into the Bürgerbräukeller on November 8, the night of what would go down in history as the beginning of the Beer Hall Putsch, the price for the three beers he ordered was 3 *billion* marks. He handed one to Hitler, who took a sip even though he already considered himself a nondrinker. With three top Bavarian officials sitting at the speaker's platform, Hitler—wearing his Iron Cross over his trench coat and grasping a whip—ordered his Brownshirts to seize control of the hall. "Quiet!" he shouted. When the crowd continued to talk in the general confusion that followed, he jumped on a chair and fired a shot into the air. "The national revolution has broken out. The hall is surrounded!" he proclaimed.

Even greater confusion followed. Hitler marched the Bavarian officials out to a side room, telling them he wouldn't accept anything but their support for his putsch. He would reward them with top positions, he vowed; if they refused, the alternative would be grim, he warned. "Gentlemen, not one of us shall leave this hall alive! There are three of you, and I have four bullets. That will be enough for all of us if I fail." By some accounts, he held a pistol to his head as he said so. No one seemed impressed, and General Ludendorff, who had arrived late but dressed in his full Imperial Army uniform, allowed the Bavarian officials to slip away after supposedly securing their assurances that they were on the plotters' side.

Hanfstaengl held an impromptu press conference, telling foreign correspondents that a new government had been formed. Cabling from Berlin, Wiegand accepted that version of events as fact and ran with it. "REBELS IN COUP SEIZE BAVARIAN RULE, BEGIN ARMED MARCH AGAINST BERLIN" proclaimed the giant two-line headline across the front page of the *San Francisco Examiner* in its November 9, 1923, edition over his story. He reported that after "the long expected coup," Hitler's storm troopers were in control of key communications in Munich and had cut off contact with Berlin, Ludendorff had taken charge of the army, and Hitler had proclaimed the end of the republic.

In reality, Hitler and Ludendorff had lost control of events as soon as the Bavarian officials had left the beer hall. Overnight, the officials made arrangements to put down the rebellion. Although they had largely toler-ated Hitler's movement up till then and sympathized with some of its aims, they weren't about to let him dictate to them. By the time Hitler and Ludendorff had ordered their troops to march from the Bürger-bräukeller to the center of the city around noon on November 9, the state police was lined up to stop them, with two machine guns at the ready. Confident that they wouldn't open fire on a war hero like Ludendorff, both the general and the ex-corporal proceeded with their plan, leading the march. They were met with machine-gun fire. Fourteen Nazis died on the spot, along with four policemen.

The American consul Robert Murphy and his German colleague Paul Drey had rushed to the scene to see what was happening. "I can testify that both Hitler and Ludendorff behaved in an identical manner, like the battle-hardened soldiers they were. Both fell flat to escape the hail of bullets," Murphy recalled. In the brief pandemonium, it was hard to see what actually transpired—and Hitler may have dropped to the ground for another reason. One of those struck by the hail of bullets was Scheub-ner-Richter, Hitler's close aide, who was marching with him arm-in-arm. Killed instantly, he may have jerked Hitler to the ground. In any case, the Nazi leader fled the scene with a dislocated shoulder.

Several top Nazis were immediately arrested and Ludendorff sur-rendered to the authorities, but he was set free after giving his officer's word that he wouldn't evade trial. Putzi, who had missed the shooting, rushed to see the outcome, and a Brownshirt medic he encountered told him that Hitler, Ludendorff and Goering were all dead. "My God, Herr Hanfstaengl, it's too terrible," he said. "It is the end of Germany." Believ-ing all was lost, Putzi advised other Nazis he met to get out of Munich immediately, crossing the border into Austria. And he promptly followed his own advice.

In fact, Hitler had managed to escape to his waiting car, along with Walter Schultze, the chief doctor for the storm troopers and others. And, unlike Putzi, he sought refuge in the Hanfstaengls' country house in Uff-ing, about an hour from Munich. "The last place it would have occurred to me to go was my own home in Uffing, where I surely would be caught and arrested," Putzi noted later.

In Hitler's case, that's exactly where he ended up, although apparently not by initial design. Still, he probably went there in part because, as Putzi put it, Hitler had developed "one of his theoretical passions" for Helen. Putzi was quick to suggest that Hitler was impotent, and that Hitler's infatuation with his wife never went beyond hand-kissing and bringing her flowers. "He had no normal sex life . . . somehow one never felt with him that the attraction was physical," he declared. Helen agreed that her admirer was probably "a neuter," but she had no doubt that he was strongly attracted to her.

Whatever the reason, Helen suddenly found herself with an unexpected house guest on the evening of November 9. She had been hearing reports about the putsch and the rumors that Hitler and Ludendorff were dead, but she didn't know what to believe. While she and Egon were having supper in the upstairs living room, a maid reported that someone was knocking softly on the door. Helen went downstairs and, without opening the door, asked who was there. "To my utter amazement, I recognized the weak but unmistakable voice of Hitler," she recalled.

Helen quickly opened the door and found herself facing a very different Hitler than the one who normally showed up: "There he stood, ghastly pale, hatless, his face and clothing covered with mud, the left arm hanging down from a strangely slanting shoulder." The doctor and a medic were holding him up from both sides, but they, too, looked "pathetically rampaged." Once inside, Helen asked Hitler about Putzi. He told her he wasn't in the confrontation because he was working on putting out the party newspaper and that he'd probably show up soon. Hitler kept talking, despondent about the deaths of his aides and possibly of Ludendorff, and furious about what he called the treachery of the Bavarian officials. He also swore to her that "he would go on fighting for his ideals as long as breath was in him."

Hitler was running a temperature and in pain from the dislocated shoulder, so the doctor and the medic eased him upstairs to a bedroom. From there, Helen heard him moaning as they tried to push his arm back into his shoulder.

During the night, the doctor explained to Helen that they, too, had tried to flee to Austria, but their car had broken down. When the driver couldn't fix it, Hitler had suggested going to Hanfstaengl's house since they could reach it by foot, although it was a long, difficult walk for the three worn-out men. What that story didn't explain was how Hitler imagined he could stay hidden in the house of one of his well-known followers.

The next morning, Hitler sent off the doctor to Munich to see if he could arrange for another car to pick him up and still get him to Austria. His arm was in a sling and he appeared to be in less pain than the previous evening, but he was pacing nervously about in a blue bathrobe, asking where the car might be. Helen's mother-in-law called to say that the police were already in her nearby house. Suddenly, an official cut her off and took the phone himself, telling Helen that he and his men would be arriving at her house next.

Helen went upstairs to let Hitler know that he was about to be arrested. Standing in the hallway, he looked devastated by the news. "Now all is lost—no use going on!" he exclaimed, throwing up his hands. Then, with a quick motion, he picked up his revolver from the cabinet. "But I was alert, grasped his arm and took the weapon away from him," Helen recalled.

Alarmed that he might have shot himself, she shouted: "What do you think you're doing? After all, are you going to leave all the people that you've gotten interested in your idea of saving the country and you take your life . . . They're looking for you to carry on."

Hitler hadn't resisted when she grabbed the gun, and he sank into a chair, burying his head in his hands. While he was still sitting like that, Helen quickly took the gun away to dispose of it, settling on a large flour bin where it easily vanished from sight as she pushed it down deep inside. Returning to Hitler, she urged him to dictate to her all his instructions for his followers before the police arrived; that way, they would know what to do while he would be in prison. She added that he could then sign each sheet containing instructions and she would make sure they would be delivered to his lawyer. "He thanked me for helping him remember his duty to his men, and then dictated the orders which were to be of such importance in carrying on the work," she recalled.

Soon, the police with guard dogs surrounded the house. Helen answered the knock at the door, and a shy young army lieutenant, accompanied by two policemen, apologetically explained that he had to search the house. Helen told them to follow her upstairs and she opened the door to the room where Hitler was standing. Startled, the three men took a step back for a moment. The Nazi leader had regained his confidence and immediately began berating the lieutenant in a loud voice, particularly when he told him he had to arrest him for high treason.

There was no use arguing, however, and even Hitler realized that. Refusing Helen's offer of Putzi's clothes to shield him from the cold, he was still dressed in the blue bathrobe, with his own coat draped over his shoulders, as the men led him down the stairs. At that moment, little Egon ran out, calling, "What are the bad, bad men doing to my Uncle Dolf?" Looking moved, Hitler patted Egon on the cheek. Then he shook hands with Helen and the maids before going out the door. Helen caught a last glance at his face when he was seated in the police car. It was "deathly pale," she remembered.

Most of the press coverage that followed, at home and abroad, quickly wrote off Hitler and the Nazis. The Beer Hall Putsch had been laughably amateurish, and now all that awaited the arrested leaders was a trial and certain convictions.

Few people realized then that the trial and even imprisonment would serve Hitler surprisingly well. And only a few insiders knew then that it was a young American woman, the wife of one of his earliest followers, who may have prevented him from taking his own life—an act that would have delivered humanity from the devastating consequences of his political resurrection later. It was Helen Hanfstaengl, née Niemeyer, who, in the worst possible way, may have changed the course of history.


Like Knickerbocker who quickly became a close friend, Edgar Ansel Mowrer of the *Chicago Daily News* was a new arrival in Berlin in 1923, showing up late that year and staying for a decade, right through Hitler's rise to power. And, like Knickerbocker, Wiegand and other correspondents, he was as much intrigued by the German capital's dynamism in the arts as by its chaotic politics. The city was "a cultural riot, the wilder for the lack of such deep traditions as still had held sway in Paris and London," he recalled. Along with his British-born wife Lilian, he was quickly swept up in that cultural riot.

At the annual Press Ball in the huge Zoo Restaurant, the Mowrers had the chance to mingle with everyone from top government officials and the high-society crowd to the playwrights Bertolt Brecht and Carl Zuckmayer, composer Richard Strauss when he was visiting from Vienna to conduct an opera, and conductor Wilhelm Furtwängler. The event brought together "the leaders of totally different worlds," Mowrer wrote. "It was as though Paris had merged the Elysée, the Opéra, and the *Beaux Arts* Ball into one vast get-together that opened with the dignity of a state reception and ended in a bacchanal."

Initially, Lilian Mowrer had been distinctly unimpressed with Berlin when she followed her husband after wrapping up the couple's affairs in Rome, their previous assignment. Arriving in March 1924, she was depressed by the figurative and literal cold and the contrast to Italy, where spring flowers were already in bloom. "In Berlin ice still covered the ponds in the Tiergarten, and the atmosphere was leaden," she noted. She was depressed, too, by "the ugliness of the city," the heavy Victorian architecture, the pompousness of public buildings—and by "the unlovely figures of the people!"

In the apartment they rented, she found canvases painted by their landlord, female nudes "in the violent tones and formless composition of the German Expressionist school" featuring massive torsos and backsides. "As if we don't see enough horrors in the street," she complained. Then there was the matter of food. "There is a great deal in the German cuisine that needs getting used to," she archly noted. Even the fact that the mark had finally stabilized had its downside as far as she was concerned: prices were now much higher for foreigners than a few years earlier.

Soon, however, Lilian began to see her new home in a different light. German Expressionism was still a puzzle to her, "but something in the passionately contorted figures and faces was beginning to arouse my interest." She loved Italian art but realized that in Rome she had been living artistically "entirely in the past." By contrast, "German modern work, half metaphysical, half barbaric, was a stimulating challenge." As for German theater, she quickly recognized it as "the most vital in Europe" and Germans as "the greatest theater-goers in Europe." And she loved the fact that Berlin was full of foreign productions as well, from the classic Comédie Française to the daring new Russian offerings of Stanislavsky and Meyerhold, which she found particularly exciting. "Nowhere in the world was there such hospitality to foreign talent as in Germany," she wrote.

Lilian's happiest discovery, though, was how open many Germans were to foreigners in everyday life, not just on the stage. "They were so wonderfully hospitable, those Weimar Republicans, they did not wait to make a *bella figura* with receptions and parties, they invited us to take potluck with them in the friendliest manner." She found everyone—bankers, politicians, writers—inquisitive, expansive and often entertaining.

Another striking aspect of life in Weimar Germany, she observed, was the role of women. At the time of her arrival, the Reichstag boasted 36 women parliamentarians—more than anywhere else. Women were studying a broad array of subjects at the universities—law, economics, history, engineering—and were entering professions once reserved for men. Lilian even met "a full-fledged slaughterer" in Berlin: Margarethe Cohn, who could kill a steer with a single blow of the mallet. "A woman could do what she liked in Weimar Germany," Lilian concluded.

Lilian was far more than just an observer of life in Berlin. She wrote articles for *Town and Country*, and she appeared in the first "super-talkie" German film, *Liebeswalzer* (The Love Waltz), which had both an English and a French version. The German actress who had been cast for the role didn't speak English as well as she claimed, and Lilian was asked to try out for it. She passed the screen test easily, but her initial elation faded when she saw how monotonous much of the work of endless reshooting was. Still, there were consolations. At another studio lot, Marlene Dietrich was shooting *The Blue Angel*, and Lilian saw her often eating lunch at the same restaurant where she took her meals. She recognized Dietrich from the stage, where she played leads in "sophisticated" musical reviews and comedies. When *The Blue Angel* catapulted her to stardom on the big screen, Lilian wasn't impressed. "It was the greatest waste of material to condemn her forever to vamp roles," she wrote.

Lilian and Edgar got to know many of the city's other most famous inhabitants, from the artist George Grosz to Albert Einstein. Meeting the physicist, Edgar asked him about a part of his relativity theory he found illogical. Einstein smiled and replied: "Quit bothering your mind about it: mine is a mathematical, not a logical theory. Here . . ." At that point, he took his violin and began playing Bach.

Little wonder that Lilian soon conceded: "I was becoming reconciled to Berlin."

American officials played a key role in bringing about the return to apparent economic normalcy that newcomers like the Mowrers immediately noticed. Ambassador Houghton had been more than just sympathetic to Germany's plight; he defied isolationist voices back home by arguing that the United States was to blame for not acting more decisively to support Germany's democratic government. "All in all, Europe is in a sorry mess," he wrote to State Department European Division Chief William Castle on February 12, 1923. "We ourselves had at one time the power to stabilize conditions . . . unless something of a miracle takes place, we may look forward confidently and happily to a time not far off when another war may lay prostrate what is left of European civilization."

Repeatedly urging Washington "to save what is left of German capital and German industry," Houghton was driven to near despair observing the devastating impact of hyperinflation on his host country, along with the strikes, riots and clashes of extremists of the left and the right. In the summer of 1923, he watched Chancellor Wilhelm Cuno's government collapse after less than a year in office. "I feel as if I had come back into the same old building, but found the beams and rafters steadily decaying and the floors increasingly unsound, and that unless steps were speedily taken to repair it, the roof and walls must before long inevitably fall in," he wrote to Secretary of State Hughes.

Those pleas didn't fall on deaf ears. With backing from the Coolidge Administration, Houghton began to make progress on his push for a new reparations settlement and other measures aimed at stabilizing Germany. In his public pronouncements, Houghton avoided chastising France and denied any intention of seeking to block her "just claims," but he stressed that Germany's economic recovery was the key to the continent's recovery. Working closely with Germany's Gustav Stresemann, who served briefly as both chancellor and foreign minister in 1923 and then stayed on as foreign minister in eight successive governments, he won support in Berlin and other European capitals for a more active American role.

The result was the Dawes Plan, named after Chicago banker Charles G. Dawes, one of a group of American experts who tackled the reparations question. The plan did not fix an exact amount of reparations that the Germans still owed, but it allowed them to make reduced annual payments until their economy improved. Accepted at the end of August 1924, the Dawes Plan immediately triggered a flood of American loans to Germany that would continue until the Depression hit. The stabilization of the currency and the subsequent economic recovery were a direct result of those measures. Speaking to the Reichstag on May 18, 1925, Stresemann left no doubt who was responsible for this dramatic turnaround. "The United States is that nation from which emanated the most important efforts directed toward the reconstruction of the economy and, beyond that, the pacification of Europe," he declared. "For no country can those efforts be more welcome than for Germany."

American loans and direct investments, coupled with growing U.S.-German trade, meant that the two countries felt increasingly linked with each other. Germany was not only open to Americans but to the broader trends identified by a new term characterizing their country's economic, social and cultural influence. "The Americanization of Europe proceeds merrily apace," Wiegand reported in a feature that was given prominent play in the *Washington Herald* on June 14, 1925. "Half in wonderment, half in protest this tired old group of nations is falling under the magic sway of that babulous 'dollar land' across the ocean."

As his article pointed out, the average German exhibited a decidedly schizophrenic attitude toward the new money culture, mass production and mass entertainment, including a flood of American movies. He is "resentful of the intrusion of a staccato pace into the easy comfort of his existence and growls and mutters guttural curses against the Americanization of his civilization," Wiegand wrote. "Then he goes and forgets his troubles to the tune of an American jazz band, beating a savage tom-tom in any of the thousand amusement places." The German listening to a band playing "My Sweetie Went Away," he added, was likely to be dressed in a brand-new suit "cut on Yale lines."

Germans flocked to the Scala variety house, where the hit of the moment was an American troupe that Wiegand described as "the eighteen dancing, prancing Gertrude Hoffman girls." In his 1925 article, he noted one key reason for the Americans' popularity. "Their slender legs and waists are not of the pattern usually favored in Berlin," he wrote.

Berlin was also beginning to experience American-style traffic problems, he reported, and had installed its first traffic lights on Potsdamer Platz, "winking its flirtatious American eyes at the street car conductors, taxi drivers and chauffeurs who get flustered in the tangle of this place where five important streets meet."

Mowrer echoed those sentiments. "By the early twenties signs of Americanization were appearing all over Europe, and nowhere so conspicuously as in Germany," he wrote. In his reports, he called 1925 "the first great American year in Europe" and explained how "that complex of factors, personal democracy, technique and standardization of practice," along with new flashy ads, "had bitten deep into the German soul." He quoted an American economist as saying that mass production was transforming Germany into "the United States of Europe."

All of which contributed to the lure of Berlin for American expats. While Paris was still their favorite city in Europe, many of them visited the German capital in the 1920s. Josephine Baker and her *Revue Nègre* took their act to Berlin, holding their opening show at the Nelson Theater on the Kurfürstendamm on December 31, 1925. Although there were protesters outside denouncing the black entertainers, and Nazis called Baker subhuman, she was elated by the enthusiasm of the audiences. "It's madness. A triumph. They carry me on their shoulders," she said.

Berlin was the city where Baker received the most gifts: she was showered with jewelry, perfume, furs. After her regular shows, the Nelson Theater was turned into a cabaret, and Baker would continue to perform. She also happily accepted invitations to other parties, at times wearing nothing more than a loincloth. Berlin's wild nightlife has "an intensity

Paris doesn't know," she declared—and she loved it. She even considered settling in Berlin but was lured back to the French capital to star at the Folies Bergère.

Both for American visitors and residents, Germany's racy sexual life was a source of constant fascination. As Edgar Mowrer put it, "The period immediately following the war saw throughout the world a sexual exuberance which, in Germany, reached an almost orgiastic intensity . . . If anything, the women were the more aggressive. Morality, virginity, monogamy, even good taste, were treated as prejudice." And when it came to "sexual perversions," Mowrer added with open amazement, old laws were simply ignored. "It is hard to conceive a much more tolerant society."

Ben Hecht, who had reported from Berlin for the *Chicago Daily News* a few years earlier, described what his successor was hinting at. He met a group of homosexual aviators at an Officers' Club. "These were elegant fellows, perfumed and monocled and usually full of heroin or cocaine," he recalled. "They made love to one another openly, kissing in the café booths and skipping off around two A.M. to a mansion owned by one of them. One or two women were usually in the party—wide-mouthed, dark-eyed nymphomaniacs with titles to their names but unroyal burns and cuts on their flanks. At times little girls of ten and eleven, recruited from the pavements of Friedrichstrasse, where they paraded after midnight with rouged faces and in shiny boots and in short baby dresses, were added to the mansion parties."

Although Hecht may have embellished some of his descriptions for his autobiography, there's no question that Berlin boasted a flourishing gay scene. For visiting young gay Americans like Philip Johnson, this was an exhilarating discovery. Drawn to Germany by the Bauhaus movement and other forms of architectural modernism emerging there in the 1920s, the future famous architect was quickly enchanted by much more than his professional interests. "The air we breathed, the people we came to know, the restaurants, the Kurfürstendamm, the sex life were all new, all thrilling to a young American," he recalled. "The world was being created here."

In a letter to his family back home, Johnson wrote: "I think if it can be told from the platform of a Berlin cabaret, it can be written to one's mother. How prudish I am getting, my, my! Recently in Berlin, it seems, the law against homosexual relations has been repealed, apropos of which the *conférencier* said that at Easter the law against relations with animals will also be repealed and the normal relation only will be prohibited. The audience thought it very funny, as I did myself, but then of course, I would not admit it."

And Johnson, like other Americans, found the Germans extremely welcoming, irrespective of sexual preferences. "The Americans were the conquerors of old Germany and the young Germans were eager to accommodate them," he recalled. "Paris was never that *gastfreundlich*."

After the aborted Beer Hall Putsch, the Nazis were no longer considered a major story. But then, in early 1924, Hitler was put on trial along with Ludendorff and the others accused of treason. Hitler used the occasion to openly proclaim his goal of overthrowing the Weimar Republic, elaborating on his stab-in-the-back theory about how its treacherous politicians were responsible for Germany's humiliating defeat and for the subsequent economic disaster. "Treason to the Republic is not treason to the real Germany," he insisted.

As the judges gave him free rein to dominate the proceedings and even cross-examine witnesses, Hitler scored point after point, ridiculing the Bavarian authorities for initially going along with him before turning against the putsch. Since everyone knew the Bavarian leaders had denounced and defied the central government in Berlin on countless occasions, Hitler sounded convincing when he testified that they "had the same goal that we had—to get rid of the Reich government." They had discussed that goal before the putsch, he added.

The clear message: Hitler had acted on his convictions, shared by all those who despised Germany's current rulers, while the Bavarian authorities had played a double game. "You may pronounce us guilty a thousand times over, but the goddess of the eternal court of history will smile and tear to tatters the brief of the state prosecutor and the sentence of this court," he told the judges. "For she acquits us."

Observing Hitler for the first time as he covered the trial, Mowrer was clearly impressed. "He spoke with humor, irony and passion," he reported. "A little dapper man, he sometimes resembled a German drill sergeant, and sometimes a Viennese floor walker." His oratory "literally tore to pieces" the claims of the Bavarian authorities. When he had finished his impassioned speech, "there was scarcely a spectator or a correspondent who did not want to applaud him," he concluded.

Hitler was sentenced to five years in prison, the minimum sentence for treason, and Ludendorff was acquitted altogether. Murphy of the American consulate summed up his conclusions in a report to Washington dated March 10, 1924: "While the putsch in November 1923 was a farcical failure, the nationalist movement behind it is by no means extinguished in Bavaria. It has simply been delayed . . . It is contemplated that upon completion of his term Hitler, who is not a citizen, will be expelled from the country. Further nationalist activity on his part, for the present at least, appears to be excluded."

In his memoirs that were published in 1964, Murphy wrote that this conclusion was "not too bad." Specifically, he contrasted it with the single mention of Hitler in the memoirs of Lord D'Abernon, the British ambassador to Germany from 1920 to 1926. The future German leader's name appeared only in a footnote, which claimed that after his release from prison, Hitler "vanished into oblivion."

Hitler was released from Landsberg Prison after serving less than nine months in pampered conditions, which allowed him to use the time to dictate his autobiography *Mein Kampf*. His jailers treated him like a guest of honor, allotting him a comfortable large room with a lovely view and allowing plenty of visitors and packages from well-wishers. After his release, he was not expelled to his Austrian homeland.

Still, Hitler's movement was beset by internal feuds during his absence, and, even when he began to mobilize his followers again and the ban on the party was lifted, the country's improved economic situation diminished its appeal. In the December 1924 elections for the Reichstag, the Nazis won a paltry 14 seats as compared to 131 for the Socialists and 103 for the German Nationalists, a less radical right-wing movement.

During the presidential elections in April 1925, the right-wing parties backed Field Marshal Paul von Hindenburg, who easily won despite the fact that he was already seventy-seven. As Hamilton Fish Armstrong, the editor of the prestigious journal *Foreign Affairs* who was visiting Germany at the time, recalled in his memoirs, the most interesting part of that presidential campaign was that the Nazis did not figure "even as a side issue." Hitler was out of prison but still barred from public speaking and, as Armstrong added, "as far as I can remember, nobody, either German or American, so much as mentioned his name to me."

In the May 1928 parliamentary elections, the Nazis dropped even lower, winning only 12 seats. The Socialists raised their tally to 152 seats, and the Nationalists dropped to 78. Little wonder that both American diplomats and correspondents, who had briefly focused on Hitler during the run-up to the Beer Hall Putsch and then through his trial, largely ignored him afterward. There was no line for interviews, no urgent queries about him from Washington to the diplomats or from the editorial home offices to the foreign correspondents.

At times, the Americans residing in or passing through Berlin appeared to be as much preoccupied with each other and fellow expats as with their surroundings. Writing to a friend on November 14, 1927, Knickerbocker tossed in this teaser: "Hemingway by the way is here in Berlin just now, hobnobbing with Sinclair Lewis." Lewis, who in 1930 would become the first American to win the Nobel Prize for Literature, spent a good deal of time in Berlin because of Dorothy Thompson, who had moved there in 1925. One of the first female foreign correspondents with celebrity status, Thompson reported for the *Philadelphia Public Ledger* and the *New York Evening Post*, and she shared a duplex apartment on Händelstrasse with the Mowrers.

Knickerbocker, who would later take over her Berlin job for the Philadelphia and New York papers, conveniently introduced Thompson to Lewis at a tea given by the German foreign minister. To make things juicier, some accounts claim that Thompson and Knickerbocker were more than colleagues, briefly linking them romantically.

Thompson had just divorced Joseph Bard, a Hungarian who had a well-deserved reputation as a womanizer, and Lewis's marriage to Grace

Hegger was in a state of collapse. The acclaimed author and the pioneering woman foreign correspondent were immediately infatuated with each other. Thompson called Lilian Mowrer one evening. "Do come on up, I have a jolly crowd here," she told her. Mowrer came to the other part of the duplex apartment they shared to find Lewis, fresh from his triumphant publication of *Elmer Gantry*, delivering sermons "in the manner of his ecclesiastical hero" to the small gathering. Turning his collar back to front, he let loose with a torrent of words, damning his listeners for their sins. "It was an amazing *tour de force*, and we quaked, deliciously conscious of our shortcomings," Lilian recalled. Lewis and Thompson soon became lovers and, once his divorce came through, they married in 1928.

That kind of social scene, along with Germany's openness to "Americanization," meant that Americans felt very much at home in Berlin. In 1928, even Hitler—then the leader of what still looked like an inconsequential party—pointed out that "Americanization" was leaving its mark in numerous ways. "International relations between nations have become so easy and close through modern technology and the communication it makes possible, that the European, often without being conscious of it, applies American conditions as a standard for his own," he declared. It was a rare case of Hitler acknowledging a new trend without immediately denouncing it.

The talk of Americanization was shorthand for what now is called globalization. It was a genuine opening up to the world. That, as much as any specifically American characteristics, represented the real attraction of Berlin. "These were the brilliant, feverish years when Berlin was, in a cultural sense, the capital of the world," Thompson wrote, repeating the sentiments of the banjo virtuoso Michael Danzi and other artists. "These were the days when the German mind was open to every stream of thought from every part of the earth. Every current beat upon Berlin."

While American reporters continued to cover the political and economic situation, the stories that stand out in this period—and thrilled readers the most—were the lighter features. And none more so than the first transatlantic passenger flight of the *Graf Zeppelin* in October 1928, a 112-hour voyage in the rigid airship from Friedrichshafen, Germany, to Lakehurst, New Jersey. The *Chicago Herald and Examiner* issued a special booklet with all the articles of the two Hearst correspondents on board. The introduction called the compilation "an authentic record of a voyage that today is second only to that of Columbus in importance."

One of the Hearst correspondents on board was Wiegand. The other was Lady Drummond-Hay, who was hailed as the first woman to cross the Atlantic by air. Both reporters filed extensively, and it was the pairing of their stories that added to the sense of adventure and romance about the voyage. Lady Drummond-Hay's writing was particularly evocative:

"The Graf Zeppelin is more than just machinery, canvas and aluminum," she filed. "It has a soul—every man who worked to build it, every man who worked to fly it, every one of us who have made this journey, has contributed to the humanization of the aerial colossus. I love the airship as if it were something alive . . . I have been supremely happy on the Zeppelin. The journey has contributed richly to my emotional life."

Some readers may have guessed another source of Lady Drummond-Hay's emotional life: the romantic attachment between her and her colleague Wiegand. In 1923 at the age of twenty-eight, the Englishwoman had married the former diplomat Sir Robert Hay Drummond-Hay, who was fifty years older than she was. Three years later, he died, leaving her a young aristocratic widow who focused on her journalistic career. Working for Hearst, she met Wiegand, and their relationship quickly became much more than professional. Wiegand was married, but, as a gallivanting foreign correspondent, he was often separated from his wife.

After the two met in 1926, they tried to cover stories together as often as they could—including the first around-the-world zeppelin voyage in 1929. When separated, the duo wrote constantly to each other. Their correspondence leaves no doubt about the nature of their relationship. "You have indeed cared for me 'tenderly' Ol' Bear, and the Cubbie-wubbie is fully appreciative and will stick close beside the Old Bear for comfort and protection, and love all her life . . . I love you very dearly and very truly," the Englishwoman wrote in one of her first letters in 1926, signing it "Cubbie-wubbie-Tum-Tum."

The Hearst newspapers loved trumpeting the exploits of the "brilliant British woman" and the "internationally-known newspaper correspondent" Wiegand. And they had no hesitation about focusing on stories about air travel when the situation on the ground looked better than it had since the beginning of the previous war. As Dorothy Thompson wrote later, the period from 1924 to 1929 seemed "full of promise . . . In that brief five years, truly remarkable progress was made in Germany." It seemed to make perfect sense to illustrate that progress with dramatic narratives about people soaring across oceans, invoking visions of a peaceful, more harmonious world.

Even in that era full of promise, many Americans in Germany sensed that, despite surface similarities, "the Germans" were different from them and many other Europeans. "Though externals of American life were becoming increasingly popular—quick-lunch bars, flashy slogans, sky-scrapers, even chewing-gum—the mental attitude towards them remained purely Teutonic," Lilian Mowrer observed. Those "Teutonic" differences were sometimes odd, sometimes comic, and, occasionally, hinted at something troubling, something sinister.

The Mowrers investigated a German social phenomenon that, at first glance, looked titillating. "Where but in Germany could one find 150,000 organized nudists?" Edgar wrote. But after visiting several nudist colonies, Lilian pointed out: "They all had the same un-erotic, purposeful atmosphere." She wrote off the more lurid stories of sexual shenanigans there as nothing more than rumors and detected something more philosophical. "These Germans were swayed by feelings half primitive, half religious, with hopes of a saner humanity in some remote future yet undreamed."

She was troubled by "the loose emotional fervor" the nudist movement engendered and its "ardent yearning for something 'different.'" Most of the young people she met at the nudist colonies voted Communist, thinking this represented the path to human betterment. Those feelings, she concluded, "could be just as easily canalized and turned in any other direction by an unscrupulous leader interested in using it for his own ends."

Thompson was struck by the German public's fascination with gruesome crimes, as evidenced by the popularity of a police exhibition chronicling a series of murders that had captured the headlines. It included a reproduction of the bedroom of a man who had trolled for his twenty-six young male victims in the toilets of the Hannover train station. "If one wants a glimpse of the miserable den in which this monster killed his victims, if one longs to see the cot where he strangled them, the table where he carved them, the buckets in which he stored them, one must stand in line for half an hour," she observed.

Americans were equally intrigued by other forms of extreme behavior. The Mowrers were taken aback by the assistant in the *Daily News* bureau who pursued a "natural" diet with almost no liquids that he claimed would ensure him a much longer than normal life span. He did so with such fervor that he lost forty pounds, his productivity dropped by 50 percent and he looked "like a death's head." When he broke down and ordered a meal of pork, potato salad and apple pie, along with plenty of beer, his body swelled up enormously and he had to be hospitalized. Still, after a six-week recovery, he declared that he simply hadn't found the right diet to prolong his life. "If only I could devote all my time to the search . . ." he said.

"Do you think Germans are madder than any other peoples?" Lilian asked her husband. "They seem so unbalanced . . . so hysterical."

"They lack coherence," Edgar replied. "They are so rich in intellect and poor in common sense. And there is almost nothing they can't persuade themselves to believe."

In an era of rampant anti-Semitism, Weimar Germany wasn't always viewed as a special case. In fact, Hecht, who claimed to be the only Jewish correspondent in the American press corps in Berlin during his stay from 1918 to 1920, offered this somewhat startling reflection about his experiences: "The strange bit of history I have to report is that in my two years in Germany, I, a Jew, saw and heard no hint of anti-Semitism. Not once in the time I spent in Germany did I hear the word Jew used as an epithet . . . There was less anti-Semitism to be heard, seen, felt or smelled in that postwar Germany than at any time in the U.S.A."

Hecht may have had a couple of reasons for deliberately overlooking the anti-Semitic rhetoric that would have been hard to miss. First, he wanted to make the point that Americans had no cause to feel smugly superior on this score. Second, writing in the immediate aftermath of World War II and the Holocaust, he was setting up his thesis that what led to this disaster was a national characteristic of the average German. No matter how educated or sophisticated the German appeared to be, Hecht claimed, "In him all morality was secondary to this morality of obeying a leader." Or put differently, it wasn't the doctrine of a leader that made Germans follow him; it was simply the fact that he demanded their allegiance and they blindly complied.

There was no denying how receptive Americans were to anti-Semitism in the aftermath of World War I. Or how energetically some Americans not only embraced anti-Semitic propaganda but promoted it. The most prominent American to do so was Henry Ford. The automaker was also a crusading pacifist who had proclaimed his worldview as early as 1915. "I know who caused the war—the German-Jewish bankers," he told Rosika Schwimmer, a Hungarian Jewish peace activist. "I have the evidence here. Facts!"

In 1919, Ford bought the *Dearborn Independent*, a small weekly that promptly launched a virulently anti-Semitic campaign, championing the *Protocols of the Learned Elders of Zion*, a fraudulent exposé of the alleged Jewish conspiracy to take over the world that had circulated earlier in Europe but only reached American shores at that time. The series of articles were soon published as a notorious pamphlet called *The International Jew*. When Annetta Antona, a columnist for the *Detroit News*, interviewed Hitler on December 28, 1931, at the Brown House, the Nazi headquarters in Munich, she noticed the large portrait of Ford above his desk. "I regard Henry Ford as my inspiration," Hitler told her.

Too much can be read into that statement of the future leader of Germany. Hitler had lived and breathed anti-Semitism long before he became acquainted with Ford's views. And his admiration of Ford had at least as much to do with his pioneering work as an automaker as with his prejudices. Once in power, Hitler would transform his idea of the Volks-wagen—the "people's car"—into reality, crediting "Mr. Ford's genius" for demonstrating that the motor car could be an instrument for uniting different classes rather than dividing them.

Still, the Ford record and other manifestations of American anti-Semitism serve as useful reminders that Germany was far from unique in harboring such sentiments in the 1920s. In fact, some Americans in Berlin were just as likely as their German counterparts to let their prejudices show. In a letter dated February 23, 1921, to Vivian Dillon, an aspiring American opera singer, Wiegand expressed shock that she was considering marrying "a prosperous, energetic, Jewish manager." He inquired "why must it be a Jew, or have you come to the conclusion that there are no others, who are prosperous and energetic?"

But anti-Semitism in Germany wasn't just a matter of all-too-ordinary bias. On June 24, 1922, Foreign Minister Walter Rathenau, the most prominent Jew in high office, was assassinated in Berlin, and other acts of right-wing violence became increasingly commonplace. Diplomat Hugh Wilson blamed a combination of factors: millions of veterans returning to a Germany where jobs were scarce and the rich and powerful included "a high proportion of Jews." Bolshevism was seen as dominated by Jews, he pointed out, as were some of the democratic parties in the Reichstag. "One could sense the spreading resentment and hatred," he wrote.

Once the country appeared to be getting back on its feet in the mid-1920s, many Americans in Germany were less alarmed by the anti-Semitic diatribes of the Nazis and other extremists. But they hardly could be as oblivious to them as Hecht claimed to be years earlier. Particularly when they were in the presence of German Jews, they were acutely conscious of the growing tensions.

One evening in 1928, S. Miles Bouton, the *Baltimore Sun*'s Berlin correspondent, ran into Thompson and Lewis at the Berlin Municipal Opera. Bouton was there with a daughter of a Jewish family that lived in his apartment building. He had not met Lewis before, and Thompson introduced them during the intermission. Since the young woman spoke no English, Lewis used only his fluent German, and at one point made a reference to Jews. He hadn't said anything critical, but Bouton was worried enough to caution him quietly in English: "Look out. The girl with me is a Jewess."

Lewis gave no indication he had heard him, but then casually re-marked: "You know, lots of people won't believe that my father was a rabbi." The young woman was suddenly all aglow. "Your father was a rabbi?" she asked.

Writing about this encounter a few years afterward, Bouton recalled: "There was still no indication in 1928 of the coming pogroms that were to sully Germany's repute five years later, but songs about spilling Jewish blood were being sung by uniformed marchers, and the swastika, emblem in Germany for hatred of the race, was ever more in evidence." For this young woman, the highlight of the evening was not only meeting the fa-mous American writer, who in reality was the son of a Wisconsin country doctor, but hearing the white lie that he was Jewish. "I hope she has never been undeceived," Bouton concluded, "but be that as it may, Lewis's alert-ness and kindness of heart brought more cheer to one unfortunate than he will ever know."

In 1925, Jacob Gould Schurman succeeded Houghton as ambassador. A former New York politician, Schurman had studied in Germany, spoke excellent German and worked hard to maintain the good will that his predecessor had earned. One of his initiatives was to raise money from wealthy Americans for a building fund for Heidelberg University; among the contributors was John D. Rockefeller, who donated $200,000 of the total gift of $500,000. Such activism made Schurman a very popular envoy.

So did his pronouncements praising the German government's com-mitment to peace and democracy. Early in his tenure, he argued that "the will to war was dead in Germany" and he later touted Germany's signing on to the 1928 Kellogg-Briand Pact outlawing war. On a visit to New York that same year, he declared, "The Republic has in general com-mended itself to the people and grows with such strength and vitality that its permanency may now be taken for granted."

Schurman wasn't as blind to the dangers of more turmoil as his pub-lic pronouncements suggested. He noted during his first year in Berlin that American financial institutions were aggressively pushing their high-interest loans, disregarding the risks involved. His embassy reported that the "itch to pour unproductive millions into German municipal coffers is rapidly becoming pathological."

American correspondents like Mowrer also began to question what was happening. Economist David Friday, who had been one of Mowrer's instructors at the University of Michigan, came to Berlin representing an investment firm eager to pump funds into Germany. Puffing on a cigar after a dinner with the Mowrers, he explained his mission: "You see we consider these people a sound proposition: hard-working, solid . . . we're going to put them on their feet again."

"At nine per cent?" asked Mowrer.

"Well, of course, we are no philanthropists," Friday replied.

As Lilian Mowrer pointed out, the influx of what appeared to be easy money from the United States and other countries led to "an orgy of spending." Traveling frequently around the country for her *Town and Country* pieces, she mentioned one example: "the stunning new railway cars and streamlined monsters on the Reichsbahn track." She also realized that "the entire rolling stock of the country had just been equipped with the new Kunze-Knorr air brakes, a little luxury that had cost close to one hundred million dollars." Britain, she added, had considered equipping its railroads with those new brakes, but had concluded it couldn't afford to.

Germany was also using loans to make reparation payments, and Schurman openly sympathized with German complaints that the financial burden was unsustainable. Even before the Wall Street crash, there were plenty of ominous signs of the shakiness of the German economy. In March 1929, Schurman received a warning from the chairman of the Reichstag Budget Committee that the country's finances were in the worst shape since the near meltdown in 1923.

Soon the Dawes Plan was replaced by the Young Plan, named after American banker Owen D. Young, the chairman of another group of experts. They produced a plan in 1929 to further reduce reparation payments but stretch them out all the way until 1988. Ferdinand Eberstadt, the most knowledgeable of the American experts about Germany's finances, bluntly told Young right at the beginning of their deliberations with the French and others: "Hey, this thing's a fake—it will bust up because they are playing politics and have no concern for economics." German officials complained the payments were still too high, and Hitler and other opposition figures denounced the whole scheme.

The Wall Street crash of October 1929 changed everything. Although the German government formally approved the Young Plan in March 1930, allowing it to receive about $300 million in new American loans, the plan was effectively stillborn. Faced with the sudden drying up of foreign loans and the domestic credit market followed by mounting unemployment, the Socialist government collapsed that same month. A new minority coalition led by the Center Party's Heinrich Brüning failed to win support for its economic program. Frustrated by the gridlock in the Reichstag, he called for new elections in September.

The stage was set for the return of the agitator from Munich.

# Whale or Minnow?

L ike so many Germans, Bella Fromm discovered that her life was turned upside down by World War I and its aftermath. Born into a well-to-do Bavarian Jewish family in 1890, she had worked for the Red Cross during the war. Her parents died early, leaving her with what looked like a healthy inheritance once the fighting stopped— certainly enough for her to live on after a brief unhappy marriage and continue doing volunteer social work. But then the hyperinflation of the early 1920s wiped out that cushion and she had to look for a paid job. "I'm going to have to start a new life," she wrote in her diary on October 1, 1928. From age ten, she had kept a diary and now she decided to write for others, not just herself. She became a journalist for the Ullstein publishing house, covering the social and diplomatic scene in Berlin.

The cub reporter quickly proposed a novel approach to her job. "Let's have society reports in the American manner," she told her editor at the *Vossische Zeitung*, a Berlin-based liberal newspaper with two issues a day. "Lively, with plenty of pictures." Her editor agreed to give this a try, and soon she wasn't only reporting in what she dubbed the American manner but mingling frequently with Americans as well, scrupulously noting her encounters in her private diary that she continued to keep.

In her diary entry of July 16, 1929, she described her experience at a Davis Cup match between Germany and Britain in Berlin's Grunewald district, famous for its lush forest. William "Big Bill" Tilden, the American tennis champion, was there to watch Daniel Prenn, Germany's top player, who was Jewish. He was playing the English star Bunny Austin. When Prenn won, Fromm noted, " 'Big Bill' beamed, for Danny had gained his victory with a racket Tilden had brought him as a present from America."

But Fromm heard a very different reaction from Count Friedrich Werner von der Schulenburg, who was a member of the Tennis Guild and would later serve as Germany's last ambassador to Moscow before Hitler's armies invaded the Soviet Union. "Of course, always those Jews!" he remarked.

"What do you mean?" Fromm asked angrily.

"The Jew would win of course," he responded. But as Fromm recorded, at least "he had the grace to blush."

Fromm had the last word. "He won for Germany. Would you have preferred to have the Englishman win?"

Perhaps precisely because of such contrasts between the Americans she met and her own countrymen, Fromm's diary entries about Americans in Germany were almost always positive. On February 2, 1930, she went to the train station to observe the arrival of the new American ambassador to Germany, former Kentucky Senator Frederic M. Sackett. In her diary, Fromm wrote that he was "a gentle-looking man with, obviously, very good background." As for his wife, she was "an attractive woman of great distinction."

In a later entry that year, she marveled at how the Sacketts were showing what entertaining American-style was all about. "Even the international diplomats are stunned," she wrote. "The Sacketts serve lobster at tea, an unheard-of luxury in Berlin."

But Fromm also observed that the new ambassador was acutely aware of the economic crisis that Germany and other countries now faced following the Wall Street crash. She sat next to him at a dinner and opera recital hosted by the Czech legation, giving her the first opportunity to speak with him. "I like Berlin. It is inspiring," he told her. "We are anxious in America to help Europe get out of the present crisis. We'd like to settle national differences at the green table instead of on the battlefield."

It wasn't just a newcomer like Sackett who liked Berlin and felt welcomed not only by Fromm but also by much of German officialdom, despite the renewed sense of crisis. On a visit to his Philadelphia home office in 1930, Knickerbocker was asked about the attitude of Germans toward American correspondents.

"Fortunately for us, we enjoy splendid prestige in Berlin," he replied. "We are treated courteously and our questions are answered intelligently. Tea is served at the Foreign Office every Friday afternoon at 3 o'clock, being attended by correspondents from every important country in the world." There, he continued, senior officials provided briefings and the newsmen made valuable contacts. He added, "Germany is the only European country, so far as I know, that has not expelled a correspondent since the World War."

Asked which country was the most interesting in Europe for a correspondent, he replied: "Germany for the moment. I consider Berlin the most important capital in Europe. For the moment (please note that I emphasize the phrase) Germany and the Soviet Union are the most pacific countries in Europe. The Soviet can't afford a war and Germany is sick of war. Yet we never know what may happen."

As Germany's economy began to unravel again, triggering new angst and unrest among a population that still had raw memories of the last crisis when so many lives and livelihoods were ruined, the Nazi movement began to gain traction. By the end of 1928, with its early signs of trouble ahead, the party boasted 108,000 dues-paying members; by the end of 1929, that number had jumped to 178,000. While Hitler was still considered a marginal political figure, he was drawing larger, more enthusiastic crowds and the party was making gains in local elections.

Not surprisingly, Wiegand was the first American correspondent to decide that it was worth interviewing the rabble rouser whom he and his colleagues had largely ignored for the past several years. After all, Wiegand had been the first American reporter to write about Hitler in the early 1920s, and he remembered well his rapid rise and apparent fall then. He also remembered his ability to play upon popular discontent—and, with that discontent growing, it was only logical to see whether Hitler could ride its wave again.

Wiegand hadn't bothered to check on Hitler since his imprisonment following the Beer Hall Putsch of 1923. But in December 1929, he traveled to Munich to meet him. "Now he is again active, and with a much larger following," he reported in his article in the *New York American* that ran on January 5, 1930. Most of his dispatch consisted of lengthy quotes from his interview with Hitler, which were delivered "with that vigor of expression that is characteristic of him."

Hitler focused his remarks on the threat of Bolshevism—and on his claim that his party was the only force capable of stopping it. "Germany is steadily, slowly, but surely slipping more and more into conditions of Communism," he declared. Pointing to the litany of economic woes—particularly the growing number of bankruptcies and rising unemployment—and "disgust with the present party system in Germany and distrust of public officials," Hitler warned that "all this tends to smooth the way to national destruction."

"The public mind of the German people is in utter confusion," he continued. "It is in this state of affairs that the National Socialists are raising the cry of home, country and nation against the slogan of internationalism of the Marxian Socialists." The goal, as he explained it, was "to save Germany from being economically enslaved to foreign powers on the one hand and on the other hand from being utterly bolshevized and falling into disorganization and demoralization."

Wiegand reminded Hitler of his earlier failed putsch and asked if he intended to try to depose the government by force again. "No, we have no thought of revolution," he replied, insisting that support for his movement was growing so rapidly that "we have no need of other than legal methods." He claimed that the party was supported at that moment by about 2.5 million Germans, and that this number would grow to about 4 million in another year.

When pressed on what kind of system of government he favored, Hitler was evasive. He called Germany's parliamentary system with its multiplicity of feuding parties "an utter farce." He indicated he saw some pluses in the American form of government, "where the president is something more than a rubber stamp and the cabinet cannot be overthrown from day to day." That kind of system, he added, has "elements of stability" that Germany was sorely lacking. But his language suggested that this was hardly the ideal solution.

Instead of clarifying what he was for, Hitler dwelled on what he was against, including the Jews who had attained, as he put it, wildly disproportionate power and influence. "I am not for curtailing the rights of the Jews in Germany, but I insist that we others who are not Jews shall not have less rights than they," he said. Any regulations about Jews, he claimed, would be no different from America's immigration laws that required immigrants to submit to medical examinations to prove they were healthy before they would be admitted. "Germany has no such protective measures," he complained. "Jewish influence expressed politically has prevented such measures being enacted. We are overrun by the elements that you reject in advance."

Finally, Hitler told Wiegand he was open to "an entente or understanding" between Germany and England and the United States. But he saw "no hope" that France would change its hostile approach to Germany, allowing for a lessening of tensions between the two.

Although Hitler attempted to sound less strident than he did at his rallies, the message he delivered left little doubt that he remained a committed foe of Germany's current system of government. Even if he no longer planned to march on Berlin, he wanted to see it come crashing down.

In the conclusion to his article, Wiegand noted that many people in Germany were surprised that Hitler was staging a political comeback. "Just how much of a factor he will be in coming difficulties in Germany, none seems to care to predict," he wrote. But by giving Hitler and his views so much play, Wiegand was signaling that the Nazi leader should once again be taken seriously.

On one point, Hitler was right on target: many Germans were experiencing "utter confusion," triggered both by the deteriorating economic situation and their growing anger at the squabbling among the politicians in Berlin as successive governments came and went. "The German people were sick of everything," Edgar Mowrer wrote. "Treaty fulfillment had not led to national recovery. Russian Bolshevism was not attractive. War was still impossible. Yet the miserable present simply could not go on."

Contempt for the current rulers cut across all social classes. Charles Thayer, who served in the U.S. Embassy in Berlin both before and after World War II, pointed out that it wasn't just the far right, big business-men and former military brass that had failed to support the Weimar Republic. "So had a majority of the professors—a most influential set in Germany, where academic degrees rank second only to military titles in establishing a person's social position," he wrote. "Most of them had openly sneered at the little Socialists of Weimar who seldom had a single 'Dr.' to put in front of their names." Their students, he added, shared that contempt for a government that they held responsible for Germany's humiliating losses of territory after World War I. And when their job prospects began to evaporate as the Depression settled in, "they flocked to the Nazis in droves."

Mowrer insisted that the lack of faith in liberal democracy extended even to those who were ostensibly its guardians. "The most remarkable feature of the Liberal German Republicans was the scarcity of Liberal republicans," he wrote. The Weimar governments had not only tolerated numerous "patriotic" private armies but also used them to suppress left-wing revolts. Hitler's Sturmabteilung, or SA, the Brownshirts, and his elite Schutzstaffel, or SS units, the Blackshirts, were hardly unique when they were formed in 1921.

Early during their stay in Germany, the Mowrers were returning by a night train from a weekend in East Prussia when they were suddenly awakened by loud shouting. The train had stopped at a small station, and two young men had boarded, turned on the light in the carriage where the Mowrers and other passengers were trying to sleep, and opened the window. From the platform, a middle-aged man wearing a trench coat and narrow leather belt was shouting at them "with the raucous voice of a drill sergeant," Lilian Mowrer recalled. She got up and turned out the light, but one of the young men brusquely switched it back on, clicked his heels and returned to the window. Edgar put a warning finger to his lips, signaling that it was better not to confront them. He explained to her afterward that the men belonged to "a secret army which the government tolerates but does not recognize."

But by the end of the 1920s, it was Hitler's political power—admittedly, backed by his not-so-secret armies—that was on the rise. When the economic crisis started to hit hard, the Nazis benefited immediately. In the September 1930 parliamentary elections, they won 107 of 577 seats, a spectacular jump from the 12 seats they had won two years earlier. Of the 35 million Germans who had gone to the polls, nearly 6.5 million had voted for Hitler's party, making it suddenly the second-largest party in the Reichstag after the Social Democrats. In 1928, only 800,000 Germans had cast their ballots for the Nazis. Hitler, it appeared, had good reason to put his faith in "legal methods" of seizing power, as he had indicated to Wiegand. The Hearst correspondent's nose for news was working well when he had decided it was time to interview him again.

For Americans living in Germany, the growing strength of the Nazis was hard to miss. Berkeley exchange student Enid Keyes arrived in Berlin in the fall of 1931, with a fellowship to study at the University of Berlin. On October 30, she accompanied Lars Mehnert, the younger son of her German hosts, to a Nazi rally in a big indoor sport stadium. She was fascinated by the policemen lined up outside in case trouble erupted, and by the scene she encountered inside. "The seats swarmed with people, old and young, all loyal to Hitler and the National Socialist program," she wrote her mother back in California. Noting how quickly the Nazis had risen from obscurity to become the largest opposition group, she added that girls passed around red cans "to collect money for the poor, or the imprisoned Nazi people. And people were generous with their pennies."

What impressed Keyes the most was the atmosphere of the rally. "The noise, the spontaneous cheers, the band, reminded me of a football game crowd," she wrote. "But the feeling here was deeper, more firmly rooted, and much more significant than a Saturday afternoon football throng. Heart and soul, Germans are concerned with the political destiny of their country. It was stirring to see the vast crowd rise as one man, when the trumpets announced the entrance of the Hitler flags, and the various divisions marched to their place on the platform." The crowd greeted the Brownshirts with the Nazi salute and "the roof was nearly raised by the Nazi song, a hymn with a catchy tune." While Keyes didn't understand much of the speeches, she needed no translation to feel the fervor of the crowd. She wrote her mother that "young Lars" came home decked out with Nazi pins and flags. "Like all the youth of Germany, he is an ardent party member," she concluded.

The rise of the Nazis wasn't simply something Americans observed; it also began having a direct impact on their lives. Edgar Mowrer recounted the story of a thirteen-year-old American boy, whom he only identified as Arthur. The boy was attending a Jesuit school in Berlin, and one day in the winter of 1931 he posed a question to his father: "Dad, what do you think of National-Socialism?"

"I don't think about it," the father replied evasively, since he knew he was treading on dangerous ground. "National-Socialism is purely a German matter which does not concern you or me."

But Arthur didn't give up. A few days later, he asked his question a different way. "Dad, if you were a German, would you be a National-Socialist?"

The father asked what was prompting his questions. "You see, nearly all my friends are National-Socialists," Arthur explained. "I like to be with them, and if you aren't one, there are so many interesting things you are shut out of."

Worried, the father told Arthur that the Catholic bishops had condemned the Nazis. "How can Catholic boys be members of a forbidden organization?"

"I don't know, Dad," Arthur continued. "But they are, and if you aren't a National-Socialist in this school, you aren't anybody. Do you think as a foreigner I could become one?"

Mowrer reported that Arthur never followed through on that wish. But by 1932, about half of the students in his class openly supported Hitler's party. Despite efforts by the Jesuits to stop the politicization of their classrooms, even the boys' rough games reflected the larger battles swirling around them. One of the most popular was "chariot bumping." Pretending to ride chariots like in the 1925 silent movie *Ben-Hur*, the boys crashed into each other. At first, the opposing forces in those contests were labeled "Romans" and "Jews." Then, the labels switched to "Centrists" and "Nazis" and the confrontations became nastier, with boys clearly seeking to hurt their opponents.

In their dispatches, American correspondents were often reluctant to make outright predictions on how far the growing backing for the Nazis could carry Hitler. But in their private exchanges with their editors, they were more willing to be blunt about the connection between the deteriorating economic conditions and its impact on politics. Writing on December 28, 1931, to C. M. Morrison, the editor of the *Philadelphia Public Ledger*, Knickerbocker painted a bleak picture of the country he was covering. He had just traveled all over Germany for a series of articles he was writing. "I never saw before with my own eyes the degree and extent of real poverty now prevalent here," he reported. Those conditions, he warned, could lead to another disaster.

Correspondents like Knickerbocker and Mowrer also enjoyed occasional lighter moments even during economically desperate times. The two American reporters were walking down Friedrichstrasse one day when they stopped two streetwalkers. Knickerbocker introduced himself and asked what the women thought of the latest government changes that represented a major setback for the Social Democrats as more conservative politicians took power.

"We are for the new gentlemen," one of the women responded.

Taken aback, Knickerbocker and Mowrer asked why.

"These damn socialists with their free love have made it almost impossible for an honest whore to earn a decent living," she said. "The gentlemen will change all that and give us a chance!"

As Mowrer sardonically noted, he and Knickerbocker filed stories on this revealing conversation, but his editors at the *Chicago Daily News* found it "too hot to publish."

For the most part, though, what Americans in Germany saw of the lives of ordinary Germans was far from amusing. Enid Keyes, the Berkeley exchange student, wrote home on November 17, 1931, about the "sad side" of life in Berlin: "I can't ever walk a block without seeing blind men, old women with galoshes stuffed with newspapers for shoes, cripples, white-haired ex-soldiers who are begging or selling matches or shoe strings. Old people with gnarled hands and round shoulders, faces blue with the cold, creep along looking for work, picking up twigs in the threadbare park, or searching the gutters for paper." The following month she noted that people were looking even more discouraged, and beggars "have increased on the streets in terrible numbers." Women approached passersby pleading that they were hungry and had children "who are crying for food," she added.

In his letter to Morrison, Knickerbocker concluded from all this that Germany not only couldn't pay reparations in the current crisis, "but will not pay reparations ever again." Any attempt by France to force the issue would backfire, he added. "Germany is like Sampson [sic]. She is prepared to pull the building down about her ears rather than continue paying 'tribute' which she, the whole nation from Communists to National Socialists, considers she does not owe."

He offered this forecast: "If Germany does get rid of reparations, does take up the Hitler banner as it seems likely she will do, and does recover with the general recovery of world business that must sooner or later come, then Germany under Hitler will sooner or later re-arm. The money we remit to Europe, one way or another, goes to increase armaments. But this is only another way of saying that this continent is going to war again."

Replying to Knickerbocker on January 8, 1932, Morrison thanked his correspondent for his impressions, particularly about German attitudes toward the reparations question. He predicted this would lead the United States to become less sympathetic to their plight. "You see defiance in Germany begets defiance on this side of the Atlantic," he wrote. But he ignored Knickerbocker's warnings about a new major conflict, focusing instead on the economic fallout of the rapid rise of Hitler. "This country has grown to expect Hitler to take over power in Germany next month. It will not come as any shock although the effects may be rather disastrous in the financial and economic situation when it does come," he added. Given Knickerbocker's far more alarming predictions, Morrison's worries looked almost sanguine by comparison.

But as the Nazis continued to gain momentum in the early 1930s, even Knickerbocker vacillated in his judgment about how much of a threat Hitler really represented. In a letter to Percy Winner, the editor of the *New York Evening Post*, on June 18, 1932, he wrote about the increasing speculation that new parliamentary elections the following month would give Hitler the opportunity to become part of a ruling coalition. Knickerbocker still considered him to be a far less powerful figure than Mussolini, in part because of his "feminine" side. And he predicted that President Hindenburg would have no problem keeping him in check.

"Hitler is a homo-sexual, effeminate corporal with a hyper-sensitive political olfactory nerve," he wrote. "Hindenburg is a granite-faced, bass-voiced Field Marshal with a commanding manner that makes little corporals tremble."

Then he offered this prediction: "If Hitler came to Hindenburg and said 'Now is the time to do away with the Republic,' Hindenburg would cry out '*Was!*' and the little corporal would wilt like a lettuce leaf in hot water."

And that wasn't the end of it. He gave Hitler high marks for his ability to exploit discontent. "Hitler is a cork," he wrote. "He floats on the crest of every wave of popular sentiment. No man in Germany can smell the trend of mass feeling and respond to it as Hitler can." This ability, he continued, made Hitler indispensable to the party. But within that same party "he is pulled from pillar to post by his lieutenants in the most astonishing way."

Finally, Knickerbocker pointed out that all the indications in Germany were pointing toward "militarism." The inclusion of the National Socialists in a coalition government, he added, would lead to "the disappearance of their 'socialist' character," leaving only the nationalist part. Still, Hitler's role would be important but limited, he insisted. He'd continue to be "the olfactory sense of the party, but I cannot see him as Germany's Mussolini, even though he may remain the official head."

The man Knickerbocker couldn't imagine as Germany's Mussolini had challenged the country's aging President Paul von Hindenburg when he ran for a second term in the spring of 1932. Hitler came up short, but placed a strong second in the first round, forcing a runoff the following month. In that round, Hindenburg won the support of more than 19 million Germans, while Hitler won more than 13 million votes. Hindenburg tried to curb the violence of the Nazis by agreeing to dissolve the SA and the SS, but his efforts to check the broader unrest failed. Triggered by the worsening economic conditions, strikes and other protests multiplied. Soon the president decided to dismiss Heinrich Brüning's government, name Baron Franz von Papen as his successor as chancellor, and call new elections. A member of the Catholic Center Party who believed he could control the Nazis, Papen convinced Hindenburg to agree to the lifting of the ban on the SA and the SS, which only intensified the bloody clashes between them and the Communists.

In the elections on July 31, 1932, the Nazis emerged victorious, winning 230 seats, more than doubling their total from two years earlier. This made them the largest party in the Reichstag, leaving the Social Democrats in second place with 133 seats. They were followed by the Center Party with 97 seats and the Communists with 89. Chancellor von Papen—whom correspondents like Mowrer labeled as dictatorial and reactionary—simultaneously weakened the left by dismissing Social Democrats from top positions and dispatching Defense Minister Kurt von Schleicher to negotiate a deal with Hitler. But emboldened by his party's stunning results, the Nazi leader wasn't ready to settle for anything less than Papen's job. Their talks ended in failure, and new elections were called on November 6, 1932. This time, the Nazis came in first once again, but lost 34 seats and 2 million votes. They won 196 seats, with the Social Democrats still in second place with 121, and the Communists gaining ground by winning 100.

As late as it was in the endgame of the Weimar Republic, many observers saw the drop in support for the Nazis as a sign that the movement was losing momentum. Their violent rhetoric and actions were backfiring with some of the electorate, and there were also new signs of splits within the party's top ranks. Schleicher, who took over the job of chancellor from Papen in early December, wanted to take advantage of those divisions by trying to lure Gregor Strasser, a popular Nazi who was considered the

leader of the party's relatively moderate "socialist" wing, into his government as vice chancellor. That proved to be fatal to Strasser, whom Hitler
had always viewed as a possible rival. Instead of joining the government,
Strasser ended up resigning his party posts.

Americans trying to sort out the meaning of the swirl of elections and
political maneuvering were often understandably uncertain what to make
of all this. Abraham Plotkin was a Jewish-American labor organizer who
arrived in Berlin in November 1932, with the avowed goal of studying
workers' conditions and the German labor movement. He would end up
spending six months in Germany, witnessing the demise of the Weimar
Republic and the first months of Nazi rule. But during his early days in
Berlin, he was far from convinced that Hitler would prevail.

Like the journalist Knickerbocker, the exchange student Keyes and
others, he was struck by the destitution of working-class Germans. In
the United States, he had worked as a West Coast organizer for the International Ladies' Garment Workers' Union, the ILGWU, losing his job
in late 1931 when the union had to trim its payroll. He knew firsthand
about the toll that the Depression was taking in his own country. But he
found that living conditions in Germany were often worse.

Initial impressions could be misleading, he noted on November 22,
1932, in the diary he kept throughout his stay. On the streets of Cologne
and Berlin, he pointed out, people "hide their poverty very well," looking
reasonably dressed. "From their appearances it would be hard to believe
that the last unemployment figures show that 44 out of every hundred
Germans are out of employment, and some of them for the last three
years."

Soon he was making the rounds with local trade union organizers,
seeing what life was like in reality. While the jobless received unemployment and welfare benefits, they were hardly enough to relieve the misery.
"You Americans have a bathroom in every apartment—is it not so?" one
of his escorts named Hans asked him. He was showing Plotkin a building with 120 inhabitants and not a single bath. "They tell me that in New
York every apartment has a toilet," Hans added. "Come. I'll show you
what we have." Leading Plotkin to the basement, he pushed open a door
and lit a match so he could see a crude toilet made of wooden boards. "Do

you know how many families use this toilet?" he asked. "Nine families. The pots in the rooms would choke you. Go to America and tell them you saw this."

Visiting another tenement house with Hans, he observed one family's diet: potatoes and herring or potatoes and margarine for the main meal, never any butter, and one pound of meat on Sundays for the four of them. The head of a district health department told Plotkin about the rapid spread of infectious diseases because of deteriorating sanitary conditions. Berlin's bathhouses had lost two-thirds of their customers, he explained, since they could no longer afford their small fees; and even families with tubs were bathing in the same water to save heating costs.

Plotkin was also "fascinated by the ladies of the streets and their easy ways." While he was drinking a beer at Alexanderplatz, a young woman approached him, asking whether he'd consider her for two marks—the equivalent of 50 cents. When he declined, she asked if he'd like one of her four friends at the next table. He turned her down again, but offered to buy her a beer and sausage. She eagerly agreed, but scoffed when he asked her about Wedding, a district known for its poverty. She complained that the women there weren't professional because they would sell themselves "for a piece of bread."

As they talked, the woman was startled to learn Plotkin had read Alfred Döblin's recently published novel *Berlin Alexanderplatz* about the down-and-out life in the city. "Do you remember that Döblin said that time is a butcher and that all of us are running away from the butcher's knife?" she asked. "Well, that's me, and that's all of us."

Meeting German Jews, Plotkin found himself besieged by questions about how conditions were for Jews in America. "Do you have a fascist party in America?" someone asked. "No, not yet—we had the Ku Klux Klan for a while, but that's over with for the present," he replied, alluding to signs that its membership had peaked earlier.

"Then the Jews of America are fortunate," one of the German Jews declared. "Here we are cursed with anti-Semitism, the most bitter anti-Semitism we have ever known." When Plotkin declared that there was anti-Semitism in the United States, too, they scoffed at the notion that it could be at all comparable. "Do they ever throw Jews out of subway cars in New York?" they asked. "Do they ever come into stores belonging to Jews and tear up all the stock and break up all the fixtures?" They pointed out that boycotts and threats were a daily fact of life. "The majority of the Jews in Germany are being driven into no one knows what," he quoted them as saying. "There is hardly a Friday night that we pray without trembling."

Yet despite all the poverty and anti-Semitism he witnessed or heard about, Plotkin was dubious about Hitler's chances of seizing power—or, if he did, how long he would be able to keep it. Many of the trade union leaders he met were convinced that his movement had already peaked. "Hitlerism is rapidly going to pieces," one of them insisted to Plotkin, adding that the Communists were on the rise. "Whenever a Hitlerite leaves the Nazis, he goes straight to the Communists, they are growing in strength."

Plotkin decided to see for himself what the Nazis represented. On December 16, 1932, he noticed posters advertising one of their rallies at the Sportpalast, with propagandist Joseph Goebbels as the featured speaker. He showed up an hour early, finding only a couple of thousand people in the hall which he estimated could hold 15,000. The young Nazis in uniforms looked disheartened. By the time the rally started, the hall contained more people, but there were still plenty of empty seats. The opening round of martial music was met with weak applause. "One felt as if the spirit had taken flight," Plotkin noted in his diary. While he gave Goebbels high marks for "showmanship," the evening proved anticlimactic. "So this was the famous menace to Germany and to the world," he wrote. "I confess my disappointment . . . I had come to see a whale and found a minnow."

Other American Jews who visited Germany in this period also weren't sure how dangerous the Nazis, with their anti-Semitic tirades, really were. Norman Corwin, a young reporter from Massachusetts who would go on to become a highly successful writer, director and producer in radio's golden age, took a European journey in 1931. In Heidelberg, he stayed at a pension where the owners were apolitical but their blond seventeen-year-old son was a committed Nazi. The boy was intrigued by Corwin, who was only four years older and probably the

first American he'd met. He followed the visitor everywhere, in Corwin's words, "like a faithful dog."

As they walked around the city taking in the sights, Corwin told his
companion about life in the United States, and the German teenager
expounded on his views of his country's future. The Nazis, he insisted,
would restore Germany to its proper place in the world and rid it of "the
pollution of the race." Corwin listened, but it wasn't until his last day,
while they were up at the Heidelberg Castle, that he told the boy that he
was Jewish. This was met with silence that neither of them broke during
their walk back to the pension.

Corwin left Germany not nearly as troubled as he should have been
by that encounter. Traveling in northern France, he tried to convince a
young woman he met that her fears about a new war were unfounded.
"We are beyond thinking of war as an instrument of political expediency,"
he told her.

The American diplomats and journalists who were based in Berlin were
increasingly curious about the man who led the movement that everyone
was talking about. On Saturday, December 5, 1931, Ambassador Sackett met Hitler for the first and only time during his three-year posting.
Carefully prearranged to avoid the appearance of an official meeting with
an opposition figure, this first-ever encounter between a U.S. envoy and
Hitler took place over tea in the home of Emil Georg von Stauss, a pro-
Nazi director of the Deutsche Diskonto Bank. Sackett, who had only
limited German, was accompanied by Alfred Klieforth, the embassy's
first secretary. Hitler was accompanied by Rudolf Hess, Hermann Goering and Putzi Hanfstaengl.

As the host, von Stauss introduced the topic of Germany's "distress-
ing" economic situation—and Hitler promptly took over by embarking
on one of his trademark monologues. Sackett would note later that he
spoke "as if he were addressing a large audience." The Nazi leader claimed
the country's plight was caused by its loss of colonies and territory, and
argued for a revision of the terms of the Versailles Treaty, including the
return of the Polish Corridor. He denounced what he characterized as

a vastly overarmed France and warned that its aggressive actions could prevent Germany from repaying its private debts, which he claimed it otherwise would do. And he insisted that the Nazis' paramilitary units were only "for the purpose of keeping order within Germany and suppressing Communism."

Writing to Secretary of State Henry L. Stimson, Sackett indicated that the meeting had left him with distinctly cool feelings. "The impression I gained of Hitler is that of a fanatical crusader," he reported. "He has a certain forcefulness and intensity which gives him a power of leadership among those classes that do not weigh his outpourings. His methods are those of an opportunist. While he talked vigorously, he never looked me in the eye." Many Germans were turning to the Nazis "in despair that former political allegiances provide no relief from present intolerable conditions," Sackett acknowledged. But he predicted that "if this man comes into power he must find himself shortly on the rocks, both of international and internal difficulties. He is certainly not the type from which statesmen evolve."

It was no accident that Hanfstaengl had accompanied Hitler to his meeting with the American ambassador. This "half American" Harvard graduate, as he liked to characterize himself, was once again seen frequently in the Nazi leader's entourage, particularly during his meetings with American journalists. After Hitler was released from prison in late 1924, Putzi and Helen had continued to see him fairly regularly for the next couple of years, but then their contacts tapered off during the period when his political appeal was waning.

Hitler was still clearly attracted to Helen. On one occasion when he was visiting the Hanfstaengls' home and Putzi had gone out, Hitler sank down on his knees in front of her and began: "If only I had someone to look after me . . ." Helen was sitting on the sofa, she recalled later, and "here he was on his knees, with his head in your lap, he was almost like a little boy." Was this a declaration of love, as Putzi would later write in his memoirs? Was he really in love with her? "I should say in a way he was," Helen explained. "As far as he was in love with anyone, maybe I was one of the ones that perhaps he was in love with."

All of Helen's qualifiers were understandable. After all, she and her husband speculated, as American correspondents and others did, about Hitler's sexuality. In his memoir, Putzi wrote: "I felt Hitler was a case of a man who was neither fish, flesh [he clearly meant "meat" here] nor fowl, neither fully homosexual nor fully heterosexual . . . I had formed the firm conviction that he was impotent, the repressed, masturbating type."

Helen had asked Hitler once, "Why don't you find a lovely wife and marry?" He replied that he could never marry because his life was dedicated to his country. But the evidence suggests that, whatever his sexual capabilities or proclivities, Hitler was at the very least attracted to several women during his life, with Helen perhaps the only one who was close to him in age. He routinely charmed older women, but whatever sexual longings he possessed seemed mostly focused on much younger ones.

As Putzi began to reengage with Hitler when the Nazis' political fortunes rose in direct response to the economic crisis, he found that suppressing information was a big part of his role. And one of the biggest near scandals that needed to be contained surrounded the nature of Hitler's relationship with his half-sister's daughter Geli Raubal. By all accounts vivacious and flirtatious, Geli had come to Munich from Vienna as a teenager ostensibly to study. But soon she seemed fully preoccupied with her uncle, who was nearly twenty years her senior. She appeared at his side at cafés, restaurants, the opera and other public places. Then she moved into his spacious new apartment on Prinzregentenplatz, which was funded by his supporters. Although she had her own room there, rumors about the couple were rife in party circles.

Putzi dismissed Geli as "an empty-headed little slut" who basked in her uncle's fame. Helen took a more charitable view. "I always had the feeling he was trying to run her life, tyrannizing her, that she was more or less oppressed," she said, looking back at that period. Others—particularly Otto Strasser, the brother of Hitler's main rival in the party—would later claim that Hitler forced Geli to arouse him by humiliating sexual practices since he was incapable of normal sex. Whatever transpired between them, Geli was found in her room, shot in the heart, on September 18, 1931, dead at age twenty-three; earlier, she and Hitler had been overheard having a loud argument. Officially, her death was ruled a suicide, but Putzi and other propagandists had to work hard to quell reports in leftist local papers that this was a possible cover-up. "The whole affair was hushed up and glossed over as much as possible," he noted.

While Putzi was busy cultivating his ties to American correspondents, he certainly didn't let them in on this story, whether it was the early party gossip and whispers about Hitler and Geli when they were parading around together or her suspicious death. Instead, he was eager to serve as the go-between for American reporters who wanted to interview Hitler, usually for the first time. Even as Hitler's domestic drama was playing itself out behind the scenes, the Nazi leader was capitalizing on the growing popular discontent that was attracting new converts to his cause. To boost Hitler's international stature, Putzi urged him to meet American reporters, particularly the most famous ones.

One of the most famous, of course, was Dorothy Thompson. While she was no longer living in Berlin, she wasn't really settled with her husband Sinclair Lewis in New York either. Europe—in particular, Germany—kept pulling her back as she churned out lengthy pieces for the *Saturday Evening Post* and other publications. She had tried to meet Hitler as far back as the aftermath of the failed Beer Hall Putsch in 1923. Hearing that he had taken refuge at the Hanfstaengls' place outside of Munich, she rushed to the house "of an American woman" only to learn from Helen that Hitler was already gone. She recalled meeting Helen in New York during World War I and claimed that even then she was "a German propagandist." Following Hitler's release from prison, Thompson made a few attempts to meet him but blamed her failure to do so on the fact that he was "lofty and remote from all foreigners."

Like many American journalists, Thompson found Putzi Hanfstaengl to be the most colorful member of Hitler's entourage. "Fussy. Amusing. The oddest imaginable press chief for a dictator," she wrote. But also like many of her colleagues, she could mock him as "an immense, high-strung, incoherent clown." To be sure, that didn't prevent her from enlisting his help when *Cosmopolitan* gave her the assignment of interviewing Hitler in November 1931. Excited by that prospect, she checked into Berlin's Adlon Hotel, where she ran into John Farrar of the

New York publishing house Farrar & Rinehart. He promptly got her to commit to writing a quickie book about the Nazi leader if her interview went well. After all, it wasn't just *Cosmopolitan* that was interested in figuring out whether this bizarre figure could become the leader of Germany and who he really was.

Thompson made full use of this opportunity, speedily turning out her short book, *I Saw Hitler!*, which made a big splash when it was published in 1932, just as its subject was figuring prominently in all the political stories flowing from Germany. In the foreword, she expressed no reservations about making sweeping judgments that others might consider more appropriate for historians—quite the contrary. "The times in which we live move too fast for the considered historian to record them for us," she grandly proclaimed. "They move too quickly to permit the writing of long books about momentary phases. Ours is the age of the reporter."

And Thompson wasn't shy about revealing her emotions and snap judgments as she set up and conducted the interview. She briefly explained Hitler's shift in tactics after he emerged from prison, abandoning talk of revolt and replacing it with a new strategy: "Gone 'legal,'" she wrote. "No longer was there to be a march on Berlin. The people were to 'awaken' and Hitler's movement was going to *vote* dictatorship in! In itself a fascinating idea. Imagine a would-be dictator setting out *to persuade a sovereign people to vote away their rights.*" This would-be dictator, she added, already had his own army and "terrorizes the streets."

Little wonder that Thompson was a popular writer: her vivid, succinct prose got right to the heart of the issue. She knew her readers wanted to know about Hitler's strategy, but, more important, whether it was going to work. And she wasn't going to disappoint them by equivocating.

Confessing that she was nervous enough about this encounter to consider taking smelling salts, she waited impatiently in the Kaiserhof Hotel for Hitler to arrive. He did so an hour late, and then kept her waiting in Putzi's room even longer. Thompson related all this, keeping the reader in suspense as well. But not for long. With a dramatic flourish, she allowed the reader to accompany her not just into her meeting but also into her mind. "When finally I walked into Adolph Hitler's salon in the Kaiserhof Hotel, I was convinced that I was meeting the future dictator of Germany," she wrote. "In something less than fifty seconds I was quite sure I was not. It took just that long to measure the startling insignificance of this man who has set the world agog.

"He is formless, almost faceless, a man whose countenance is a caricature, a man whose framework seems cartilaginous, without bones," she continued. "He is inconsequent and voluble, ill-poised, insecure." Then, referring to the title of a bestselling novel of that era by German writer Hans Fallada, she added: "He is the very prototype of the Little Man."

In quick brush strokes, she completed the physical portrait of Hitler: the lock of hair falling over "an insignificant and slightly retreating forehead," a large nose "badly shaped and without character," and his movements "awkward, almost undignified and most un-martial." But his eyes, she pointed out, were notable, because "they have the peculiar shine which often distinguishes geniuses, alcoholics, and hysterics." At the same time, she confessed he had "the soft, almost feminine charm of the Austrian!"

She contrasted his "actor's face . . . capable of being pushed out or in" to President von Hindenburg's face "cut out of rock" and Chancellor Brüning's "head of an eighteenth century cardinal-statesman." This caused her to involuntarily smile and think, "Oh, Adolph! Adolph! You will be out of luck!"

As Thompson also pointed out, the interview itself was difficult, since Hitler, as usual, spoke as if he were addressing a mass meeting. But it wasn't the content of her interview that was important; it was her reading of the man and his prospects. While she dutifully marched the reader through his ideas as he spelled them out in the interview and in *Mein Kampf* ("The Jews are responsible for everything," as she summed it up— adding "take the Jews out of Hitler's program, and the whole thing . . . collapses"), the real message was her conclusion that "Hitler's tragedy is that he has risen too high." Her prediction: "If Hitler comes into power, he will smite only the weakest of his enemies." In that case, she concluded, the key question would be who would come after him.

American readers probably found Thompson's descriptions and conclusions reassuring. After all, the message was that, in all likelihood, Hitler would never make it to the top—and, if he did, it would be only for a brief, ineffective moment. When *I Saw Hitler!* was published, Nazi activist Kurt Ludecke, who shared Putzi's ambitions to educate Hitler about the United States and saw the press chief as a pompous fool, told the Nazi leader that he was going to quote him something from "Mrs. Lewis, the wife of one of America's most famous novelists." He then translated the part about how quickly she had realized that he wasn't going to take power.

"Who is this Mrs. Lewis anyway?" Hitler asked. Ludecke explained that she was Dorothy Thompson, the correspondent Putzi had brought to him. "Ja, ja, now I remember," Hitler replied. "Hanfstaengl again! He brought this woman to me . . ."

But Hitler seemed more amused than irritated by Thompson's conclusions, much to the disappointment of Ludecke. In fact, he had good reason to welcome and encourage any coverage that downplayed the threat he represented—and he usually did so with Americans when Hanfstaengl was the facilitator, taking advantage of his American and, on occasion, Harvard ties.

One of Putzi's classmates and best friends at Harvard was Hans V. Kaltenborn, who would become a nationally famous radio broadcaster. The son of German immigrants who had settled in Milwaukee, he learned German at home, and in college he became the vice president of the Deutscher Verein, the German Union, while Putzi served as its president. In the 1920s, Kaltenborn visited Europe often and, in Germany, Hanfstaengl arranged for him to meet various Nazis. But he hadn't met Hitler, since he was rarely willing to spend much time waiting around for a possible interview. As Kaltenborn recalled, though, Putzi "felt that any newspaper correspondent or radio commentator should be willing to waste at least a week in prayerful hope that the Führer might condescend to receive him."

But on August 16, 1932, while he was visiting Berlin, Kaltenborn received a telegram from his old classmate, who was in Munich, informing him that an interview was arranged for the next day in Berchtesgaden, Hitler's Alpine retreat. Louis Lochner, the Associated Press bureau chief in Berlin, called him to let him know he had received a similar telegram so they would be going together. The two took the night train to Munich, and Putzi met them at the station. Both journalists were disappointed to learn from him that Wiegand, the Hearst correspondent, would also be included. The session felt less and less exclusive.

Putzi had arranged for Hitler's car and driver to take them to Berchtesgaden. Once they arrived, they were treated to lunch on the terrace of a little hotel, while Putzi went over to Hitler's "Swiss chalet," as Kaltenborn called it. Wiegand had argued that he had to have a separate interview, and the two other journalists were pleased when Putzi managed to arrange this. They were even happier when the Hearst correspondent angrily returned from a mere fifteen minutes with Hitler. "That man is hopeless," he told them. "He gets worse every time I see him. I get nothing out of him. Ask him a question and he makes a speech. This whole trip has been a waste of time."

Kaltenborn took that as a lesson and decided that he would confront Hitler immediately about his feelings about the Jews. "Unlike Lochner, I wasn't stationed in Germany and did not need to be discreet to escape expulsion," he noted later. They walked over to Hitler's house, and their host, dressed all in black, including his tie, came out to meet them. Hitler's laundry, hung out by his half-sister Angela, was fluttering in the breeze, the view of the Bavarian Alps was majestic, and despite a few Nazi guards stationed on the paths outside, "everything suggested peace," Kaltenborn noted. But he also felt an atmosphere of "latent hostility" when Putzi whispered to Hitler who they were.

As soon as they sat down, Kaltenborn fired off his first question: "Why does your anti-Semitism make no distinction between the Jews that flooded into Germany during the postwar period and the many fine Jewish families that have been German for generations?"

"All Jews are foreigners," Hitler shouted back. "Who are you to ask me how I deal with foreigners. You Americans admit no foreigner unless he has good money, good physique, and good morals. Who are you to talk about who should be allowed in Germany?"

From then on, Kaltenborn continued tossing in as pointed questions as possible, while Lochner focused on more tactical queries about Hitler's next political moves. As Kaltenborn noted, Hitler didn't really answer his questions, no more than the first one, since "he has no capacity for logical consecutive thought." As usual, he denounced the parliamentary system that, he argued, "has never functioned in Europe," and called for authoritarian rule. He expected to take power, he maintained, but with the support of the German people. "A dictatorship is justified once the people declare their confidence in one man and ask him to rule," he insisted.

Kaltenborn was as interested in Hitler's behavior as in his answers. At one point, Hitler's wolfhound came to the porch and approached his master. Instead of petting him, Hitler sternly commanded "*Platz!*"—the standard German order for a dog to back off and lie down. The dog obeyed, and soon took advantage of Hitler's absorption in his own rhetoric to slink away. "I could understand that a man with Hitler's temperament, background and experience might not care to make a friendly gesture towards an American correspondent, but it was surprising to see him observe the same stern aloofness towards his own dog," Kaltenborn wrote.

The interview lasted forty-five minutes, and Kaltenborn emerged distinctly unimpressed with the man everyone was talking about. But the conclusion he drew was startling. "After meeting Hitler I myself felt almost reassured," he recalled. "I could not see how a man of his type, a plebeian Austrian of limited mentality, could ever gain the allegiance of a majority of Germans." He arrived at that judgment despite the fact that the Nazis had already garnered more votes and more Reichstag seats than any other party.

Yet Kaltenborn deserves credit for honestly admitting that he was no prophet. Many others would have been tempted to airbrush their memories; he didn't. "Most people who met Adolf Hitler before he came to power in January, 1933 were apt to underestimate him," he wrote in his autobiography. "I was no exception."

## 4

## "I Will Show Them"

There were those who saw what was coming, those who were blind to it until the very last moment and those who continued to insist that the fears about Hitler and the Nazis had been blown out of all proportion, dismissing all the evidence to the contrary. That was true of Germans; it was also true for Americans who lived and worked in their midst.

There was also a special category of German politicians: those who believed that they could outmaneuver and outsmart Hitler. On June 1, 1932, Franz von Papen, the newly appointed chancellor, took the AP's Louis Lochner aside at a lunch in the Reich Chancellery, assuring him that he knew how to more effectively contain the Nazis than his predecessor had. His strategy, he explained, would be to loosen rather than tighten the restrictions on them. "I'll give the Hitlerites enough freedom to show them up in all their absurdity," he told the American reporter.

After he was replaced as chancellor by General Kurt von Schleicher, who had served as his defense minister, Papen began promoting a new approach. In his dealings with the octogenarian President von Hindenburg—who according to Lochner and others was increasingly "senile"—

he argued that the best way to keep Hitler under control would be to appoint him chancellor.

Schleicher was pursuing a different policy toward the Nazis, trying to split them by luring Gregor Strasser, the head of the "socialist" faction within the party, into his government as vice-chancellor. Although that maneuver failed, the chancellor would prove to be as naïve in his own way as Papen. After taking power in early December, he quickly convinced himself that he had managed to usher in a new era of *"Ruhe, Ruhe, Ruhe* [Quiet, Quiet, Quiet]," as he told Lochner during the Christmas holiday.

"As you see, I have succeeded," he declared. "Germany has for a long time not been as quiet as now. Even the Communists and the Nazis are behaving. The longer this quiet continues, the more certain is the present government to reestablish internal peace." Lochner later observed that it was "sophomoric" for Schleicher to mistake the normal Christmas lull in Germany as a sign of better times.

New reports of fissures in the Nazi movement, combined with the dip in their support in the November 6 elections, had led others to nurture such illusions as well. American Ambassador Sackett was more worried about the fact that the third-place Communists had increased their number of seats in the Reichstag, since he viewed the left as more dangerous than the far right. To counter the Communist threat, he argued, "it was obviously important at the moment to have a strongly centralized more or less military Government." While Sackett had warned Washington that Hitler appeared determined to "rule alone" and that he and Goebbels "are past adepts at twisting events to suit their fancies and purposes, and indefatigable spellbinders," he still sounded somewhat dismissive of the Nazi leader, calling him "one of the biggest show-men since P. T. Barnum."

Abraham Plotkin, the Jewish-American labor organizer who had arrived in Berlin in November, continued going to political rallies to figure out for himself what the Nazis represented. He saw Goebbels perform for the second time in early January. The Nazi propagandist stirred little emotion at first but then fired up the crowd by blaming Jews for the murder of a young Nazi. This prompted Plotkin to reflect in his diary that day about the possible parallels to the Ku Klux Klan back in his home country. The Klan had looked to be ascendant in the mid-1920s, controlling several governorships, he wrote, but then abruptly the movement had collapsed politically. "I am told that in Germany it will not be so easy for the Hitlerites to collapse, but it strikes me that any movement that depends on the intensity of emotion such as I saw tonight must either win power quickly or its foundations of hatred and feeling will collapse," he wrote.

The following day, Plotkin returned to the same theme. "The Nazi meetings are dispirited, as if beaten and know it," he noted. But he added a cautionary note: "The only disquieting factor is the number of killings that are political in their origin." Three days later, he attended another Nazi rally, where Goebbels once again denounced "the bloody Jews," whipping up the crowd to such frenzy that Plotkin thought for a moment that it would "run out of his control." But when the rally was over, the American was struck by the sight of the young Nazi troops in uniform waiting for their orders "like a bunch of schoolboys, and like a bunch of schoolboys bought hot dogs when the hot-dog men started to circulate among them." The wording of this diary entry suggests he found it hard to believe that these young men eating hot dogs could be truly dangerous.

Even with the mounting reports of violence by just such young men, some wealthy German Jews didn't seem all that disturbed by the Nazis either. Edgar Mowrer recalled a dinner at the end of 1932 in the home of "a banker named Arnholt." Mowrer probably misspelled his host's name; if so, the banker in question may have been Hans Arnhold, who was forced to flee Germany after Hitler's takeover (his villa now serves as the home of the American Academy in Berlin). In any case, all the men around the dinner table except Mowrer were Jews.

Over coffee, several of them boasted that they had given money to the Nazis at the urging of non-Jews like Hjalmar Schacht and Fritz Thyssen. Although Schacht had served as the currency commissioner in the critical year 1923, when he was credited with ending hyperinflation, and then as president of the Reichsbank until 1930, he had become an increasingly vocal supporter of the Nazis; so had industrialist Thyssen.

Mowrer didn't hide his surprise, prompting his host to ask what he was thinking. "Merely wondering how the People of Israel have managed to survive so many thousands of years when they obviously have a strong suicidal urge," the American responded.

"But you don't take this fellow seriously," his host inquired.

"Unfortunately I do—and so should you."

"Just talk," the banker declared, and all the others nodded in agreement. As Mowrer noted, they "thought me incapable of understanding the German soul."

Schacht, who had once aligned himself with the democratic forces of the Weimar Republic, wasn't about "just talk." Shortly before Christmas, Mowrer ran into him and asked politely about his plans for the holidays. "I am going to Munich to talk with Adolf Hitler," he declared.

"You too, my fine Democrat!" Mowrer responded, abandoning any pretense of politeness.

"*Ach*, you understand nothing. You are a stupid American," Schacht shot back.

"Granted. But tell me what you expect from Hitler in words of one syllable and I'll try to understand."

"Germany will have no peace until we bring Hitler to power."

Three weeks later, Mowrer met Schacht again, and asked him how his conversation went with the Nazi leader. "Brilliantly," the German banker replied. "I've got that man right in my pocket."

As Mowrer recalled in his memoirs, "From that moment I expected the worst."

He wasn't the only one. Bella Fromm, the Jewish social reporter, found herself seated next to Wiegand at a dinner party in Berlin on December 8. The Hearst correspondent wasn't living full-time in Berlin then, but had a knack for appearing on scene "whenever a political melodrama is about to sweep the stage," Fromm noted in her diary.

"When are the National Socialists going to seize the government?" she asked him bluntly, using the old journalistic ploy of asking a question in a way that implied she knew the score already.

Wiegand looked taken aback but offered a crisp response: "It won't be long now."

And what would that mean? "Hitler intends to abolish the treaty of Versailles," the American correspondent continued, drawing upon his past meetings with Hitler. "He wants to unite all Germans. He has no desire for the return of colonies if he finds a way for new *Lebensraum* [living space] within Central Europe, to install all the regained German subjects. One of Hitler's early associates, Professor Karl von Haushofer, has been studying the *Lebensraum* problem for years. He has persuaded Hitler that an expansion to the east, peaceful or by force, is an inevitable necessity."

On December 22, Fromm attended a reception hosted by American Consul General George Messersmith, who had been stationed in the German capital for the past two years and monitored the Nazi movement. While Ambassador Sackett was increasingly convinced that the Schleicher government had successfully contained the Nazi threat, Messersmith took a different view. "The German government had better act quickly, and strongly," he said at the reception. "It's really upsetting to find so many people of importance in the National Socialist party. There are going to be fireworks here pretty soon, unless I'm badly mistaken."

Fromm added this final line to her diary entry that night: "I do not think that my friend Messersmith is mistaken."

At an "intimate" dinner for twelve guests hosted by Chancellor von Schleicher and his wife six days later, on December 28, Fromm was able to relay Wiegand's prediction of a Nazi takeover directly to the man currently in charge. Schleicher laughed it off. "You journalists are all alike," he told her. "You make a living out of professional pessimism."

Fromm pointed out that these views were widely held, not just by her and Wiegand. And that everyone knew that Papen and others were "trying to bring the National Socialists to power."

"I think I can hold them off," Schleicher insisted.

Referring to the aging President von Hindenburg, Fromm cautioned, "As long as the Old Gentleman sticks to you."

Later the two of them were briefly alone in Schleicher's study. The chancellor once again talked about bringing Gregor Strasser into his government. Fromm was hardly reassured. While Strasser represented the left wing of the Nazi Party, he shared the anti-Semitic views of the rest of the leadership. "What about the church and Jew-phobia of the party?" she asked.

"You ought to know me better than that, Bella," Schleicher replied. "All that will be dropped entirely."

Once again, Fromm added a line of commentary to her diary entry of that night. "The National Socialist Party is not in the habit of dropping anything that suits its purposes," she wrote. "They scuttle men quicker than they scuttle doctrines."

But even during the fateful month of January 1933, Americans in Berlin were hearing constant reassurances that Hitler and his movement were fading as a threat. Chancellor von Schleicher, they believed, really knew both what he was up against and how to outplay his opponents. On January 22, Abraham Plotkin met with Martin Plettl, the president of the German Clothing Workers' Union, in a packed Berlin restaurant. Plettl explained to the American labor organizer that Hitler was "dancing between four masters and any one of the four of them may break him." The four: two camps of industrialists, and two camps within the Nazi Party. As a result, Plettl maintained, Hitler was facing a choice of either accepting a position within the current government or allowing his party rival Strasser to do so. "Hitler will lose either way," he insisted.

Plettl's reasoning was that Schleicher was probably using Hitler "as a cat's paw." And "Hitler on the downgrade, supplying Schleicher with provocative means for eliminating the Communists, will clear the roads for Schleicher in the coming elections." When Plotkin indicated he was skeptical, Plettl argued that it was a strategy that could easily work, allowing Schleicher to use the Nazis to destroy the Communists but prompting deeper fissures within the party itself as some leaders would be compromised by joining a coalition government. Hitler's party would no longer be a pure opposition force, and its base of support would weaken.

But the previous chancellor, Papen, had by that time already effectively undercut his successor. On January 4, he met with Hitler in Cologne at the home of banker Kurt von Schröder. The two politicians worked out a deal to oust Schleicher, with Papen assigned the task of winning the support of President von Hindenburg. Even when word of their meeting leaked out, Schleicher professed himself "in no way alarmed by the alleged plot against him." Neither were the top diplomats at the American Embassy, who believed that the meeting was mostly focused on dealing with the Nazis' ailing finances. The "rapidly increasing" party debt, chargé d'affaires George Gordon reported, was threatening to undermine the movement. Its financial backers, he added, were both trying to solve that problem and encouraging Hitler to participate in the government, not topple it.

In the last few days of January, those interpretations were proven grievously wrong. Facing a growing political revolt fanned by Papen, Schleicher asked Hindenburg for his support so that he could dissolve the Reichstag. The president refused, triggering the resignation of the Schleicher government. Next, he turned to Papen to negotiate a new arrangement with the political parties. This gave Papen the green light to do what he had been advocating all along. On January 30, Hindenburg formally asked Hitler to form a new government, appointing him chancellor and Papen as vice chancellor. While Ambassador Sackett reported this "sudden and unexpected triumph" for the Nazis, the AP's Louis Lochner indicated that Papen remained convinced that he had truly outsmarted the new chancellor. "We have hired Hitler," he told his friends. In other words, Lochner concluded, Papen was still convinced that he would be "in the driver's seat."

Even before the debate about whether Hitler could truly take power was settled by his dramatic ascension, Americans in Germany were split about what such a development would mean. Were Hitler's speeches and *Mein Kampf* a true indication of what Nazi rule would look like, or were they merely tools for his emotional campaign? If the latter, it would be logical to believe that, once in power, Hitler would tone down his rhetoric, moderate his program and seek accommodation with many of those he had been denouncing at home and abroad.

Among the correspondents covering Germany, no one had a longer track record than S. Miles Bouton of the *Baltimore Sun*. He had arrived in Germany in 1911, working at first for the Associated Press. He had covered World War I, written the book *And the Kaiser Abdicates*, married a German woman and left no doubt that he considered himself the preeminent authority on the country. "It requires no great skill at reading between the lines to discover that I have no very high opinion of the quality of the reporting done from Germany for the American press," he declared in an interview for his own newspaper on a visit to the United States in 1925. He claimed he wasn't blaming his fellow correspondents but only their editors, who were guided by their prejudices. Nonetheless, he was scathing about those colleagues. "Some of them are, it is true, much less well informed about the situation there than they might be."

A well-informed correspondent, he emphasized both before the Nazis took power and after, would have no doubt who was to blame for what went wrong in Germany. Speaking to the Rockford, Illinois, Women's Club in March 1935, he pointed out that he had denounced the Versailles Treaty from the beginning. "Read that treaty and understand the things that are happening today," he said. "The allies heaped oppressions, humiliations, and exactions upon Germany."

Bouton had first encountered Hitler in September 1923 before the Beer Hall Putsch that made the Nazi leader famous. At the party headquarters, he was met by a young man who began explaining how Hitler would restore Germany's honor, saving it from the Communists and the Jews. "It was several minutes before it occurred to me that this was Hitler, talking about himself in the third person," Bouton recalled in an unpublished manuscript. "I had never before met and have never since met a man who so completely identified himself with his supposed mission."

When Hitler's party regained momentum once the Depression hit, Bouton was at first skeptical of its chances, reporting in 1930 that it "does not come into consideration at all as a government party." (In 1935, he would claim to have been much more prescient, telling his audience at the University of Georgia: "For the last five years of the Republic I prophesied time and again that Hitler and the National Socialists would come to power.") But in March 1932, he reported that the strong second-place finish by Hitler in the presidential election "represents a remarkable personal triumph, and it becomes the more astounding when one considers the circumstances in which it was gained." From there, he launched into an account of what he characterized as the story that his American colleagues had routinely failed to report: it was about "the methods used by both the Reich and the state governments against Hitler, since these methods make a mockery of all protestations by the men in power that they believe in democracy."

In other words, the real story that needed to be reported from Germany was not about the brutal methods and ideology of the Nazis but the attempts by the Weimar government to muzzle them, forbidding them to broadcast their message on the radio, suppressing their party newspapers, and banning some of their leaders from speaking in public, as happened to Hitler after he emerged from prison. He scornfully referred to all the talk of the "menace of Hitlerism" that was "disturbing the peace of mind of the outside world in general and of America in particular." Americans, he added, saw Hitler as "a mere rabble-rouser and shallow demagogue." Quoting Dorothy Thompson's description of Hitler as "the very prototype of the Little Man," he declared that his extensive experience in Germany had taught him to be hesitant about making such judgments about both Hitler and his followers, who were dismissed as "a strange collection of heavy doctrinaires and helpless neurotics."

"I am pretty sure that these confident critics are wrong," he wrote. "There are probably few if any Americans in Germany who have as wide a circle of German friends and acquaintances as I have." Those acquaintances, he added, were highly educated—"for the greater part academicians, professional men of high standing, high government officials, etc." At least 80 percent of them had voted for Hitler, he claimed. Of the others, 10 percent refused to vote for Hindenburg, and the remaining 10 percent were Jews. "Even some of them would have voted for Hitler had it not been for the anti-Semitic plank in his platform."

At the end of his long article, he tossed in what he called "one more significant fact." Many of his German friends had American wives who "without any exception are more ardent Hitlerites than their German husbands." His interpretation of this phenomenon: "Theirs is the American brand of patriotism, the brand which has happily made Marxism and internationalism unthinkable in our country." His message: Germans supported Hitler for the same "patriotic" reasons, and American readers shouldn't be swayed by the anti-Nazi accounts of his colleagues in the American press corps.

Some of those colleagues had come to their own conclusions about why Bouton was offering such contrarian views. Writing on December 11, 1932, to his daughter Betty, who was a student at the University of Chicago, the AP's Lochner recounted an incident triggered by a photograph of Chancellor von Papen and a few journalists, including Lochner and Bouton, that ran in the Nazi weekly *Illustrierter Beobachter*. The caption read: "*Von Papen und die jüdische Weltpresse*" (Von Papen and the Jewish world press). "That they put me down as one of the Chosen People doesn't matter much, but the unkindest cut was that Miles Bouton, of all people—he who himself is an ardent Nazi—should have been put down as 'Sally Bouton-Knopf.' The whole American colony is laughing about it," Lochner wrote.

Lochner explained that the Nazi publication listed Bouton's first name as Sally "as that is a favorite Jewish name" and that they had translated Bouton as *Knopf* (German for "button") and hyphenated his last name. "Miles nearly hit the roof," Lochner added with evident glee. "He was furious—all the more so as he had travelled around with Hitler in an airplane. We both protested not because we were called Jews—we both have very dear friends among the Jews and neither of us are anti-Semitic—but because from the whole ideology of the Nazis it is evident they meant to insult us by calling us Jews."

Lochner reported that he heard Hitler was furious about this "boner" by the Nazi weekly, and several Nazi leaders called him to say they were "ashamed" that someone from their camp had played such a dirty trick on them. Lochner wrote to the editor of the weekly demanding he print a retraction. "He did—but in a way that makes the readers think we objected to being called Jews, when our point was that we objected to being insulted by the Nazis," he reported to his daughter. Nonetheless, Lochner was pleased that the Nazis had made Bouton squirm. "We've had lots of fun," he concluded.

*    *    *

No issue crystallized the question of Hitler's intentions more than what Nazi rule would mean for the Jews. A correspondent like Edgar Mowrer, who was Bouton's polar opposite when it came to his assumptions about the party and what it represented, had covered the attacks of Brownshirts on "foreigners and Jews," in some cases going out in armored police cars. His wife Lilian recalled anxiously waiting for hours until he returned from "the front." The young thugs wearing heavy leather boots and carrying revolvers were "always insolent and swaggering," she added, and they would gather at a number of cafés and beer houses, hanging huge swastika flags outside. The owners of these establishments had no choice but to tolerate "these invasions."

Before the Nazis came to power, Edgar made a habit of going into such hangouts to buy the brawlers beers and try to learn more about their views. As Lilian described it, these young toughs rallied to slogans like "We spit on freedom" and "Beat the Red Front to pulp." Their favorite toast: "Germany awake, perish the Jew!"

"But just where did you learn all this interesting stuff about the Jew?" Edgar asked on one occasion.

"*Aber Herr*, everybody in Germany knows that the Jews are our misfortune," one of the Nazis replied.

"But just how? Why?" Edgar persisted.

"There are too many of them. And then, Jews are not people like the rest of us."

"But in my country the proportion of Jews is much higher than in Germany. But we lost no war, have not starved, not been betrayed to foreigners; in short, have suffered none of the evils you attribute to the presence of the Jews in Germany. How do you account for this?"

"We don't account for it. We simply know it is true," the Nazi replied, complaining that the Jews were getting the best jobs for themselves by "stealth and fraud." Germans were waking up to that, he added, "and no matter how hard the Jew works, he won't be on top long."

"Then you admit the Jew works harder?" Edgar asked.

"Of course."

"But doesn't the hardest worker deserve the best jobs?"

His interlocutor suddenly sounded uncertain. "Yes—that is, no; not if he is a Jew."

"Is that logical, is that clear thinking?"

"*Ach*, thinking!" the exasperated Nazi replied. "We are sick of thinking. Thinking gets you nowhere. The *Führer* himself says true Nazis think with their blood."

And this kind of lack of thinking was everywhere. The Mowrers' young daughter, Diana Jane, came home from school one day and said, in German, that she had to ask her mother a question. Lilian insisted, as always, that she speak English at home. "But I have only heard about these things in German and I must know if I am saying the right words," she replied.

Lilian assented.

"Mutti, am I a Jew or a Christian?"

"You are not a Jew, my dear. What makes you ask?"

The girl said that all the talk at school about who was or wasn't Jewish had made her wonder about her own identity. "It isn't good to be a Jew," she concluded.

Nineteen thirty-two was a big year for Edgar Mowrer. He would win the Pulitzer Prize for his reporting then, and his deepening fears about where Germany was heading prompted him to write his book *Germany Puts the Clock Back*, which he finished in November and was quickly published in the United States at the beginning of 1933 just as Hitler was taking power. His book chronicled the disintegration of the Weimar Republic, how Germans had grown "sick of everything" and how "the depression brought voters by the carloads to Hitler." By way of explanation of the Nazi leader's appeal, he wrote, "A little man has taken the measure of still smaller men."

Yet even Mowrer wasn't quite sure what Hitler represented—and what to expect if he took power. "Did he believe all that he said?" he asked. "The question is inapplicable to this sort of personality. Subjectively Adolf Hitler was, in my opinion, entirely sincere even in his self-contradictions. For his is a humorless mind that simply excludes the need for consistency that might distress more intellectual types. To an actor the truth is anything that lies in its effect: if it makes the right impression it is true."

Sigrid Schultz of the rival *Chicago Tribune* recalled one incident that proved Mowrer's point about Hitler's acting ability, which allowed him to ingratiate himself with those who were normally skeptical. After the Nazis' string of electoral wins in 1932, Hanfstaengl invited a dozen American and British correspondents to meet Hitler at the Kaiserhof Hotel. Schultz was among them, and she watched with fascination as Hitler greeted the first correspondent in line by clutching his hands and staring into his eyes. Encountering Schultz, he merely shook her hand. When he reached a correspondent who was normally known for his irreverent style, Schultz expected some fireworks. Instead, she recalled, "I could see the man's face as Hitler went into his routine and, to my horror, those usually cynical eyes responded adoringly to whatever message Hitler was giving out."

Mowrer credited Hitler and the Nazis with doing everything possible to achieve the maximum effect at every such opportunity. "While others slept, they had labored. While opponents talked once, they talked ten times," he wrote. "Hitler believes chiefly in the personal contact, the spoken word, personality." He added ominously, "In the great game of fooling the public he is an incomparable master."

As for the true intentions of his anti-Semitic campaign, Mowrer sounded alarmed in some moments but uncertain in others. "A suspicion arises that Adolf Hitler himself accepted anti-Semitism with his characteristic mixture of emotionalism and political cunning," he wrote. "Many doubted if he really desired pogroms."

In January 1933 after Mowrer had completed his book and Hitler was coming to power, the *Chicago Daily News* reporter won an election, too. He was elected president of the Foreign Press Association. It was a confluence of events that would ultimately lead to a dramatic ending of the Mowrers' stay in Germany.

Putzi Hanfstaengl would claim in his postwar memoir that he had felt "singularly unmoved by that clamour and hysteria of that January 30 in

1933 when the Nazi Party came to power." He added, "Certainly it was an exciting moment, but I had too many reservations concerning the danger-ous turbulence of the radicals to feel unduly confident about the possible march of events."

If he really had any reservations then, Putzi disguised them well. He congratulated Hitler when he returned to the Kaiserhof Hotel after his meeting with President von Hindenburg and immediately talked with a steady stream of foreign journalists coming to see him. And soon he was directing propaganda films, publishing a book of "caricatures"—or sketches—of Hitler, and designing his own personalized Nazi Party uni-form. Putzi didn't want to don the standard shirt and trousers that Hitler offered him from the party's clothing store. Instead, he noted, "I sent for a superb length of chocolate-brown gabardine from a London tailor and had it made up with a delicate little gold epaulette."

Hanfstaengl boasted that his first appearance in his new uniform, at a dinner party hosted by the AP's Lochner and his German wife, Hilde, "was, needless to state, the talk of the town." Lochner remembered the evening well. It was April 27, 1933, and his guests included U.S. Consul General George Messersmith, Sigrid Schultz, some former German of-ficials and banker Curt Sobernheim and his wife, Lilli, who were Jewish. In typical German fashion, all the guests had arrived promptly at eight, except for Putzi. Hilde was ready to seat them at eight-fifteen when the Nazi press officer suddenly appeared. "In strode an enormous bulk of masculinity in a brand-new Nazi brown uniform," Lochner recalled. "It was Putzi, who had hitherto made sarcastic remarks about the official Nazi garb and had never dressed in one."

Lochner added that Lilli Sobernheim—"a short stubby person who was nearly as round as she was small"—nearly fainted. Trembling, she whispered, "The Gestapo." Putzi bowed to Hilde and apologized for his tardiness, explaining that his butler hadn't properly prepared his evening dress suit, which was why he had to wear his party uniform. As Louis noted, nobody believed him; Putzi's own account of that evening makes clear that his appearance in uniform was fully planned, although he never mentioned his lie. Nor did he mention what happened next. According to Lochner, he politely bowed and kissed the hand of Lilli Sobernheim. Her husband, Curt, then stated, with a look of professed innocence: "I believe, Dr. Hanfstaengl, we are somewhat related."

Putzi was visibly startled. After all, a Jew was telling him that he was related to him. "How interesting! What do you mean?" he asked.

Sobernheim began explaining that a relative had married someone in Hanfstaengl's family, and the two men retreated to a corner where they talked further. Lochner recalled that this had everyone chuckling since "it seemed like accusing someone of treason to tell a Nazi he was related to a Jew."

As the evening progressed, the tension appeared to dissipate. Hanfstaengl even spent time chatting amicably with former Minister of Defense Wilhelm Groener, who had supported a ban on the SA during his term in office. "Only you unofficial people can stage a dinner like this," Messersmith, the U.S. consul general, told Lochner. "There ought to be more like it. Maybe they would exert a good influence upon the Nazis."

But as Hanfstaengl made the rounds of the parties hosted by diplomats and journalists during those early days of the new government, he charmed some of his hosts and alienated others. Messersmith soon concluded that he was "a court jester," but one who "thought that his position as Hitler's favorite and his uniform permitted him to do anything." Since the consul general had become increasingly critical of the new regime, Hanfstaengl registered his displeasure by what was meant as a pointed put-down at an American Embassy dinner party. "Oh, so this is the famous Messersmith who knows everything that is going on and doesn't like it," he told him.

Putzi's rudeness didn't stop there. He began rubbing the leg of the woman seated next to him at the dinner table. As Lilian Mowrer pointed out later, "I knew he was crazy about women and could not keep his hands off them." Most guests pretended not to notice Putzi's antics, but Messersmith bluntly and openly reprimanded him. The consul general reported with evident satisfaction that Putzi acted like "an exemplary guest" from that point on.

Later, Hanfstaengl would seek to take revenge by spreading rumors that Messersmith was Jewish. He had used the same tactics against Edgar Mowrer when the correspondent began reporting on attacks against Jews during those first months of the new regime, claiming that Mowrer was a "secret" Jew. Meeting with James G. McDonald, the visiting head of the New York–based Foreign Policy Association, Putzi declared: "Of course, he is a Jew and so is his wife"—and then proceeded to name other reporters who he claimed were Jews or served Jewish interests.

Mowrer's friend Knickerbocker heard a group of Nazi leaders repeating this story. "Edgar a Jew? Of course!" he replied. Then referring to the revered general from World War I who had marched with Hitler in the Beer Hall Putsch, he added, "As Jewish as Ludendorff!"

Those kinds of personal battles were hardly surprising given the escalating political tensions from the moment that Hitler took power. According to Putzi, Hitler initially liked Knickerbocker, not for his reporting but for his excellent German, lively personality and red hair—although, of course, none of that would matter later when his dispatches became increasingly irritating to the Nazis. Knickerbocker was on hand for all the major events in early 1933, including "the greatest torchlight procession in its history" on January 30, when Hitler became chancellor.

"Hitler stationed himself at the window of the Chancellor's palace and Hindenburg at another window," Knickerbocker wrote. "From eight o'clock in the evening until midnight the thirty-five thousand Brownshirts of Berlin marched past and their flaming torches turned the streets into rivers of fire. The aged president stood in a bath of searchlights, the young Chancellor in another. All Berlin tried to reach them to cheer them and the music and the shouting brought many stout Teutons to tears."

At first, the representatives of the new regime reached out to Americans to deliver messages of reassurance. "The Nazis will make no attempt to carry out any of their well-known demagogic reforms," Hjalmar Schacht, the former president of the Reichsbank who would soon regain his old post, told Alfred Klieforth, the embassy's first secretary, over dinner. Sackett, who would end his posting in Berlin in March, initially believed that the government was genuinely divided in its responsibilities, with the Nazis taking charge only of "the purely political and administrative departments" while others would continue to deal with the economy, finance and the remaining daily chores of government. He believed Papen, the vice-chancellor, was continuing to play a major role, along with

Nationalist Party leader Alfred Hugenberg, who had been appointed minister of agriculture and economics. The ambassador described him as "practically economic dictator."

But the next rapid sequence of events would dispel all such illusions about competing power brokers. On February 27, the Reichstag was set ablaze by Marinus van der Lubbe, a twenty-four-year-old Dutchman who had been a member of a Communist youth group. Suspicions were immediately aroused that the arsonist was "a dupe of the Nazis" and that he had been set up to provide them with an excuse for a massive crackdown. Subsequently, many historians have concluded that the Dutchman may have indeed acted alone. But whatever the case, Hitler seized on the opportunity to lash out against the Communists and other alleged conspirators, and to transform Germany into an absolute dictatorship.

Based on a hastily prepared emergency decree "For the Protection of People and State," Hitler banned opposition publications and rallies, and ordered the arrests of thousands of Communists and Social Democrats, claiming they were plotting more attacks. SA troops wreaked havoc, breaking into homes, beating and torturing the victims they dragged out. With new elections scheduled for March 5, everything happened so fast that it ensured that opposition parties wouldn't have a chance to mount effective campaigns.

On February 28, the day when Hitler had convinced the increasingly feeble President von Hindenburg to sign the emergency decree that suspended the key civil liberty sections of the Weimar constitution, Fromm attended a reception at Sackett's residence. Everyone was abuzz with the latest speculation about how far the crackdown would go. It was then, according to Fromm, that Sackett revealed he had asked Washington to send him home. He was disappointed by the failure of American efforts to stabilize the German economy, the Jewish reporter wrote in her diary, and "deeply displeased with German domestic politics."

Despite the Nazis' rampage against their opponents, the party garnered only 43.9 percent of the votes in the March 5 elections. That made them the strongest party in the Reichstag but still not the majority party. They had to include Hugenberg's Nationalists in the government to give them the majority they needed. But Hitler had no intention of allowing anything to slow him down. On March 23, he had the Reichstag approve the "enabling act," effectively shifting all key powers from the legislative body to him. As chancellor, he would draft the laws that would be enacted by the cabinet—even, as the act specified, when they "might deviate from the constitution." There would be no more restraints on his power.

Or on the attacks on anyone deemed a political opponent and on Jews. April 1 marked the official start of a boycott against Jewish businesses, allegedly as a response to slanderous campaigns against Germany by Jews abroad. Calling what happened next "a tragedy," Knickerbocker reported: "The nation turned into a huge hunting party and for another fortnight all attention was absorbed in chasing the Jews."

Dorothy Thompson, who was back on the continent but no longer living in Berlin, had arrived in the German capital on the night of the Reichstag fire and stayed long enough to witness some of the rampages that followed. When the Jewish boycott started on April 1, she wrote from Vienna to her husband Sinclair Lewis, who was back in New York: "It is really as bad as the most sensational papers report . . . the S.A. boys have simply turned into gangs and beat up people on the streets . . . and take socialists and communists & Jews into so-called 'Braune Etagen' [brown floors] where they are tortured. Italian fascism was a kindergarten compared to it." She also despaired of "incredible (to me) docility" of the liberals and confessed she felt the urge to go around Berlin reciting the Gettysburg Address. And she was worried about her colleagues who were still stationed there, particularly Mowrer. "Edgar is constantly threatened, but has no intention of leaving Berlin & doesn't think he is in actual danger."

Thompson sent another letter to a friend in London, the pianist Harriet Cohen, who knew British Prime Minister Ramsay MacDonald. She explained that she had seen many victims of Nazi violence with her own eyes. The SA thugs had gone "perfectly mad" as they hunted down new victims, she wrote. "They beat them with steel rods, knock their teeth out with revolver butts, break their arms . . . urinate on them, make them kneel and kiss the *Hakenkreuz* [the swastika]." Noting the silence of the German press and the exodus of such writers as Thomas Mann, Erich Maria Remarque and Bertolt Brecht, she let loose with her frustration.

"I keep thinking what *could* be done . . . I feel myself starting to hate Germany. And already the world is rotten with hatred. If only someone would speak . . ." Cohen understood this to be an appeal for her to show the letter to MacDonald, which she did.

Not that such messages had any impact. The Nazis continued to usher in their new order with new drama. On the evening of May 10, propaganda chief Joseph Goebbels presided over the infamous "burning of the books"—"the auto da fé of 'un-German literature,'" as Knickerbocker described it, "when throughout the Reich 100,000 students gathered to destroy 'Jewish, Marxist, anti-German, immoral' publications of 280 authors, many of them bearing world-famous names." It was "a circus of historical significance but one that furnished immense entertainment for the participants."

Addressing the crowd, Goebbels declared: "These flames do not only illuminate the final act of the old era, they also light up the new. Never before have the young men had so good a right to clean up the debris of the past . . . Oh, my century, it is a joy to be alive." Along with the predictable volumes of Marx, Engels and Lenin, books by Remarque, Brecht, Hemingway and even Helen Keller (*How I Became a Socialist*) went up in flames, all part of an estimated total of 20,000 copies incinerated that night while the crowd cheered and sang.

Several correspondents witnessed the spectacle, and the cumulative effect of the Nazi actions was a growing sense of repulsion among many of them. Even the *Baltimore Sun*'s Bouton, whom Lochner had scornfully referred to as "an ardent Nazi" earlier, underwent a fundamental transformation and started filing increasingly hard-hitting stories, warning "that the truth [about the Nazis' tactics] is ten times worse than the reports." Just over a year after Hitler took power, the German Foreign Ministry ordered Bouton to "change his style of reporting or leave the country." Within a short time, he was gone.

Most of Bouton's colleagues, including Lochner, very much wanted to keep covering what was the most exciting story of the moment. Besides, their home offices didn't want dramatic exits—they wanted to keep their reporters in Berlin. "Our orders from our bosses were to tell no untruth, but to report only as much of the truth, without distorting the picture, as would enable us to remain at our posts," Lochner wrote in his memoirs. Cautious by nature, the AP veteran would follow those instructions.

Other Americans exhibited even greater caution, but sometimes for other reasons. Despite all the violence and intimidation—in fact, directly because of the seemingly unbridled nature of the almost daily attacks on anyone deemed a political opponent—the outsiders were often puzzled and still suspended judgment on what exactly was driving this fury.

Writing in the *American Federationist*, the house organ of the American Federation of Labor, Abraham Plotkin summed up the desperate situation of his German counterparts in an article that he published shortly after his return to the United States in May 1933. "The Nazis have turned loose forces that they themselves do not understand," the Jewish-American labor organizer insisted. "It may surprise many to learn that the most exciting things that have happened in Germany have come as an upsurge from below, and not from the government itself." Citing as an example the anti-Jewish boycott in Munich, which was formally disavowed by Hitler's government, he claimed it had been started by SA troops and "it gained such momentum within a few hours that not one among the Nazi leaders dared to make an effort to head it off."

Plotkin was far from the only American subscriber to the notion that Hitler and other top Nazis were seeking to restrain their supporters rather than incite them to ever greater violence. Consul General Messersmith initially believed that Hitler had to ride the violent wave of his followers since otherwise he might be replaced by "real radicals." Growing protests back in the United States, such as the one held in Madison Square Garden on March 27, were only whipping up "what was almost hysteria" among those German leaders who wanted to pursue a moderate course, he warned. Unlike Plotkin, he believed that the subsequent boycott of Jewish businesses in Germany had been ordered from the top, but to contain the popular resentment and control it. When the government officially abandoned the boycott on April 4, he was pleased to report that the number of anti-Semitic incidents dropped quickly.

Not even the fact that a growing number of Americans were caught up in the violence could shake Messersmith's belief that the reality of what was happening was far more complicated than it appeared—and that it would be counterproductive to pin all the blame on Hitler. In early March, Nathaniel Wolff, a painter from Rochester, New York, was nabbed by the SA when he was overheard denouncing both Communists and Nazis. Before he was allowed to leave the country, he had to sign a statement promising that he would never return. "I am a Jew," it read. "I certify that no physical violence has been done to me and none of my property has been stolen."

Others were not so lucky. Some, like editor Edward Dahlberg, a visiting *Scribner's Magazine* editor, were beaten on the street. The American wife of a German Jew had to watch storm troopers, who had burst into their apartment, beat her husband, ostensibly for having four suits in their closet. "Four suits, while for fourteen years we have been starving," one of his tormenters shouted. "Jews. We hate you."

On March 31, the SA snatched three Americans and took them to a makeshift prison, where they were stripped and left to sleep on the cold floor. The next day, their tormentors beat them unconscious before leaving them out on the street. American correspondents knew of this and other incidents, but Messersmith convinced them to hold off any reporting on what happened to the trio of Americans on March 31 for forty-eight hours. He explained this would allow him to press the authorities to take the proper actions first. As Messersmith reported with evident satisfaction, the police took "rapid action" and the guilty Brownshirts were "sharply reproved" and expelled from the ranks.

Messersmith and other embassy officials kept protesting when Americans were assaulted, as they continued to be. But they also looked for signs of hope in any case where the authorities seemed willing to help. During the summer of 1933, America's famous radio broadcaster H. V. Kaltenborn returned to Berlin for a visit with his son Rolf. He told Messersmith that American reporters like Mowrer were surely exaggerating in their stories about incidents of Nazi brutality. A few days later when his son Rolf failed to salute the Nazi banners carried in one of the frequent parades, a storm trooper hit him. Learning of the incident, the Propaganda Ministry promptly issued his father a written apology "in the hope that I would not feature my son's misadventure in a broadcast," Kaltenborn recalled. He added, "I had, of course, no intention of exploiting a personal experience."

Some Americans, it seemed, didn't want to see what was really happening, even when it was happening to them.

There were other American visitors during those early days of Hitler's rule who were keen to understand just how dramatically the situation had changed in Germany—and not to downplay the implications. James G. McDonald, the head of the Foreign Policy Association who would soon become the League of Nations' high commissioner for refugees, was alarmed by what he heard from the moment he arrived in Berlin on March 29, 1933. That first day, Putzi Hanfstaengl painted "a terrifying account of Nazi plans," McDonald recorded in his diary, and didn't conceal what this would mean for Jews. "The Jews are the vampire sucking German blood," Putzi told his American visitor with a laugh. "We shall not be strong until we have freed ourselves of them."

Later, McDonald was so disturbed by Hanfstaengl's vitriol that, unable to sleep, he walked around the Tiergarten. It was a beautiful night, the park was peaceful, with lovers scattered about, "and yet these ghastly hatreds breeding such shocking plans for heartless oppression of a whole section of the people," he noted.

Making his rounds, McDonald found nothing to lessen his fears. At dinner with the Mowrers, he could see that both of them were "highly overwrought." He wrote in his diary: "I have never seen them so tense. He could talk of little but terror and atrocities." Since a waiter was hovering within earshot, they could not talk all that freely. When they met again several days later, Mowrer was even more scathing in his remarks. "To him the leaders are thugs, perverts, and sadists," McDonald wrote. Separately, Knickerbocker reported to McDonald that he believed that the Nazis were already holding more than 40,000 political prisoners.

During the Jewish boycott, McDonald was chilled by the sight of an old Jew surrounded by a taunting crowd and, on another occasion, "laughing, jeering children making sport of a national shame." Meeting

German officials, he was struck how they refused to acknowledge that there could be anything wrong with what was happening. He was reminded of meetings he had in Moscow with militant Communists. "In each case the discussion was completely dogmatic"—in particular, when it came to their racial theories.

Two months before his visit to Berlin, McDonald had met with Henry Goldman of Goldman Sachs, who also was planning a trip to Germany. McDonald asked him then whether the intense anti-Semitism of Germany's new government didn't signal that something was wrong with the German people. Goldman, the son of the German-Jewish immigrant founder of the company, brushed off McDonald's question. "No, there is no more anti-Semitism in Germany than in the United States," he declared. McDonald considered Goldman a longtime "apologist for Germany," but he was startled by how he looked when they met at the Adlon Hotel on April 8. "I saw that he was a broken old man," McDonald noted.

Based on what he had seen and heard, Goldman had radically revised his views of Germany. "Mr. McDonald, I never would have believed that the worst of the fifteenth and sixteenth century would return in this twentieth century and of all places in Germany," he said. When McDonald asked him how long he was staying, he replied: "Just as long as I can bear it."

Later that same day, Hanfstaengl had arranged for McDonald to meet Hitler, giving him the opportunity to ask him directly about "the Jewish question." As the American visitor entered his office, Hitler "sized me up from head to foot with glances obviously half suspicious," McDonald recorded. But he appeared almost nonchalant in replying to his queries about his anti-Semitic policies.

"We are not primarily attacking the Jews, rather the Socialists and the Communists," Hitler declared. "The United States has shut out such people. We did not do so. Therefore, we cannot be blamed if we now take measures against them. Besides, as to Jews, why should there be such a fuss when they are thrown out of places, when hundreds of thousands of Aryan Germans are on the streets? No, the world has no just ground for complaint."

McDonald observed that Hitler had "the eyes of a fanatic, but he has in addition, I think, much more reserve and control and intelligence than most fanatics."

That was what McDonald recorded of his encounter in his diary right afterward. Later, when he returned to the United States, he offered an additional description of what Hitler said. "His word to me was, 'I will do the thing that the rest of the world would like to do. It doesn't know how to get rid of the Jews. I will show them.'"

# "Get Out, and Fast"

Hamilton Fish Armstrong, the editor of *Foreign Affairs* who had visited Germany and charted its politics during the Weimar era, showed up in Berlin on Hitler's birthday, April 20, 1933, less than two weeks after McDonald's departure. That morning, on his way from the train station to the Adlon Hotel where he was staying, Armstrong saw groups of boisterous Brownshirts preparing for the festivities. By noon, a crowd was gathered on Pariser Platz in front of his hotel, but sleet and rain kept the enthusiasm level down, despite the attempt to stir up emotions with a loudspeaker that broadcast Nazi slogans.

Armstrong knew many officials and professors from the Weimar era, along with some of the diplomats and correspondents stationed in Berlin. He found that some of the British and American correspondents were wary of reporting all the stories of Nazi atrocities that were floating about, but they realized that it was enough to quote the statements of the Nazis themselves to convey the draconian nature of their new policies.

Among the American diplomats, he considered George Messersmith the most knowledgeable—and the most upset about what was happening on a daily basis. "He could hardly restrain himself when he talked about the Nazis, biting his cigar into two pieces and tossing them away in disgust as he catalogued his difficulties in trying to protect American citizens from molestation," Armstrong recalled. Messersmith expressed his frustration at the powerlessness of government officials to restrain the Nazis; the militarism of the party activists, he continued, was making it increasingly unlikely that peace in Europe would last long.

Reconnecting with Germans he had known earlier, Armstrong heard a very dubious take on the new Hitler regime. Foreign Ministry officials like Hans Dieckhoff, who would later serve as the German ambassador to Washington, "were holding on to their offices and keeping quiet," he noted. Their message to him was that the Nazis were "a flash in the pan," and these officials insisted that they were trying to minimize the damage to German interests and foreign policy, waiting until a new government would take over. If Hitler did stay in power, they added, he could end up charting a more moderate course as he came to grips with the realities of the world. "They were not unintelligent men but I knew in my bones that they were wrong," Armstrong wrote later.

Part of the reason for Armstrong's pessimism was his realization that so many of the people he had consulted on previous visits—academic luminaries like agricultural expert Karl Brandt, economist Moritz Bonn and Ernst Jäckh, the founder of the Hochschule für Politik, some of whom had contributed articles to *Foreign Affairs* or worked closely with the Council on Foreign Relations, its parent organization—were nowhere to be found. "They had disappeared, I was told, and in any case it was better for them that I should not try to look them up," he recalled. Many members of the intellectual elite in such fields as medicine, science and literature had already lost their jobs, and several had fled the country to avoid more serious persecution. "It was staggering to think of what the resulting intellectual vacuum would mean in a country bled white and defeated in a devastating war," Armstrong later noted.

Like McDonald, the visiting editor was determined to meet the man who was responsible for these dramatic changes, the new leader who was the focal point of all the speculation about the country's future. As a first step, he went to meet Hjalmar Schacht, whom Hitler had reappointed to his old job as president of the Reichsbank as a reward for his support. It was a bizarre experience. Arriving at the Reichsbank, Armstrong was led to the big empty kitchen. Schacht was posing for a sculptor who was making a bust of him. Since the sculptor wanted to view him from an angle from below just as others would view the bust later, he had him seated on a chair placed on a large table. So while the sculptor worked and struggled, as Armstrong recalled, with shaping a likeness of his "screwed-up ugly face," Schacht explained to Armstrong how the Nazis were going to correct the excesses of capitalism, providing a more stable, reliable economic system. He also promised to write an article for *Foreign Affairs*, which he did a year later.

Armstrong was bemused by what he considered to be this moralizing about capitalism from a man who had drummed up support of German capitalists for Hitler, but he wasn't about to show it. His goal was to get the banker's help in lining up an interview with Hitler. If that meant playing to Schacht's "great vanity," as Armstrong put it, he was happy to do so.

Those tactics worked. On April 27, a week after his arrival in Berlin, Putzi Hanfstaengl showed up at the Adlon to take him to his interview. Armstrong was startled to see Putzi in his new Nazi uniform, the one that he would wear that evening to the Lochners' dinner party. As Armstrong recalled, "nothing matched" in the bizarre outfit: the tunic, shirt and breeches were all different shades of brown—"olive drab," "yellowish brown" and "a rather sickly greenish brown."

"Why, Putzi, I've never seen you in uniform before. How magnificent!" Armstrong declared.

Hanfstaengl took his compliment deadly seriously. "Yes, it is rather good, isn't it?" he replied. "Don't tell anyone, but it's English stuff. That does make a difference."

When he was escorted into Hitler's office at the Chancellery, still filled with potted flowers that had been birthday gifts, the German leader greeted him with a handshake, motioned him to a table and, as Hanfstaengl and another aide looked on, quickly launched into an opening monologue stressing his commitment to peace. "His general appearance was insignificant," Armstrong recalled, noting his large nose and small wrinkles about his eyes. But if those wrinkles made him appear inquisitive, that was totally misleading. "Although I had come from the West where his policies had aroused such fierce antagonism," Armstrong pointed out, "he did not ask me a single question or by any remark or reference reveal that he was in the least concerned by what the world thought of him or of the position in which he had placed his country." When Hitler spoke, he didn't look at Armstrong, instead keeping his eyes "fixed on the upper distance, which made it seem as though he were in communication with God."

Hitler's presentation about Germany's peaceful intentions quickly was transformed into his standard denunciation of the Versailles Treaty and of the "impossible and intolerable" border with Poland. He portrayed the eastern neighbor as a monster hovering over Germany. "Poland holds a naked knife in her teeth," he said, clenching his teeth for added effect, "and looks at us menacingly." Germany had been forced to disarm and was surrounded by such threatening neighbors, he insisted. The armies of France, Poland, Czechoslovakia and Belgium had fifty soldiers for every German soldier, he added, which meant that if there was any outbreak of fighting, the responsibility would clearly be theirs.

As Armstrong recalled, a lock of Hitler's hair came down menacingly over his eye as he forcefully punctuated his argument with what he believed was irrefutable logic: "To say the contrary is to say that a toothless rabbit would start a battle with a tiger."

Hitler had no problem combining his withering attacks on Poland, the most anti-Bolshevik country in the region, which had fought a war with Russia in 1920, with his thesis that the world's key countries should unite to defend themselves against the threat of Bolshevism. "We are armed today with spears, bows and arrows and swords," he continued. "Does that condition represent a danger to the peace of the world? Or does the danger of war come from the vast arms produced by Poland?" The only means to right those wrongs, he insisted, was for Germany to rearm. "We cannot and will not wait longer. The *sine qua non* of any agreement which Germany will join must be, at the very minimum, equality in arms."

Armstrong tried to interject other questions during the rare moments when Hitler paused in his monologues, but the German leader had no interest in anything resembling a give-and-take. As Hitler escorted him to the door, Armstrong slipped in his barbed thanks for addressing him rather than the usual millions of Germans. The German leader missed the irony completely and declared he had enjoyed their "animated talk."

On the way back to the Adlon, Hanfstaengl was effusive, claiming that Hitler was more open than he had ever been with a foreign visitor. "Wasn't he lovely to you?" he asked rhetorically. Besides, he added, it was such a great compliment that he had escorted his guest to the door, which he normally didn't do.

But Armstrong was feeling anything but "lovely" about the new Germany, which was so different than the country he had visited in the 1920s. Returning to New York, he quickly wrote a slim volume called *Hitler's Reich: The First Phase*, which was published in July 1933. Its opening words offered a dramatic—and devastatingly accurate—description of the country's brutal transformation:

> *A people has disappeared. Almost every German whose name the world knew as a master of government or business in the Republic of the past fourteen years is gone. There are exceptions; but the waves are swiftly cutting the sand from beneath them, and day by day, one by one, these last specimens of another age, another folk, topple over into the Nazi sea. So completely has the Republic been wiped out that the Nazis find it difficult to believe it ever existed . . .*

Anyone who did not accept Hitler's rule, pledging full allegiance to the man and his movement, wasn't just wiped out: "It is pretended that he never was. His name is not mentioned, even in scorn. If one asks about him, a vague answer is given: 'Oh, yes—but is he still alive? Maybe he is abroad. Or is he in a nursing home?' This does not apply merely to Jews and communists, fled or imprisoned or detained 'for their own protection' in barbed-wire concentration camps . . ." Then he went on to mention several national, state and city officials who were also in the category of the persecuted, the broken or now in exile. "The men who ruled Germany in these fourteen years have been swept away, out of sight, out of mind, out (according to the program of Dr. Goebbels, propagandist-in-chief) of history."

Armstrong neatly conveyed the strategy of the Nazis as they resurrected "Teutonic mysticism" and the notion of "the German super-man," but had to explain why the superior warrior was defeated in the previous war. "Either he is not a super-man, or there is an alibi," he wrote. "The alibi is furnished by the Jew, the traitor within the gates."

Despite this stark portrait of the new Germany that he painted, Armstrong asked near the end of his book whether Hitler, "having given the German spirit an opportunity to purge itself of part of its store of resentment and hate and envy," might chart a more moderate course, more like his predecessors who tried to redress their country's grievances in a more patient, long-term manner. "The first phase of the revolution is over," he concluded. "But we cannot pretend that as yet there is any real evidence to cause our fears to diminish, or that our questions can as yet be given any conclusive answers."

Armstrong was reluctant to give in completely to pessimism— something that he noted with a tinge of regret in his memoirs, since if he had done so he would have been proven completely vindicated by events. But the main import of his slim treatise was clear: Hitler's Germany was stirring up real fears for good reason—and anyone who downplayed the dangers was dangerously self-delusional.

In early 1933, shortly after Hitler had taken power in Germany, another new leader appeared on the world scene: Franklin D. Roosevelt. Coming to power in the midst of the Great Depression, he was understandably preoccupied with his domestic agenda. In his inaugural address on March 4, 1933, the same day that the Nazis won the most seats in the Reichstag elections, he focused on the need for national recovery, only making a brief mention of "world policy" during which he pledged that the United States would be "the good neighbor."

But Roosevelt faced an almost immediate decision about whom to send to replace Sackett, Herbert Hoover's envoy to Germany whose tour ended in late March. Despite the pull of his domestic agenda, Roosevelt understood that this was an increasingly important post and sought to fill it with someone who would have a chance of playing a constructive role there. He first offered the job to James M. Cox, who had been the Democratic presidential candidate in 1920 and shared the ticket with FDR as his running mate. "I regard Berlin as of special importance at this time," Roosevelt wrote him, imploring him to accept the post. Cox turned him down, citing his need to attend to his business interests, including his publishing company. The president was no more successful in his subsequent overtures to former Secretary of War Newton Baker, businessman Owen D. Young and a couple of prominent New York politicians.

While he struggled to find a new Berlin envoy, Roosevelt signaled his intent to pursue a global disarmament agenda. On May 16, he appealed to world leaders to begin scrapping all offensive weapons and to pledge not to engage in acts of aggression. The next day, Hitler appeared at the Reichstag to deliver his own "Peace Speech." Calling the American president's proposal "a ray of comfort for all who wish to co-operate in the maintenance of peace," Hitler professed his country's willingness to renounce all offensive weapons and "to disband her entire military establishment" if her neighbors would do the same thing. War was "unlimited madness," he added, calling for an end to old enmities and insisting that Germany was ready to live in peace with everyone.

"The speech was the best thing I have heard Hitler do," Lochner wrote to his daughter Betty afterward. He had presided over the AP bureau's extensive coverage of the event, and he was still feeling optimistic when he wrote his letter on May 28. The Nazis would have been furious if any Weimar chancellor had delivered such a conciliatory speech, he added. "That's the interesting thing about dictatorships, anyway: When it comes to foreign policy, they are tame as lambs . . . for they know they have so much trouble consolidating their power at home that they want to avoid everything possible that might look like trouble with foreign nations. It is quite obvious that Hitler doesn't want war."

Lochner wasn't completely credulous. "Whether, however, when you instill the military traditions in a people, war won't come anyway, is another question. Certainly, Germany looks like an armed camp," he wrote, mentioning the proliferation of uniformed Nazis, paramilitary units and police. "Hitler had to explain that the 'Private Armies' are harmless ping-pong affairs!"

Despite the generally positive coverage Hitler's speech received, Roosevelt was hardly sanguine about relations with Germany and continued to be frustrated by his inability to recruit someone for the Berlin post. But he perked up immediately when, at a meeting on June 7, Secretary of Commerce Daniel Roper suggested his friend William E. Dodd. A professor of history at the University of Chicago who specialized in the Old South, Dodd was born in North Carolina, studied at the Virginia Polytechnic Institute and then went on to get a doctorate at the University of Leipzig. Dodd, who was sixty-three, was both a Democratic partisan and "a democrat in the full American sense of the word," noted fellow historian Charles A. Beard. Beard added that Dodd was a Baptist who believed in "separation of Church and State, religious liberty and freedom of conscience."

The very next day, Roosevelt called Dodd at his University of Chicago office. "I want to know if you will render the government a distinct service," he told the startled professor. "I want you to go to Germany as Ambassador."

When Dodd recovered from the initial shock, he asked for some time to think the proposition over. "Two hours; can you decide in that time?" Roosevelt persisted, adding that he was sure the German government would not object to a book he had written about Woodrow Wilson or any of his other writings. "That book, your work as a liberal and as a scholar, and your study at a German university are the main reasons for my wishing to appoint you. It is a difficult post and you have cultural approaches that would help. I want an American liberal in Germany as a standing example."

Dodd quickly called his wife and talked with university officials, but there was little doubt in his mind what his answer would be. Suddenly, he had received an offer to be a participant in history, not just an observer. Besides, as his daughter Martha pointed out later, the call from the president aroused "an almost sentimental nostalgia for the Germany of his youth, the country that had opened up the tremendous cultural horizons to him, softened his heart by the kindness and generosity of its people, both simple and educated." Dodd had criticized the harsh terms of the Versailles Treaty when it had been unpopular to do so, and he had admired the attempt by the Weimar-era politicians to construct a democratic system.

If both Roosevelt and his appointee were inclined to believe that a cultured, liberal, democratic American ambassador might have a salutary effect on relations with Germany, they knew that they couldn't expect miracles. Over lunch at the White House on June 16, the president discussed trade and financial issues, and then turned to the question of the Jews. "The German authorities are treating the Jews shamefully and the Jews in this country are greatly excited," he said. "But this is also not a governmental affair. We can do nothing except for American citizens who happen to be made victims."

At the beginning of July, Dodd met with a group of prominent New York Jews, who appealed to him to do what he could to defend their persecuted brethren in Germany. While explaining that he could not intervene officially, he vowed to "exert all possible influence against unjust treatment of German Jews." But during another call in New York, Dodd received a dramatically different message. Philanthropist Charles R. Crane, who had endowed a chair at the University of Chicago's history department and also funded the Institute of Current World Affairs, discussed both his hatred of Russia's Bolsheviks and his admiration for the new regime in Germany, including its treatment of the Jews. "Let Hitler have his way," Crane advised Dodd.

Little wonder that Dodd boarded the *Washington*, the ship that would take him, his wife and their grown children Bill and Martha to Hamburg, in a serious mood. He was still excited by this unexpected new opportunity but recognized that Roosevelt's description of Berlin as "a difficult post" was certainly an understatement. He would have to deal with the Nazis and professional foreign service officers who had a reputation for snobbishness, and he had to try to resurrect his German language skills that had atrophied since his student days. As the ship prepared to depart, a group of New York newspapermen asked Dodd and his family to pose for photos on the front deck. As the new envoy noted sheepishly in his diary, "My wife, son and I yielded reluctantly and, unaware of the similarity of the Hitler salute, then unknown to us, we raised our hands." The last image of the departing appointee, then, was one of him and his family seemingly mimicking the Nazi salute.

On the voyage over, Dodd practiced his German and insisted that his son Bill and daughter Martha listen to him read aloud so that they would begin to understand the language. He also read Edgar Mowrer's new book *Germany Puts the Clock Back*. After taking the train from Hamburg to Berlin on July 13, Dodd immediately found himself answering questions about the kinds of issues that Mowrer wrote about. The *Familienblatt*, a Hamburg publication, had written that Dodd had come to Germany to speak up for the Jews. At his first briefing at the U.S. Embassy the next day, he told reporters that this was not the case.

Among the reporters present was Mowrer, who came up to greet him afterward. The new envoy told the famous *Chicago Daily News* correspondent that he had read his book with interest, but didn't say anything about the fact that it was banned in Germany and that, as he already knew, the Nazis were demanding that Mowrer resign his post as president of the Foreign Press Association.


In the memoir she published a few years later, Lilian Mowrer described the sense of solidarity that blossomed among many of the American and British correspondents who gathered in Berlin late most evenings at Die Taverne, an inexpensive Italian restaurant near the Kurfürstenstrasse, during those early months of Hitler's rule. "No group of professional men co-operate so easily as foreign correspondents," she wrote. "Spontaneously in those first awful days, each accepted the common task of telling the world, and for the purpose laid aside any thoughts of personal competition." Sitting on wooden benches at long tables under low ceilings, the reporters swapped stories, including of desperate late night phone calls or visits from Jews, Catholics, Socialists and others who told terrifying tales of arrests, beatings and torture. In one case, the Mowrers met a recently released Jew who showed them "his back beaten to pulp," as Edgar recalled.

But if most reporters were increasingly aware of the brutality around them, not all reacted the same way—or certainly not the same way the Mowrers did. When the Nazis had announced the boycott of Jewish stores, Lilian took her American passport and "pushed past these bullies" to shop at Kaufhaus des Westens, a Jewish-owned department store that was almost empty of customers, except for a few other foreigners. Edgar made it a point of visiting a Jewish doctor at the same time to have the cast removed from his leg, the result of an earlier skiing accident. The doctor was so frightened that he only reluctantly entered his own consulting room.

Since the publication of Mowrer's book, the Nazis had been openly angry at him. A senior press official at the Foreign Ministry suggested that he resign from his post as president of the Foreign Press Association; otherwise, he warned, the government would boycott it. Mowrer turned to Foreign Minister Konstantin von Neurath, a holdover from the pre-Nazi government who routinely tried to assure foreigners of Germany's good intentions, but received no help. He was as unhappy with Mowrer's book as were his new masters. Accompanied by Knickerbocker, Mowrer next managed to arrange a meeting with Goebbels, who was equally dismissive. "You claim to have reason to speak with me?" the propaganda chief greeted them.

Unable to stave off a boycott of the Foreign Press Association, Mowrer called a general meeting and offered his resignation. But a large majority of the members voted to refuse his offer, or "to allow social and personal pressure to hinder them in the freedom of their criticism in so far as their work was based on authentic material." A month later, the Pulitzer Prizes were announced for reporting in 1932, and Mowrer won for "best correspondence from abroad."

While not changing his mind on the boycott, Goebbels suddenly took a softer line with Mowrer, offering him some journalistic "favors." He allowed him to join a group of correspondents on a visit to the Sonnenburg concentration camp, with the aim of proving that political prisoners were held in humane conditions. At the time, the early camps of the Nazi regime didn't have the full range of horrifying associations that they would have later, but stories about brutal treatment were already circulating.

Recognizing that they would be given a show tour, Mowrer and Knickerbocker worked out a strategy to find out how one of the most prominent prisoners—Carl von Ossietzky, the editor of a pacifist weekly—was
treated. When they asked to see him, Ossietzky was brought out but
surrounded by guards. Allowed to ask a few questions, Knickerbocker
inquired whether he was able to receive books.

"Certainly," Ossietzky replied to the satisfaction of the guards.

Knickerbocker asked what kind of books he liked to read, and Ossietzky said: "Whatever you have ... history perhaps."

Mowrer jumped in, asking what period interested him the most. "An-
cient, medieval, modern—which do you prefer?"

Ossietzky was silent, then briefly looked him in the eyes as he replied in
a monotone voice, "Send me a description of the Middle Ages in Europe."

As Mowrer recalled later, the two American journalists understood
his message all too well, and they watched silently as the prisoner was led
"back into Europe's New Dark Age."

The AP's Lochner was also part of the group, but he came to a
somewhat different conclusion. After questioning the prisoners, he was
convinced that some of them "were indeed badly beaten up, but that apparently all cruel treatment has now stopped," he wrote in the same letter
to his daughter Betty where he had described Hitler's "Peace Speech." He
was troubled, though, by the lack of charges against the prisoners, and the
uncertainty they faced about their fate. "Hence, if the purpose of our visit
to Sonnenburg was to convince us that no bodily harm was being done
to the prisoners, the purpose was served," he concluded. "But if the Nazis
think that any of us came away enthusiastic over Sonnenburg, they are
far mistaken."

During the visit to the camp, the Nazi officer in charge put on a show
of friendliness for the visiting correspondents—and made a special point
of singling out Mowrer. "You know, Herr Mowrer, we were very angry at
you at one moment," he said, implying that this was no longer the case.
"We even thought of sending a detachment of SA lads to beat you into
reason. What would you have done about that?"

"If there had been anything left of me, I suppose I should have staggered
to a typewriter and written what I thought about it," the American replied.

The Nazi wanted to know what he would have thought exactly. Mowrer promptly told him: "That it was a typical Nazi victory."

"And what do you imply by that?" the Nazi persisted.

"Fifteen armed men against one unarmed man," Mowrer noted, bringing their exchange to an end.

The "sugar period" in relations between the correspondents and the Nazis, as his wife, Lilian, called it, didn't last long. Certainly not for her husband, who continued to pursue the stories that only deepened his gloom about where Germany was headed. He wasn't just saddened—he was angry and increasingly impatient with those who refused to see the danger signals the way he did. When two prominent American editors visited him in Berlin—Oswald Garrison Villard of the *Nation*, and George Shuster of *Commonweal*—he tried to convince them that Hitler was really intent on war, but only antagonized them instead. "If such intelligent Americans refused to face the facts, how be confident that the West would react in time to prevent the worst?" he wrote.

One of Mowrer's sources was a doctor who was the son of the Grand Rabbi in Berlin. Every couple of weeks, the American would phone and complain of a pain in his throat, asking for an appointment. When the doctor would start to examine his "patient," he would find an excuse to send his assistant out of the room. As soon as she stepped away, he would quickly push a rolled-up piece of paper into Mowrer's breast pocket, chronicling the latest assaults and arrests. On one such visit, the doctor told him: "You are a marked man and were followed here. I can't afford to see you any more."

But see each other they did. Mowrer suggested an alternative scheme, whereby each Wednesday at 11:45 A.M. they stood at adjoining urinals in the public restroom under Potsdamer Platz. The two men never spoke, and they left by separate entrances so no one trailing them would suspect anything. But the doctor would drop messages on the floor that Mowrer picked up as he continued to gather information on the plight of the persecuted. When Jews asked him for advice, he was unhesitating in his answer: "Get out, and fast," he'd say—even providing those who listened with a map of the border between Germany and Czechoslovakia.

Despite all the rising tensions, Mowrer didn't completely lose his sense of humor. It was a tradition of the Foreign Press Association to hold a dinner for the German foreign minister each June where the minister would expound on his policies. Since the Nazi government was still boycotting the association in June 1933 because of its anger at Mowrer, the association decided instead to hold a lunch for the diplomatic corps. To the surprise of the correspondents, along with almost all the foreign ambassadors, two German officials they had invited showed up: Reichsbank president Schacht and Heinrich Sahm, Berlin's famously tall (6 feet 6) mayor.

When Mowrer rose to greet everyone, he pretended to encounter difficulties with German grammar. "In this country where we are—I mean *have* been—so happy . . . that some of us have sought relief—I mean recreation—abroad . . ." he said, reeling off a string of such "corrections" of his wording that soon had all the ambassadors laughing uproariously.

An angry Schacht demanded the right to reply. He charged that the foreign press should report facts, not opinions, implying that the latter was the reason why Germany's image was tainted in the world. Mowrer thanked him with the same kind of ironical humor he had used before, saying that he was pleased that Schacht so valued American journalism, which was justifiably famous for its factual reporting. Once again, he left the diplomats chuckling while Schacht fumed.

The Nazis certainly weren't laughing, and Mowrer could feel their mounting displeasure. In July, Colonel Frank Knox, the publisher of the *Chicago Daily News*, arrived in Berlin, still skeptical about some of the stories that his correspondent was filing from there. But by the time he left, he concluded two things: Mowrer was right about the rising terror, and it was time for his correspondent to leave. He informed Mowrer that he wanted to transfer him to Tokyo, since he was convinced that the Nazis could do him physical harm otherwise.

Mowrer didn't want to go but recognized that at some point he would almost certainly be expelled if he didn't go voluntarily. He was also more outspoken than ever, not hiding his antipathy to Germany's new masters. When he had the chance to talk to Dodd at social occasions, Mowrer expounded on the brutality of the regime but found the new ambassador cautious to the extreme, considering the correspondent too emotional on the subject. After a dinner party at the Dodds', the ambassador noted in his diary: "I felt at the end that Mowrer was almost as vehement, in his way, as the Nazis, but I could understand his point of view."

Dodd's reluctance to accept Mowrer's dark vision of what was happening in Germany led the American correspondent to write off the ambassador's appointment as "a blow to freedom." It was a harsh judgment, but understandable given the contrast to the increasingly bold behavior of the far more experienced George Messersmith. The consul general vigorously protested the mistreatment of any Americans, including the correspondents, and, as a result, had developed close ties with them. In the Mowrer household, Messersmith's number was written on three stands, since he would be the first person to call if anything happened to Edgar. "At this point, when even foreigners were dividing into sheep and goats, this American not only 'stood up' to the country to which he was accredited—a rare phenomenon!—but came out in the open in defense of everything finest in the American tradition," Lilian Mowrer wrote. Messersmith's earlier doubts had largely evaporated about the extent to which Nazi terror reflected Hitler's will.

Late one night in August, Edgar received a frantic phone call from the wife of Paul Goldmann, the Berlin correspondent for the Vienna *Neue Freie Presse*. "Oh, Mr. Mowrer, they have just arrested my husband!" she declared. Goldmann was sixty-eight, ailing, a Prussian Jew and one of the founders of the Foreign Press Association. He had been picked up in retaliation for the arrest and deportation of the German press officer in Vienna, and his wife was understandably terrified that he wouldn't last long in a Nazi prison.

When he hung up, Edgar let loose with his feelings. "The sons of bitches! Why don't they pick on someone their own size?" Lilian recalled that she had never seen him so angry.

Once he had calmed down, Edgar and Knickerbocker concocted a scheme to spring Goldmann. Knickerbocker told Goebbels that Mowrer would resign as president of the Foreign Press Association if they let Goldmann go. What he didn't tell him was that Edgar knew already that he was going to be transferred to Tokyo soon. Learning about this, some other American correspondents told Gestapo chief Rudolf Diels that they were willing to spend a day each in jail in exchange for Goldmann's freedom. The Nazis happily took Mowrer up on his offer, promptly releasing their prisoner.

There was just one catch: the authorities also confiscated the German passport of Goldmann's wife to make sure he didn't try to leave the country or do anything "unfriendly." But she was an Austrian by birth and immediately filed for divorce so that she could reclaim her Austrian citizenship—and an Austrian passport.

Lilian Mowrer asked "the plucky old lady" whether it didn't hurt her to take such drastic action after so many years of marriage. "No, my dear," she replied, although the tears in her eyes told a different story. "It is true that I shall divorce him, but that is merely a matter of expediency. I shall continue to live with my husband . . . in sin."

When some of Mowrer's American and British colleagues filed stories about how he had outwitted the authorities since he was going to be transferred to Tokyo anyway, the Nazi press proclaimed that they had succeeded in getting rid of a "sworn and proven enemy" from the top job at the Foreign Press Association. Storm troopers showed up outside Mowrer's office and apartment, followed him around town and often followed his acquaintances as well. Messersmith was so concerned about him that he made a point of always leaving him a phone number where he could be reached when he went out in the evenings. Lilian lived in constant anxiety about her husband. The presence of the Brownshirts was "a horrible menace," she recalled, "for there was practically nothing they could not have done at that period."

The climax came quickly. The Mowrers had originally planned to move to Tokyo in October, but the Nazis kept cranking up the pressure that August. The German ambassador in Washington, Hans Dieckhoff, whom Mowrer had once considered a friend, informed the State Department and Colonel Knox that because of "the people's righteous indignation" his government could no longer guarantee his physical safety. The Nazis were particularly anxious to force his departure before the party's annual celebration in Nuremberg on September 2, which he was still hoping to cover.

Worried that his reporter was in severe jeopardy, Knox sent a telegram telling Mowrer to leave right away. Edgar still wanted to resist, at least delaying his departure until after the Nuremberg event to show that he would not be intimidated. But Ambassador Dodd urged him to leave sooner. "If you were not being moved by your paper anyway, we would go to the mat on this issue, but it only means hastening your departure by six days," he told him. "Won't you do this to avoid complications?" While Mowrer bitterly resented the new ambassador's reluctance to take a stronger stand against the regime, even Messersmith and Knickerbocker concurred with Dodd's judgment. They figured that the risks were too high for their friend and it was time for him to get out.

Mowrer finally agreed to leave on September 1, with Lilian and their daughter staying behind for a short while to pack up. Before Edgar's departure, his British and American fellow correspondents presented him with a silver rose bowl inscribed to a "gallant fighter for the liberty of the Press." And as he prepared to board a train for Paris from the Bahnhof Zoo, Messersmith rushed over from a dinner party to give him an embrace.

Others were at the train station in a more official capacity, making sure that the correspondent who had been such an irritant really departed. Shortly before his departure, a young German official sardonically asked him: "And when are you coming back to Germany, Herr Mowrer?"

"Why, when I can come back with two million of my countrymen," the correspondent replied.

It took a moment for the official to absorb the import of his statement: Mowrer was envisaging a day when American soldiers would march into a defeated Germany. "*Aber nein.* Impossible," the official protested loudly.

Mowrer didn't let that pass; he wasn't about to leave Germany without having the last word. "Not for the *Führer,*" he said. "The *Führer* can bring anything about . . . even that."

# "Like Football and Cricket"

Martha Dodd was twenty-four when she arrived in Berlin in the summer of 1933 with her father, the new American ambassador, her mother and brother. Recalling her state of mind later, she stressed how naïve and uninformed she was about politics, with almost no idea about what Germany would be like—or what its new Nazi rulers represented. While her father had evident misgivings and mentioned several times that he wasn't sure how long their Berlin assignment would last, Martha seemed largely oblivious to them. "I do not remember any of us being especially disturbed by the thought of living under a dictatorship," she wrote in her Berlin memoir *Through Embassy Eyes.*

She was hardly alone in that respect. Many Americans were still agnostic about Hitler and his movement, including some of the country's leading literary figures. At a farewell dinner for the Dodds hosted by the German-American societies in Chicago, Martha sat between Thornton Wilder and Carl Sandburg. Wilder urged Martha to learn German quickly and spend her time with Germans instead of the foreign community in Berlin, while Sandburg offered this bit of advice: "Find out what this man Hitler is made of, what makes his brain go round, what his bones and blood are made of. Before your eyes will pass the greatest pageant of crooks and gangsters, idealists, statesmen, criminals, diplomats, and geniuses. You will see every nationality in the world. Watch them, study them, dissect them. Don't be frightened or diffident, don't let them or your experiences spoil you or your eagerness for life. Be brave and truthful, keep your poetry and integrity."

All of which inspired Martha to view this journey into the unknown as a great adventure, which she planned to experience with the "eagerness for life" that Sandburg commended to her. As for the other qualities—bravery, truthfulness, integrity—there would be plenty of disagreement among those who met Martha in Germany whether she lived up to them, along with endless gossip about her behavior, particularly with a procession of men of various ages and nationalities. If her father often appeared to be stumbling through his time in Berlin, not quite sure what he should or could be doing, Martha was anything but "frightened or diffident." In that sense, she took Sandburg's words very much to heart.

Growing up in Chicago, Martha had gone to University High School, which was labeled by students from rival schools as "Jew High." By her own admission, Martha was also "slightly anti-Semitic." As she put it, "I accepted the attitude that Jews were not as attractive physically as Gentiles and were less socially presentable." She recalled that when she went to the University of Chicago, even some of her professors "resented the brilliance of Jewish colleagues and students."

After college, Martha got a job as the assistant literary editor of the *Chicago Tribune*. She also married "for a short period unhappily." But in matters of the heart, she wasn't quite the naïve young woman that she appeared to be politically. She didn't bother to inform most of her new acquaintances in Berlin that she was married—and not yet divorced. "I suppose I practiced a great deception on the diplomatic corps by not indicating that I was a married woman at that time," she noted with evident amusement. "But I must admit I rather enjoyed being treated like a maiden of eighteen knowing all the while my dark secret."

While no maiden, Martha succeeded in charming many of those who met her for the first time. Upon seeing her arrive with her parents in

Berlin on July 12, 1933, Bella Fromm described the daughter of the new ambassador as "a perfect example of the intelligent young American female." When William Shirer, the new bureau chief of the Universal News Service and soon-to-be-famous CBS broadcaster, arrived in Berlin the following year, he noted in his diary that Martha spent many evenings at Die Taverne, the restaurant where American correspondents gathered almost every evening after filing their stories. Shirer described her as "pretty, vivacious, a mighty arguer."

But Martha also triggered other feelings, particularly among the embassy wives. Kay Smith returned with her husband, Truman Smith, the military attaché who had been the first American official to meet Hitler in 1922, for a second tour at the Berlin embassy in 1935. "Martha had an apartment of her own on the top floor of the Embassy," she wrote in her unpublished memoir. "She was small, delicate looking, blue eyed, pink and white complexion, a little Dresden figurine. Appearances are deceiving. Martha had a way with the gentlemen and it was said no scruples. As time went on I heard rumors that she entertained men at all hours in her apartment."

Martha certainly had a predilection for romance, both political and personal. When it came to politics, her first judgment as a new arrival was that Germany and its new rulers had been unfairly condemned by world opinion—and she needed to help set the record straight. "We liked Germany, and I was enchanted by the kindness and simplicity of the people . . . everything was peaceful, romantic, strange, nostalgic," she recalled. "I felt that the press had badly maligned the country and I wanted to proclaim the warmth and friendliness of the people, the soft summer night with its fragrance of trees and flowers, the serenity of the streets." When she made the rounds of reasonably priced restaurants, she found herself comparing her experiences to what she knew of France: "The Germans seemed much more genuine and honest, even in the merchant class."

Soon after her arrival, Martha met fellow countryman Quentin Reynolds, who was also a newcomer to Germany. Reynolds had been sent to Berlin in early 1933 by the International News Service to fill in for the regular correspondent, who had run afoul of the new Nazi rulers. He went straight from writing baseball stories about the superstar Ty Cobb to covering the biggest foreign story of the era. By his own admission, he had only "saloon German" and "no special grasp of current events." But he credited fellow correspondents with giving him a crash course in local politics. Knickerbocker urged him to read *Mein Kampf* right away. "No American I know of has taken the trouble to read it seriously, but it's all there: his plan for the conquest of Europe," he told him.

By the time he met Martha Dodd, Reynolds was also friendly with Putzi Hanfstaengl, who regularly dropped by Die Taverne. "I regret to say that on first acquaintance he struck me as a likeable fellow," Reynolds recalled later. "He was a tremendous man physically, with heavy features, dark eyes, and a mane of coal-black hair that he kept tossing back. With an ingratiating manner, he was a compulsive and amusing talker and, unlike other Nazis I later had to do business with, he went out of his way to be cordial to Americans. You had to know Putzi to really dislike him."

Martha was impressed that Reynolds, who had only been in the country a few months, already knew "such legendary figures" as Hanfstaengl and arranged for her to be introduced to him. At a party thrown by an English journalist—"a lavish and fairly drunken affair," as Martha recalled—the Nazi propagandist lived up to her expectations. "Putzi came in late in a sensational manner, a huge man in height and build, towering over everyone present," she noted. "He had a soft, ingratiating manner, a beautiful voice which he used with conscious artistry, sometimes whispering low and soft, the next minute bellowing and shattering the room. He was supposed to be the artist among the Nazis, erratic and interesting, the personal clown and musician to Hitler himself . . . Bavarian and American blood produced this strange phenomenon."

Like other Americans, Martha would find herself frequently in Hanfstaengl's company, dancing with him at parties and gladly taking advantage of his offers to introduce her to Nazi luminaries. But Reynolds was already developing a healthy sense of skepticism about him while remaining careful not to show it. About a month after Reynolds arrived, he ran into Hanfstaengl at the bar of the Adlon Hotel. "You've been here a month now, and you haven't asked me about our so-called

Jewish problem or written anything about it to annoy me," Putzi told him. "How come, Quent?"

"Give me time, Putzi," Reynolds replied. "I haven't been here long enough to know what's going on."

By the time he met Martha, Reynolds not only knew more but was eager to explore more for himself. In August, he suggested to Martha and her brother Bill that they take their Chevrolet and travel to southern Germany and Austria together with him—an idea that immediately appealed to Martha. As they drove south, she recognized the word "*Jude*" in banners strung across the road; they realized this was anti-Semitic propaganda but, as Martha put it, "we didn't—at least I didn't—take it too seriously."

In fact, Martha was so swept up by the sight of marching Brownshirts and the apparent enthusiasm of the people, she responded equally enthusiastically. When Germans saw their special license plate with a low number, they assumed the trio of Americans were top officials—and welcomed them with "*Heil Hitler*" greetings. "The excitement of the people was contagious and I 'Heiled' as vigorously as any Nazi," she recalled. Although Reynolds and her brother mocked her behavior, "I felt like a child, ebullient and careless, the intoxication of the new regime working like wine in me," she admitted.

Around midnight, the Americans stopped for the night in Nuremberg. As they reached their hotel on Königstrasse, they were surprised to find the street filled with an excited crowd and speculated that they may have run into a toymakers' festival. As he registered, Reynolds asked the hotel clerk if there was going to be a parade. The clerk laughed. "It will be kind of a parade," he replied. "They are teaching someone a lesson."

The visitors walked out to join the crowd. Everyone seemed in a good mood, with the sound of a band adding to the festive atmosphere. Then they saw Nazi banners and swastikas, and the source of the music: a marching band of Storm Troopers. Two tall troopers were dragging someone between them. "I could not at first tell if it was a man or a woman," Reynolds wrote. "Its head had been clipped bald, and face and head had been coated with white powder. Even though the figure wore a skirt, it might have been a man dressed as a clown." As the Brownshirts straightened out their victim, the Americans spotted the placard around its neck: "I wanted to live with a Jew."

As the "lesson" continued, the Americans learned from the crowd that this was a woman named Anna Rath. The reason for her harsh punishment: she had tried to marry her Jewish fiancé, defying the ban on mixed marriages. Martha remembered the image of her "tragic and tortured face, the color of diluted absinthe." She also was startled by Reynolds's reaction. She had believed him to be a "hard-boiled" journalist, but "he was so shaken by the whole scene that he said the only thing he could do was to get drunk, to forget it."

The Nazis wound up the evening by playing the "Horst Wessel Song" as about 5,000 people stood singing, their right arms extended—and then everyone disappeared. Although she suddenly felt nervous and cold, with her earlier elation fully gone, Martha still tried to convince Reynolds that he shouldn't file anything about the incident. She argued that her presence and that of her brother would make this a sensational story, and, after all, who knew what the Nazi side of the story really was. And it had to be an isolated case.

Although Martha claimed that the three of them made good on Reynolds's vow to get drunk, proceeding to tank up on red champagne, the journalist was sober enough when he went up to his room. He promptly called Hudson Hawley, his bureau chief in Berlin, excited that he had proof of exactly the kind of atrocity story that many journalists had heard about but not witnessed—and the Nazis routinely denied. Hawley cautioned that he might not be allowed to wire it and suggested he send it by mail instead. He also advised him to leave out any mention of the presence of Martha and Bill Dodd to avoid negative repercussions for the new ambassador. "Writing the story, I found myself trembling," Reynolds recalled. "The grotesque white face of Anna Rath haunted me." The next morning he mailed it in.

By the time he and the Dodds returned to Berlin a week later, the story had received big play. Hanfstaengl had left a message for him, requesting an urgent meeting. "There isn't one damn word of truth in your story!" Putzi shouted at Reynolds, dropping all pretense of conviviality. "I've talked with our people in Nuremberg and they say nothing of the sort happened there."

But the veteran British correspondent Norman Ebbutt had followed up on the story, getting one of his reporters to confirm it. He told Reynolds that the reporter had learned that Rath had been locked up in a mental hospital.

The Foreign Ministry didn't bother to deny the story the way Hanfstaengl did. In fact, they dispatched officials to the Dodds' residence to apologize for what they characterized as an incident of isolated brutality—providing the explanation that Martha had already suggested to Reynolds. They also claimed that the perpetrators would be punished. That, apparently, was enough to allow Martha to continue to nourish her initial illusions that the only problem with the new Germany was that it was misunderstood by the outside world.

As for Reynolds, he was rapidly shedding any illusions he still had not just about the nature of the Nazi regime but also about Hanfstaengl. Because of the Anna Rath incident, he got to see the real Putzi, not just the jocular one who charmed many Americans. When Reynolds's parents visited Berlin, the correspondent threw a big dinner party for them, inviting Martha and Bill Dodd along with several of his journalistic colleagues and German acquaintances. Showing up late as usual, Putzi sat down at the piano and turned to Reynolds's mother, announcing that he would sing a song for her that he had written himself. "Putzi serenaded my mother with a foul song in which the Third Reich's enemies were jingled out as Jews, Catholics, and Negroes," Reynolds recalled. Putzi had lowered his voice so only the small group at the piano could hear his words, which indicated he knew very well what he was doing. He was paying Reynolds back for the Anna Rath story by targeting his mother as the correspondent looked on.

Reynolds felt like hitting him right there, but another German guest talked him out of making a scene that would only reflect badly on him. Relishing his sense of self-importance, Putzi soon announced that he had to leave early because Hitler wanted him at the Chancellery to play some Liszt. Escorting Putzi to the door, Reynolds summoned enough self-control to look like he was the genial host sending his guest off with a pleasant good-bye. But his final words, delivered so only Putzi could hear, couldn't have been blunter: "Never come to my house again, you louse."

\*　　　\*　　　\*

Writing to his daughter Betty at the University of Chicago on June 30, 1933, the AP's Louis Lochner mused about President Roosevelt's decision to send historian William Dodd to represent the United States in Berlin. "Roosevelt must have a sense of humor to send this exponent of the most liberal Jeffersonian democracy . . . into this anti-democratic country," he wrote. "He'll fit into here about like a square peg into a round hole!"

When Dodd arrived in Germany in July, he began cautiously exploring his new surroundings, gauging the reception he received, and sizing up the political situation. Meeting Konstantin von Neurath, Dodd found the foreign minister "most agreeable." Hans Luther, Germany's ambassador to the United States, who was also in Berlin that July, visited his new American counterpart to discuss Hitler's plans for economic recovery and tariff policy. As for the touchier issues of how the Nazi government would treat its immediate neighbors, Luther sought to be reassuring. "He showed no belligerent spirit toward France and did not mention the Polish corridor," Dodd wrote in his diary.

Dodd was particularly interested in the views of his fellow academics, and what he heard left him with an uneasy feeling. Professor Otto Hoetzsch of the University of Berlin, a former member of the Reichstag and "well-known internationalist," as Dodd wrote, expressed "his comparative satisfaction with the Hitler regime." As the new ambassador observed, "So far nearly all university men seem to acquiesce in their own intimidation, but one sees that it is fear of unemployed status rather than a willing surrender."

On July 28, Dodd described "the saddest story of Jewish persecution I have yet heard." Acclaimed chemist Fritz Haber came to ask him whether he could emigrate to the United States. He had been fired from his post and denied a pension by the Nazis, all the while suffering from heart problems. Dodd told him that there were no places left in the immigration quota, and there were no special provisions for scientists of his stature. While Haber did have an alternative plan to try to go to Spain, Dodd reflected: "Such treatment can only bring evil to the government which practices such terrible cruelty."

Like Consul General Messersmith and other American diplomats, Dodd found himself trying to intervene in the growing number of cases where Americans were beaten by Brownshirts, especially after they failed to give *Heil Hitler* salutes. Foreign Minister von Neurath assured him that he would do everything possible to prevent such incidents in the future, but he maintained that the Brownshirts "are so uncontrollable that I am afraid we cannot stop them."

In a Columbus Day speech to the American Chamber of Commerce luncheon at the Adlon Hotel, Dodd decided to make some broader points about the nature of government and the perils of repressive actions. With representatives of the Foreign, Economics and Propaganda ministries present, he warned that new social experiments could easily end in disaster. "It would be no sin if statesmen learned enough of history to realize that no system which implies control of society by privilege seekers has ever ended in any other way than collapse," he declared. As an alternative, he pointed to Thomas Jefferson's belief that "to develop the ideal social order was to leave every man the utmost freedom of initiative and action and always to forbid any man or group of men to profiteer at the expense of others."

Dodd was immensely gratified by the "extraordinary applause" his declaration produced, although he noted the high level of tension in the room. He also recognized that the authorities were showing signs of irritation with his pronouncements and his persistent inquiries about the assaults on Americans. "It is evident some dislike of me is arising here now in official circles," he wrote. "I believe it is simply Nazi opposition."

On October 17, the ambassador was able to present his case directly to Hitler. His first impression: "He looks somewhat better than the pictures that appear in papers." When Dodd raised the issue again of attacks on Americans, Hitler sounded accommodating. As the ambassador wrote in his diary, "The Chancellor assured me personally that he would see that any future attack was punished to the limit and that publicity would be given to decrees warning everyone that foreigners were not to be expected to give the Hitler salute."

But when Dodd asked Hitler about his recent announcement that Germany was withdrawing from the League of Nations, the chancellor "ranted" about the Treaty of Versailles and the many alleged indignities a victimized Germany had faced at the hands of the victors of World War I. Dodd conceded that the French had been unjust, but he tried to strike a more philosophical note. War is always followed by injustice, he argued, citing the example of how southern states were treated after the U.S. Civil War. But Hitler wasn't exactly the eager student of history: he remained conspicuously silent as the former professor tried to illustrate his point.

A few days earlier, Dodd had tried to take a similarly philosophical tack with Roosevelt in discussing the nature of what was happening in Germany. In an October 12 letter to the president, he wrote about the need for reserving judgment on that country's new rulers, implying that there was still reason for hope. "Fundamentally, I believe a people has a right to govern itself and that other peoples must exercise patience even when crudities and injustices are done. Give men a chance to try their schemes."

Dodd tried to draw Hitler out on what his schemes might be—specifically, whether a border incident with any of Germany's neighbors could trigger a new war. "No, no," Hitler protested. But when Dodd asked whether he would try to call a European conference if there were any flare-up in the Ruhr Valley, he replied: "That would be my purpose, but we might not be able to restrain the German people." Dodd noted in his diary, "I saw that meant the violent Nazis whom he has trained to violence." The ambassador's conclusion: "My first impression was of his belligerence and self-confidence."

Still, Dodd wasn't convinced that Hitler had the full support of the German people and questioned how strong his grip on power really was. Two days before he met the chancellor, he had gone to the movies and observed that Hitler's appearance in a newsreel only triggered tepid applause. "Hitler is surely not so powerful with the people as Mussolini, the Italian despot, has been," he observed. But Dodd certainly understood the physical danger represented by his movement. On the last Sunday in October, he was walking along the Tiergartenstrasse at noon and spotted a procession of Storm Troopers approaching. "I walked into the park to avoid embarrassment," he recorded in his diary. Understandably, he did not want to become a cause célèbre by not giving the Hitler salute and possibly paying the price as other Americans already had.

Nonetheless, Dodd was intent on continuing to do what he could to make the case that Germany should put some brakes on repression, preserving a modicum of liberty and decency. Asked to speak at the German-American Church Forum on November 19, which was designated as Martin Luther Day, the ambassador lectured about Luther's life "just as I would have done before an American audience," he noted with visible pride. The audience was about two-thirds German and one-third American, and both groups applauded him enthusiastically. "It was clear to me that Germans wished me to say in public what they are not allowed to say in private, especially about religious and personal freedom," he concluded.

Dodd had by no means shed all illusions about Hitler's intentions. In early December, Sir Eric Phipps, his British counterpart in Berlin, dropped by his house to brief him on Hitler's renewal of an earlier proposal to discuss a disarmament deal with France. Under its provisions, Germany would be able to maintain a 300,000-man army along with guns and "defensive airplanes." Now, Hitler was adding that he would include a ten-year pledge not to go to war, and accept international supervision of German armaments and of its 2.5 million SA and SS troops. Dodd promised to cable a report summarizing this offer to Washington, and noted optimistically in his diary, "It looked to me like a real move towards disarmament . . ."

But if the ambassador continued to hold out hope that Hitler might prove to be more reasonable than his rhetoric and program indicated, he was hardly at ease in his company—and sensed that the German leader was equally ill at ease with him. On January 1, 1934, Berlin's diplomatic corps gathered in the Presidential Palace to pay their respects to eighty-six-year-old President von Hindenburg. When Hitler showed up, he and Dodd exchanged New Year's greetings. Then, seeking to find a seemingly neutral subject of conversation, the American told him that he had recently spent a few very pleasant days in Munich, where Hitler had spent part of the holidays. Dodd mentioned that he had met "a fine German historian"—a Professor Meyer who had studied with him in Leipzig. When Hitler indicated he had no idea who Meyer was, Dodd mentioned some other academics at Munich University. But, once again, Hitler didn't display any signs of recognition, "leaving the impression that he had never had contacts with the people I knew and respected."

"I was afraid he thought I was trying to embarrass him a little," Dodd wrote in his diary. "I was not. There was, however, no diplomatic or political subject we could mention these touchy times." Hanfstaengl, who had made a point of cultivating his ties with both the ambassador and his daughter Martha, would later claim that there was another reason for the awkwardness between the chancellor and the American envoy. "*Der gute* Dodd, he can hardly speak German and made no sense at all," Hitler told Putzi. In the eyes of *Der Führer*, Dodd's earnestness left almost no impression. The German leader was only too happy to dismiss him as an inconsequential figure representing a country that was "hopelessly weak and could not interfere in any way with the realization of . . . [his] plans."

Hanfstaengl shared his leader's scorn for Dodd. "He was a modest little Southern history professor, who ran his embassy on a shoe-string and was probably trying to save money out of his pay," he wrote in his postwar memoir. "At a time when it needed a robust millionaire to compete with the flamboyance of the Nazis, he teetered round self-effacingly as if he was still on a college campus."

The notion that a flashier, wealthier envoy could have "competed" with the Nazis is, to put it mildly, a bizarre argument that says more about Hanfstaengl than it does about Dodd. Putzi still proudly strutted about town as Hitler's propagandist, while Dodd was at least trying to push back against the Nazi tide—even if it was proving to be a futile effort.


In the first year of Hitler's rule, there was at least one American visitor who had come to a quick judgment about what was happening and decided to issue a blunt warning to the Nazis. He was Sherwood Eddy, a Protestant missionary and YMCA national secretary who had traveled and taught in Asia, Russia and Germany, writing several books about his experiences and views. The Carl Schurz Society, named after a German-American politician and journalist who had served as a general in the Union Army during the Civil War and then become the first German-

American elected to the U.S. Senate, was hosting a reception for the annual American Seminar in July 1933, and Eddy was the leader of the visiting delegation. In fact, as he pointed out to his hosts, this was his twelfth visit to Germany.

The continuation of such meetings was supposed to send a signal of reassurance that the new regime was committed to peace. At the reception, the German speakers praised Hitler's recent Reichstag speech on international relations. According to reporter Bella Fromm, who as usual was present at such social events, they delivered a double-edged message: "Any possible concern in foreign countries as to the aggressive intentions of Germany should disappear. After all, the *Führer* principle is also represented in America under Roosevelt."

Eddy responded with a polite profession of his love for Germany and delicately edged into the subject of the new regime. "I noted the unity of enthusiasm and zeal in what you call the 'New Germany.' I have always approved of enthusiasm and zeal." But then he quickly made his point. "Besides my love for Germany, I have another, even stronger love in my heart: the love for humanity." And that love, he continued, made him into a firm proponent of "impartial justice; freedom of speech, press, and assembly; fundamental moral and economic principles." In case anyone didn't get the point, he added, "These freedoms have to be accepted by all nations who claim cultural integrity."

Eddy mentioned that he had upheld the same principles in Russia and refused to remain silent about the blatant violations of them there. "As a friend of Germany, I state that you are acting against the principles of justice," he continued, making the Nazis in the audience "gasp in consternation," as Fromm noted. "There is no room for a twofold justice, one for 'Aryans' and 'Nordics,' and another one for Social Democrats, Communists, Liberals, Jews, and Pacifists. Don't say it's your affair. It concerns the whole world when we in the United States conduct a lynching . . . The world is also concerned when you commit similar injustice."

As he warmed to his topic, Eddy addressed the Germans even more bluntly: "In your country, injustice is committed every day, every hour. What are you doing to Catholics, Communists, Social Democrats, Jews?

What atrocities are committed behind the wall of your horrible concentration camps? I see your papers."

With that, Eddy held up that day's edition of the Nazi daily *Völkischer Beobachter* with the headline "70,000 Jews Immigrated into Germany Within the Last 15 Years." He called the statement not only wrong but "an instigation of youth, a kindling of race-hatred, a signal for cruel and wanton destruction." Mentioning that he had heard the "Jew baiting" at meetings in Germany, he warned: "This must lead to a massacre . . . I am deeply worried about this country, which I love."

Many of the foreigners in the audience applauded him. "The Nazis, pale, with rage, sat immobile, in cold silence," Fromm recorded. But she wasn't about to get the chance to write anything about this extraordinary performance by the visiting American missionary in her newspaper. Instead, another reporter plucked out the most innocuous parts of Eddy's opening remarks and ended with his alleged pledge to urge friendly understanding for the new Germany in his home country. "I gasped when I read the piece," Fromm wrote in her diary. But there was nothing she could do to set the public record straight.

In his clarity of vision and willingness to deliver his tough message, Eddy was unlike almost any other early American visitor to the "new Germany." There were others who were troubled by the behavior of the Nazis, but very few who truly understood the sweeping nature of the transformation of the country and its people, and the danger this represented.

Often, American visitors would exhibit no more than a vague uneasiness. Future novelist Wright Morris, then only twenty-three, hopped a freighter from New York to Antwerp in October 1933, setting off to explore Europe. During his sojourn there, he briefly passed through Germany, checking into a youth hostel in Heidelberg. The dormer window of his room looked out on a park where blond children were playing, the weather was beautiful, and, as he walked about the city, he was keenly aware of its romantic tradition. "On the bridge over the Neckar I stood long and long, looking at the castle, my fancy on the Rhine maidens and the mists behind it," he wrote in his travel memoir.

But he also felt his "first presentiments that something was rotten in this picture of perfection. Behind the light and the shadow, the trilling voices of the children, lurked a danger in which we were all complicit." When he entered a tobacco shop to look at some pipes, he caught sight of someone spying on him through a curtain. "In the shopwoman's smiling, unctuous manner there was something both disturbing and false," he recalled. "I could hear muttered whisperings behind the curtain. My sense of apprehension was unused and rudimentary, since I had felt it so seldom, but in the eyes and furtive manner of this woman I felt, and shared, a nameless disquiet." Nonetheless, Morris was quick to add, "Back in the sunlight I soon forgot it."

Others were keen to overlook any disquieting signs, convinced that the key to international harmony was recognition of the notion that every country was free to choose its own path and that people everywhere have more in common than they realize. No one believed that more passionately than Donald B. Watt of Putney, Vermont, who in the summer of 1932 took his first small group of young Americans to Europe, launching the Experiment in International Living. The highly successful exchange program, which includes stays with local families, continues to operate today. As Watt put it, his aim was "to create a controlled human situation which would produce understanding and friendliness between people and different cultures in a limited period of time."

Watt's enthusiasm for "making friends out of 'foreigners'" made him shrug off—and even mock—all those who warned him against taking his young idealistic travelers to Germany in the summer of 1933 for the second "Experiment" after Hitler had taken power. "From its war-like reputation, one would have expected Germany to have been most inhospitable toward a group interested in making peace," Watt wrote. "Just the opposite materialized: the Nazi organizations made us feel most welcome ... The picture which the [American] newspapers gave and what we actually saw in our families could scarcely have been more different." Specifically on the subject of violence, he added, "The suggestion of personal danger to foreigners is no less laughable to those who spent the summer in that country than the thought of German courtesy failing."

Watt did concede after the trip that there was an "excess of order" and "hypnosis of the masses" orchestrated by the Nazis. But the only real danger for a visiting foreigner, he felt, was not to be swept up by "the power of suggestion" of the constant saluting and "to use all his restraint if he does not wish to join the saluting throng." Despite the widespread reports of beatings of visiting Americans who failed to join in the Nazi salutes, Watt maintained that his charges were free to do whatever they pleased. Living with German families, they began to understand that they had been victims of propaganda back in the United States. "All they had learned of Hitlerism in America was definitely unfavorable, but here they actually saw some good features of it," Watt wrote.

Even when it came to Jews, he reported that everyone in his group concluded that "relatively few [were] roughly handled." The main cause of anti-Semitism in Germany, he added, was the fact that "a large proportion of all business was in Jewish hands." The young Americans were also impressed how Germans "are surmounting their relative poverty by a return to simple folk ways." But the key takeaway, as Watt put it, was the one he had come searching for—and was determined to find no matter what happened. "Perhaps most important of all, we realized that the people whom we met were very much like us," he concluded. "The Second Experiment in International Living was an interesting and successful demonstration of tolerance."

The American social scientists who studied the new Germany were distinctly less Pollyannaish, but they were far from uniform in their judgments of the country's New Order. Political scientist Frederick Schuman—who, like Dodd, taught at the University of Chicago—spent eight months in Germany in 1933. He had arranged his research trip before Hitler had come to power, but that event now changed both the nature of his stay and its purpose. "I journeyed toward a land I had already known and enjoyed as the home of music, philosophy, and *Gemütlichkeit* and as the birthplace of my Prussian and Hanoverian ancestors, now strangely transmuted into 'Aryans' and 'Nordics,'" he wrote. "Upon my arrival in April of the year of the Nazi seizure of power I found the Reich in process of violent, if orderly, transition from parliamentary democracy to Fascism."

Schuman made the focus of his research the newly triumphant Nazi movement, gathering materials for his 1935 book *The Nazi Dictatorship: A Study in Social Pathology and the Politics of Fascism*. Given the nature of his encounters, its analytical but highly critical tone was hardly surprising. "By the older German officials I was invariably received with courtesy and granted as much co-operation as was consistent with considerations of political and personal safety," he recalled. "By the newer Nazi administrators I was invariably received with evasions and complex circumlocutions or, as in the case of Hanfstaengl, with gross and clownish discourtesy bred of psychic insecurity and conceit."

While Schuman insisted he was interested in "explanation, not condemnation," he left no doubt that any accurate picture of the new movement would inevitably be seen as partisan. "Like every form of highly emotionalized and subjectivized mass mysticism, National-socialism demands acceptance or rejection," he wrote. "Objectivity is equivalent to rejection." By the time he produced his book, he would offer a dire— and accurate—prediction about the likelihood of a new war inspired by "pathological hatreds, lusts, and longings for extinction." His conclusion: "Fascism itself will be consumed by its war-mad sons. With it will perish the remnants of an age that has outlived its time."

Columbia University sociologist Theodore Abel was also fascinated by events in Germany. When Hitler was appointed chancellor on January 30, Abel wrote in the private notebook where he regularly recorded his observations: "Germany wants to become a world power again, it wants to conquer[,] it wants an emperor. The danger of communism is great and it might come to civil war in Germany. All peace measures will go into the discard meanwhile..."

But Abel was far more restrained—even at times, complimentary— about Germany's new rulers than Schuman; he also would later question some of Schuman's findings. On February 2, he wrote: "Struck by Hitler's manifesto appealing in noble terms to patriotism and setting forth as its goal reestablishment of unity of Germans who he claims are on the brink of dissolution." He approvingly noted that Hitler had vowed to fight unemployment and boost agriculture, while at the same time emphasizing his commitment to peace and disarmament. "I consider it a noble document and while it sounds genuine I hope it is meant," he wrote.

As for the means Hitler was using, Abel seemed willing to give him every benefit of the doubt. "Parliamentarianism and dictatorship are not, therefore, antithetical but means of solving problems, adequate for specific conditions," he wrote on March 7. Even when the Nazis staged their burning of the books in May, Abel was intrigued rather than outraged. Calling the book-burning "a futile but a symbolic gesture," he asserted: "I am impressed by the vitality and sweeping enthusiasm of the Hitler movement, its idealizations[,] its emotional fervor, its revolutionary aspects. They certainly are swayed by an idea, no matter how ludicrous it may seem to us who have no idea to live for. I envy the fascists, the nationalists, the communists, all those who are working for something to be realized." This was a stunning admission about what could attract an American intellectual to the most radical movements of the time.

In the summer of 1933, Abel visited Germany and was struck by the willingness of many people, especially Hitler's followers, to discuss their political experiences. This gave birth to his idea, nurtured during a period when he found it impossible to find a full-time job, to do a major research project on the Nazis. By June 1934, with the backing of Columbia and the agreement of the German authorities, he announced a contest "For the Best Personal Life History of an Adherent of the Hitler Movement." Only those who had joined the party before January 1, 1933—prior to Hitler's coming to power—were eligible to submit the autobiographical essays. Prizes ranging from 10 to 125 marks were to be awarded to the best entries. "Completeness and frankness are the sole criteria," he explained in the announcement.

It was an inspired initiative, attracting 683 submissions before the deadline in the fall of 1934. A series of mishaps delayed shipment of the essays to Abel in New York for two years, and his final product based on his analysis of those submissions—a book entitled *Why Hitler Came into Power*—wasn't published until 1938.

Abel was intent on showing what prompted so many Germans to follow Hitler. He took careful note of the disillusionment spawned by defeat in World War I, the Treaty of Versailles and the revolutionary uprisings in Germany that followed. A young soldier wrote: "Heroism had become cowardice, truth a lie, loyalty was rewarded by dastardliness."

Eighteen percent of those who submitted autobiographies had participated in some type of postwar military activities, whether to fight against the rebels of the left or the right or in fighting in Upper Silesia or the Ruhr Valley. Some professed to be shocked by "the spirit of Jewish materialism" and motivated by their nationalist upbringing. "We knew nothing of politics, yet we felt that therein lay the destiny of Germany," one of them declared.

Then came Hitler's failed Beer Hall Putsch of 1923 and his treason trial that only built up his reputation. "From that time on I had no thought for anyone but Hitler," another essayist wrote. While many of the contributors also mentioned the harsh economic conditions in Germany, Abel offered a somewhat different picture of Hitler's followers than scholars like Schuman did. "Schuman concludes that at the bottom of the Hitler movement was a collective neurosis, a psychological malady of the *Kleinbürgertum* [lower middle class] . . . the disorganized and pathological personality of a whole class of the German population."

Dismissing this approach as too reliant on group psychoanalysis, Abel maintained that Schuman and other scholars had painted a misleading portrait of Hitler's core supporters. Based on those who submitted essays, he offered his description of a fictional average Hitler supporter:

> *He is male, in his early thirties, a town resident of lower middle-class origin, without high school education; married and Protestant; participated in the World War, but not in the revolutionary activities during the revolution of 1918 or later outbreaks; had no political affiliations before joining the National Socialist party and belonged to no veteran or semi-military organizations. He joined the party between 1930 and 1931, and had his first contacts with the movement through reading about it and attending a meeting. He was strongly dissatisfied with the republican regime in Germany, but had no specific anti-Semitic bias. His economic status was secure, for not once did he have to change his occupation, job, or residence, nor was he ever unemployed.*

Abel played up the differences between his portrayal of Hitler's supporters and the characterizations of Schuman and others, although there was overlap in many areas. The key difference was that Abel's average Nazi supporter comes across as more balanced emotionally, and somehow less sinister, than those portrayed by others. In his introduction, he pointed out that many of the contributors "frankly state their disagreement with certain policies, as, for example, anti-Semitism." But he is conscious of the danger of appearing to accept the declarations of the Nazi contributors at face value. "In presenting these facts and opinions without comment, I do not intend to convey the impression that I agree with them," he insisted.

The essays Abel collected point to a broad array of factors that contributed to Hitler's appeal. By giving his followers a chance to present their own narratives, Abel produced a significant addition to the growing body of literature in the United States about the Nazi movement, a resource that would prove to be highly valuable to future researchers. But it isn't hard to understand why several American publishers rejected his manuscript before Prentice Hall finally agreed to take it on. Abel's attempt to maintain a nonjudgmental, academic detachment while studying the Nazis felt like an artificial exercise—and he often slipped in judgments anyway. As Schuman had pointed out, Hitler's movement demanded acceptance or rejection. The problem with Abel was that, just as he had when Hitler first came to power, he still seemed to want to give the Nazis the benefit of the doubt whenever possible.

The American journalists who had witnessed the rise of Hitler firsthand were more interested in his drive for total control at this point than in debating what attracted so many Germans to his movement in the first place. The hardworking Knickerbocker filed a slew of pieces during the spring and summer of 1933 that left no doubt about the extent of *Der Führer*'s power grab. "Adolf Hitler has become the Aryan Messiah," he wrote, explaining that he had committed everything to his campaign for "racial purity." Reporting on the latest anti-Semitic booklet, he noted that it listed six types of Jews: "Bloody Jews; Lying Jews; Swindling Jews; Rotten Jews; Art Jews and Money Jews." He added: "The fact that such a publication could appear is best proof of the good judgment of the refugees abroad." Hitler had emerged as "the supreme boss," he wrote in another article, and his authority "transcends . . . that of any political boss known to democratic regimes."

Drawing on his prior reporting experience in Moscow, Knickerbocker also pointed out how the Nazis were following the Bolshevik lead when it came to new forms of terror. "The latest Soviet method to be taken over by the Nazis is the taking of political hostages," he wrote. Aside from effectively holding "all the Jews of Germany hostage for the good behavior of their racial compatriots abroad," he explained that the Nazis now were targeting relatives of any anti-Nazi Germans who fled abroad. As in the Soviet Union, he wrote, this "distasteful" practice was proving highly effective. "The bravest man, willing to risk his own life, will shrink at risking the lives or liberty of his loved ones," he reported.

Knickerbocker found one exception to all this forced subservience. "German nudists are the only successful rebels against Nazi control," he wrote. While Hermann Goering and other top Nazis decreed that the nudists put their clothes on, the journalist reported that this was the one area where the authorities appeared to be willing to turn a blind eye at times, inspiring a degree of defiance. "The nude cult has gone the way of all popular movements suppressed by an unpopular law. It has gone bootleg." But this was hardly total defiance. The committed nudists were joining the Nazi movement, he added, working from the inside for their cause. "They intend to appeal to Adolf Hitler, who, like the nude culturalists, does not drink, smoke or eat meat." Although Hitler had given no indication he would accept the centerpiece of their agenda—stripping naked—the nudists weren't giving up hope. "Hitler must understand us," Knickerbocker quoted them as saying.

The nudists provided a rare lighter subject in an otherwise alarming drumbeat of stories. And nothing was more alarming than the question that Knickerbocker posed in the opening to his book *The Boiling Point*, based on his crisscrossing of the continent during the year after Hitler's ascension and published in early 1934. "Europe is in uniform," he wrote. "Will she go to war?"

Knickerbocker was one of the most astute young journalists of his time, someone whose reputation had already spread far beyond his readers in New York and Philadelphia. Running an interview with him on November 12, 1932, the Polish newspaper *Express Poranny* called him "the most talked about reporter in the world." He didn't pull his punches when reporting on Hitler's brutal tactics at home, prompting angry protests from the Nazis who claimed he was spreading anti-German slanders. They pressured his editors to send him home early, but initially to no avail. There was little reason to think that Knickerbocker would be any less straightforward in trying to answer the question he was asking about the risk of war—a question that was on the minds of so many people on both sides of the Atlantic.

Yet his book opened with a stunning first chapter devoted to Danzig, the Baltic port with an overwhelmingly German population that had been designated a "Free City" by the League of Nations after World War I. Polish-German tensions over the status of the city, which was surrounded by Polish territory, looked like they could easily spark the next major conflict. Knickerbocker stated a contrary view right from the start:

DANZIG . . . *Ten million lives of Europeans and Americans have been saved in this city of Danzig. That many lives were lost on the battlefields of 1914–1918. At least that many would be lost in the next war. That war was scheduled to begin in Danzig. Today it is evident that war is not going to begin here, and Hitler the Warmaker has become Hitler the Peacemaker as the Lord of Danzig.*

*For today Danzig is Nazi, and for the first time in thirteen years Danzig is at peace with the Poles. For the first time since the war Danzig has been eliminated from its number one place in the list of the probable seats of war.*

As Knickerbocker explained, the Nazis won the city elections on May 28, 1933, sweeping into power "a tornado of Brownshirts that drove fear through the heart of every Pole and Jew in the city and made Europe hold its breath." But while the Nazis quickly consolidated their hold on the city, Hermann Rauschning, the president of the Danzig Senate and Hitler's lieutenant, immediately went to Warsaw and signed agreements on trade and rights for Polish citizens in the Baltic city. "The Poles were amazed, suspicious, but pleased," Knickerbocker reported. Danzig and Warsaw played a friendly soccer match, and suddenly tensions eased all around. Hitler had ordered a truce for Danzig, he added, and it was working—at least so far.

What should readers make of this? "Its lesson for Europe is that Hitler can keep the peace if he wants to," Knickerbocker wrote. But he warned that this could be merely a tactical truce to buy time for Hitler to rearm. Still, "it means peace in this corner of the European cockpit at least for years to come."

But as Knickerbocker chronicled the other parts of his journey— through Central Europe, the Balkans and Western Europe—he emphasized the caveats as well as the cold calculations. Hitler doesn't want war because his country wasn't prepared for a new conflict, he maintained. "The odds are too great against Germany for anyone but a mad German to consider making war now against France and her allies," he wrote. "Contrary to a considerable body of opinion abroad, it may be positively asserted that there are no madmen running Germany today."

While he deplored the racial doctrines and terror tactics of the Nazis, he called them "masters of power politics." Which meant that they were trying to change the balance of power before they would consider triggering a new war. The key, he warned, would be how soon Hitler would feel confident about winning an eventual conflict. Among the experts he consulted, the consensus was that the answer was five to ten years. Knickerbocker ascribed Europe's pessimistic mood to the fact that the new arms race was already under way. Hitler was insisting over and over again that he wanted only peace. "It is the peace to make the world safe for armaments," Knickerbocker wrote, ending on a far more ominous note than in his opening section. "Armaments have never kept the world safe from war."

Hitler launched World War II by attacking Danzig only five years later, and Knickerbocker would certainly have liked the chance to pull back that opening chapter. Still, his book is instructive, including in that section. It demonstrates how much a highly critical journalist felt compelled to hedge his bets—even when, as the final chapters indicate, he shared much of the pessimism about where Hitler's policies would ultimately lead.

Knickerbocker's critical faculties were certainly still intact, which is much more than could be said about some other Americans living in Berlin. At about the same time that *The Boiling Point* appeared in print in early 1934, Sir Philip Gibbs, a famed British correspondent during World War I and later a novelist, visited the German capital. He, too, was asking the question whether Europe would go to war. Observing marches of the SA and the Hitlerjugend, along with the shouts of *Heil Hitler*, he admitted: "It was impossible not to be impressed by the splendour of that German youth . . . There was something stirring in the sight of this army of young men." But he also felt a sense of apprehension. "This pride and discipline of youth could be so easily used by evil minds for sinister purpose, later on."

There was little doubt in his mind that Hitler could be the one to push the country to disaster again. "He was the mesmerist who had put a spell on the German people so that they followed him blindly," he noted. The German leader kept insisting he wanted peace, but this veteran journalist observed that every German magazine he picked up was full of pictures of soldiers in steel helmets and scenes from the last world conflagration.

Among the most notable meetings he had on his visit to Berlin was with an American woman who had been married to a German for a long time. At tea with her in the Fürstenhof Hotel, where he was staying, Gibbs came straight to the point. "Most people in England and everybody in France believe Germany is preparing for a new war," he told her.

"But that is impossible! It's ridiculous!" she replied with genuine astonishment. "Why should they believe such an absurdity?"

He recounted his observations about the militarism of the Nazis, their belief in racial dogmas and persecution of Jews, their crude anti-intellectual theories and all the talk in *Mein Kampf* and elsewhere about Germany's expansive dreams. Men like Nazi ideologist Alfred Rosenberg were preaching barbarism and the reign of instinct and biological force, he added.

"My German friends laugh at Rosenberg's nonsense," the American woman said. "As for all this marching and drilling, it means nothing as far as war is concerned. Germans like it, just like the English like football and cricket."

She assured him she knew plenty of young Nazis. "They talk very freely to me, because I am the wife of a German and therefore, in their minds, German. They never talk of wanting war. On the contrary, they hate the idea of it." They only talk about war, she continued, when discussing the possibility that they might be attacked by France and her allies. In that case, they would "naturally" defend the fatherland. "Wouldn't any other nation feel the same?"

By then, Gibbs was keenly aware of several waiters hovering around their table. He suggested they move to a quiet corner. "We are having an audience," he pointed out.

Once they had switched tables, the American woman talked about Hitler, whom she knew and admired. "He is all for peace," she declared. "Foreigners don't believe in his sincerity. But I'm certain he wants to make a friendship with France. It is his strongest wish . . . Why doesn't France accept the offer?"

Gibbs was hardly reassured, but he was convinced that the American woman was utterly sincere in her belief that Hitler and his followers wanted nothing but peace. Like Martha Dodd, she felt the new Germany and its leaders were misunderstood and unfairly maligned—and no one more so than Adolf Hitler.

# Dancing with Nazis

On Saturday, June 30, 1934, Martha Dodd drove off early with her date, someone she identified as "a young secretary in a foreign embassy," in a Ford roadster, with the top down, to a private lake in Gross Glienicke on the outskirts of Berlin. It was a beautiful, warm, sunny day, and she and her companion spent it on the lakeside beach, working on getting as much of a suntan as possible, knowing that summer doesn't normally last long in northern Europe. In the late afternoon, the couple began slowly driving back to the city, "our heads giddy and our bodies burning from the sun," as Martha recalled, perfectly content. "We were not thinking of yesterday or tomorrow, of the Nazis or of politics."

They drove into the city at six. "I pulled down my skirt and sat up straight and proper as befits a diplomat's daughter," she wrote. But something looked and felt different in the German capital; the atmosphere had changed since their departure that morning. There were fewer people on the streets, mostly clustered in small groups, and, as they got closer to the center, they saw an unusual number of army trucks and machine guns, along with soldiers, SS men and Nazi police. The normally ubiquitous SA troops—the Brownshirts—were nowhere to be seen. Reaching Tiergartenstrasse, they saw that regular traffic was banned completely, and only their diplomatic plates got them through the thickening military and police checkpoints. The young diplomat dropped Martha off near her father's ambassadorial residence, and then quickly drove to his embassy to find out what accounted for the tense atmosphere.

With the sun still beating down hard on her, Martha rushed to her father's residence, feeling slightly dizzy, her eyes briefly blinded as she entered what looked to her like a dark house. She started up the stairs and saw the murky outline of her brother Bill.

"Martha, is that you?" he asked. "Where have you been? We were worried about you. Von Schleicher has been shot. We don't know what is happening. There is martial law in Berlin."

General Kurt von Schleicher had served as defense minister and then briefly as the last chancellor before Hitler came to power. He had pursued a policy of trying to split the Nazis by offering Gregor Strasser, the head of the "socialist" faction and a possible rival to Hitler, the post of vice chancellor. Schleicher was one of the politicians who had assured the AP's Louis Lochner and other correspondents that his government was succeeding in reestablishing "internal peace." On that morning of June 30 while Martha Dodd and her date were on their beach outing, SS men had arrived at Schleicher's villa, rung the bell and shot him dead when he opened the door. They then shot his wife as well. At noon, Gregor Strasser was arrested at his house in Berlin and brought to the Gestapo prison on Prinz Albrechtstrasse, where he was shot a few hours later. Strasser had never accepted Schleicher's offer to join his government and he had withdrawn from politics altogether, but that wasn't enough to save him from Hitler's wrath.

Those murders in Berlin were only one part of the bloody score-settling known as the "Night of the Long Knives." Bullet-ridden bodies were left scattered in houses and prisons across Germany. Henry Mann, the Berlin representative of the National City Bank, found the body of one of his neighbors on his front steps; the victim had been lured out of his house and murdered in front of the American's house. The body lay there for an entire day before the police came and took it away, instructing

Mann's servants to wash up the blood. Mann had earlier expressed the belief to Ambassador Dodd that he and other American bankers could work with Germany's new rulers. But as Dodd noted in his diary, Mann "showed no patience with the Hitler regime now."

The primary targets on June 30 were the leaders of the SA, the Storm Troopers who had provided the muscle for Hitler during his rise to power. In particular, tensions had been growing between the Reichswehr, the regular army, and Ernst Röhm, the flamboyant head of the SA, whose numbers had swelled to 2.5 million after the Nazis came to power. Röhm was a famed veteran of the movement, who had teamed up with Hitler even before the 1923 Beer Hall Putsch.

The Brownshirts were responsible for much of the violence that followed Hitler's rise to power—the attacks on Jews, Socialists and anyone else seen to be an opponent of the regime, along with the random American or other foreigner who failed to greet the Brownshirts with a Nazi salute. While there was no doubt that they saw themselves as carrying out Hitler's will, the Nazi ruler would later claim that they were threatening to spin out of control. He was receiving constant complaints from the Army, and even from the ailing President Hindenburg, about their lack of discipline. And Röhm was increasingly defiant, portraying his thugs as the vanguard of an ongoing revolution. "The SA and the SS will not allow the German Revolution to fall asleep or be betrayed half-way there by non-fighters," he proclaimed, vowing to carry on "our struggle." Hitler responded in blunt terms, although not mentioning Röhm by name. "Only fools thought the revolution was not over," he declared.

The opulent living of the SA leaders, with widespread stories of heavy drinking and open homosexuality, hardly helped their cause. Röhm occupied a villa on Prinzregentenplatz in Munich, outfitted with centuries-old Florentine mirrors and French armchairs. A truce negotiated between the Reichswehr and the SA in early 1934 did little to lessen the rising tensions. Early in the morning on June 30, Hitler personally led a small armed contingent of police that drove in three cars from Munich to Bad Wiessee, the lakeside resort where Röhm and other SA leaders were sleeping off another night of partying.

Breaking into Röhm's room, they declared him a traitor; in another room, they found Edmund Heines, the leader of the Breslau SA, in bed with a young male lover. Rounding up Röhm's contingent, they took them back to a Munich prison in a bus. Several were shot immediately. Hitler initially appeared undecided about his old comrade Röhm, and it was only the next day that the SA leader was offered a pistol so he could shoot himself. He refused, and two SS men dispatched him. The regime issued a terse announcement about the man who was once a key figure in Hitler's rise to power: "The former Chief of Staff Röhm was given the opportunity to draw the consequences of his treacherous behavior. He did not do so and was thereupon shot."

Appearing at the Propaganda Ministry on that same day, Hermann Goering told a group of hastily assembled foreign correspondents that the Nazis were forced to act to prevent a planned rebellion against Hitler. As the *Chicago Tribune*'s Sigrid Schultz recalled, the Luftwaffe (Air Force) commander had arrived "in full regalia, with his officers, strutting as stiffly as he could." After making his terse declaration, Goering started to march out, but, spotting Schultz, whom he knew from earlier social encounters, he stopped short. "And by the way, General von Schleicher was shot, trying to escape," he told her loudly. He then looked at her "piercingly," Schultz recalled. It was his way of saying, she concluded, that the Nazi brass could get away with anything they wanted.

The sweeping nature of the killings and the disparate backgrounds of the victims indicated that Hitler and the SS, whose leaders hated Röhm and the SA, had decided to eliminate anyone they regarded as a past or potential opponent. The body of Gustav von Kahr, the Bavarian leader who had presided over the suppression of the Beer Hall Putsch before retiring from politics, was found hacked to pieces. Other victims included the secretary and several associates of Vice Chancellor Franz von Papen, the scheming former chancellor who had helped undermine Schleicher and give Hitler his shot at total power.

Papen was the politician who had assured the AP's Lochner that "we have hired Hitler" and that he and other veteran politicians would keep him under control. He was personally spared, although roughed up and briefly placed under house arrest until he was dispatched as Hitler's envoy to Vienna. On July 25, 1934, less than a month after the Night of the

Long Knives, Austrian Nazis assassinated Chancellor Engelbert Doll-fuss, who had amassed dictatorial powers but opposed Hitler's move-ment. Still, Papen didn't hesitate to accept his new assignment, which would involve preparing the way for Austria's *Anschluss* (unification) with Germany in 1938.

His willingness to continue serving the regime he had helped ma-neuver into power earned him broad contempt from those foreign-ers and Germans who were alarmed by what they saw happening. At the American Embassy's Fourth of July Party at the Dodds' residence, the Jewish journalist Bella Fromm noted that everyone was on edge, but there was agreement on one thing: "There was general regret that Schleicher was the one to lose his life while Papen only paid with a couple of teeth."

On July 1, Dodd and his daughter Martha had made the point of driving by Papen's residence. Martha spotted the young son of the vice chancellor standing behind the curtains, and he later told the Dodds that his family was grateful for this sign of solidarity at a time when no other diplomats dared to venture near their house. Ambassador Dodd also sent his card with a message: "I hope we may call on you soon." According to Martha, her father had no sympathy for Papen, whom he viewed as "black with cowardice, devious with espionage and betrayal." But this was his way of expressing his displeasure with the brutal methods of Ger-many's new rulers.

At the Fourth of July party, the Dodd residence was festooned with red, white and blue flowers that artfully decorated the tables, along with small American flags. While the orchestra played American music, the American expats, both diplomats and journalists, mingled with the Ger-man guests. Martha and her brother Bill sardonically greeted the Ger-man arrivals with what had become the most frequently asked question since the Night of the Long Knives: "Lebst du noch?" Translation: "Are you still alive?" Some of the Nazis were visibly irritated.

At one point, the butler told Martha that Papen's son, the one they had seen in the window three days earlier, had arrived. Visibly nervous, he talked with Ambassador Dodd, protesting how ludicrous were the charges that his father was somehow involved in a conspiracy with Röhm,

Schleicher and the others against Hitler. A few days later, once his father was freed and out of immediate danger, the two Papens openly came to visit Dodd, prompting the American journalists to rush over for information about the politician who was still formally in Hitler's government but had come so close to becoming one of his early victims. Despite Dodd's personal misgivings about Papen, it was a way for the vice chancellor to demonstrate that he had American support. As Martha put it, this indicated "that the Germans were still respectful, and a bit awed by American public opinion at this time."

Her father was reaching a different conclusion, even if he had contributed to Papen's salvation so that he could go on serving his new masters. That same week a professor from the University of Berlin came to see him, ostensibly to discuss a lecture Dodd was supposed to give to the History Department on July 13. Given the tense situation, they agreed to call off the lecture. The German was despondent about the savagery the Nazis were arousing among his countrymen, stunned that they were capable of such barbaric behavior. He made a point of praising an editorial in London's *Times* that described the Night of the Long Knives as a return to medieval practices. "Poor Germany, she cannot recover in decades to come. If I could go to any other of the greater countries, I would leave the university at once," he declared.

In his diary entry of July 8, Dodd admitted to feeling a similar deepening pessimism. He hosted a visiting American delegation, but they had asked that no press be allowed to cover the event because they didn't want to be attacked at home for their presence in Germany. Hitler's killing spree had hardened hostility to the country in the United States and elsewhere. As for Germany itself, Dodd noted, "I can think of no country where the psychology is so abnormal as that which prevails here now."

The ambassador was increasingly questioning the sense of his own mission. "My task here is to work for peace and better relations," he wrote. "I do not see how anything can be done so long as Hitler, Goering and Goebbels are the directing heads of the country. Never have I heard or read of three more unfit men in high place." Reading the diary at this point, you can almost hear Dodd sigh as he concluded, "Ought I to resign?"

\*　　　\*　　　\*

On February 23, 1934, William Shirer, who was living with his Austrian wife, Tess, in Paris, turned thirty—but he wasn't exactly thrilled by his situation. Back in 1925, he had left Cedar Rapids, Iowa, right after college and pursued the adventurous life of a young reporter eager to explore the world. He worked for the *Chicago Tribune* out of Paris, where he got to meet the likes of Ernest Hemingway, F. Scott Fitzgerald and Isadora Duncan; he also snagged assignments that allowed him to wander all around Europe and as far afield as Afghanistan and India, where he befriended Mahatma Gandhi and contracted malaria and dysentery. In 1932, as the Depression worsened, he lost his job and he had a skiing accident that caused him to lose sight in one eye. He and Tess then tried to live off his savings in Spain while he worked on a novel and an early memoir, failing to publish either. When they returned to Paris, he got a job offer from the Paris edition of the *New York Herald* in January 1934. But as he noted in his diary on his birthday the following month, it was "the worst job I've ever had."

The big stories seemed to be happening elsewhere—in Germany, Russia, Italy, where strong leaders were all in command. France was buffeted by strikes and unrest, but looked rudderless by comparison. "The Paris that I came to in 1925 at the tender age of twenty-one and loved, as you love a woman, is no longer the Paris that I will find day after tomorrow," he wrote right before his return in January 1934.

On June 30, he excitedly recorded in his diary that the phone lines to Berlin were down for several hours. "And what a story!" he exclaimed. He cited the reports of the arrest of Röhm by Hitler in person, and the shooting of several SA leaders. "The French are pleased. They think this is the beginning of the end of the Nazis," he continued.

While Shirer didn't record any judgment of his own, he realized that the biggest story of his life was unfolding nearby. "Wish I could get a post in Berlin," he concluded. "It's a story I'd like to cover." Two weeks later, after more details about the breadth and brutality of the purge had come to light, Shirer added: "One had almost forgotten how strong sadism and masochism are in the German people."

In his largely forgotten novel *The Traitor* that he wrote after the war, Shirer expounded on his feelings at the time. His protagonist, the aspiring American journalist Oliver Knight, discusses his plans to go to Europe with his college instructor. The instructor tells him that Paris would be great fun, but he would be just "another young American in Paris," likely to spend endless hours with wine and women, "babbling about a Europe you were woefully ignorant of." Besides, France is "too static," he continued, and "nothing very world-shattering is likely to come out of France in our time."

Not so with the Germans, the instructor continued. Despite Bach, Beethoven, Schiller and Goethe, their culture was "a mere veneer so thin that their barbarism—the pagan barbarism of the German forests—is continually threatening to break through and engulf them." The big story was developing in Germany, his instructor insisted, and any young man who wanted to make his mark in journalism should go there, not Paris. To be sure, Shirer wrote his novel with the benefit of hindsight, but it undoubtedly reflected his gut feelings in 1934. He desperately longed to get to Berlin.

On August 2, President von Hindenburg died at the age of eighty-six. Once considered a towering figure, he had looked largely irrelevant and impotent once Hitler had become chancellor. "Who *can* be president now? What will Hitler do?" Shirer asked in his diary when he heard the news. The next day he knew the answer: Hitler had announced he would take over all presidential powers along with his current ones, and the Army would be required to swear an oath of "unconditional obedience to Adolf Hitler, the *Führer* of the German Reich and people, Supreme Commander of the Armed Forces." It wasn't an oath to serve the country; it was deliberately fashioned as an oath to serve one man whose power was now unquestioned and unlimited.

Shirer was impressed with the sheer audacity of such a move. "The man is resourceful," he wrote in his diary on August 4. Hitler also announced that a plebiscite would be held on August 19 to approve his seizure of all political and military powers. He justified his actions in large part by the alleged plot against him and the Army that he claimed triggered the June 30 crackdown. After attending a meeting of the American

Chamber of Commerce in Berlin, Fromm noted in her diary: "Nobody believes that Hitler's life was endangered or that a counterrevolution was planned."

But on August 3, Knickerbocker, the veteran correspondent who had been so perceptive in many of his earlier dispatches, reported that Röhm's Brownshirts had planned "what would have been the most extraordinary massacre in modern political history." Its supposed victims: the leaders of the Reichswehr, including the chiefs of the General Staff—which, according to Knickerbocker, was why the generals were willing to accept "a one-time corporal" as their commander-in-chief and swear a personal oath to him. While Knickerbocker indicated he was relaying a version of events from Berlin sources, presumably top Nazi officials, he didn't include anything to suggest he was skeptical of this interpretation.

Wiegand, the Hearst correspondent, didn't comment on Hitler's claims but offered a more critical view of his power grab on the same day. Noting that "Hitler has attained a position quite without parallel in any country in the world," he added: "Until yesterday it was possible to say he was the instrument of the Reichswehr. Today the army is his weapon. Fear, not freedom, promises to rule the voters Aug. 19."

Within days of Hindenburg's death and Hitler's quick moves to consolidate all power in his hands, Shirer got his wish: he received a call from one of the bosses at Hearst's Universal News Service, who offered him a job as its correspondent in Berlin. Elated, Shirer immediately agreed. "Must brush up my German," he wrote in his diary. On August 25, he and Tess took a train from Paris, arriving at Berlin's Friedrichstrasse Bahnhof at about ten in the evening. As soon as Shirer stepped off the train, two plainclothesmen grabbed him and demanded to know if he was "Herr So-and-So," as Shirer recalled, since he didn't catch the name they kept repeating. "I had expected to meet the secret police sooner or later, but not quite so soon," he wrote. After examining his passport, the plainclothesmen finally let him go. As he thought of the new chapter that was about to begin for him, Shirer ended his first Berlin diary entry that evening with what he admitted was a bad pun: "I'm going from bad to Hearst."

That same morning, another foreign correspondent, far more famous at the time than Shirer, had boarded a train to go in the opposite direction, from Berlin to Paris. Dorothy Thompson had the distinction of exiting Nazi Germany for the last time because she had been presented with an expulsion order. Thompson, or Mrs. Sinclair Lewis as she was known because of her novelist husband, had gone to Austria after the murder of Chancellor Dollfuss on July 25, eager to cover what the Nazis were up to there. In early August, she decided to drive from Austria through Munich up to Berlin, reacquainting herself with her old stomping grounds, stopping in towns and villages along the way to get a sense of the popular mood. She may have badly misjudged Hitler when she interviewed him in late 1931, but she was now intent on discovering what he was doing to Germany.

Thompson wasn't exactly sure when she crossed into Germany since no border guard stopped her, but then she noted the sudden appearance of houses decked out in Nazi flags. Along the road, she saw a Storm Trooper wearing a black armband, which she assumed was in honor of Hindenburg. But when she asked him, the SA man said it was "for Röhm." Thompson also noticed the election banners everywhere in preparation for the plebiscite that coming Sunday to affirm Hitler's power grab following Hindenburg's death. Compared to other countries where voters chose between competing candidates, "in Germany Hitler made himself President and it was a law, and then people voted, whether they liked the law or not," she wrote later. "If they liked it, that meant he was President; and if they didn't, that meant he was President anyhow."

Thompson found the roads in Germany clogged with cars, motorcycles and bicycles, almost all driven by young men. "I was in a procession of young men," she recalled. "I had the feeling that there were only young men in Germany, thousands and thousands of young men, all very strong and healthy, and all working furiously to get somewhere." Then there were the election posters that Thompson described as "sentimental, evangelical," proclaiming "We are with thee, dear leader."

In Garmisch, an American visitor from Chicago told Thompson that he had been in Oberammergau, the Bavarian village famed for its Passion Plays. "These people are all crazy," he said. "This is not a revolution, it's a revival. They think Hitler is God." During the scene in the Passion Play when Judas received his thirty pieces of silver, a woman sitting next to him declared: "That is Röhm, who betrayed the Leader."

In the Bavarian town of Murnau, a Hitler Youth camp filled with "beautiful children," as Thompson put it, sported a huge banner proclaiming WE WERE BORN TO DIE FOR GERMANY. When she arrived in Munich, Thompson had letters of introduction to people she hadn't met before. "I went to see them but they wouldn't talk," she reported. "They were frightened to death; you could see that."

At another stop, she met a Catholic priest who was willing to talk. "The Nazi Revolution is the greatest blow to Catholicism since Martin Luther," he told her. "But it is also a blow to all Christianity . . . In the Nazi outlook nationalism is elevated to a mystic religion, and the state claims not only the bodies of the people but the souls. Force, and not goodness, is the measure of all things." Who would win in this struggle between Christianity and the Nazis, she inquired. "They are getting the children," the priest replied. "That is their program—to get the children." In other words, the Nazis were aiming to replace Christianity with their own "mystic religion," and they were well on their way to doing so.

When Thompson finally arrived in Berlin, she headed straight to the Adlon Hotel, which felt "like home," the smiling barman ready with his popular dry martinis. "Oh, I was so glad to be back!" she recalled. Everything was perfect in the hotel. "It was all the courtesy, all the cleanliness, all the exquisite order that was Germany." But her journalistic colleagues warned her not to use the hotel phones, since they were monitored. So Thompson found a cheap saloon with a phone booth in the back, which she used to place calls to some of her German acquaintances.

The American reporter had lunch with a young woman who worked as a stenographer in a state bank. She had "eyes as candid as water," Thompson noted. "When you look at her you know she never told a lie in her life."

"Do you find it's so bad here as the outside world seems to think?" the woman asked Thompson. When the reporter replied that she had come back to Germany to see the situation for herself, the woman explained that she hadn't been a Nazi in the beginning, but that even in her bank conditions had changed since Hitler came to power. Over-all, wages were lower than before, but the biggest cuts were among the directors and other senior staff. And regular staff felt that they were treated better, with fewer social distinctions. "It's as though we all belonged to a big family," she said. While there was talk of food rationing, she claimed everyone was willing to make sacrifices as long as they were employed.

Thompson asked her about the Night of the Long Knives. She professed it was "an awful shock" to learn that some of the Nazi leaders had been "acting dreadful" and were corrupt. "That is why Hitler had to execute them," she concluded, as if that was a perfectly logical solution.

When Thompson pointed out that in the United States people were tried before they were punished, the German woman didn't seem to understand her point. "It was funny," Thompson mused. "I never met anyone in Germany except a few intellectuals, who minded that these people did not have a trial. It was as though they had forgotten that there ever had been such a thing as law."

Thompson also met a Brownshirt she had known earlier. While admitting there were clashes within the Nazi movement and some of the SA leaders wanted to get rid of Goering or Goebbels, he insisted there was never any talk of undermining Hitler's regime or of acting in any way against him. "Hitler sold us out," he said. "There wasn't any plot. No one was treasonable to Hitler." He described how Nazi firing squads gunned down far more of his colleagues than reported, with the victims numbering about 300 instead of the 77 mentioned by Hitler.

Thompson also met Otto, a German journalist who had earlier been a staunch defender of free speech but who now "writes articles that free speech isn't any good," as she put it. Over coffee and plum cake, he calmly explained that revolutions aren't made by pleasant people. "Revolutions need terrorists," he said. "Afterward, when the revolutions succeed, the people who made them are in the way." The Russians could send those who fell out of favor to Siberia, but in Germany "there was nothing to do but shoot them." He admitted that shooting former Chancellor von Schleicher's wife "made a bad impression abroad" and the cleanup was "not pretty." But the result was a stronger Germany, he insisted. "I doubt if any revolution in history has been made with greater order. It is now consolidated. It will last for years."

While listening to Otto, Thompson was thinking of some of the other murders on June 30. A music critic in Munich by the name of Willi Schmidt was shot because he was mistaken for a storm trooper with the same name who had already been shot earlier that same day. Dr. Erich Klausener, a Catholic leader, was killed for no reason that she could ascertain. He was cremated and his ashes were sent to his wife by registered post, according to an account she had read in a British newspaper. "I kept thinking how it must have been when the postman rang the bell," she recalled, imagining a scene of the postman asking the unsuspecting widow to sign for the package and then tipping his hat. "They are awfully polite in Germany," she observed. To Otto, she said aloud: "Yes, Germany is an orderly country."

Thompson spent only ten days in Berlin. One day the porter called. "Good morning, madam, there is a gentleman here from the secret state police," he announced. A young man in a trench coat that looked like the one Hitler wore came up with an order for her to leave the country within forty-eight hours. "In view of your numerous anti-German publications in the American press, the German authorities, for reasons of national self-respect, are unable to extend to you a further right of hospitality," it read.

While other reporters had been pressured to leave, this was the first outright expulsion and it generated front-page stories back in the United States. "The general feeling of the foreign colony here over the incident is that Nazism has once again demonstrated its utter inability to understand any mentality but its own," wrote Frederick Birchall, the *New York Times*'s Berlin correspondent.

Several American and British correspondents came to see Thompson off to Paris, giving her American Beauty roses for her journey. As the train pulled out of the station, she leaned out of the window, clutching the roses, "a little tearful about such a demonstration of comradeship," Birchall added.

In her own account, Thompson identified the real reason for her expulsion as "blasphemy." As she explained, "My offense was to think that

Hitler is just an ordinary man, after all. That is a crime against the reigning cult in Germany, which says Mr. Hitler is a Messiah sent by God to save the German people—an old Jewish idea." Returning to New York in September, she had attained new supercelebrity status, with reporters rushing to get her views on the country that had given her the boot. "Germany has gone to war already and the rest of the world does not believe it," she declared.

At about the same time, Shirer, the new arrival, was contrasting his new home with the city he had first visited in the 1920s. "I miss the old Berlin of the Republic, the care-free, emancipated, civilized air, the snub-nosed young women with short-bobbed hair and the young men with either cropped or long hair—it made no difference—who sat up all night with you and discussed anything with intelligence and passion." Instead, Shirer found a city where there were the constant shouts of *"Heil Hitler,"* Brownshirts and SS guards marching everywhere, and the endless clicking of heels, all of which grated on his nerves. Barely a week into the new assignment that he had been so anxious to get, Shirer admitted he was already "in the throes of a severe case of depression."

Whether the correspondents were coming or going, they recognized that Germany had undergone a remarkably swift and chilling transformation. No one was casually writing off Hitler anymore.

Back in the United States, Sinclair Lewis, Dorothy Thompson's husband, drew heavily on his observations of Germany as he dashed off his new novel *It Can't Happen Here* in two frantic months of writing. Published in 1935, it envisaged the coming to power of a fascist dictator in the United States. Like Hitler, Berzelius Windrip, Lewis's antihero, claims to have all the answers to all the country's economic problems, while proclaiming his people's superiority. "My one ambition is to get all Americans to realize that they are, and must continue to be, the greatest Race on the face of this old Earth," he declares. Once in power, he abolishes Congress and employs the Minute Men, his equivalent of the Brownshirts, to bash anyone who dares to resist.

The book was a huge success, eventually selling more than 300,000 copies, and stirring controversy as the American Communist Party and others on the far left embraced its message with particular enthusiasm.

Lewis liked the praise, but was uneasy about the source. "There is no excuse for any one to swallow the Bolshevik claim to be the one defense against Fascism," he wrote. But he had succeeded in his primary aim: convincing many of his countrymen that fascism was a threat that they should take seriously, wherever it manifested itself.

As new American correspondents came on the scene, they were prone to start from the premise that they were going to report from a bizarre, increasingly sinister but always intriguing place. Pierre Huss of the *International News Service*, whom Shirer characterized as "slick, debonair, ambitious, and on better terms with Nazi officials than almost any other," came to call it both "Hitlerland" and "Naziland." And, of course, no one was a more intriguing figure in that land than Adolf Hitler. Both the veteran Berlin correspondents and the new arrivals were always looking for opportunities to see him in person, trying to take the measure of the man and his movement. Reflecting on the eight years that he would spend in Berlin, right up until a month before the United States and Germany went to war in December 1941, Huss wrote: "You had to work hard and long, frequently taking your food and sleep on the wing to keep up with Hitler."

In January 1935, Huss's efforts to get an interview with Hitler paid off at just the right moment. The Nazi leader was in his Alpine chalet in Obersalzberg, waiting for the results of the plebiscite in the Saar, the territory that had been administered during the previous fifteen years by Britain and France under a League of Nations mandate. There was little doubt that the Saar's inhabitants would vote as Hitler wanted them to, ensuring the return of the territory to Germany. Huss calculated he would find *Der Führer* in good spirits, which would make this an opportune time to meet him.

He wasn't mistaken. Arriving at the chalet, he saw Hitler examining the returns, his eyes "alight with joy." He was dressed in what Huss characterized as "his golf suit," while Goering stood nearby in a huge white sweater, joining his boss in celebrating the outcome of the voting. Hitler promptly greeted his American guest by insisting that he join him on his regular walk in the mountains before lunch. As usual, he didn't allow his bodyguards to accompany him, instead only taking along his white Hungarian shepherd dog, his walking stick made of knotted wood, and a Luger automatic pistol in his pocket.

With the dog leading the way through the snow, Hitler kept up a brisk pace that left Huss nearly out of breath as they reached the crest of a hill. Hitler told him it was good exercise, enjoying the fact that his guest was struggling a bit. Then he pointed down to the chalet that they had just left, which was surrounded by hills like the one they had just climbed. "A good rifle shot, aiming through telescopic sights, could easily pick me off from here while I am sitting on the porch or in that back room there," he told Huss. He added that he was buying all the land in the area, closing it to outsiders "so [SS leader Heinrich] Himmler can quit worrying." The road that Huss had traveled up the mountain would also be closed to all but authorized traffic.

Hitler next pointed in the direction of Salzburg, saying that Himmler and some army officers had claimed that "a few well-directed cannon shots from there some dark night could blow us out of bed." With a forced laugh, he explained that he had told Himmler that he'd have to be patient since "I cannot just walk over the border and take a piece out of Austria." He added, "I am a fatalist and all those things take care of themselves."

Huss felt Hitler was taking a risk by walking in the hills alone, whatever measures were used to secure the area. He pointed to two woodcutters a couple of hundred yards ahead, indicating that they or someone else could attack him while he was out on one of his walks. At that point, Hitler told Huss to pack a hard snowball and throw it far. When Huss did so, Hitler pulled out his pistol and fired off a dead-on shot: the snowball burst apart in the air. Seeing Huss's skeptical expression, he told him to throw a second snowball. Once again, his aim was perfect. "You see, I am not entirely defenseless," he said—and went on to boast that the SS and Army brass considered him better than many of their best marksmen.

The amiable mood of their walk was broken when Huss ventured to suggest that Hitler would be courting a major conflict if he insisted on carrying out every part of his party's 25-point program first proclaimed in 1920, including its call for a Greater Germany with new territory and colonies. Hitler abruptly stopped, and "like a flash he changed from the Bavarian alpine rambler to Adolf Hitler," Huss recalled. Hitler shot back, "Sooner than give up one little point of my program, I'd go over to that tree and hang myself." Although the Nazis had departed from several parts of their original program already, he insisted "it can only be fulfilled to the letter because it expresses the will of Germany."

Huss's conclusion about Hitler after his walk in the hills: "He is a fanatic, every inch of him, going into a passion or fury when the occasion demands."

Veteran correspondents like Lochner and Wiegand worried that the fanaticism of Germany's new rulers was impacting their ability to do their jobs. "Reporting from Germany ceased to be a pleasure when the Nazis seized power in 1933," the AP bureau chief noted with typical understatement. In a letter to William Randolph Hearst dated August 5, 1933, Wiegand told his boss that he had been warned "that in one way or another every effort allegedly will be made to persuade you to transfer me from Germany." Mentioning the increased monitoring of cables, phones and mail, along with the sweeping crackdown on any freedom of expression inside Germany, he wrote: "It is no pleasure to a freedom-loving man to work in Germany these days . . . Hitler's proud claim is that there is order and discipline in his Germany. So there also is in St. Quentin and Sing Sing."

The Nazis realized that they often lost the propaganda war if they forced correspondents out, since those reporters then enjoyed the spotlight when they returned home. But that only prompted them to try new methods to compromise those they disliked. Supposedly anti-Nazi Germans started approaching correspondents with offers to provide secret military information. On more than one occasion, Sigrid Schultz threw men out of her *Chicago Tribune* office when they made such an offer and warned her colleagues to stay clear of them. In April 1935, she returned home one day to discover that an envelope with "important information" had been delivered in her absence by what sounded like one of the same men. Opening it, she saw the design for an airplane engine, which she promptly burned in her fireplace; she knew that, if found on her premises, this would be perfect incriminating evidence in a spy trial.

On her way back to the office, Schultz spotted three men, who looked familiar from her earlier encounters with the secret police, heading toward her home. Stepping in front of them, she told them not to bother going there since she had burned the envelope. As they stood speechless, she hailed a cab and loudly instructed the driver to take her to the American Embassy.

Schultz was convinced that Goering was behind that effort to set her up because they had had several tense exchanges earlier about the country's expanding concentration camps. At a lavish lunch in the Adlon Hotel for him and his new bride, Emmy Sonnemann, on May 2, the feisty reporter told him quietly but firmly what happened, blaming his *agents provocateurs*. Startled, Goering kept saying, "You are imagining things." When Schultz stuck to her story and added that she had informed the embassy of the details, he snapped angrily: "Schultz, I've always suspected it: you'll never learn to show proper respect for state authorities. I suppose that is one of the characteristics of people from that crime-ridden city of Chicago." An amused acquaintance in Goering's Air Ministry later told her that around his offices she became known as "that dragon from Chicago." But no more attempts were made to set her up.

Despite such incidents, the Nazis still sought to impress as much as to intimidate, particularly with the displays of adulation of their leader. For most correspondents, the best chance to observe Hitler and his followers up close came during the annual *Parteitag*, the weeklong Nazi Party Congress in Nuremberg. The party leaders, from Hitler on down, were only too happy to have the foreign press observe these lavishly orchestrated demonstrations of their popularity and power.

"Like a Roman Emperor Hitler rode into this medieval town at sundown today past solid phalanxes of wildly cheering Nazis who packed the narrow streets . . . The streets, hardly wider than alleys, are a sea of brown and black uniforms," Shirer wrote in his diary on September 4, 1934. The new correspondent got his first glimpse of Hitler as he drove past the Württemberger Hof, where the reporters were staying. *Der Führer* stood up in his open car, wearing a worn trench coat, fumbling with his cap and "acknowledging the delirious welcome with somewhat feeble Nazi salutes from his right arm."

Shirer was struck by Hitler's lack of expression—"though there *is* something glassy in his eyes, the strongest thing in his face." But he had expected something more powerful and theatrical, prompting him to observe that "for the life of me I could not quite comprehend what hidden springs he undoubtedly unloosed in the hysterical mob which was greeting him so wildly." And hysterical they were. That evening, Shirer found himself "caught in a mob of ten thousand hysterics" in front of the Deutscher Hof, Hitler's hotel, shouting: "We want our *Führer*." He wasn't prepared for the faces he saw in the crowd, especially those of the women when they caught sight of Hitler as he stepped out briefly on the balcony.

"They reminded me of the crazed expressions I saw once in the back country of Louisiana on the faces of some Holy Rollers who were about to hit the trail," he wrote. "They looked up at him as if he were a Messiah, their faces transformed into something positively inhuman. If he had remained in sight for more than a few moments, I think many of the women would have swooned from excitement."

The next day, Shirer began to understand how Hitler was generating such fanatical admiration. At the opening meeting of the Party Congress in Luitpold Hall, he noted that the Nazis were putting on "more than a gorgeous show; it also had something of the mysticism and religious fervour of an Easter or Christmas Mass in a great Gothic cathedral." There were brightly colored flags, a band that fell silent when Hitler made his dramatic entrance and then struck up a catchy marching tune, and the roll call of the "martyrs"—the Nazis who had died in the failed Beer Hall Putsch. "In such an atmosphere no wonder, then, that every word dropped by Hitler seemed like an inspired Word from on high," Shirer recorded. "Man's—or at least the German's—critical faculty is swept away at such moments."

By the end of the Nuremberg festivities, Shirer confessed he was "dead tired and rapidly developing a bad case of crowd-phobia." But he was pleased that he had come. "You have to go through one of these to understand Hitler's hold on the people, to feel the dynamic of the movement he's unleashed and the sheer, disciplined strength the Germans possess," he noted.

To be sure, the foreign correspondents took a more jaundiced view of the proceedings than the Germans in attendance. Shirer, Knickerbocker and a couple of British reporters were in a room overlooking the moat of Nuremberg's castle when they saw Hitler driving by again. "Though Hitler is certainly closely guarded by the S.S., it is nonsense to hold that he cannot be killed," Shirer wrote. He and the other correspondents in the room agreed that it would be simple to throw a bomb from the room onto Hitler's car, and then escape by running into the crowd.

Along with four other reporters, the AP's Lochner was invited to join Hitler's motorcade as it made a triumphal tour of the city before going up to the Burg, Nuremberg's medieval castle. The reporters were put in the car directly behind Hitler's so that they could see the reaction of the crowds. "His followers were simply beside themselves with hysteric joy when they see him, and they actually think of him as a God-sent superman whom they do not hesitate to liken to Christ," Lochner explained in a letter to his daughter Betty back in Chicago, echoing Shirer's observations.

When the motorcade reached the castle courtyard, Hitler got out of his car and approached the reporters to greet them. But before he could reach out his hand to Lochner, the AP correspondent declared: "Mr. Chancellor, I welcome you here in the city of my forebears."

Hitler was startled. "How come?" he asked. "You're an American, aren't you?"

"Yes, indeed," Lochner replied. "I am an American, but my family for centuries lived continuously in this city until my grandfather and father emigrated to the United States. I think therefore I have the right to greet you here."

Lochner hadn't considered how this declaration would be received. As the reporter recalled, "Hitler blushed in anger, turned on his heel, and stalked into the castle." It was then that Lochner realized that he had inadvertently reminded *Der Führer* that he wasn't a born German. "I had struck an exceedingly sensitive nerve," he concluded. And he blamed this incident for the fact that Hitler never invited him for a personal meeting again, although he would remain in Germany until their two countries went to war with each other seven years later.

The Nuremberg rallies became a standard event for reporters from many countries, often with special seats in the motorcade that were meant to ensure that they reached the right conclusions. Two years later, in 1936, a young United Press correspondent, Richard Helms—the future director of the Central Intelligence Agency—was one of the chosen ones. After sitting in the back seat of a car alongside Nazi ideologist Alfred Rosenberg and a Polish reporter, Helms offered this evocative description of his experience as they followed right behind Hitler's car:

> *There was, I must admit, something mesmerizing about this ride. Only a seasoned movie star might have resisted the weird, vicarious sense that somehow some of the blind adulation of the crowds, who could have had no idea who was riding in the limousine directly behind Hitler, was meant for oneself. It was not difficult to imagine the feelings of the provincial Nazi Party functionaries in the cars that followed.*
>
> *However much one loathed Nazis, and I certainly did, this was heady stuff. There could be no question about the German people's intoxication with their leader. It is easy today to forget that in his prime—the word sticks on one's tongue—Hitler was a masterful politician.*

While many of the regular American correspondents in Berlin failed to get personal meetings with Hitler, Putzi Hanfstaengl was still in the business of trying to connect influential Americans with *Der Führer*. One person he targeted was Hearst, the powerful publisher, who traveled frequently to Europe and made a special point of declaring how much he liked Germany. He was particularly enchanted with Munich—"the city, the surroundings, the climate, the bright and happy Bavarian people, the shops, the theaters, the museums—and the beer," he told a reporter. "In fact, it is such a delightful place that one has to be careful not to want to live here instead of going home and attending to business."

Catching up with Hearst, who was on another European trip during the summer of 1934, Hanfstaengl tried to convince him to come to Nuremberg to attend the Nazi Party rally. After the two men met in Munich, Putzi published an article in Germany that was cited in the *New York Times* on August 23. Putzi quoted the publisher as saying that the results of the plebiscite backing Hitler were "a unanimous expression of the popular will." Hearst added: "Germany is battling for her liberation from the mischievous provisions of the Treaty of Versailles . . . This battle, in fact, can only be viewed as a struggle which all liberty-loving peoples are bound to follow with understanding and sympathy." In his account, Putzi also reported that Hearst would attend the Nuremberg rally the following month.

Hanfstaengl had spoken too soon. Worried that his presence in Nuremberg could be viewed as an even stronger endorsement of Hitler's movement, Hearst declined. Nonetheless, after some initial hesitation, he accepted Putzi's invitation to meet the Nazi leader in Berlin on September 16, once the Nuremberg spectacle was over.

When they met in the Chancellery, Hitler—speaking through Hanfstaengl, who served as the translator—immediately asked: "Why am I so misrepresented, so misunderstood in America? Why are the people of America so antagonistic to my regime?"

Hearst reportedly explained that Americans "believe in democracy and are averse to dictatorship."

Hitler replied that he had been elected by the German people, who had reaffirmed their support for his policies. "That is democracy, is it not?"

"That might be democracy, but it is also dictatorship in view of what those policies are," Hearst said.

If accurate, that account, which was provided by his traveling secretary Harry Crocker, would indicate that Hearst wasn't a completely uncritical admirer of Hitler as his critics back home were charging. But there's no doubt that Hanfstaengl had achieved his goal of making Hearst see Hitler in a more positive light. Fromm noted in her diary that Putzi had been "bragging about what he considers his latest achievements"—namely, orchestrating the Hearst-Hitler session at which the German leader "turned on all his charm to *impress* the great man."

"Hitler is certainly an extraordinary man," Hearst wrote to his friend and secretary Colonel Joseph Willicombe after their meeting. "We estimate him too lightly in America. He has enormous energy, intense enthusiasm, a marvelous facility for dramatic oratory, and great organizing ability." He did throw in a note of caution, however: "Of course, all these qualities can be misdirected."

"Hitler needs a woman," Hanfstaengl declared to Martha Dodd during her early days in Berlin. "Hitler should have an American woman—a lovely woman could change the whole destiny of Europe." Then, with his typical dramatic flourish, he proclaimed, "Martha, you are the woman!"

Martha recognized that "this sounded like inflated horse play as did most of Putzi's schemes," but she wasn't sure he wasn't serious. "I was quite satisfied by the role so generously passed on to me and rather excited by the opportunity that presented itself, to meet this strange leader of men," she wrote. She was still convinced that Hitler was "a glamorous and brilliant personality who must have great power and charm."

In her recollection of the day of her encounter, Martha added a somewhat sardonic note, which nonetheless reveals her state of mind: "Since I was appointed to change the history of Europe, I decided to dress in my most demure and intriguing best—which always appeals to the Germans: they want their women to be seen and not heard, and then only as appendages of the splendid male they accompany."

Putzi and Martha went to the Kaiserhof, Hitler's favorite hotel, where they met Jan Kiepura, a Polish singer. They drank tea and chatted until Hitler, accompanied by his bodyguards and driver, sat down at a table nearby. Kiepura was called over to Hitler's table and the two men talked for a few minutes. Then, Putzi walked over to *Der Führer*, bending his tall frame down to whisper something to him. Visibly excited, he returned to Martha, telling her that he had agreed to meet her. When Martha walked over to his table, Hitler stood up and kissed her hand, murmuring something that she didn't catch since her German was still rudimentary then. Their encounter was very short, with Hitler kissing her hand once again as she went back to her table. From time to time, she recalled, he cast "curious, embarrassed stares" her way.

That meeting left her "with a picture of a weak, soft face, with pouches under the eyes, full lips and very little bony facial structure." She barely noticed his famous mustache, but she observed that his eyes were "startling and unforgettable—they seemed pale blue in color, were intense, unwavering, hypnotic." Overall, she found the Hitler she met that afternoon to be "excessively gentle and modest" and "unobtrusive, communicative, informal." She was struck by "a certain, quiet charm, almost a tenderness of speech and glance."

When Martha returned home that evening and told her father about her meeting with Hitler, the ambassador didn't hide his amusement at how easily she was impressed by him. He did admit that Hitler could turn on personal charm, and, teasingly, told her not to wash her hands for a long time since she should preserve the extraordinary blessing of Hitler's kiss. If anything, he persisted, she should wash carefully around the spot where his lips had blessed her. Martha was irritated by this ribbing, but she tried not to show it.

Nothing more clearly demonstrated the difference in perceptions of Hitler up close than another even more fleeting encounter, this one with Robert Lochner, the teenage son of the AP bureau chief. Robert and his stepmother were at the opera in Berlin one evening, waiting for his father to arrive, when suddenly a phalanx of SS men burst in, clearing a path for Hitler. As the leader followed in their wake, there were shouts of "*Heil Hitler*," and the Germans shot their right arms out in the obligatory right-handed salute. Instead of following suit, Robert lapsed into the pose of a surly American teenager. "I ostentatiously kept both of my hands in my pockets and demonstratively chewed gum, which the Nazis disapproved of," he recalled. For a split second, this prompted Hitler to focus his attention on him, and the teenager was startled by the menacing intensity of his "piercing look."

Angus Thuermer, a cub reporter who worked in the AP bureau where Robert's father was the boss, recalled how the younger Lochner explained his feelings after that short incident. "Ever afterwards, I could understand how young officers, or anyone else, for that matter, would be terrorized by Hitler's eyes," he said.

Young as he was, Robert Lochner certainly understood Germany better than Martha Dodd—and was more attuned to the atmosphere of fear and intimidation that accompanied Hitler and the Nazis. But this wasn't only a difference in the views of two young Americans. It also underscored how Hitler succeeded in favorably impressing women on so many occasions, particularly when in their company for the first time. Louis Lochner recalled attending a reception hosted by Joseph and Magda Goebbels in 1935, with many theater and movie people in attendance. Hitler appeared to love the company, pressing the hand of famed actress Dorothea Wieck, who blushed as he greeted her. Inviting her over to his table, he laughed and told stories, even slapping his thigh as he did so. And there was one thing that Lochner heard women saying over and over: "Once you look into Hitler's eyes, you are his devoted follower forever."

Aside from Hitler, Martha Dodd was initially attracted to many German men who showed up on the endless diplomatic social circuit. She wasn't that taken with the young Reichswehr officers she met, whom she dismissed as "extremely pleasant, handsome, courteous, and uninteresting." But aside from Putzi, she was happy to be in the company of the likes of Ernst Udet, the World War I flying ace who took her up in his plane (Martha later wrote *Sowing the Wind*, a mediocre novel about an Udet-like character); Prince Louis Ferdinand, the grandson of Kaiser Wilhelm II and a frequent guest of the Dodds and the Lochners; and numerous young Foreign Ministry and SS men. One of these young men she dated, whom she at first considered to be part of the "blond Aryan wholesome-looking talent," pressed her repeatedly for information about her father's views on events in Germany. Finally recognizing what he was doing, she confessed that he was "one of the first disillusions I had in German official life."

While she was still in what she characterized as her "most violent pro-Nazi period," Martha met a young French diplomat, who began taking her out with her parents' permission. Not that Martha cared much about such formalities. Although her German male friends warned her that he was a French spy and she considered herself anti-French and pro-German, she was drawn to "the tall boy, romantic and perfect of feature." When he denounced the militarism of the Nazis, she argued with him— but later she conceded that some of his arguments made her begin "to think a little." Sylvia Crane, one of Martha's friends, maintained that her political thinking was always guided by her love life. "She just liked sleeping with attractive men, and that's how she learned about politics and history," she said.

Martha was certainly eclectic in her tastes. Early in her stay, she met the Gestapo chief Rudolf Diels. He was a frequent visitor to the Dodds' residence, often to assure the ambassador that he was doing what he could to prevent violence against Americans. Martha's father and other diplomats viewed him as more sympathetic to their grievances than other German officials. Nonetheless, he was also presiding over the early concentration camps, and Martha admitted she heard from several people that "at least twelve people a day" were killed during that period. But none of that prevented Martha from going out with him, dancing in nightclubs and taking long drives in the country together. "I was intrigued and fascinated by this human monster of sensitive face and cruel, broken beauty," she declared. Nor, of course, did it matter that Diels was married; Martha dismissed his wife as "a pathetic passive-looking creature."

A young Jew who met Martha at several cocktail parties warned her that Diels was using her as protection, probably in some internal Nazi battles. "Martha, you are very silly, and you are playing with fire," he said. But she wasn't about to be dissuaded and kept seeing the Gestapo chief. "I was extremely interested in his type and his conversation," she wrote. "He gave me, consciously and unconsciously, a picture of the backstage workings of espionage that I could have not got anywhere else." It was a revealing comment that later could be read as an indirect admission about her own spying for a different regime.

Martha was soon infected by Diels's evident nervousness about his rivals within the party, and in December 1933 even told Messersmith, the U.S. consul general, that he feared for his life. He wanted Messersmith to write a letter to the Nazi authorities praising him, suggesting that he was doing a lot to keep U.S.-German relations on an even keel. Messersmith and Ambassador Dodd sympathized with him but didn't feel they could write such a letter.

Martha worried both about inadvertently saying something to Diels about her German friends that might lead to their deaths, and about Diels himself. After one late night of dancing, Diels came into the Dodds' residence for a drink in the library before going home. It was evident he wanted to talk about whatever latest intrigues he had on his mind. Martha grabbed a pillow from the sofa. When Diels asked her what she was doing, she indicated she was going to cover the phone. That prompted a fleeting sinister smile, as Martha recalled, and a nod of approval.

While Martha continued to take such measures, she admitted she got herself into "a nervous state that almost bordered on the hysterical." She began replaying conversations in her head with various Germans, wondering if they were recorded or overheard. From her second-floor bedroom, she was suddenly prone to hear ominous footsteps on the gravel driveway, see moving shadows, and to assume any popping sound was a gunshot. As for Diels, in the period leading up to the Night of the Long Knives, he was like "a frightened rabbit," Martha recalled, clinging to her. Diels survived the bloodletting of June 30, 1934, but earlier he lost his post of Gestapo chief, never attaining that prominent a position in the Nazi hierarchy again.

Martha Dodd claimed that a variety of factors—everything from the crudeness of German propaganda to her exposure to a widening circle of friends—transformed her from an apologist for the Nazis into a fervent opponent in the spring of 1934. Not coincidentally, this was also the period when Martha began what was probably her most passionate affair. Her new lover was Boris Vinogradov. In her 1939 memoir *Through Embassy Eyes*, she never mentioned him by name, but he was "the young secretary in a foreign embassy" who took her to the lakeside beach on June 30. He was a tall, blond, handsome first secretary in the Soviet Embassy, and, because he had served earlier as the press secretary, was well known to American correspondents in Berlin. They found him to be good company when Martha would bring him by Die Taverne, the Italian restaurant where they gathered in the evenings.

The other important new person in Martha's life was Mildred Harnack, a fellow midwesterner who found herself in Germany. She had met Arvid Harnack, a German exchange student, at the University of Wisconsin and soon married into his distinguished, scholarly Prussian family. In 1929, the couple moved to Germany, and Mildred at first taught classes on American and British literature at the University of Berlin and later at a night school for adults. Watching the impact of the Depression on her students, she noted their sense of weariness since they knew "they had no future." Like her German husband, she was troubled by the rise of the Nazis, but she was confident that they would fail to seize power. "It is said by people who are capable of estimating the present situation that no such dictatorship as is in Italy can be erected in Germany," she wrote on July 24, 1932.

Mildred's confidence flowed from her faith that there was already an alternative model that would serve as the solution to the crisis of the capitalist system. She and Arvid had visited Russia, where she was awed by the atmosphere of "hopefulness and achievement." She enthusiastically explained in a letter to her mother that the country was "the scene of an enormously important experiment in loving your neighbor as yourself." Back in Berlin, the Harnacks became regular guests at Soviet Embassy receptions.

Once the Nazis came to power, the Harnacks had to be careful to hide their political views, and Mildred avoided any more pro-Russian commentaries in her letters home. But when she met Martha, the two instantly hit it off. Mildred and Martha, with her new political outlook and Soviet lover, felt free to share their private thoughts with each other. And they were both quick to pass judgment on those who they felt hadn't seen the light the way they had. Martha professed herself "amazed at the naïveté" of any Americans who still could have profascist leanings, seemingly oblivious to the irony that she would make such a statement so soon after her own conversion.

On May 27, 1934, Mildred, Martha and Boris—along with Heinrich Maria Ledig-Rowohlt, the son of the publisher Ernst Rowohlt—drove to the farm of writer Hans Fallada, whose 1932 novel *Little Man, What Now?* was a huge bestseller in Germany and a major hit abroad. While the Nazis liked his grim portrayal of life in Weimar Germany, they were highly suspicious of him. Fallada tried to skirt current politics and even sought to ingratiate himself with the Nazis on occasion. Nonetheless, as numerous press attacks on him indicated, the lack of ideology in his books was enough to make the authorities discern an undercurrent of dangerously independent thinking.

But Martha was irritated by Fallada's decision to concentrate on his life on the farm with his wife and children, and his ostensibly apolitical writing. "He was isolated from life and happy in his isolation," she wrote reproachfully. From their conversation, she continued, "though I got the impression that he was not and could not be a Nazi—what artist is?—I felt a certain resignation in his attitude." Mildred was less judgmental, telling her companions that Fallada was a man with a conscience. "He is not happy, he is not a Nazi, he is not hopeless," she said. In fact, Fallada's last novel, *Every Man Dies Alone*, which he wrote right after World War II, would prove to be one of the most powerful fictional portrayals of the horrors of life in Germany under Hitler—and of the terrifying price that anyone paid who dared to resist the Nazis.

That summer, with Vinogradov's help, Martha made her first pilgrimage to her new ideal state: Russia. "I had had enough of blood and terror to last me for the rest of my life," she declared by way of explaining why she was eager to take a break from Germany. And, of course, what other country was freer of blood and terror than the Soviet Union? From the moment she set foot in Moscow, and probably even before she made her trip, her blind admiration of Stalin's Russia knew no bounds, even exceeding her earlier zeal for Hitler's Germany. There was a complete lack of militarism, arrogance, insolent behavior and regimentation, she giddily reported. The Bolshevik Revolution had been a triumph for humanity. "One felt in Moscow that the struggle was over, that the fruits of victory were being cherished and enjoyed by everyone."

While she confessed that there was still some startling poverty, everything was being done to eliminate it, she insisted. Stalin was setting an example by living modestly, the workers were living happily in their workers' state, and "the conscience and idealism that lie latent in most mankind were being stimulated and awakened in me," she wrote. That didn't prevent her from boasting that she was served caviar three times a day on a Volga cruise ship, along with "marvelous nourishing Russian soups, excellent meats, butter, ice cream, fish . . ." Or from "marveling over the fact that everything good in life was being supplied for the vast majority of the population." Unlike Germany, she added, Russia was "almost like a democratic country," and threatened no one.

Despite her new anti-Nazi, pro-Soviet orientation, Martha was still the same woman when it came to matters of the heart. When she returned to Germany, she was, as always, more than eager to associate with any man who looked glamorous to her, no matter what his views. This was certainly the case with Thomas Wolfe, whose novel *Look Homeward, Angel* was a smash hit in Germany as elsewhere. When he visited Berlin in 1935, the young but already widely known writer was treated like a conquering hero. Arriving in Berlin, he was greeted at the American Express office by a huge number of letters, telegrams and phone messages from journalists, diplomats and admirers, all seeking to see him. Describing all this in a letter to his editor Max Perkins, Wolfe marveled that "for the last two weeks at least I have been famous in Berlin."

As Martha put it, "Tom, a huge man of six foot six, with the face of a great poet, strode the streets, oblivious of the sensation he created . . . To the desolateness of the intellectual life in Germany, Thomas Wolfe was like a symbol of the past, when great writers were great men." Wolfe had visited Germany in the mid-1920s, and his fond memories of that era combined with his recent literary successes there prompted him to feel that Berlin was still a magical place. In his letter to Perkins from Berlin, he declared: "I feel myself welling up with energy and life again . . ." He had finally finished a new novel, *Of Time and the River*, and he was reveling in the adulation he found in Germany, going from party to party, where he was always the center of attention.

"Part of Tom's uncritical attitude towards Nazism can be explained by his own state of delirium," Martha wrote. Her own forgiving attitude was just as easy to explain: she loved escorting a celebrity like Wolfe around town and adding him to her list of conquests. It was a tempestuous affair, with Martha often reprimanding him for his heavy drinking. Decades later, Ledig-Rowohlt, the son of his German publisher, revealed to an interviewer a conversation that he and Wolfe had about Martha. Wolfe told him that Martha was "like a butterfly hovering around my penis."

Wolfe indicated that he did notice some "disturbing things" during his 1935 visit to Germany, but it wasn't until he returned in the summer of the following year that his intoxication with his reception there wore off and he began to recognize what Nazi rule meant in practice. In an interview that Ledig-Rowohlt arranged for him with the *Berliner Tageblatt*, he still waxed poetic about Germany's virtues. "If there were no Germany, it would be necessary to invent one," he declared. "It is a magical country. I know Hildesheim, Nuremberg, Munich, the architecture of Germany, the soul of the place, the glory of her history and art." But, as Martha explained, Wolfe returned to Germany "a much soberer person, this time eager to learn what lay beneath the surface of Nazi success and effectiveness."

After that visit, Wolfe wrote *I Have a Thing to Tell You*, a novella that was spread over three issues of the *New Republic* in March 1937; he later expanded his story and made it part of *You Can't Go Home Again*, one of two novels that were published after his death from a brain disease in 1938, before he reached his thirty-eighth birthday. The novella is unabashedly autobiographical in terms of Wolfe's feelings about Germany. It is the story of an American writer as he leaves Germany, "that great land whose image had been engraved upon my spirit in my childhood and my youth, before I had ever seen it . . . I had been at home in it and it in me."

But this Germany is one that the narrator realizes he must leave for the last time. A German friend frets about losing his job, his mistress and possibly even his life because "these stupid people"—the Nazis—are capable of anything. At the same time, he warns the American that he must not write too truthfully about what he observed, since the authorities would then ban his books and destroy his exalted reputation. "A man must write what he must write," Wolfe's narrator and alter ego replies. "A man must do what he must do."

As the narrator's train leaves Berlin behind, he muses that the people he knew there were "now remote from me as dreams, imprisoned there as in another world."

Soon, though, the American finds himself cheered by his lively, friendly companions in his compartment. Even "a stuffy-looking little man with a long nose," who fidgets throughout the trip and initially made the other passengers uncomfortable, gradually loosens up and joins in the convivial conversation. Reaching the frontier at Aachen, they all get out for fifteen minutes while the locomotive is changed. The little man says something about needing to pick up a ticket for the rest of the journey, and slips away. The others walk around before returning to the platform to reboard.

As the returning passengers look from the outside, they see the fidgety man—his face now "white and pasty"—sitting in their compartment facing a group of officials. The leader of his interrogators is "a Germanic type . . . His head was shaven, and there were thick creases at the base of his skull and across his fleshy neck." Even before he learns that his fellow passenger was a Jew who was trying to escape and smuggle money out in the process, the American narrator felt "a murderous and incomprehensible anger" welling up in him. "I wanted to smash that fat neck with the creases in it," he writes. "I wanted to pound that inflamed and blunted face into jelly." But he admits to his sense of helplessness, which is shared by everyone around him. Feeling nauseated, he watches as the officials escort the man off the train.

As the train pulls out of the station, the narrator and the others look at him for the last time. He looks back. "And in that glance there was all the silence of man's mortal anguish," Wolfe writes. "And we were all somehow naked and ashamed, and somehow guilty. We all felt somehow that we were saying farewell, not to a man, but to humanity."

The American's sense of remorse and anger is only heightened by the advice of an attractive blond woman in the compartment, whom he had found seductively appealing, with "an almost shameless physical attraction." She tries to talk the others in the compartment out of their glum mood. "Those Jews!" she says. "These things would never happen if it were not for them! They make all the trouble. Germany has to protect herself."

As the German friend in his novella had predicted, the publication of *I Have a Thing to Tell You* led to the banning of Wolfe's books in Germany, and he never returned to that country. In an interview in the *Asheville Daily News*, his North Carolina hometown paper, Wolfe talked about his last trip to Germany. "I came away with the profoundest respect and admiration for the German people, but I feel that they are betrayed by false leadership," he declared. Reflecting more broadly on his European experiences, he added: "I saw a certain perfection and finish in European life that we do not have here. However, there is a poisonous atmosphere of hatred. I finally wanted to come back home."

Despite the title of his posthumous novel, Wolfe did make it home.

✦ ✦ ✦

# "A Mad Hatter's Luncheon Party"

During the summer of 1936 when Thomas Wolfe visited Berlin for the last time, it was "the season of the great Olympic games," as he wrote in his novel *You Can't Go Home Again*. George Webber, his alter ego and main character, observed how "the organizing genius of the German people . . . was now more thrillingly displayed than he had ever seen it before. The sheer pageantry of the occasion was overwhelming, so much so that he began to feel oppressed by it." Webber—in reality, Wolfe—felt oppressed because he was acutely conscious of the ominous nature of this pageantry. "It so evidently went beyond what the games themselves demanded . . . It was as if the games had been chosen as a symbol of the new collective might, a means of showing to the world in concrete terms what this new power had come to be."

The irony was that Hitler and the Nazis had a long history of virulent opposition to the whole idea of holding the Olympics or other international sporting events in Germany. In 1923, the Nazis had protested against the German Gymnastics Festival that was held in Munich because it was open to "Jews, Frenchmen and Americans," as a petition that Hitler signed put it. In 1932, right before taking power, the Nazi leader called the Olympics a "plot of Freemasons and Jews"—even though the decision to bring the games to Berlin had already been taken a year earlier. And once the Nazis were in command, they still chafed at the notion of an international competition that would include Jews and blacks. The *Völkischer Beobachter* fumed that it was "a disgrace and a degradation of the Olympic idea" that blacks could compete with whites. "Blacks must be excluded," it concluded. "We demand it."

But Hitler and the Nazis also insisted that the young should be physically fit, engaging in a broad array of sports training on a regular basis. The idea was to strengthen the bodies and aggressive character of their young followers, as well as their allegiance to the movement. "For us National Socialists, politics begins in sport—first, because politics guides everything, and second, because politics is already inherent in sports," declared Bruno Malitz, who was in charge of sports for the Berlin storm troopers.

Right after the Nazi takeover, Theodor Lewald, the president of the German Olympic Committee and a fervent promoter of hosting the games in Berlin, set up a meeting with Hitler, Goebbels and Interior Minister Wilhelm Frick to convince the new rulers to support his cause. He argued that the games would more than pay for themselves because of the revenue they would generate—and, more important, there would be an "enormous propaganda effect." Conjuring up the image of about 1,000 journalists converging on Berlin for the games, he pointed out that nothing could "even remotely match" their propaganda value. This proved to be a winning argument.

For precisely the same reason, many Jewish groups in the United States, along with an array of other activists, particularly from the left, pushed hard for a boycott of the Berlin Olympics. They pointed out that the Nazis' record of discrimination against Jews was in direct contradiction of the Olympic ideal that all competitors were welcome. Avery Brundage, the president of the American Olympic Committee (AOC), initially sounded sympathetic to that argument. "My personal, but unofficial opinion is that the Games will not be held in any country where there will be interference with the fundamental Olympic theory of equality of all races," he declared.

Prodded by Lewald, the Nazis responded that Germany would welcome "competitors of all races," but also stipulated that the composition of the German team was its own affair. In September 1934, Brundage traveled to Germany, supposedly to investigate whether German Jews were getting fair treatment. German sports officials gave him a quick tour of their sports facilities, also acting as translators when he talked to Jews. Arno Breitmeyer, a top Nazi sports official, even came dressed in his SS uniform for a meeting with Jewish sports leaders. Brundage didn't stop to consider the intimidating effect of those arrangements on the Jews he met; he appeared satisfied that he was getting their candid assessments. He also reported that the Germans had assured him that there would be "no discrimination in Berlin against Jews." Pleased by those declarations, he added: "You can't ask for more than that and I think the guarantee will be fulfilled." In one of his more expansive moments, Brundage suggested a common bond with his hosts, pointing out that his men's club in Chicago didn't admit Jews.

Charles Sherrill, another member of the AOC, traveled to Germany in 1935 to try to convince the Nazis to name at least one Jew to the German team, unabashedly arguing that they needed the equivalent of "the token Negro." But in a personal meeting with Hitler, he called himself "a friend of Germany and of National Socialism" and didn't seem at all bothered by Hitler's adamant opposition to including any Jews in Germany's Olympic squad. According to the Nazi leader, this would contaminate the Aryan contingent. Sherrill described his meeting with Hitler as "wonderful," and used similarly effusive terms in describing his subsequent four days as Hitler's personal guest at the annual Nuremberg Nazi Party rally in mid-September. "It was beautiful!" he wrote. "You could almost hear the [Nazi] units click, as each fitted into place, exactly on time."

As the battle lines were drawn back home between the pro- and antiboycott factions, including within the AOC and other athletic organizations, several top American diplomats in Germany were offering a far more accurate picture than "fact finders" like Brundage and Sherrill. Ambassador Dodd met with Jewish sports officials privately, avoiding the kind of staged sessions that had been arranged for the visitors. He reported to Washington that his interlocutors described "flagrant discrimination" against Jewish athletes and widespread intimidation of the few who were admitted to Olympic training camps.

As early as 1933, Consul General Messersmith, who had made a habit of not allowing himself to be fooled by the Nazis, had predicted that the new regime might make a show of allowing a few Jews to compete in the Olympic trials. But he warned that "this will be merely a screen for the real discrimination that is taking place." He and Raymond Geist, another top embassy official, kept reporting on the discrimination, trying to counter the "whitewash" of Sherrill and others. After his transfer to Vienna in 1934, Messersmith continued to urge Secretary of State Cordell Hull to oppose American participation in the Olympics. The Berlin event, he argued in a cable in December 1935, "has become the symbol of the conquest of the world by National Socialist doctrine." If the Olympics were stopped, "it would be one of the most serious blows which National Socialist prestige could suffer within an awakening Germany." He added that many "wise and informed observers" believed the fate of the games would have a major role "in determining political developments in Europe"—and that he fully concurred with this view.

Despite the impassioned opposition to the Berlin games by Jeremiah Mahoney, the president of the American Athletic Union, and several other sports officials back in the United States, the Brundage-Sherrill view narrowly prevailed. Hull was largely unmoved by the pleas from his diplomats in Berlin and Vienna, and Roosevelt remained studiously silent on the controversy. As David Clay Large wrote in his authoritative study *Nazi Games: The Olympics of 1936*: "A consummate politician, FDR certainly understood that throwing his weight behind either position carried more risks than taking no position at all." Besides, Large continued, his administration was already perceived as too "Jew friendly," and even Judge Samuel I. Rosenman, one of his Jewish advisors, warned him against supporting a boycott.

When the games got under way, they were every bit the triumphant pageant that both their proponents and opponents had predicted. Wolfe offered this vivid description in *You Can't Go Home Again*:

> *The daily spectacle was breath-taking in its beauty and magnificence. The stadium was a tournament of color that caught the throat; the massed splendor of the banners made the gaudy decorations of America's great parades, presidential inaugurations, and World's Fairs seem like shoddy*

*carnivals in comparison. And for the duration of the Olympics, Berlin*
*itself was transformed into a kind of annex to the stadium . . . the whole*
*town was a thrilling pageantry of royal banners . . . banners fifty feet in*
*height, such as might have graced the battle tent of some great emperor.*

All of which served as the stage for every triumphant appearance of
the modern emperor. "At last he came—and something like a wind across
a field of grass was shaken through that crowd, and from afar the tide
rolled up with him, and in it was the voice, the hope, the prayer of the
land," Wolfe continued. As Hitler arrived, standing stiffly in a shining car,
he raised his hand "palm upward, not in Nazi-wise salute, but straight-up,
in a gesture of blessing such as the Buddha or Messiahs use."

It wasn't only Hitler's followers who were impressed. "Berlin is now a
handsome, hustling place to be at home in," the *New Yorker's* Janet Flan-
ner wrote. "The past year has been closer to physical prosperity and far-
ther from political nervousness than any Germany has known since the
war, and its capital city shows it." Everything was done to convey exactly
that impression to the foreign visitors. Rudi Josten, a German staffer in
the Associated Press bureau, recalled the abrupt revival of many of the attractions of the Weimar era. "Everything was free and all dance halls were
reopened," he said. "They played American music and whatnot. Anyway,
everybody thought: 'Well, so Hitler can't be so bad.'" The Nazis even allowed 7,000 previously banned prostitutes to ply their trade once again
in the German capital.

Whether it was on the streets or in what passed for the new high society, the visitors were given every opportunity to revel. "A glittering swirl
of Olympic receptions," Fromm wrote in her diary. "The foreigners are
spoiled, pampered, flattered, and beguiled." Shirer was depressed by the
degree to which the visitors were taken in by the lavish show. "I'm afraid
the Nazis have succeeded with their propaganda," he noted as the games
were ending.

Carla de Vries, an older American woman, was so caught up in the
fervor that she managed to elude Hitler's bodyguards and kiss *Der Führer*
on the cheek during his visit to the swimming stadium. Swimmer Eleanor
Holm Jarrett, the twenty-two-year-old wife of bandleader Art Jarrett and

a gold medalist at the 1928 Los Angeles Olympics, had already partied so hard on the transatlantic crossing that Brundage had her dropped from the team. She remained in Berlin anyway, convincing Hearst's International News Service to give her an assignment to report on the festivities. She did her job enthusiastically, showing up at receptions hosted by top Nazi leaders. When Goering gave her a silver swastika pin, she happily wore it on her chest for everyone to see.

But none of this was enough to completely satisfy Hitler. Fromm recorded in her diary that he applauded German winners in "an orgasmic frenzy of shrieks, clappings, and contortions," but that he displayed a "disgusting" lack of sportsmanship when others emerged victorious— especially Jesse Owens and his fellow black American athletes. "It was unfair of the United States to send these flatfooted specimens to compete with the noble products of Germany," he complained. "I am going to vote against Negro participation in the future."

When Owens scored one of his victories, Wolfe was sitting in the diplomatic box with Martha Dodd. He let out "a war whoop," Martha recalled, which didn't go unnoticed by the Nazi leader, who was also in attendance. "Hitler twisted in his seat, looked down, attempting to locate the miscreant, and frowned angrily." In fact, the German leader was ignoring some of the guidelines of his own regime. A Nazi directive to the German press had warned that "Negroes should not be insensitively reported . . . Negroes are American citizens and must be treated with respect as Americans."

Although such instructions were inspired by cynical calculation that an appearance of respectful reporting could fool the world into believing that the Nazi movement was based on tolerance, the irony was that many Germans were genuinely enthusiastic about the black American stars, especially Owens. Cheers went up in the Olympic Stadium whenever he appeared. The black American sociologist and historian W. E. B. DuBois, who spent nearly six months on a fellowship in Germany in 1935 and 1936, wrote: "Jesse Owens ran before the astonished eyes of the world. He was lauded and pictured and interviewed. He can scarcely take a step without being begged for his 'autogramme.' He is without doubt the most popular single athlete in the Olympic Games of 1936." And while

Hitler and other top Nazis bitterly complained about the black American Olympians, some of those athletes were invited by ordinary German citizens for coffee or dinner.

Little wonder that Owens and his black teammates returned from Germany with less bitterness than many of their countrymen expected—especially since these athletes all too often would see no change in the discrimination they faced at home. Richard Helms, the young United Press reporter in Berlin and future CIA chief, happened to be crossing the Atlantic on the *Queen Mary* with Owens after the games. In their conversations, the runner shrugged off all the stories about how Hitler had allegedly snubbed him. "Owens was a quiet, modest man," Helms recalled. "He did not feel he had been insulted, as conventional reporting had it, when Hitler failed to award him the gold medal."

Reflecting on his stay, DuBois elaborated on the reasons why black Americans would have mixed feelings about their experiences in Hitler's Germany. "I have been treated with uniform courtesy and consideration," he reported. "It would have been impossible for me to have spent a similarly long time in any part of the United States, without some, if not frequent cases of personal insult or discrimination. I cannot record a single instance here."

He observed that Germany felt "contented and prosperous" under its new rulers, but also that it was "silent, nervous, suppressed" and all opposition was banned. He certainly noticed the "campaign of race prejudice carried on openly, continuously and determinedly against all non-Nordic races, but specifically against the Jews, which surpasses in vindictive cruelty and public insult anything I have ever seen." The situation, he added, was "so complicated that one cannot express it without seeming to convict one's self of deliberate misstatement." All of which got him back to the Olympics, concluding that "the testimony of the casual, non-German-speaking visitor to the Olympic Games is worse than valueless in any direction."

Many of the American athletes, black or white, gave little or no thought to such considerations. They were there for the competition—and, just like the spectators, out for a good time. In at least one case, this led to a German-American personal drama that played itself out almost as publicly as the races on the field.

Leni Riefenstahl, Hitler's favorite film director, who had already im-
mortalized the Nuremberg Nazi rallies in *Triumph of the Will*, was busy
filming the games for what would become her second major work, *Olym-
pia*. Fromm clearly detested the glamorous young director and former
actress. "Wearing gray flannel slacks and a kind of jockey cap, [she] is ob-
trusively in evidence everywhere," the Jewish reporter wrote in her diary.
"On and off she sits down beside her *Führer*, a magazine-cover grin on
her face and a halo of importance fixed firmly above her head." It wasn't
the Nazi leader, however, who made Riefenstahl lose control of her emotions; it was the American decathlon winner Glenn Morris.

On the second day of the decathlon, the German champion Erwin
Huber introduced Riefenstahl to Morris, who was lying on the grass
resting with a towel over his head. "When Huber presented Morris to
me, and we looked at one another, we both seemed transfixed," the film
director wrote in her autobiography, slipping into the tone of a sappy romance novel. "It was an incredible moment and I had never experienced
anything like it. I tried to choke back the feelings surging up inside me . . ."

After Morris won the competition, breaking a world record, he
stood with two other Americans on the podium for the medals ceremony. Riefenstahl watched, but was unable to film the ceremony because it was getting dark. As Morris came off the podium, he headed
straight toward the film director. Here, her memoir goes from romance
novel to bodice-ripper mode. "I held out my hand and congratulated
him, but he grabbed me in his arms, tore off my blouse, and kissed my
breasts, right in the middle of the stadium, in front of a hundred thousand spectators. A lunatic, I thought," she wrote. "But I could not forget
the wild look in his eyes . . ."

Riefenstahl claimed she tried to avoid Morris after that, but ended
up encountering him again at the pole vault. "We couldn't control our
feelings," she wrote, describing how they immediately became lovers in
the midst of the Olympic events and her film shoots. "I had lost my head
completely," she confessed, and imagined he was the man she would marry.
When Morris left to be feted for his triumphs in a New York ticker-tape
parade, she was despondent. Then she read that he was engaged to an
American teacher. He still wrote to Riefenstahl, and she still believed she

loved him. Although she finally decided to break off their affair, she sent him her stills of him in action in Berlin, which helped him get the part of Tarzan in a Hollywood movie. Later, she learned he divorced in 1940 and died of alcohol and drug abuse in 1974.

By pointing out "his sad fate" in her memoir, Riefenstahl implied that Morris would have done better if he had stayed with her. In the midst of the pageantry of the Olympics, Hitler's favorite film director had fantasized about a whole other life with the American who couldn't have cared less what movement she was working for.

Truman Smith, who had been the first American official to meet Hitler, returned to Berlin in 1935 for a second tour, this time as the senior military attaché. It wasn't until a couple of years later that he met the Nazi leader again, although he had observed him from afar on several occasions, including at the Olympics. At an official function at the Chancellery, Smith worked his way through the reception line and shook Hitler's hand. Preparing to move on, he felt Hitler's hand on his sleeve.

"Have I not seen you before?" Hitler asked.

"Yes, Mr. Chancellor, in Munich in 1922," the startled attaché responded.

"Oh, yes, you introduced me to Hanfstaengl," Hitler recalled.

It was a vivid demonstration that the German leader, like many skilled politicians, possessed an uncanny memory for significant faces and events in his life even after a long interval.

Returning to Berlin, Truman and his wife, Kay, were immediately struck by its transformation since the early 1920s. "Berlin was so familiar," Kay wrote in her unpublished memoirs. "It was the same yet not the same. The streets, the buildings were all as I had known them. But now no more shabby fronts and broken fences. All was clean, freshly painted . . . It was as in a dream; all is familiar but changed . . . The crowds well dressed, the people looking well nourished, energetic." Without any irony, she also observed: "Berlin was a very safe city at this time, as all the drunks, bums, homosexuals, etc. had been put in concentration camps."

If such remarks betrayed her own prejudices, Kay wasn't blind to what she characterized as "a certain tenseness" in the air, the product of a regime that was ready to target anyone. When she and Truman returned to the house one day, a servant told them that telephone repairmen had visited the house and insisted on "checking" their connections, despite her protestations that the phone was working well. After that, the Smiths made a habit of putting an overcoat over the phone to foil any listening devices, and postponing any sensitive conversations to when they took walks in the Grunewald, the forest on the outskirts of the city. The couple assumed that it wasn't only the Nazis who could be spying on them. According to Kay, Truman tried to engineer the removal of an American secretary in his office, a longtime Berlin resident with strong leftist views who he suspected was giving information to the Russians.

Kay also pointed out parallels between the Nazis and the Communists. The Nazis, like the Communists, hoped to replace Christianity with another doctrine—what she identified as "the old Germanic religion," but in reality was the idea that Nazism superseded all previous beliefs. According to one of Kay's Catholic friends, a Nazi leader had ordered schoolchildren to replace the standard grace at meals with "Dear Jesus, stay away from us. We eat gladly without thee." When Rochus von Rheinbabin, a German acquaintance from their first tour, arrived decked out in Nazi insignia, proudly boasting about his early membership in the party, Kay questioned him about the party's beliefs. After he finished, she said, "But Rochus, what is then the difference between National Socialism and Communism?" Her German visitor threw up his hands. "Hush Katie," he declared. "One may not say that."

When Colonel Charles Bennett, the chief of the attaché section of the Military Intelligence Division of the War Department, had asked Smith to return to Germany, he was counting on his getting privileged access to the new regime. "Your past relationship with Hitler, [Minister of War and Army Commander-in-Chief Werner von] Blomberg, and others who are at the head of affairs in Germany, would enable you to do a service that no one else, however well qualified they might be in other respects, could do," he wrote. Of course, Smith could no longer drop in on Hitler the way he first had in Munich; in fact, his brief encounter with him on the reception line was the only time he spoke to him directly again. But his extensive contacts from those earlier days gave him a tremendous advantage over the other military attachés in Berlin, more than justifying Bennett's faith in him.

Unlike many of his counterparts in other embassies, Smith had no money in his office budget to pay for spies. What he did have was a long list of German officers he knew, some of whom he had met during his first tour in Germany or later when he was an instructor at the Infantry School at Fort Benning, Georgia, from 1928 to 1932. The assistant commandant of the Infantry School was George C. Marshall, then a lieutenant colonel, who treated Smith as an aide and translator when it came to dealing with visiting Germans.

After the Nazis took power, they made a rule that a German officer could not visit the house of a foreigner unless he knew the foreigner previously. This meant most military attachés were effectively prevented from inviting German officers to their homes. But Smith was in a different category. When he and Kay held a party upon their return to Berlin, Kay recalled, "The other attachés were dumbfounded to find so many German officers at our reception. They were green with envy and Truman became their prime target in their attempt to get news."

By comparison, Kay noted, the British and the French, who relied heavily on paid spies, "were remarkably bare of contacts." That was true for most of the other attachés as well, making Truman a celebrity in their ranks. Only the Poles, she conceded, may have had better contacts than her husband.

Truman used everything he could to learn about the German military plans and deployments. Early in his second tour, German officers still wore insignia of their regiments on their shoulders. He carefully noted what units were represented, piecing together valuable information, even enlisting Kay and their young daughter Kätchen to help him in this task. "Katchen and I were coached to scrutinize their shoulders well and to describe their marks," Kay wrote, omitting the umlaut that her daughter has always insisted belongs on her name. "Whenever we drove out in the car together she would take one side and I the other, our faces pressed against the window pane. It made an amusing game for us and we had the feeling of helping solve the riddle."

Kätchen, who was born in 1924, still relishes similar memories. Her father suspected that their driver Robert was reporting on them, she recalled, so Truman took them out for drives in the country on Sundays when he had the day off. Kätchen would sit in the back with her dog, a chow called Tauila, and Truman would often ask her to be the lookout. "Don't be too obvious, but turn your head and see if you can see a big building in there," he told her on one occasion as they were driving on a road surrounded by woods. He was looking for signs that a new factory had been built to produce engines for the Luftwaffe.

When Kätchen traveled to The Hague by train with her friends the daughters of the Dutch ambassador, she observed the gun emplacements on the German side of the border with Holland—and promptly sent a postcard to her parents describing them. "People thought that he must have had spies in Berlin, but I was the only spy," Kätchen laughed, thinking of herself at about age twelve taking on that role.

But there was one riddle Truman realized early he would have trouble solving. For all his contacts in the army, he had few contacts with the Luftwaffe—and no more knowledge "of air corps organization and tactics than did the average American infantry officer," as he put it. He also had "negligible" knowledge of the technical side of air power. Captain Theodore Koenig, the assistant attaché who was supposed to monitor Germany's growing air capabilities, was a capable officer, but Truman was worried that his small team was poorly equipped to do so, forced to rely on "their wits alone" to make up for their lack of resources.

The urgency of such tasks was underscored by Hitler's push to reassert Germany's power, which Truman took extremely seriously. When German troops reoccupied the Rhineland in March 1936, reversing the demilitarization that had been mandated by the Treaty of Versailles, he rushed home. "How fast can you and Katchen get away from here?" he asked Kay. Looking around the apartment, she replied that it would probably take movers three days to pack up their things. "Three days!" Truman replied. "Thirty minutes is all you will have if the French react as they must. The bombers will be here in half an hour. Pack two suitcases. Tell Robert to put enough cans of gas in the car to take you to France." When Kay asked what he would do in that situation, he declared he would "stay with the embassy." Kay did as she was told, but the French failed to respond at all to Hitler's calculated gamble.

Two months later, Kay and Truman were having breakfast in their apartment when she pointed out a front-page story in the Paris edition of the *Herald Tribune*. It reported that Charles Lindbergh had visited an airplane factory in France. Over the next few days, Truman began wondering if the famous airman, whose transatlantic voyage had captured the imagination of people everywhere, couldn't gain the same kind of access to German airplane factories as he did to French ones. He checked with aides to Luftwaffe Commander-in-Chief Goering, and they reacted as he had hoped they would, saying that they would be pleased to show Lindbergh their combat units and factories. Truman then wrote a letter to Lindbergh on May 25, relaying this invitation. Smith had never met Lindbergh before, but he didn't hesitate to make a forceful case.

"I need hardly tell you that the present German air development is very imposing and on a scale which I believe is unmatched in the world," he wrote. Pointing out that the Luftwaffe's buildup had been shrouded in secrecy until recently, he added that the Germans had already demonstrated an increasing willingness to show more of what they were doing to Americans than to representatives of other countries. "General Goering has particularly exerted himself for friendly relations with the United States," he continued, emphasizing that the invitation was extended directly by the Luftwaffe commander and his Air Ministry. "From a purely American point of view, I consider your visit here would be of high patriotic benefit," Smith concluded. "I am certain they will go out of their way to show you even more than they will show us."

Smith's appeal to Lindbergh, who at that point was living with his wife, Anne, in England to escape the constant publicity about them in the United States following the kidnapping and murder of their son in 1932, would prove to be a fateful initiative. Lindbergh's response that he would be "extremely interested in seeing some of the German developments in both civil and military aviation" led to a series of visits to Germany—and charges that the aviator was sympathetic to Hitler's regime. But it would also prove to be just the kind of breakthrough in military intelligence-gathering that Smith had hoped for.

*       *       *

Smith was certainly aware that the Germans would seek to exploit Lindbergh's visit for propaganda purposes, and he hoped to keep the press away from the famous aviator as much as he could. But when the dates for the first visit were set for July 22 to August 1, 1936, that meant the last day coincided with the opening of the Olympics. The Germans insisted that Lindbergh attend the opening ceremonies as Goering's special guest. Smith understood this would attract just the kind of publicity he was hoping to avoid, but there was nothing he could do to prevent it. Instead, he focused on getting the Germans to agree to a long list of airplane factories, research facilities and Luftwaffe units that Lindbergh would be allowed to inspect, accompanied by either Captain Koenig or him. That way, the American attachés would be able to both view these installations and make valuable new contacts.

When the Lindberghs flew to Berlin in a private plane, they were greeted by Air Ministry officials, Lufthansa executives, other representatives of German aviation and the American military attachés. Truman and Kay had offered to put them up in their apartment, and the two couples immediately struck up a friendship. "Colonel Smith is alive, questioning, and talks well," Anne Morrow Lindbergh recorded in her diary. "She is observant, intelligent, and amusing."

Anne's diary entries reflected her newcomer's credulity about the new Germany ("The neatness, order, trimness, cleanliness . . . No sense of poverty . . . The sense of festivity, flags hung out"), but also contained numerous wry asides. At their official greeting, "Everyone is in uniform; lots of clicking of heels. 'Yah.' Clipped speech. They hardly notice me; very few women." When she is separated from Charles, who is driven off in an open car accompanied by German officers while she and Kay and Kätchen Smith "drive behind quietly" in a closed car, she notes: "Ah, yes—subservience of women in Germany!" And as for the formalities: "This raising of the arms business adds to the complications of life. It is done so often and takes so much room."

On the first full day of his visit, Charles was the guest of honor at an Air Club luncheon attended by senior German officials and American diplomats. Knowing that he would be asked to speak, he had prepared a text and showed it to Truman ahead of time. His message was a somber one. "We, who are in aviation, carry a heavy responsibility on our shoulders, for while we have been drawing the world closer together in peace, we have stripped the armor from every nation in war," he declared. "The army can no more stop an air attack than a suit of mail can stop a rifle bullet."

Air power had changed "defense into attack," and made it impossible "to protect our families with an army. Our libraries, our museums, every institution we value most, are laid bare to bombardment." All of which underscored the importance of how the "revolutionary change" of aviation would be handled. "It is our responsibility to make sure that in doing so, we do not destroy the very things which we wish to protect," Lindbergh asserted. His speech received widespread international coverage; the German press printed the text without offering any comments. According to Kay, "the Germans were not too pleased with the speech." Later, while discussing plans for Lindbergh's subsequent visits, one Air Ministry official added, "But no more speeches."

The most important social event during Lindbergh's visit was a formal luncheon at Goering's official residence on Wilhelmstrasse. It was attended by many of the most important aviation officials, including the legendary World War I pilot Ernst Udet. Arriving in a black Mercedes escorted by several motorcycles, the Lindberghs and the Smiths were treated as honored guests. For Truman, this was the first time he had the chance to talk with the Luftwaffe's chief—and he took full advantage of the occasion to observe him. "Goering showed many facets of his personality," he noted. "In turn he was magnetic, genial, vain, intelligent, frightening, and grotesque. Despite excessive corpulence, it could be seen that in his youth he had been both handsome and formidable looking."

Anne Lindbergh wrote that the forty-three-year-old Goering was "blazoned in white coat, with gold braid, good-looking, young, colossal—an inflated Alcibiades . . ." The host shook her hand but didn't look at her. Anne was seated on Goering's and his wife Emmy's right and Kay on their left, but the host focused all his attention on Charles. When he asked who had been his copilot and checked his instruments on one of his longer recent flights, Kay volunteered that it was Anne. In response, he used a familiar German expression that directly translates as: "I find that to laugh to death." In other words, he didn't believe her.

Lunch was an elaborate affair, with five different wines, one for each course, leaving Kay to marvel: "I have never tasted such nectar." But if this display suitably impressed Goering's guests, they were also curious about some of his stranger habits. Charles asked if they could see his pet lion cub, and the host happily obliged. They walked through large halls, decked out with old tapestries, illuminated as if they were pictures, and other artwork. Then they assembled in a library, and the doors were dramatically opened for the young lion. Kay estimated he was about three feet tall and four feet long, and "not too happy" when he saw the large gathering of people there. "I want you to see how nice my Augie is," Goering announced. "Come here Augie."

Goering was sitting on a sofa and the lion bounded to him, jumping up into his lap and licking his face. Kay kept a safe distance, with a table between her and this scene, but could clearly see what happened next. One of the German aides laughed. "The startled lion let loose a flood of yellow urine all over the snow white uniform!" Kay recalled. "A wave of red flowed up Goering's neck." The host pushed off the lion and jumped up, "his face red with anger, his blue eyes blazing." Emmy Goering rushed over, putting her arms around him. "Hermann, Hermann, it is like a little baby," she pleaded. "There are too many people!" Goering calmed down, conceding that the animal was like a little baby.

Truman had turned away, pretending not to witness all of this, and Anne had the same instinct. "I see and say nothing," she recorded in her diary. While the guests studiously admired the library's artwork, Goering rushed off to change. Returning, he was dressed "in a pongee suit, whiffs of eau de Cologne, and a diamond pin," Anne wrote.

Although Kay had worried that Goering would hold this incident against Truman and the others in the room, the luncheon started a relationship that allowed the military attaché to maintain contact with the Luftwaffe chief for the rest of his tour in Berlin. When Goering's lion grew too difficult to handle and was sent back to the Berlin Zoo, Truman arranged for his daughter to see the animal there and even hold it on her lap. In the photo of that scene, Kätchen is looking at the camera, flashing a weak smile while wearing gloves to avoid touching the lion directly. "I was scared to death," she recalls. "My father loved that picture."

The lunch wasn't the only occasion where Truman didn't know what to say in Goering's presence. As he recalled, during a meeting at the Air Club a year later, Goering kept going on about his devotion to Hitler. His eyes were moist when he declared: "Smith, there are only three truly great characters in all history: Buddha, Jesus Christ, and Adolf Hitler." Referring to himself as usual in the third person in his writing, Truman noted: "This remark reduced the military attaché to speechlessness."

But the real payoff of Lindbergh's visit came in the form of the daily visits to Germany's air installations. At Rostock, for instance, Lindbergh and Koenig, the assistant attaché, were allowed to inspect the new Heinkel He 111 medium bomber. Lindbergh concluded that it was comparable to British and American bombers, and superior to French ones. They also watched Udet fly the He 112, the prototype of a new fighter—and saw the plane disintegrate during a dive, forcing the famed pilot to parachute to safety. Still, based on what they saw of those and two other Heinkel planes (the He 70 observation plane, and the He 118 dive bomber), along with the company's modern factory for navy planes at Warnemünde, the Americans were suitably impressed. "I have never seen four planes, each distinct in type and built by one manufacturer, which were so well designed," Lindbergh told Smith when he returned to Berlin that evening.

Writing to the banker Harry Davison, Lindbergh pointed out that "we have nothing to compare in size to either the Heinkel or Junkers factories." In another letter, he professed he was struck by "a spirit in Germany which I have not seen in any other country," and the fact that the country's new rulers had already built up "tremendous strength."

Captain Koenig continued to be allowed to visit more airfields and factories after Lindbergh's first visit, which meant that his reports about Germany's air capabilities were packed with increasingly detailed rundowns. Based on such observations and the second visit by Lindbergh in October 1937, Smith reported to Washington that, if current trends continued, Germany would "obtain technical parity with the USA by 1941 or 1942." If the United States slowed down its program for any reason, he warned further, "German air superiority will be realized still sooner."

Goering may have deliberately exaggerated some of his claims to Lindbergh about Germany's capabilities, but his guest was inclined to take them all seriously. At a cocktail party hosted by Ambassador Dodd's wife, the society reporter Bella Fromm overheard Lindbergh telling Udet: "German aviation ranks higher than that in any other country. It is invincible." And German officials boasted that Lindbergh would prove to be "the best promotion campaign we could possibly invest in."

Smith and Koenig remained convinced that Lindbergh's visits provided them with crucial information about Hitler's aviation buildup, which they regularly conveyed to Washington. At the end of World War II when some columnists attacked Smith for his close ties to Lindbergh, FDR advisor Bernard Baruch wrote to then Chief of Staff General George Marshall on June 13, 1945: "How well and how timely were his [Smith's] warnings about German preparations! And what little attention we paid to them!"

Of course, the reason why the Smith-Lindbergh relationship became controversial in the first place was the political trajectory of the aviator and his wife that can be traced to that first visit to Germany, which ended with his brief appearance at the opening ceremony of the Olympics in a VIP seat. By inviting Lindbergh and rolling out the red carpet for him everywhere, the Nazis hoped to demonstrate the strengths of the new Germany—both political and military. They would continue to do so during his subsequent four visits before the outbreak of the war in 1939.

Right after their first visit to Germany in 1936, both Charles and Anne were full of the kind of impressions that their hosts had tried so hard to convey. In a letter to her mother from Copenhagen on August 5, Anne wrote: "I have had ten days in Berlin—bursting to talk about it . . . The feeling that one was right in the center of the volcano of Europe . . ." She described the shock of seeing in person what she had been viewing through "the strictly puritanical view at home that dictatorships are of necessity wrong, evil, unstable, and no good can come of them, combined with the funny-paper view of Hitler as a clown."

As for the real picture, as Anne saw it, "there is no question of the power, unity, and purposefulness of Germany. It is terrific. I have never in my life been so conscious of such a *directed* force. It is thrilling when seen manifested in the energy, pride, and morale of the people—especially the young people." But Anne admitted this unity could also be terrifying as "a weapon made by one man but also to be used by one man." Hitler, she added, "is like an inspired religious leader, and as such fanatical—a visionary who really wants the best for his country." She pointed out many things she disliked about the new Germany: "their treatment of the Jews, their brute-force manner, their stupidity, their rudeness . . ." But she concluded "it could be a force for good in the world" if only the world would seek to acknowledge Germany's new rulers, turning them "in the right direction" rather than ignoring or insulting them.

Also from Denmark, Charles wrote to Truman: "While I still have many reservations, I have come away with a feeling of great admiration for the German people." As for Hitler, Lindbergh wrote in a letter to the banker Harry Davison, "he is undoubtedly a great man, and I believe he has done much for the German people." While conceding that Hitler and the German people exhibited fanaticism, he added: "It is less than I expected . . ." And many of Hitler's accomplishments would have been impossible "without some fanaticism."

The event that would cement Lindbergh's reputation as pro-Nazi took place on October 18, 1938, during the flyer's third visit. Hugh Wilson, who had recently returned to Germany to take up the post of ambassador, hosted a stag dinner that included Goering and other German aviation officials and experts. When Goering arrived with his aides, he greeted Wilson and then, with the ambassador at his side, made straight for Lindbergh. Holding a small red box in his hand, the Luftwaffe chief made a short speech in German and awarded Lindbergh the Service Cross of the German Eagle, one of the highest decorations for civilians. As Wilson confirmed later in a letter to Lindbergh, both of them were caught by surprise by this award, which was given for his services to aviation. Truman Smith, who was also present, noted there was "no possibility" for Lindbergh to have turned down the decoration. "To have done so would have been a personal affront to Ambassador

Wilson, his host for the evening, and to Minister Goering, who in a sense was a host in Germany," he wrote.

Lindbergh's subsequent vocal campaign to keep the United States out of the war in Europe, his involvement in the isolationist America First movement, and his conviction that the Soviet Union represented the real threat to European civilization—and that, in a war between those two powers, "a victory by Germany's European people would be preferable to one by Russia's semi-Asiatic Soviet Union"—only confirmed how well he had been played by the Nazis. His critics were right that he had become, in effect, an apologist for Hitler. Ironically, though, the flyer's political blindness also allowed him to help Smith and his team gather more data on the Luftwaffe's modernization and ambitions than any of their counterparts in other embassies. For his part, Lindbergh was pleased to be part of this effort; as he saw it, this information on Germany's growing strength only bolstered his argument that the United States should avoid any new conflict with that country.

Not all of the intelligence Smith gathered was on target—and, by his own admission, he overlooked the early signs of German plans for rocketry. He also made some erroneous predictions about the degree of disaffection between the Nazis and the military, and certainly about "Hitler's realistic and reticent foreign policy," as he put it in 1937. But on balance, the regular air intelligence reports Smith sent to Washington demonstrated his team's accomplishments. And Smith's reputation as the best-informed attaché in Berlin on the Luftwaffe was fully merited, something he always stressed was only thanks to the fact that Lindbergh had cooperated with him so extensively and opened so many doors.

At a reception at the British Embassy in 1938, Cardinal Pacelli, the Vatican secretary of state who had served earlier as the papal nuncio in Germany, sent an aide over to Smith asking him to join him. "I was astonished when . . . he quizzed me in perfect English as to the state of readiness of the Luftwaffe," he recalled. "One of his questions that I remember distinctly was, what did we Americans think of Germany's new two-motored fighter: the Messerschmitt 110." A year later, Pacelli was elected pope and took the name Pius XII.

\* \* \*

Of all the people Hitler surrounded himself with, Putzi Hanfstaengl was a special case—and he liked it that way. It wasn't just the fact that his mother was an American or that he had gone to Harvard that made him different from most of the Nazi leader's entourage. He would later explain to everyone and anyone that he had wanted to educate and civilize Hitler, but unfortunately he was thwarted at every turn by the radicals around him. "I could feel that the rabid extremists of the Party had got their claws into him again and the arguments of the more reasonable of us were constantly being countered," he wrote in a typical passage of his memoir.

Note the wording: "the more reasonable of us." What he really meant was that he was the only reasonable one. When John Toland, the Hitler biographer, interviewed Hanfstaengl in 1970, he asked him whether there were any intelligent men in Hitler's circle. "No!" Putzi shouted.

Hanfstaengl would also claim that his misgivings about Hitler's leadership grew steadily. "It would be reasonable to ask why, in view of all my misgivings about the character and intentions of Hitler and his circle, I continued for so long in association with them," he wrote. His answer: "I was an idealistic National-Socialist, I make no bones about it."

While many Americans in Berlin, especially the correspondents who relied on him to gain access to Hitler, viewed Hanfstaengl as a highly useful contact—and some, like the AP's Lochner, considered him to be a friend—others were more suspicious and antagonistic. Even Wiegand, the veteran Hearst correspondent who had often taken advantage of Hanfstaengl's interventions to get to his boss, found himself in tense exchanges with Putzi after Hitler came to power. In a memo dated October 23, 1933, Wiegand wrote that Hanfstaengl complained to him that Hitler was holding him responsible for the fact that the American correspondent was now "one of my most bitter opponents." There were also tensions over money; from Wiegand's correspondence, it's clear Putzi had taken fees for articles he may have either contributed or helped on in the past, although he wanted to return some of the money after Hitler came to power.

William Randolph Hearst took an active interest in Wiegand's memos and letters about Hanfstaengl. The propagandist "probably likes to make a little money occasionally for news features," he wrote Wiegand on November 20, 1934. "That is not a crime. The thing I think is unfortunate is the fact that he is such an extremist and may not be giving his boss the best advice on these religious situations. First the Jews were alienated, then the Catholics, and finally many Protestant sects." Still, he urged his correspondent to be patient. "Do not be displeased with Dr. Hanfstaengl and others in the Government who seem antagonistic," he wrote. "Give them good advice and try to guide them towards a greater liberality which will gain approval both at home and abroad."

By then, many of the Berlin correspondents no longer nurtured those kinds of illusions. As for Putzi, the reporters who were new to Berlin were particularly scathing in their evaluation. Observing him at the Nuremberg party rally in September 1934, Shirer described him as "an immense, high-strung, incoherent clown who does not often fail to remind us that he is part American and graduated from Harvard." But he admitted that many of the American and British correspondents "rather like him despite his clownish stupidity."

When it came to Hanfstaengl's postwar assertions that he had disagreed with the Nazis' anti-Semitism, they were flatly contradicted by his behavior. On numerous occasions, he had lashed out at outspoken American diplomats and correspondents, like George Messersmith and Edgar Mowrer, by labeling them as Jews. Bella Fromm ran into Putzi at the entrance at the Dodds' farewell party for Messersmith on May 12, 1934.

"I wonder why we were asked today," Hanfstaengl told her. "All this excitement about Jews. Messersmith is one. So is Roosevelt. The party detests them."

"Dr. Hanfstaengl, we've discussed this before," the Jewish reporter replied. "You don't have to put on that kind of an act with me."

"All right," he said. "Even if they are Aryan, you'd never know it from their actions."

Putzi ended their exchange by offering her a fruit drop. "Have one. They are made especially for the *Führer*."

Fromm had enjoyed eating similar fruit drops as a child and she politely took one. Then, as she was about to put it in her mouth, she noticed the swastika on it. "Try as I would to make the hideous mark disappear, it remained leering at me until I had finished the drop," she noted.

A month later, Hanfstaengl made a much-publicized visit to the United States to attend his twenty-fifth class reunion at Harvard. The news sparked heated controversy on and off campus. A committee of Jewish organizations argued that Americans should show "no discourtesy of any kind" toward him, but columnist Heywood Broun warned of "bloody riots" during his visit and called for his deportation as an undesirable alien. Noting that Broun was a class ahead of him at Harvard, Putzi dismissed his attacks as "class jealousy." Talking to reporters who met him as he disembarked in New York, he was equally dismissive of questions about German Jews. "The situation of the Jew in Germany is fairly normal," he said. When some Jewish reporters asked for five minutes to discuss the issue further, he brushed them off.

While protesters gathered a short distance from his ship and shouted "Down with Hitler," the on-campus debate was conducted in more muted tones. Benjamin Halpern, a Jewish student, wrote a letter to the *Harvard Crimson* titled "Heil Hitler" questioning the initial decision by Elliott Carr Cutler, the chief marshal at the reunion, to ask Hanfstaengl to serve as his aide during the ceremonies. Seeing the backlash, Cutler backed off that idea and asked Hanfstaengl to come as an ordinary alumnus. Still, the *Crimson* appeared to reflect the prevailing view on campus about the whole affair. "To object to the presence of a Harvard man among other Harvard men in any capacity, on purely political grounds, is an extremely childish thing to do," it editorialized.

While Putzi would find it increasingly difficult in the next couple of years to convince Americans in Berlin that he was the reasonable face of the regime, he also was encountering problems with Hitler and his inner circle. The Nazi leader was contemptuous of Putzi's assertions that he knew how to handle relations with the United States in order to prevent it from opposing Germany. When the Roosevelt Administration established diplomatic relations with the Soviet Union in November 1933, Hitler told him: "There you are, Hanfstaengl, your friends the Americans have teamed up with the Bolsheviks." Earlier, Hitler had told him bluntly: "I see America from where I sit much more clearly than you have ever known it."

Putzi would later claim that, in the first period of Hitler's reign, he began to notice its absurdities and how detached from reality his entourage was. Returning from his Harvard reunion to the aftermath of the Night of the Long Knives, the bloody purge of the SA leaders and assorted other targets of the Nazis, he was summoned to Heiligendamm, the Baltic Sea resort where Hitler, Goebbels and others were vacationing. "It was really like something out of Lewis Carroll, a mad hatter's luncheon party," he wrote. "With the whole of Germany groaning under this atmosphere of murder, fear and suspicion, there was Magda Goebbels doing the honors in an airy summer dress, with several other young women at the table, even one or two from the aristocratic families . . ."

It was around this time, Putzi added, that he came to realize that, once Hitler was ensconced in power, "the demon had entered into him." But even with the benefit of hindsight, he blamed Goebbels and others for pushing Hitler to the point of no return, and admitted he continued to nurture the hope that he could moderate his excesses. Amid all the self-justification, Hanfstaengl's real concern was much less policy than his own position. Putzi could see it was weakening rapidly. Others were openly criticizing and mocking him, and Hitler didn't seem interested in doing anything about it. The invitations to play the piano for the Nazi leader were becoming less frequent.

When Truman and Kay Smith returned to Berlin in 1935, they visited Putzi in his small apartment, which was in back of the Chancellery. The living room was dominated by a large bust of Hitler and a grand piano, and Truman casually hung his hat on Hitler's head as he walked in. "Putz hastily snatched it off," Kay recalled, pointing out that he treated this as bad manners on Truman's part, not something to joke about. Over coffee and cake, the old acquaintances caught up on their news. "It was plain that all was not rosy between Putz and Goebbels," Kay continued. "Putz intimated that Goebbels was jealous of his . . . influence over Hitler and was keeping him away from Hitler."

The jealousy factor was almost certainly overblown, since Hanfstaengl's influence had been on the wane for some time. That was typical Putzi talk—making himself out to be more important than he was. But there was certainly truth in his assertion that Goebbels had no use for a competing propagandist, and there was increasing evidence that he wanted to cut him out of the inner circle completely.

Hanfstaengl claimed that he considered resigning, but that others talked him out of it. More likely, he clung to every shred of power and influence as long as possible, even when his foreign press office was unceremoniously moved further away from the Chancellery. For nearly two years, he wasn't invited to any events with Hitler at all. At the end of the last luncheon he ever attended with him, Hitler asked him to go to the piano "to play that thing of yours." When Putzi asked him what piece he meant, he said, "Your funeral march." Hanfstaengl played it with, as he recalled, "a sense of foreboding."

In 1936, Putzi felt that he lost another connection to Hitler when his wife, Helen, divorced him. She was the American woman who had possibly prevented Hitler from committing suicide after the Beer Hall Putsch, and who had been the object of his clumsy affection in those Munich days. Helen had long put up with her philandering husband but refused to join him in Berlin—and eventually decided to make their de facto separation permanent. Like Putzi, Helen would later claim that she had grown disaffected with Hitler and the Nazis, especially after the Night of the Long Knives. But even when discussing her feelings with John Toland in 1971, she never mentioned anything else she objected to, not even the Holocaust, and remained fascinated by her association with this historic figure. "Yes, he was extraordinary," she declared. "After all, when you think of a man from very modest background, to put himself on the map so to speak, he was an extraordinary man. Yes, he was."

After not seeing Helen for a long time, Hitler once asked an acquaintance of hers what had happened to her. When he learned she had divorced Putzi, he declared, "Oh, fine, fine. I'll send a telegram congratulating her." Then, he added, "Oh no, that won't do." Helen, who provided this account, was visibly pleased that Germany's leader was still thinking about her even after he had attained absolute power. She returned to the United States in 1938, where she spent the war years; still, Hitler appeared to hold a special place in her memory until the end of her life.

On August 17, 1932, three American correspondents interviewed Hitler at Berchtesgaden. From left on the porch of his Alpine retreat: Hearst's Karl von Wiegand; famed broadcaster H. V. Kaltenborn; Hitler; AP Berlin bureau chief Louis Lochner.

Wiegand had a separate interview and quickly emerged complaining: "I get nothing out of him." After the two others had a longer session, Kaltenborn concluded that Hitler "has no capacity for logical consecutive thought." He added: "I could not see how a man of his type, a plebeian Austrian of limited mentality, could ever gain the allegiance of a majority of Germans."

Less than six months later, Hitler took power.

At Hoboken's City Hall in 1912 or 1913, Helen Niemeyer, the daughter of German immigrants, dressed up as "Liberty" holding the American flag. She later married Ernst Hanfstaengl (opposite page). The couple then moved to Munich, where they befriended Hitler.

Hitler developed a particular fascination with Helen. After the Beer Hall putsch of 1923, he took refuge in her home. As the police closed in to arrest him, he despaired that all was lost and picked up a revolver. Helen grabbed it from him, possibly preventing his suicide. He went on trial in early 1924. Below, General Erich Ludendorff, center, Hitler and the other defendants on April 1, 1924.

PERNET DR. WEBER KRIEBEL LUDENDORFF HITLER RÖHM WAGNER
FRICK BRUCKNER
PHOTO: HOFFMANN

4

Ernst "Putzi" Hanfstaengl, who had an American mother and a German father, became Hitler's propagandist. Above, Hitler and Putzi (right) on a campaign swing during the 1930 elections.

Below, Putzi at his 25th reunion at Harvard in 1934. Those who protested his presence for political reasons, the *Crimson* wrote, were exhibiting "childish" behavior.

5

6

In 1922, Karl von Wiegand was the first American correspondent to interview and write about Hitler, describing him as the leader of a rising "Fascisti" movement and as "a magnetic speaker having also exceptional organizing genius." But in the mid-1920s when Germany appeared to be recovering and the Nazis faded from prominence, readers were far more interested in stories like the ones Wiegand and fellow Hearst correspondent Lady Drummond-Hay (above) filed about the first trans-Atlantic flight of the Zeppelin, issued in a special booklet by *The Chicago Herald and Examiner* (below).

*The* First Trans-Oceanic
## VOYAGE
*of an*
## AIR LINER
*By*
**Karl H. Von Wiegand
Lady Drummond Hay**

Issued By The Circulation Dept. of the Chicago Herald and Examiner

7

8

9

*Chicago Daily News* correspondent Edgar Mowrer (above) sounded the alarm about Hitler and the Nazis early and often. Fellow correspondent Dorothy Thompson, here with Sinclair Lewis in 1928 after they were married, totally misjudged Hitler during her interview with him in November 1931. She was struck by his "startling insignificance." Later, she radically revised her views.

The Brownshirts (below, in 1926) were soon a rising force. After Hitler took power, Mowrer was threatened and driven out of Germany on September 1, 1933.

10

11

On July13, 1933, William Dodd took the train from Hamburg to Berlin to take up his post as U.S. ambassador. President Roosevelt had tapped the University of Chicago history professor for the job, telling him: "I want an American liberal in Germany as a standing example." Here Dodd is shown arriving in the German capital with his wife and daughter Martha (right). Martha quickly scandalized the embassy with her procession of lovers.

12

From left, publisher Heinrich Maria Ledig-Rowohlt, Martha Dodd, Mildred Harnack and German novelist Hans Fallada at the Fallada farm on May 27, 1934. Initially enchanted by Hitler, Martha would end up spying for Moscow. Her friend Mildred, along with her German husband Arvid Harnack, would become members of the "Red Orchestra" spy ring. Harnack was the only American woman executed by the Gestapo.

George Messersmith, U.S. Consul General in Berlin from 1930 to 1934, went on to become the ambassador to Austria (left, with Austrian State Secretary General Wilhelm Zehner in Vienna). Messersmith was a fervent opponent of the Nazis, issuing increasingly dire warnings about their intentions.

14

Truman Smith (above) served twice as a military attaché in the U.S. Embassy in Berlin. In 1922, he became the first American diplomat to meet Hitler, recording his astute impressions in a notebook. On his second tour, he came up with the plan to have Hermann Goering's Air Ministry invite Charles Lindbergh (below, with General Erhard Milch) to Germany. As Smith hoped, Lindbergh was granted access to the Luftwaffe's airfields and factories, providing valuable intelligence that he freely shared with the military attaché. This part of the Lindbergh story was soon overshadowed by the aviator's pro-German leanings and his campaign to keep the U.S. out of the war.

15

Kätchen, the daughter of Truman and Kay Smith, with Hermann Goering's lion after the Luftwaffe commander dispatched the animal to the Berlin Zoo. Its offense, as witnessed by both the Lindberghs and the Smiths: urinating on Goering's white uniform when he was showing his pet off to his guests. Kätchen recalls that she was "scared to death" while holding the lion, and wore gloves so she wouldn't touch it. Today, the photo still hangs on her refrigerator door in Connecticut.

17

Thomas Wolfe in Berlin in 1935 (top). The writer was treated like a literary superhero, and initially he reciprocated the warm feelings of the Germans. But by his next visit in 1936, he became much more aware of the horrors of the Nazi regime, vividly describing them in his novella *I Have a Thing to Tell You.*

At the 1936 Olympics in Berlin, track star Jesse Owens (below) was the most popular athlete, despite the Nazis' racist ideology.

18

After the *Anschluss*, the annexation and occupation of Austria in March 1938, a triumphant Hitler received a hero's welcome in Vienna on April 9. Here he is led by the Lord Mayor; Rudolf Hess and Joseph Goebbels are walking behind Hitler. American journalists like William Shirer were stunned by how quickly Vienna was decked out in Nazi flags and took on the look of "any German city in the Reich."

In March 1938, former President Herbert Hoover visited Berlin (top, with Reichsbank President Hjalmer Schacht and U.S. Ambassador Hugh Wilson on right). Meeting Hitler, he was subjected to Hitler's usual tirades. Nonetheless, Hoover continued to argue that "we must live with other nations." Wilson, the last American ambassador to Nazi Germany, agreed with those sentiments.

Below, Britain's Prime Minister Neville Chamberlain is greeted by Hitler on September 15, 1938.
His visit produced the infamous Munich agreement that doomed Czechoslovakia.

22

On November 9, 1938, Germany erupted in the frenzy of anti-Semitic violence known as Kristallnacht. Jews flocked to the U.S. Embassy, begging for visas, as consular official Charles Thayer recalled, in the hopes that they could be saved "from the madness that had seized the city." Above, smashed windows of Jewish shops in Magdeburg.

Below, German troops search the rubble in Danzig after Hitler launched World War II by invading Poland on September 1, 1939.

23

24

On September 16, 1940, while Hitler's armies were on the march in Europe, President Roosevelt signed America's first peacetime draft legislation (above, with Secretary of War Henry Stimson on left and Army Chief of Staff Gen. George Marshall second from right).

American correspondents in Germany were already covering the war. Below, from right, the AP's Louis Lochner, the Propaganda Ministry's Karl Boehmer and the International News Service's Pierre Huss.

25

William Shirer (broadcasting for CBS in 1940) was one of the most discerning American correspondents, anti-Nazi from the beginning.

After Germany declared war on the United States on December 11, 1941, U.S. diplomats and reporters based in Berlin were interned in a deserted spa hotel in Bad Nauheim, outside of Frankfurt. The AP's Angus Thuermer reads in his room, while other Americans pass the time in the main lobby.

29

On May 12, 1942, the Americans were released from Bad Nauheim in exchange for the release of the German diplomats and journalists who had been interned in far more luxurious conditions at the Greenbrier, the plush resort hotel in West Virginia. Here, the Americans are arriving at the Bad Nauheim train station where they would begin their journey to Lisbon—and freedom.

Seeing how tenuous his position had become, Putzi began smuggling out gold and platinum objects to London. He claimed he also helped some of the victims of the Nazis, winning the release of the daughter of a German-American couple who had been put in a concentration camp in Saxony for criticizing the regime. Above all, though, he kept looking nervously over his shoulder, often sleeping at friends' apartments and keeping a valid passport with visas to several countries in his pocket.

According to Putzi's dramatic account, he was in his Munich apartment on February 8, 1937, when the phone rang. The Chancellery was requesting that he report urgently to Berlin. A special plane was waiting to take him there. Putzi was delighted that he might be returned to favor. Although the special plane never materialized, he caught a Lufthansa flight to Berlin, where he reported to the Chancellery. There, he was told he was to fly immediately to Spain to help German correspondents who were covering the civil war. Putzi couldn't understand the urgency, and complained that this could at least wait till he celebrated his fiftieth birthday two days later. But the officials insisted he stick with the plan, and one of them assured him that, if he did well in Spain, he would be back in Hitler's good graces. They knew that this was what Putzi still craved.

Informed that he was on a secret mission that would last five or six weeks, Putzi was rushed to Staaken Airfield where he was to board a military plane. Along the way, one of his escorts told him that he would use the name of August Lehman and would pose as a painter and interior decorator in Spain. A cameraman recorded their trip to the airport. By this point, Hanfstaengl was deeply suspicious, and he became even more alarmed when Colonel Kastner, the commandant at the airfield, handed him a parachute, ordering him to put it on.

Once aloft, the pilot, who introduced himself as Captain Frodel, called him up to the copilot's seat. He had recognized who "August Lehman" really was and asked him what instructions he had. When Putzi told him he was to report to a general in Salamanca, Frodel offered him some chilling news. "Herr Hanfstaengl, I have no orders to take you to Salamanca," he said. "My instructions are to drop you over the Red lines between Barcelona and Madrid."

Putzi was stunned. "That is a death sentence," he protested. "Who gave you such orders?"

Frodel told him he received them right before he took off, and they were signed by Goering. When Putzi protested further, Frodel added, "I was told that you had volunteered for this mission."

As Hanfstaengl described it, the rest of this episode played out like a thriller, without the pyrotechnics. After only about half an hour, one of the engines made a noise and Frodel turned it off. Casting Putzi a meaningful look, the pilot told him that there was something wrong. "I shall have to put down and have it seen to," he said.

They landed at a quiet airfield near Leipzig, where the mechanics had already left for the day. Over drinks in the canteen, Frodel announced that a car would be ready soon to take them into town since there was no hope of getting the plane repaired until the next day. After ordering another round of drinks, Putzi said his stomach was bothering him and slipped out. It was dark, and he quickly made his way to the road near the airfield, and, meeting a peasant woman, discovered that there was a train station nearby. From there, he took a train to Leipzig, where he spent the night before hopping a morning train to Munich. He spent only about an hour in his hometown before boarding a third train, this time to Zurich. It was his fiftieth birthday when he arrived there, and he wouldn't return to Germany until after the war.

Did the top Nazis really concoct such an elaborate plan to arrange the death of someone who had been so eager to serve Hitler for so long? Goering wrote to Hanfstaengl later that the whole affair was "a harmless joke" aimed at getting him to reconsider "some rather over-audacious utterances you have made," and he would be perfectly safe if he returned to Germany. David Marwell, currently the director of the Museum of Jewish Heritage in New York, extensively researched this incident in Germany and concluded that the entire scheme was indeed "an elaborate hoax"; its purpose, he maintained, was to humiliate Hanfstaengl rather than to kill him. But Putzi always remained convinced that he had narrowly escaped a death plot.

Back in Berlin, some of the American residents were puzzled by Hanfstaengl's abrupt disappearance. In previous years, Putzi had hosted a Washington's Birthday party in his apartment, inviting people like Ambassador Dodd, Truman Smith and Louis Lochner, along with a few Germans. The invitations had already gone out for the party on February 22 before the host's disappearance, and it was only a day or two before that his secretary called the invited guests to say the party was canceled, without giving any explanation. Lochner suspected Putzi was in trouble and began picking up strands of the story, including reports that he had managed to avoid a plane ride over Spain that probably would have ended badly.

At a cocktail party hosted by Martha Dodd on March 17, Lochner and other guests speculated about Putzi's whereabouts. "There's nothing mysterious about Hanfstaengl," an assistant naval attaché declared. "Why, I ran into him at the bar of the Hotel Bauer au Lac in Zurich only yesterday."

Lochner hastily left the party and placed a call to the Zurich hotel. "How did you find out I was here?" Putzi asked. Lochner replied with the standard line that a newsman never reveals his sources. Since he already had his story, it gave the AP correspondent huge satisfaction that Hanfstaengl refused all calls after that.


By the time that Putzi made his escape, Ambassador Dodd was nearing the end of a four-year tour in Berlin that had proven more frustrating than productive. His early alienation from Hitler and his regime was fully understandable—and, in many ways, morally commendable. But it didn't help his effectiveness as an envoy. After the Night of the Long Knives, he wrote in his diary that he would try to avoid meeting Hitler whenever he could. "I certainly would not ask to see any man who has committed a score of murders the last few days," he wrote on July 4, 1934. And again and again throughout his four years, he ruminated about whether it made sense for him to stay in a post when he could see no hope of more positive developments.

At the State Department, his superiors were often frustrated as well. "What in the world is the use of having an ambassador who refuses to speak to the government to which he is accredited?" complained Undersecretary of State William Phillips. Since Dodd did maintain some contacts with German officials, this was overstating things—but not by much. And the scholar-turned-envoy didn't help his case by his open disdain for many of the State Department officials he had to deal with and foreign service officers in general. As he rightly noted, they acted like pampered members of an exclusive fraternity, the products of privilege and Ivy League schools. They were highly critical of an outsider like himself, and he made no effort to temper their feelings.

In fact, Dodd reinforced them by almost obsessively pushing for budget cuts, including shorter cables. His embassy did produce numerous well-done reports during his tenure, including some lengthy ones; they demonstrated a deeper understanding of the Nazi regime than the reports of many other missions, including those of France and Britain. But by penny-pinching, he contributed to the impression that there was a "telegram deficiency," as he acknowledged. He argued that he was only trying to eliminate three- or four-page telegrams when "one or two hundred words" would do, adding defensively: "I do not send what I think I should have to contradict in a week. This is my explanation. It may not be what the Department likes."

Dodd wasn't popular with his military attachés either. Truman Smith described him as "a historian of repute, and a pacifist." According to Smith, he showed "a marked distaste for military matters" and a lack of interest in the work of the military attachés or in the rapid expansion of the German Army and Air Force. "The question perforce arises with respect to Dr. Dodd's fitness for the ambassadorial post in Germany at this particular period in history," Smith wrote later. In her unpublished memoir, Kay dispensed with any diplomatic wording. Claiming that Dodd's pacifist beliefs prompted him to forbid Smith or other attachés to appear in uniform when they attended official ceremonies together, she declared: "I have seldom met a man for whom I developed so much contempt."

Dodd hardly deserved that level of opprobrium. And as his biographer Robert Dallek and others have pointed out, it would be impossible to argue convincingly that a different ambassador, no matter how skillful, could have produced better results. But Dodd's final period in Berlin was marked by his acute sense of disappointment—and the knowledge that many of the people he worked with were disappointed in him. By the end of 1936, he was considering resigning again—and openly saying that "four years' service is enough." After a two-and-a-half-month visit to the United States to deal with his deteriorating health, he returned to Germany in late October 1937. "In Berlin once more," he wrote in his diary on October 29. "What can I do?"

But when it really came time to leave, Dodd changed his mind, arguing that his term should be extended. By then, Roosevelt was no longer in sympathy with the envoy he had dispatched to Berlin in 1933, still hoping the new regime might be influenced by a convinced democrat like the historian from the University of Chicago. On one initiative of his envoy, the president was even in basic agreement with Hitler: neither leader had the least patience for Dodd's push for a new world peace conference.

Dodd left Berlin for the last time on December 29, 1937, nurturing a sense of grievance that, in the end, he was forced to resign sooner than he wanted to. "There were and are still officials in the State Department who do not like me or the things I stand for," he wrote. After retiring to his farm in Virginia, his physical condition kept declining. When World War II broke out, the man who was often labeled a pacifist wrote to Roosevelt: "Hitler intends to conquer the whole world. If we do not join England and France, we shall have a hard time." He died on February 9, 1940, at the age of seventy, long before his country joined the fight.

Dodd hadn't left Berlin alone; his family went with him. That, of course, included his daughter Martha, whose conversion to a new cause had prompted her to take some extraordinary actions during the latter part of her stay in Berlin. Although Boris Vinogradov, her lover, was recalled to Moscow, she arranged to meet him there and in Paris—and, when he was transferred to the Soviet Embassy in Warsaw, she visited him there as well. But it wasn't only romance that kept her connected to the Soviet regime. In the memoir she wrote of her Berlin days, she discreetly commented: "The Russians of the Embassy in Berlin were, on the whole, charming people—natural, informal, sprightly and clever."

One of the charming people was an agent named Bukhartsev, the Berlin correspondent for the Soviet daily *Izvestia*. By most accounts, he took over from Vinogradov as her handler for the NKVD, the Soviet secret police and spy agency. According to a NKVD memo, "Martha argues that she is a convinced partisan of the Communist Party and the USSR." In January 1936, Bukhartsev reported that he had met with Martha several times and that she "frankly expressed her willingness to help the Soviet Embassy with her information. Now she is studying hard the theory of communism [and] 'Matters of Leninism' by Stalin. Her teacher is [Arvid] Harnack to whom she goes often."

Harnack was the German husband of Mildred Harnack, Martha's American friend, a teacher who had also enlisted in the Communist cause. Like Martha, Mildred had to be careful to hide her allegiances in Germany—but, unlike the daughter of the ambassador, she would remain in Berlin, with fateful consequences.

Although Martha was hardly a patient, faithful lover, she still had her heart set on Vinogradov. On March 14, 1937, she petitioned the Soviet government, saying "we have agreed to ask official permission to marry." Two weeks later in Moscow, she met with the head of the NKVD's Foreign Department, Abram Slutsky. At his request, she prepared a statement elaborating on her willingness to serve the Kremlin: "It goes without saying that my services of any kind and at any time are proposed to the party for use at its discretion. Currently, I have access mainly to the personal, confidential correspondence of my father with the U.S. State Department and the U.S. President." It was clear her father had no idea what she was doing.

Then she switched course in her statement, pointing out that she had lost almost all personal connections with German society, and that her extensive diplomatic contacts yielded meager results. In other words, her usefulness was ending in Berlin. "Is the information which I get from my father, who is hated in Germany and who occupies an isolated position among foreign diplomats and therefore has no access to any secret information, important enough for me to remain in Germany?" she asked rhetorically. "Couldn't I conduct more valuable work in America or in some European organization such as the International Conference for Peace . . . ?"

She also noted that, while she was trying to get her father's tour in Berlin extended, it was likely to end soon. With that in mind, she was positioning herself to help Moscow elsewhere. And, at the same time, she clearly hoped that might still bring her and Vinogradov back together.

But after the Dodds returned to the United States, Vinogradov was recalled to Moscow from Warsaw. It was 1938, and Stalin's purges were at their height. Among the prime targets: anyone who had contacts with foreigners. It made no difference if that person was carrying out direct orders from Moscow. Martha's lover was arrested. Not knowing his fate, Martha responded to a letter he wrote to her at the NKVD's behest. She wrote back in a jaunty tone on July 9. "Boris, dear! Finally I got your letter . . . Are you happy? Did you find a girl you can love instead of me?" she asked. Then she added: "You haven't had time yet to know that I really got married. On June 16, I married an American whom I love very much."

Vinogradov never read that letter. Before it arrived, he was executed.

# "Uniforms and Guns"

I n the summer of 1936, just after graduating from Tulane University in New Orleans, Howard K. Smith was working at a local newspaper, earning $15 a week, when lightning struck: he won $100 for a short story he had written. Feeling flush but still savvy enough to calculate where his windfall would support him the longest, he decided to go to Germany. At that moment, Germany was the cheapest country in Europe for an American, he noted. His young friends in New Orleans, none of whom could afford such a voyage, had often discussed what the new regime in Germany represented, "whether it was workable, if it afforded solutions to problems we had in America," as Smith recalled. In essence, he explained, they were asking: "Was Nazi Germany a Good Thing or a Bad Thing?"

While their liberal arts education made Smith and his friends inclined to disapprove of dictatorships, the Great Depression had shaken many core beliefs, and they felt that everything was debatable. Thus, Smith embarked on what he dubbed his "fact-finding" journey with an open mind. "Like a political Descartes, I tried to wash all preconceptions and prejudices out of my mind," he declared. Hiring himself out as a deckhand on a cargo ship crossing the Atlantic, he experienced a common reaction to his first glimpses of the country he had set out to examine. "Germany captivated me before I set foot inside it," he wrote. "Crawling up the Weser from Bremerhaven, we passed one fancy-tickling miniature town after another, all spotless with rows of toy houses and big, sunny beer gardens along the river bank."

Looking back at his first exposure to Nazi Germany, Smith, who would much later become a famed TV anchor back home, reported not just on the country but on how his reactions to it changed over time. Based on the evolution of his thinking during what turned into a nearly six-year sojourn in Germany, most of it as a junior reporter for United Press, Smith developed a theory about how Americans and other foreigners tended to evolve in their thinking about that country. He broke the process down into four stages:

"On first glance, Germany was overwhelmingly attractive, and first impressions disarmed many a hardy anti-Nazi before he could lift his lance for attack," he wrote. "Germany was clean, it was neat, a truly handsome land. Its big cities were cleaner than big cities ought, by custom, to be ... The impression was one of order, cleanliness and prosperity—and this has been of immense propaganda value to the Nazis." On what he called "my first magic day in Bremen," a dockworker pointed out to him that Germans were "neat, clean and able to do an amazing lot with amazingly little long before Hitler came to power." The clear message was that visitors were wrong to credit all of what they saw to the new regime.

But, in most cases, they did exactly that. Some visitors never got beyond this stage, which, according to Smith, "bespeaks the sensitivity of a rhinoceros's hide and the profundity of a tea-saucer." He mentioned a group of American schoolgirls he saw in Heidelberg as perfect examples. "The principal obstacle in the way of their further progress was, I think, the fact that German men are handsome and wear uniforms."

During stage two, the most noticeable characteristic of Nazi Germany was "uniforms and guns; the amazing extent to which Germany, even then, was prepared for war. It took my breath away." The proliferation of men in uniforms—*homo militaris*, as Smith put it—suddenly transformed Nazi rearmament into a concrete reality. But visitors at stage two were titillated by what they observed. "Or, more than that, it was downright exciting," Smith admitted. He watched from a window in Nuremberg "a broad undulating river of ten, twenty thousand men in uniform, stamping in unison down the cobble-stone streets below, flooding the valley between the houses with a marching song so loud the windows rattled, and so compelling your very heart adopted its military rhythm."

As the mesmerizing spectacles of militarism began to loosen their hold, Smith continued, many visitors would progress to stage three, which was less passive and involved coming to some unnerving conclusions. "You began to grasp that what was happening was that young humans, millions of them, were being trained to act merely upon reflexes," he wrote. All this drilling was aimed at teaching them "to kill, as a reflex ... On terse commands which altered their personalities more neatly than Doctor Jekyll became Mr. Hyde, they were learning to smash, crush, destroy, wreck."

The next level was characterized by "a strange, stark terror." Those who reached stage four were often overcome with alarm that the rest of the world had no idea what was rising to confront them; they also feared that the unsuspecting outsiders would be no match for the dark forces unleashed in Germany. Once he reached that stage, Smith fretted that the Nazis were "a real, direct and imminent threat to the existence of a civilization which gathers facts and discusses." The democratic world, for all its admirable qualities, was weak, while Hitler's world was "mighty, powerful, reckless. It screamed defiance at my world from the housetops. One had to be deaf not to hear it."

Smith pointed out that some people made the journey from stage one to stage four in as little as a week. Others remained stuck at stage one or two. And still others got to stage three but didn't necessarily make it to stage four.

Of course, Americans who made only short visits to Germany often failed to get beyond stage one or two—at least, during their actual journeys. Like many wealthy undergraduates, John F. Kennedy took off for Europe in the summer of 1937 after his freshman year at Harvard. Traveling with his friend LeMoyne Billings, he drove around France and Italy before spending five days in Germany, accompanied by a young German woman—"a bundle of fun," as Kennedy put it—whom they had apparently picked up at the border.

Kennedy's cryptic diary entries suggest the American visitors came across as somewhat rowdy. The morning after they went to a Munich nightclub "which was a bit different," he noted that at the Pension Bristol where they stayed there was "the usual amount of cursing and being told we were not gentlemen." In an entry marked Nuremberg-Württemberg, he wrote: "Started out as usual except this time we had the added attraction of being spitten [*sic*] on."

Still, he did make a couple of political observations. "Hitler seems so popular here, as Mussolini was in Italy, although propaganda seems to be his strongest weapon," he wrote in Munich. Following the Rhine to Cologne, he added: "Very beautiful as there are many castles along the way. All the towns are very attractive, showing the Nordic races certainly seem superior to the Latins. The Germans are really too good—it makes people gang against them for protection . . ." A year later, his father, Joseph Kennedy, was appointed ambassador to Great Britain, where he quickly gained a reputation as an envoy with pro-German leanings.

Because of his father's views, it's easy to read more into John Kennedy's brief diary entries than they merit. At a minimum, however, they demonstrate the sense of innocence—and ignorance—of many young Americans who visited Nazi Germany in this period.

A year later, in 1938, John Randolph and his wife, Margaret, spent the summer traveling through Europe before returning to his job as an assistant professor of mathematics at Cornell. Unlike Kennedy, they pinched their pennies, staying at youth hostels and biking whenever they could. Randolph's observations from Germany, where they spent almost all of June, are filled with minute details: the cost of their lodgings, meals and bike rentals, the exact times of the trains they caught, their panic when a suitcase went astray. Also, there are the standard exclamations about the tourist attractions. "The trip up the Rhine from Koblenz to Bingen was wonderful," he wrote. But there are only a couple of the most tangential allusions to politics, and it's clear that the Randolphs were oblivious to most of what was happening.

"The morning was nice and bright," he noted on June 6 in Heidelberg. "All the people and all the swastikas were out in full color." After arriving on their bikes in Tübingen, he wrote:

"Of all things, we had a private room in a house of the Hitlerjugend and even so paid only one RM [Reichsmark] for two of us. The room had two very nice cots, two little stands, a table, a chair, a large clothes chest, and a telephone. Very nicely furnished with painted walls and ceilings (white) hard wood floors, and large window. The whole hostel was especially built in 1935 and is modern and nice in every way."

Randolph appeared to believe that the country they were visiting, like their room in the Hitlerjugend house, was nice in every way. When they happened to be caught in an air raid drill in Munich, he dismissed it as "not very interesting." A German engineer Randolph met on their trip wrote to him in December 1938, angered by what he construed to be anti-German propaganda in the United States. "You realize don't you that in Germany there is not a single unemployed, and no man that goes hungry in winter or freezes, and this is not so for any other country except Italy which is also under state's direction. In Germany order and discipline rule. You were here yourself and saw it." Nothing in Randolph's diary or papers suggests that he paused to question those claims. He had simply skimmed the surface of Germany and returned as uninformed as when he arrived.

One factor that encouraged such blindness was how, when it came to people-to-people contact, young Americans found Germans friendly and welcoming. After his first summer in Germany in 1936, Howard K. Smith had returned to a job as a reporter for the *New Orleans Item*, but then felt the lure of Germany again the following summer. Eager to continue his investigation of that country's political system, he hitchhiked to save money and was surprised to find how easy it was to get around that way. "I simply draped a small American flag over my single bag and those simple, friendly people stopped every time," he recalled. "The friendliness, the overwhelming hospitality of Germans to foreigners—and especially to Americans—was phenomenal." Smith believed the impressive performance of the American athletes in the Olympics a year earlier was one reason why "Americans appeared to be the German people's favorite foreigner." With that kind of a welcome, many visitors comfortably remained innocents abroad, missing most of what was happening around them.

Yet there was nothing innocent about Nazi Germany by then, especially in 1938. It was a year punctuated by three major events: the Anschluss, Munich and Kristallnacht. The first and second of those events—the annexation and occupation of Austria in March, and then British Prime Minister Neville Chamberlain's and French Premier Edouard Daladier's agreement to allow Germany to seize the Sudetenland from Czechoslovakia—represented major triumphs for Hitler, transforming his Greater Germany rhetoric into reality and setting the stage for the *Drang nach Osten* ("Drive to the East"). The third, the attacks on Jewish businesses and homes all over Germany on November 9 and 10, marked a dramatic escalation of Hitler's anti-Semitic policies.

Those American reporters who had already spent considerable time in Berlin were, as a rule, stripped of most illusions about the new Germany—and some had been sounding the alarm about the country, its rulers and their intentions for quite some time. William Shirer was certainly in that category. But as he marked his third anniversary in Hitler's Germany in August 1937, he found himself without a job, the victim of his news agency's cutbacks. He then received a telegram from Salzburg asking if he'd come for dinner at the Adlon Hotel. It was signed "Murrow, Columbia Broadcasting."

Shirer had only a vague recollection of the name, but he certainly knew the company and its radio broadcasts. When he met Edward R. Murrow, the European manager of CBS, and they had ordered their martinis at the Adlon's bar, Shirer was struck by Murrow's handsome face. "Just what you would expect from radio," he noted in his diary. But he also found him disarmingly sincere: "Something in his eyes that was not Hollywood." As soon as Shirer passed a voice test, Murrow called to say he was hired.

As the new CBS correspondent, Shirer was supposed to make Vienna his base instead of Berlin. Although his Berlin days were far from really over—he would return there soon enough—Shirer and his Austrian wife, Tess, were relieved to be leaving the German capital in the fall of 1937. Summing up their three years there, he wrote in his diary on September 27: "Personally, they have not been unhappy ones, though the shadow of Nazi fanaticism, sadism, persecution, regimentation, terror, brutality, suppression, militarism, and preparations for war has hung over all our lives, like a dark, brooding cloud that never clears."

And exactly as Howard K. Smith had described those foreigners who had acquired a real understanding—and sense of horror—about what they were witnessing, Shirer was increasingly alarmed by how oblivious most of the outside world still was about Hitler's Germany. "Somehow I feel that, despite our work as reporters, there is little understanding of the Third Reich, what it *is*, what it is up to, where it is going, either at home or elsewhere abroad . . . Perhaps, as the Nazis say, the Western democracies have become sick, decadent, and have reached that stage of decline which Spengler predicted . . . Germany is stronger than her enemies realize." Exasperated, he recalled his futile attempts to convince visitors of those dangers. "How many visiting butter-and-egg men have I told that the Nazi goal is domination!" he wrote. "They laughed."

Shirer reserved special scorn for the drop-in journalists who took Nazi protestations about their peaceful intentions seriously. "When the visiting firemen from London, Paris, and New York come, Hitler babbles only of peace," he wrote. "Peace? Read *Mein Kampf*, brothers." And he concluded what he thought was his farewell diary entry from Berlin "with the words of a Nazi marching song still dinning in my ears: *Today we own Germany, Tomorrow the whole world.*"

Stationed in Vienna as Hitler ratcheted up the threats and pressures aimed at forcing the Anschluss with Austria in March 1938, Shirer watched the takeover unfold with sorrow and frustration. At 4 A.M. on March 12, he wrote in his diary: "The worst has happened . . . The Nazis are in. The Reichswehr is invading Austria. Hitler has broken a dozen solemn promises, pledges, treaties. And Austria is finished. Beautiful, tragic, civilized Austria! Gone." But his frustration also stemmed from his inability to report the story on CBS; the Nazis would not permit him to broadcast. And his mood wasn't improved by his family situation: he was worried about Tess, who was still in the hospital recovering from a difficult Caesarean birth of their daughter two weeks earlier.

Although Shirer knew Austria well enough not to romanticize it—he observed how Austrian anti-Semitism "plays nicely in the hands of the Nazis"—he was still startled by how quickly many Austrians not only accepted but embraced their new rulers. After his daily visit to the hospital to check on Tess and the baby, he emerged from the subway at Karlsplatz to find himself swept up in "a shouting, hysterical Nazi mob" marching through the city. "The faces!" he wrote. "I had seen these before at Nuremberg—the fanatical eyes, the gaping mouths, the hysteria."

As the crowds sang Nazi songs, he spotted a group of policemen looking on in evident good humor. "What's that on their arm? A red-black-white Swastika arm-band! So they've gone over too!" And then there were the immediate attacks on Jews. "Young toughs were heaving paving blocks into windows of the Jewish shops," he wrote. "The crowd roared with delight."

Dropping in at the Café Louvre, the hangout of the foreign correspondents, he found his colleagues in a state of high excitement, rushing back and forth to the phone to call in the latest reports and rumors, while other regulars were saddened, even close to tears. Emil Maass, an Austrian-American who had worked earlier as Shirer's assistant, stopped by his table. He had posed as an anti-Nazi before, but now he didn't just walk in—he strutted in, as Shirer noted. "Well, *meine Damen und Herren*, it was about time," Maass announced with a smirk. Then he ostentatiously turned over his coat lapel, revealing a hidden swastika button, unpinning it and repinning it on the outside of his coat. Two or three women shouted, "Shame!" And a Major Goldschmidt, whom Shirer described as a Catholic who was also half-Jewish, got up from his table. "I will go home and get my revolver," he declared.

After another futile attempt to arrange a broadcast from Vienna, Shirer took Murrow's advice to fly to London. It wasn't that simple, though. As night turned into morning and he set out for the airport, he observed the proliferation of Nazi flags flying from houses. "Where did they get them so fast?" he wondered. At the airport, all the seats on the

London flight were taken. "I offered fantastic sums to several passengers for their places. Most of them were Jews and I could not blame them for turning me down," Shirer wrote. But he succeeded in getting on the flight to Berlin. From there, he found a prompt connection to London, where he could finally make his broadcast.

"This morning when I flew from Vienna at 9 A.M. it looked like any German city in the Reich," he told his listeners, describing the Nazi flags hanging from most of the balconies and people in the streets greeting each other with Nazi salutes and shouts of *"Heil Hitler!"* "Arriving in Berlin three hours later I hardly realized I was in another country," he added. The transformation of Austria was already complete. As for Shirer, he was more than ever convinced that Hitler was only beginning his march of conquest—and that the outside world urgently needed to wake up to the danger.

But that was hardly the prevailing view at the time. Other Americans came to radically different conclusions. Former President Herbert Hoover embarked on a trip to Europe in February 1938. After visiting several other countries—France, Belgium, Switzerland and Czechoslovakia—he went to Germany. His aim was to bolster his credentials when he held forth on key international issues. In particular, he wanted to strengthen his case that the United States needed to stay clear of "entanglements" abroad.

In Berlin, U.S. Ambassador Hugh Wilson told him that Hitler wanted to meet him. Initially, Hoover balked, explaining that he was traveling as a private citizen. Besides, according to his friend Samuel Arentz, Hoover told Wilson that he had been inclined to believe "that Hitler was actually a front man for a group of the brains who were actually running the Nazi party and everything it was doing." But Wilson pressed him to reconsider, especially in light of his own inability to get to see Hitler. Hoover finally gave in.

Wearing a khaki jacket with a swastika, Hitler greeted the American visitor at the Chancellery on March 8. As they talked, Hoover concluded that Hitler was well informed on issues such as housing, foreign exchange rates and international trade. But according to Arentz, a few key words would set Hitler off and "all of a sudden [he] would jump to his feet and just went to raving talk—tantrums—that showed he was crazy." Those words were "Jew," "Communist" and "democracy."

At one point, Hoover claimed to have interrupted Hitler, declaring, "That's enough; I'm not interested in hearing your views." He told Arentz that if Hitler would face an American jury "there wouldn't be any question about him being declared insane." Nonetheless, neither Hoover nor Hitler appeared to take serious offense at anything the other said, and the American emerged with a revised view of the German leader. He no longer believed he was merely someone else's puppet; he could see that he was a force in his own right.

The next day, Hoover had lunch with Goering at his "hunting lodge" east of Berlin, a lavish complex full of tapestries, painting and sculptures. Greeted by sixteen costumed trumpeters, the American was brought up short by the life-sized bust of a woman placed as a centerpiece on the table where they were having lunch. "Yes, that's solid gold; that's my first wife," Goering told him. Knowing about Hoover's background as a mining engineer, his host pressed him to tell him his views of Russia's mineral resources. The American gave an optimistic account, telling Arentz later that he'd prefer to have the Germans go east rather than west if they were planning any action in the future.

After Germany, Hoover continued his European journey, visiting Poland, Latvia, Estonia, Finland and Sweden. On a final stopover back in England, he spoke with the press. While he acknowledged "many menaces to peace," he asserted that he did not "believe that a widespread war is probable in the immediate future." Back in New York, he summed up his views in a speech to the Foreign Policy Association on March 31. Between his meeting with Hitler and that speech, Hitler had completed the annexation of Austria, but that had not altered Hoover's opinion about the need for America to avoid getting caught up in any new European war. Such a conflict, he said, would "have all the hideous elements of the old religious wars." His conclusion: "If the world is to keep the peace, then we must keep peace with dictatorships as well as with popular governments. The forms of governments which other peoples pass through in working out their destinies is not our business."

Hoover's message was the direct opposite of Shirer's. Yes, the situation in Europe was dangerous. And, yes, while Hoover believed Germany was not yet ready for military action, he privately conceded that it could take that step later—in all probability, targeting the East. But for him, this was an argument for leaving Hitler's Germany to its own devices, not for issuing a wake-up call aimed at mobilizing Western nations, including the United States, to try to stop him. He came to Germany with that conviction, and left Germany with his beliefs not only intact but reinforced. Not even his face-to-face encounter with Hitler, complete with tirades and tantrums, could shake his conviction that the only rational American response to the new Germany was, in effect, a shrug of the shoulders.

Jacob Beam was still short of his twenty-seventh birthday when he arrived in Berlin in February 1935 to take up his assignment as third secretary in the U.S. Embassy, with responsibility for reporting on the country's internal affairs. He would spend a total of five years working in the German capital—"a longer period than can be claimed by any other American official," as he wrote in his unpublished manuscript about that period.

Despite his youth, Beam was well prepared for his post. His father was a German professor at Princeton, where the younger Beam studied as an undergraduate before continuing his education at Cambridge. Working in the Geneva consulate when he got word of his pending assignment to Berlin, he made a point of seeking "instruction" from Edgar Mowrer, the *Chicago Daily News* correspondent who had been forced out of Germany in 1933 and was then based in Geneva. "He gave me introductions to representatives of the old regime as well as anti-Nazi dissidents who were to be approached by a cut-out," Beam recalled. "He even furnished me with a list of women to be avoided."

While acknowledging that many of those contacts were not representative of the new Germany, he insisted they were still "the most knowledgeable and influential Germans to whom I could have access." Among them were ardent German nationalists, often from aristocratic families, who considered themselves far superior to the country's new rulers. "Although cold and severe in their demeanor, they had a code of justice which abhorred Nazi excesses, particularly the mistreatment of the Jews," he wrote.

Several of these nationalists had American wives. When IBM's boss Thomas Watson came to visit the company's German subsidiaries in the summer of 1937, he hosted a large dinner at the Adlon Hotel. Among the guests was Beam, who found himself seated at a table with Norman Ebbut, the Berlin correspondent of the *Times* of London, a gauleiter (Nazi district leader), and the Count and Countess Seherr-Thoss from East Prussia. The daughter of the former American ambassador to France Henry White, Muriel White had married Hermann Seherr-Thoss in 1909; she was also the sister of one of the diplomats stationed at the U.S. Embassy in Berlin. Beam and Ebbut witnessed her exchange with the gauleiter as the dinner was ending.

"Is it true that the Party sometimes rewards deserving Jews by making them honorary Aryans?" she asked.

When the gauleiter conceded that this happened on occasion, the countess followed up with a line that she must have been mulling over for quite some time. "Can you tell me then how I could become an honorary Jew?"

That kind of bold behavior was hardly typical by then, either for Germans or their American spouses. And Beam's implicit message that many American wives of German nationalists were at heart anti-Nazi is contradicted by the account of the *Chicago Tribune*'s Sigrid Schultz. "Foreign women married to Germans often became fervent Nazis," she wrote. "One American-born countess refused to be introduced to me because I 'maligned Nazi Germany.'" Schultz had helped found the American Women's Club in Berlin, but resigned from it before the outbreak of World War II because, as she explained, it had become "a hot-bed of Nazi propaganda" and "a regular rendezvous for American women married to Germans and for their Nazi intimates."

Schultz observed the broader phenomenon of how the Nazis "commanded a hysterical fanaticism among some foreign women, Americans included." Elizabeth Dilling, a shrill anti-Communist crusader from Chicago who saw President Roosevelt as the embodiment of all evil, visited Germany in 1931 and again in 1938. On her second visit, she was delighted by "the great improvement of conditions there." She added, "Personally I thank God for the opposition Germany is making against communism." On yet another visit a short time later—this one paid for by her German hosts—she attended the Nuremberg Party rally and proclaimed, "The German people under Hitler are contented and happy . . . don't believe the stories you hear that this man has not done a great good for this country."

Schultz recalled seeing Dilling in the dining room where the foreign press and other visitors ate. Dressed in a bright red hat, Dilling went from table to table, pointing to the journalists and "doing a lot of agitated whispering." After such exchanges, the people she had been talking to would fall silent whenever one of the journalists was nearby. Her curiosity aroused, Schultz caught up with a young American woman who was accompanying Dilling. She demanded to know just what the older woman was doing.

"You are an enemy of Germany, and we must see that our friends do not speak in front of you," the young American declared.

"And what makes you think I am an enemy of Germany?" Schultz inquired.

"Because of the reports you write against us."

Schultz emphasized that the young American used the word "us," leaving no doubt that she and her mentor identified with the Nazis.

Later, Rolf Hoffmann, a local Nazi propagandist, came up to Schultz and apologized for Dilling's behavior. He told her that the American visitor had insisted that both she and Wallace Deuel of the *Chicago Daily News* should be expelled from the country. He explained to Dilling that, even if Schultz was critical in her reporting, she tried to be fair. "These foreign sympathizers are so swept away by their emotions, they don't know how to express their enthusiasm," he said, smiling.

Like many of the veteran journalists, Beam had little patience for the likes of Dilling: Americans who came to Germany and admired the Nazis. Early in his tour, however, he did offer a positive assessment of the Arbeitsdienst, the Nazi-organized compulsory six months of labor service for males between the ages of eighteen and twenty-five. Henry Leverich, an embassy colleague, had been allowed to spend time at three of the Arbeitsdienst camps and was impressed, as Beam recalled, by "the magnificent physical condition of the camp inmates; their pride in their camp and their work . . ." He noted later that this would prove good training for military service when many of these men would be called up during the war.

Beam was also given his chance to view a Nazi program firsthand—Kraft durch Freude, Strength Through Joy, that offered cheap cruises for workers to boost their morale. Permitted to travel on a one-week cruise of the North Sea, he concluded, "The tours were well-organized, without undue overcrowding, and the satisfaction of the group appeared to be genuine." As Beam later pointed out, his and Leverich's positive reporting on those programs contributed to the judgment of some of their superiors back in Washington that they were soft on the Nazis.

But Beam quickly became a perceptive observer of his surroundings, coming to share the far more critical views of many of the other Americans who knew Germany well. He noticed both the pageantry and propaganda, and the bizarre and the brutal.

To mark the anniversary of Hitler's coming to power in 1933, every January 30 the Nazis would hold a torchlight parade, and the Foreign Ministry would invite diplomats from various embassies to witness the procession. In 1937, the Americans and the Brazilians were invited. Beam and his colleague James Riddleberger came from the U.S. Embassy, and they were positioned at a window next to the balcony from where Hitler reviewed the SS troops carrying the torches.

After the parade, the American and Brazilian diplomats thought they would be escorted out. Instead, an excited Hitler came up to them, asking for their reactions. When they obliged by saying they were impressed, he invited them next door to the president's palace, which earlier had been occupied by Hindenburg and was now the scene of a party. As they entered a room that was full of Nazis in uniform, Hitler called over the waiters to make sure each of the diplomats was offered a beer. Then, he clapped his hands and shouted the first words of the "Horst Wessel Song," the Nazi anthem, as he ordered the crowd to make a path for him. This was the prelude to one of his stranger performances, a rare attempt at humor on his part.

As Beam recalled, Hitler goose-stepped across the room "ostensibly imitating a somewhat slovenly stormtrooper with a protruding stomach." Reaching a bust of himself, he saluted, turned around and marched back, this time adopting "the style of the SS, with stomach tucked in and lips tightly buttoned." The assembled Nazi brass didn't know how to react. After they awkwardly applauded, one of Hitler's aides nudged the Americans and Brazilians out the door.

There was nothing even vaguely amusing about the Nazis' ferocious enforcement methods. Beam concluded that they blotted out their "most vaunted domestic achievements." One bit of evidence that impressed upon him their "blood-lust and brutality" was provided by his colleague, Marselis Parsons. The American vice-consul was sent to witness the cremation of the body of a man who was executed for allegedly trying to assassinate Julius Streicher, the rabidly anti-Semitic founder of the Nazi newspaper *Der Stürmer*. The victim had claimed American citizenship, which was why a representative of the embassy was present to collect his remains. But before the coffin was pushed into the fire, Parsons noticed how short it was. The reason: the victim had been beheaded, and his head was placed "in the crook of his elbow."

Like many of the career foreign service officers at the American Embassy, Beam was pleased to see Ambassador Dodd depart at the end of 1937. He considered him to be "dignified, considerate, sound in his judgment of the Nazis, but very inarticulate." And he shared the view that the historian had "embarrassed the U.S. government" with his undiplomatic statements—although Beam stressed that this was "not because of their anti-Nazi content but because they had set off press speculation that the German Government would soon feel compelled to demand his removal." He also faulted Dodd for "antagonizing most of the State Department's high command."

For all those reasons, Beam welcomed the appointment in early 1938 of foreign service veteran Hugh Wilson, who had first served in Berlin for a few months back in 1916 and then from 1920 to 1923. His track record as a diplomat and in Washington, where he served as assistant secretary of state before he was sent to Berlin again, convinced Beam that their new boss was a seasoned professional. "We respected Mr. Wilson's competence," he noted. The new envoy was, in Beam's words, "a veteran, 'you have to show me' type diplomat who disapproved of his predecessor's disorderly performance."

But, as Beam soon realized, Dodd may have been more accurate in his critical assessment of the Nazi regime than his more experienced replacement. Wilson was "somewhat skeptical of the negative views held by some of us on his staff who had spent a couple of years or more in Berlin," Beam recalled. He also pointed out that this wasn't an uncommon experience "since we found it took some time to educate official newcomers to the facts of living with the Nazis."

Wilson knew that other foreign service officers with extensive Berlin experience, especially former Consul General Messersmith, saw the Nazi regime as an extremely dangerous enemy. But if Messersmith and some others held this stage-four view, Wilson arrived with an attitude that wasn't marked by the naïve admiration characteristic of stage one—but was still far from viewing Hitler's Germany with alarm. Determined to reach his own judgments, Wilson wanted "to concentrate on the diplomatic aspects of the peace in Europe," as Beam put it. He didn't want a confrontation with the Nazis over their internal policies or their broader ambitions; he wanted to use the traditional tools of diplomacy to keep the peace.

For those American diplomats like Beam who were no longer willing to suspend judgment on the Nazi regime, the arrival of Wilson proved to be a classic case of the perils of getting what you wish for. Beam and several of his colleagues also quickly concluded that Wilson "was 'not on the inside track' either in Berlin or in Washington when it came to dealing with the affairs of state at the highest level." Dodd had maintained personal relations with Roosevelt, despite his antagonistic relationship with the president's appointees at the State Department. And while he was ineffective in his dealings with the Nazis, the former ambassador had quickly shed any illusions that they might moderate their policies.

Wilson, by contrast, believed that there should be no rush to judgment on Hitler's regime, even in 1938, and that traditional diplomacy could avert a confrontation with it. This was precisely the kind of mindset that would be eagerly embraced by Britain and France, setting the stage for Munich.

*          *          *

After Wilson presented his credentials to Hitler on March 3, 1938, he promptly wrote to Roosevelt. He found that "the principal impression I carried away is the lack of drama in this exceedingly dramatic figure," he reported. "He was clad as I was in a dress suit, and wore only one order, the Iron Cross. He is more healthy looking than I had anticipated, more solid, more erect. The complexion is pale, but there is more character in his face than I had imagined from the photographs. He speaks with a strong Austrian accent, but was quite easy to follow."

Wilson added: "He is a man who does not look at you steadily but gives you an occasional glance as he talks. In our conversation at least he was restrained and made no gestures of any kind." When Wilson politely told his host he was interested in meeting the man who had pulled his country out of such poverty and despair and produced prosperity and pride, Hitler was reluctant "to assume for himself the credit for the work which is being done." The envoy found that appealing, although he confessed that their talk was "colorless" and "the very negative nature of my impressions was surprising." When he had met Mussolini earlier, Wilson had the feeling that he could have happily invited him for dinner and further conversation over a beer. "I had no such desire on leaving Hitler," he declared.

After a subsequent meeting on March 12, he wrote again to Roosevelt, pointing out that the frequent descriptions by Germans of Hitler as an artist were on target—"in the sense of a man who arrives at his conclusions and undertakes his actions through instinct rather than ratiocination." He indicated that Hitler was well informed, "but his reasoning, while making use of this knowledge, tends to justify an emotional concept." As a result, he concluded, "if we think of Hitler as an artist, it explains a great deal."

That was the same day as the Anschluss, when "the artist" orchestrated the annexation of Austria. In his diary entry for that day, Wilson assessed that event with cool detachment. "One may judge the action from the moral point of view with condemnation," he wrote. "One may deplore the brutality of it. One must admire the efficiency of the action."

In a letter to Secretary of State Hull on March 24, Wilson argued that since "the smoke and dust of the Austrian Anschluss have begun to settle," it was time to view what had happened with just that kind of dispassionate judgment. "Whether we like it or not, the Germans' economic predominance through this region is now, I believe, a fact," he wrote. By seizing Austria, he continued, Hitler had completed two parts of his original Nazi program—"the union of all Germans on the basis of self determination" and "the equality of rights of the German people vis-à-vis other nations and the cancellation of the peace treaties of Versailles and St. Germain." Only the third part—the push for *Lebensraum*, German territorial expansion into Russia—remained unfulfilled. In a subsequent letter to Undersecretary of State Sumner Welles, he pointed out that even Germans who were secretly opposed to Hitler "confess that their hearts swelled with pride when Austria was annexed."

Wilson was intrigued by what he was observing, but nowhere near as alarmed as Beam and others felt he should be. "This place is all so darned absorbing and interesting," he added in his letter to Welles. His real feelings came out most strongly in reply to a letter from Hoover, which the former president wrote to him after returning to the United States and delivering his March 31 speech urging Americans to steer clear of any involvement in Europe's conflicts or domestic affairs. Enclosing a copy of his speech, Hoover argued that it had served its purpose "of bringing our people to a realization we must live with other nations." Wilson responded that he had read the speech "with a lot of satisfaction." And he echoed its sentiments: "I wish our people in general could understand how little is gained by scolding other people, and how much is gained by trying to work with them."

Wilson wasn't blind to the persecution of the Jews, although he did hold out hope in a letter to Roosevelt on June 2 that there could be "an attempt to work out some kind of acceptable solution" to the continued Nazi confiscations of Jewish property. And he worried about the dangers of another major war, mentioning the parallels to 1914 in a letter to William Bullitt, the American ambassador in Paris. But his conclusion was always the same. Writing again to Welles on June 20, he declared: "Twenty years ago we tried to save the world and now look at it. If we tried to save the world again, it would be just as bad at the end of the conflict. The older I grow the deeper is my conviction that we have nothing to gain by entering a European conflict, and indeed everything to lose."

In his letters and reports, Wilson repeatedly emphasized that Hitler enjoyed the active or passive support of most Germans and that it was wishful thinking to believe that his regime could collapse—or that the minority who opposed it could do anything to make that happen. But as Hitler increased the pressure on Czechoslovakia at the end of the summer, Beam, who had nurtured his contacts with conservative opponents of the Nazis, returned to the embassy with a report that raised the possibility that Wilson was wrong on that score. He had stumbled on what looked like nothing less than a plot to assassinate Hitler.

Among Beam's acquaintances was Erwin Respondek, whom he described as "a valuable informant" passed along to him by Douglas Miller, the embassy's commercial attaché, who had left Berlin in 1937. A Catholic economist who despised Hitler and his movement, Respondek had served in the Reichstag in the early 1930s, when the Center Party's Heinrich Brüning was chancellor. Brüning's attempts to ban the SA and the SS won him the enmity of the Nazis, and he fled the country in 1934. But Respondek could afford to stay in Berlin, since he was hardly a famous figure. While he was banned from politics, he continued to monitor information on the country's economy and finances, passing reports along to both the American Embassy, through Miller, and Brüning. In the second week of September, when the crisis of Czechoslovakia was building to its climax, Beam was invited to a *Herrenabend*, a men's evening, at Respondek's house on the outskirts of Berlin.

It was a small gathering. Aside from Beam and his host, there was Professor Hermann Muckermann, a former Jesuit priest who wrote about science and Christian ethics, and ventured into the discussions about racial theories and eugenics. The other guest was a Luftwaffe colonel. Once Respondek's wife served dinner and left the men alone, Respondek declared, "Let's get down to business and talk about the matter we came here to discuss." As Beam recalled, the talk then turned to Hitler's apparent determination to seize the Sudetenland from Czechoslovakia. From the comments of both Respondek and the colonel, it appeared that they were part of a conspiracy against Hitler that included General Franz Halder, who had recently replaced General Ludwig Beck as the army's chief of staff. Beck had sought assurances from Hitler that his plans for Czechoslovakia wouldn't lead to a war, only to be dismissed. Now, if Respondek and the Luftwaffe colonel's information was accurate, his successor and several other senior officers appeared to be contemplating a stunning act of resistance.

As Beam wrote, "The plan was to assassinate Hitler if he moved to the point of making war." Muckermann was visibly nervous about that kind of talk, and around midnight he whispered to the young American: "Let's get out of here fast." Making their excuses, Beam drove Muckermann back to the city center, both of them breathing a sigh of relief as he did so.

Back at the embassy, Beam wrote a report for Wilson on what had transpired, showing it first to Truman Smith. The military attaché made light of Beam's account, claiming that no such plot was conceivable in Hitler's highly disciplined army. Beam submitted his report to Wilson anyway, and he believed that the ambassador passed it along to one of Hull's advisors. But he never heard anything back either from Wilson or Washington.

After Britain's Chamberlain and France's Daladier acceded to Hitler's demands for the Sudetenland later that month, Beam encountered Respondek again and inquired what had happened with the alleged Halder plot against the German leader. "He said that since Hitler had not gone to war, the coup had been abandoned," Beam wrote later. This was consistent with what Halder and several other Wehrmacht (Army) officers claimed at the end of World War II. They were undoubtedly eager to play up their purported opposition to Hitler, and much of what they had to say was greeted with understandable skepticism by the victors, especially at the Nuremberg Trials. But Beam's account indicates that they had at least seriously discussed the option of striking at Hitler then.

Once the German leader successfully pulled off the Munich Pact, however, the situation changed radically. France and Britain had caved to Hitler's demands for the Sudetenland, marking the apogee of the policy of appeasement and setting the stage for the dismemberment of Czecho-slovakia that would culminate in the German takeover of what was left of Bohemia and Moravia in March 1939. As Field Marshal Erich von Manstein explained after the war: "We had watched Germany's precari-ous course along the razor's edge to date with close attention and were increasingly amazed at Hitler's luck in attaining—hitherto without re-course to arms—all his overt and covert political aims. The man seemed to have an infallible instinct."

But if Munich eliminated any chance of a revolt of Hitler's military brass prior to World War II, Ambassador Wilson—like Britain's Cham-berlain and France's Daladier, who had signed onto the ignominious pact—viewed the outcome there as a step toward sanity. In a letter that he wrote to Secretary Hull soon after, which for an unexplained reason he never mailed, Wilson drew a contrast between "the spontaneous out-burst of joy, relief and hope for the future" that greeted news of the Mu-nich Pact in Western Europe with the "rather reluctant appreciation given in the press of our country."

His judgment on which reaction was more justified came through loud and clear. The British and the French, he wrote, "have perhaps a deeper knowledge and appreciation of the problems of Europe than the American people, remote from Europe, can have . . . it is far easier to be dogmatic in one's judgments with a wide stretch of sea between our coun-try and a possible enemy." According to Beam, Wilson wrote to "his Brit-ish colleague"—presumably that country's ambassador in Berlin—about the "stout piece of work" he had done to help produce the Munich Pact.

Roosevelt had sounded a similar note when he had congratulated Chamberlain on the "peace" deal. But at the very least, there was a grow-ing awareness in Washington that the pact had come at a very high price. Writing in his diary on September 28, Jay Pierrepont Moffat, the State Department's chief of the Division of European Affairs, noted: "I do think the chances of preserving the peace have immeasurably improved but it likewise is difficult for me to see how this can be done except at the expense of Czechoslovakia."

Beam, who returned to the United States on home leave in October, found Washington's mood to be "completely different" from the one that was predominating in diplomatic circles in Berlin. "There was a general sense of outrage over the Austrian take-over, as high-lighted by the plight of resident Jews, as well as over the Nazis' unopposed and clearly pre-destined subjugation of Czechoslovakia," he recalled. At a meeting he attended with Hull, the secretary of state "vented his frustration in Biblical predictions of impending European disaster."

It wasn't just many Americans back home who took a different view. So did some of the Americans reporting from Germany, most notably Shirer, who was back in Berlin as Hitler pushed Europe to the brink. Sitting in the balcony just above Hitler as the dictator issued his demands in a speech on September 26, Shirer recorded in his diary: "He's still got that nervous tic. All during his speech he kept cocking his shoulder, and the opposite leg from the knee down would bounce up. Audience couldn't see it, but I could." Shirer added that "for the first time in all the years I've observed him he seemed tonight to have completely lost control of himself."

Shirer had been hoping all along that the Czechs would fight, even if the British and the French wanted to convince them otherwise. "For if they do, then there's a European war, and Hitler can't win it," he wrote in his diary on September 19. When the appeasement deal was struck, Shirer was practically sickened by the cheers for peace—"a curious commentary on this sick, decadent continent," he wrote. And he observed the physical change in the German leader. "How different Hitler at two this morning . . . I noticed his swagger. The tic was gone!"

Shirer understood that Hitler had been allowed to score a victory that, far from ensuring "peace for our time" as Chamberlain famously claimed, would have disastrous consequences. His gloom only deepened for another reason: Max Jordan of NBC managed to air the text of the Munich Pact an hour before Shirer did. For the CBS man, this amounted, in his own words, to "one of the worst beatings I've ever taken."


Angus Thuermer was another young American who was eager to explore Hitler's Germany, arriving there in 1938. After he graduated from the University of Illinois, his father had suggested that he should spend six months studying German in Berlin, and then six months studying French in Paris. "He was giving me an extra year of college," Thuermer recalled, looking back at that life-changing experience more than seven decades later. But instead of going on to France, he stayed in Germany, not only studying the language but also picking up work from American correspondents there. Soon, he was offered a full-time job for the Associated Press, working under bureau chief Louis Lochner right up until the United States entered World War II in December 1941.

While he was still living in Hegel Haus, a dormitory for foreign students in Berlin, in late 1938, Thuermer took a trip to Munich, eager to see the Nazis' annual observance of "The Ninth of November"—the anniversary of the 1923 Beer Hall Putsch when sixteen members of the movement were killed. Arriving in that city, Thuermer met a young American missionary who spoke fluent German and managed to convince an SS man to admit the two of them to the VIP grandstand so that they could see how the "martyrs" were honored. (The SS man didn't know the American was a missionary.) As a result, Thuermer had a clear view of the procession of Nazi luminaries, which included Goebbels, Hess, Himmler, Goering and Hitler.

"Loose as the formation was, in the midst of his Brownshirt chums, Hitler, the Leader, walked just slightly apart," Thuermer wrote in his unpublished memoir. "By his stature, his gait, the cut of his jib, a sailor would say, he was not impressive. If I had not known for whom to look, I might have passed him by in a general glance over the group."

But the ceremony itself was solemn and, for the party faithful, moving. A man carried "the Blood Banner" in front of the leaders. "The configuration was reminiscent of the acolyte carrying the cross up the nave of the church," Thuermer noted. Every 50 yards or so, there was a 20-foot-high bright red temporary obelisk bearing the name of one of "the fallen." When they reached Königsplatz, two white stone mausoleums, each containing eight bronze coffins, were flanked by hundreds of motionless SS men. As a speaker called out the names on the coffins, the SS men answered in unison "*Hier!*" The ceremony ended with the "Horst Wessel Song," the Nazi anthem that, as Thuermer put it, was "a genuine rouser."

It included the words: "Comrades shot by the red front and reactionaries march in spirit in our ranks."

Once the ceremony was over, Thuermer bought himself a third-class ticket and boarded the overnight train to Berlin, stowing his bicycle in the baggage car. Lulled to sleep in the train, he had no idea what was happening that night around the country. Arriving in the capital, he retrieved his bike and rode from the station to Hegel Haus, hoping to make it in time to get a cheap breakfast there. Suddenly, he heard "the smash and tinkle of breaking glass." Applying his hand brake, he saw a shattered show window just ahead of him. Unbeknownst to him, he was witnessing part of what would be called Kristallnacht. Although most of the violence had taken place during the early morning hours, he saw thugs with Nazi armbands still smashing shop windows, and someone inside the store breaking a grand piano to pieces. He saw a typewriter come flying out of another window and land on Unter den Linden—"one of the great avenues of Western Europe."

After a brief stop at Hegel Haus, Thuermer and a Dutch student rode their bicycles around the city to see more. Down one street, they saw smoke from a burning synagogue, but they decided not to risk getting closer, fearing they would be arrested. "I was seeing, eye-witnessing an unreal frenzy . . . it was the n-th power of what I had seen at Nazi rallies," he recalled. "That was sound. This was fury." Since Jewish shops had the names of their owners written in white paint on the front window, they were easy to spot. Thuermer saw one shop with a new sign announcing THIS SHOP IS BEING PURCHASED BY AN ARYAN. Later that same day, the sign was changed to THIS HAS BEEN PURCHASED BY AN ARYAN. The unmistakable message: it should no longer be targeted.

Eager to see as much as possible, Thuermer and an English student took buses to other parts of the city. While they stopped to observe the spectacle, the locals were doing just the opposite at first. "The citizens were just walking along staring straight ahead, pretending they didn't know what was happening," he said. By the afternoon, though, crowds were no longer pretending; they watched the destruction in the areas with the most Jewish shops. Some of those who were continuing to smash at will were boys in their teens; others were grown men. Very few police were in sight. As Thuermer observed, "Those who were there were un-characteristically unobtrusive, obviously following orders not to interfere with the rowdy Brownshirts."

Thuermer offered two possible explanations for the lack of any op-position to this orgy of anti-Semitic violence: most Germans, by this time, "believed in it all" when it came to Nazi ideology; or they were too frightened to say anything. "By the autumn of 1938 everyone knew what happened to opponents of the regime," he wrote.

Other Americans also witnessed Kristallnacht and felt its conse-quences. Charles Thayer, a diplomat assigned to the Berlin consulate, heard horror stories from all around the city. One of his friends wit-nessed how Nazis threw a small boy from a second-floor window into a mob below. "His leg broken, the boy tried to crawl on hands and knees through the forest of kicking black boots until my friend plunged into the mob and rescued him," he recounted. While synagogues burned, the thugs ransacked Jewish-owned department stores. At Wertheim, they pushed grand pianos off the gallery level so that they would smash to pieces on the main floor six floors down.

As the violence continued for two days, the American consulate's staff had to duck in and out of the building through the fire escape in the back because, in the front, panicked Jews blocked the entrance as they tried to get in. "All day long Kempinskis, Wertheims, Rosenthals, some of the oldest and most famous names in Berlin, trembled in front of our desks, pleading for visas or passports—anything to save them from the mad-ness that had seized the city," Thayer recalled. His small apartment, he added, "was crammed with Jewish families seeking refuge until the storm subsided."

Thayer appeared to be more generous than Thuermer in his assess-ment of the reaction of ordinary Berliners to those events, explaining that "the many Berliners who were neither Nazis nor Jews stood by looking aghast and ashamed but helpless at the sordid spectacle." Still, after the war he confessed that he had a less forgiving attitude than that. During the heavy Allied bombing raids on German cities, especially those with historic Old Towns like Hamburg, he wondered whether the destruc-tion was really necessary. "But for Berlin I seldom felt a qualm," he wrote.

"That ugly old city, it seemed to me, had been the seat of too much evil to deserve either remorse or sorrow when it was smashed to pieces like the pianos at Wertheims."

For all the shattered glass, however, it still remained possible for American visitors to come to Germany and miss much of what was happening around them. Phillips Talbot, who had studied along with Thuermer at the University of Illinois and would become a well-known Asian specialist and diplomat, visited Berlin soon after Kristallnacht. He had been a cub reporter for the *Chicago Daily News* and was invited by Wallace Deuel, its Berlin correspondent, to stay in his apartment. Talbot met up with Thuermer, who pointed out the evidence of what had just transpired. "Do you see that?" he asked, pointing to a second-story shattered window on the Kurfürstendamm. "I watched them break that one on the big night."

Speaking about his brief experience in Germany long afterward, Talbot admitted that if it hadn't been for what he learned from Thuermer and Deuel, he could have easily missed much of what was happening. And he still came away with, at the very least, mixed impressions. "Measured by efficiency, it [Germany] didn't look bad," he recalled. In a letter dated December 27, 1938, written shortly after his German visit, he wrote: "But it would be unfair to mention the evidences of the anti-Jewish campaign without some of the other things I saw." He listed "the physical results of Nazism . . . the super-roads, the busy slum clearance and new housing, the bridges and public buildings," which "all give the country a flavor of newness." He did add, though, that "some of the stories of methods told by people who should have no ax to grind are chilling."

For many of those Americans who had been monitoring these chilling developments, it was no longer possible to pretend that the new Germany represented anything like a normal mixture of good and bad, and should still be treated like a normal country. In a letter to Assistant Secretary of State Francis B. Sayre on November 14, Wilson finally admitted that it was futile to keep hoping that reasonable officials within the German government would succeed in producing "some moderation of the National Socialist racial policy, at least to the extent of permitting orderly emigration of Jews with a fairly substantial portion of their property." He concluded, "The events of the last few days apparently dispel such hopes."

Facing growing outrage against the Nazi regime, the Roosevelt Administration recalled Wilson to Washington for consultations the next day. He would formally remain ambassador to Germany until August 31, 1939, the eve of Germany's invasion of Poland, but he never returned to Berlin during that period. After Wilson's departure, the embassy was run by lower-level diplomats. Although he had been disappointed by Wilson's performance, Jacob Beam noted that the decision not to replace him "dealt our Embassy a sad blow." Without an ambassador to maintain ties at the senior level with Nazi officials, he wrote, "a bizarre state of noncommunication was allowed to develop to our overall disadvantage."

Many of the embassy staffers were focused increasingly on determining Germany's war capabilities and intentions, and no one was more experienced in that department than Truman Smith. The veteran military attaché was constantly on the lookout for new opportunities to gather more intelligence. He had engineered Lindbergh's visits to Germany that had provided an inside look at many of the Luftwaffe's factories and airfields. At the same time, he took advantage of the arrival of two other U.S. Army officers who were provided with a different kind of inside look at another aspect of the German military—in this case, its officer training program and its engineering capabilities.

Remarkably and inconspicuously, the United States and Germany had agreed in 1935 on an exchange of students in its officer training schools—the Command and General Staff School at Fort Leavenworth, Kansas, and the German War College, or Kriegsakademie, in Berlin. The program was to start the following year, but the Germans failed to avail themselves of this opportunity, probably because of their belief that their officers could get better training at home. "It was suggested tactfully that the Germans did not think very highly of the U.S. course of instruction at Leavenworth," wrote Albert C. Wedemeyer, the American officer who enrolled in the German War College, staying for the full two-year course from 1936 to 1938.

At the time a young captain from Nebraska, the "tall and handsome" Wedemeyer, as Kay Smith noted, immediately hit it off with her husband. Kätchen Smith, their daughter, recalled that Wedemeyer and Paul Thompson, another young officer from the Midwest who was also studying in Germany, would often come over for Sunday brunch. Thompson was an army engineer and he was enrolled at the Technical University in Berlin.

According to Kay, Thompson was "out-going, hard-working, modest, handsome with rosy cheeks, brown eyes and dark hair and a winning personality. He was very young and naïve socially but not professionally." Or, as Kätchen recalls, "Paul was wet behind the ears—truly innocent." Her parents worried about his relationship with a German woman named Friedl, fearing that she could be taking advantage of him. When he announced to the Smiths that he was going to marry her right before he was due to sail back home, Truman told Kay: "I hope she is not just getting a trip to the United States as so many have." But the Smiths attended their civil wedding and saw them off.

Since Thompson had already acquired considerable experience dealing with flood control on the Mississippi River, he didn't feel he was learning much in his courses in Berlin. Truman managed to get him assigned to a German Army engineer battalion instead, where he closely observed the Germans' methods and equipment. His subsequent report, according to Kay, "brought Thompson to the attention of his superiors in his branch and from then on . . . his rise was spectacular." He later trained U.S. Army engineers for the D-Day invasion and landed on Omaha Beach, where he was shot through the jaw. He survived and was decorated for bravery. After the war, he retired from the Army and started a second career as a senior executive at *Reader's Digest*.

But of the two young American officers who studied in Germany in this period, it was Wedemeyer—who would later rise much higher in the military hierarchy, succeeding General Joseph Stillwell as commander of U.S. forces in China—who gathered the most valuable information. The young captain took his duties as an exchange student at the German War College extremely seriously, keeping a meticulous record of everything he learned and observed over two years, which he summarized in a 147-page report for his military superiors. It offered the military brass valuable insights into the training provided to many of the best German officers who were destined to fight in World War II.

In his report, Wedemeyer left no doubt how much he admired the German training program and its mix of in-depth military history and practical exercises of "Troop Leading," allowing the officers to simulate battlefield conditions they were likely to face so that they could apply new tactics. "The situations presented at the Kriegsakademie involve War of Movement, special emphasis being placed upon speed, in anticipation of the employment of mechanized and motorized forces," he wrote. Officers were taught to make quick decisions, recognizing "that a fair decision given in time for aggressive execution is much better than one wholly right but too late."

All of which indicated that the Germans were preparing for new forms of combat. "They visualize rapidly changing situations in modern warfare and gearing their command and staff operations accordingly," he wrote. In essence, he was previewing the blitzkrieg tactics that Hitler would first unleash on Poland the following year.

In his postwar memoir, Wedemeyer openly stated what he had clearly implied. Deeply impressed by "German methods and quality of the instruction," he concluded: "The German pedagogy and curriculum were, in my judgment, superior to our own." By comparison, he felt that the instruction he had received at Fort Leavenworth was "much more theoretical" and the instructors mostly "mediocre." In Berlin, his chief instructor was Major Ferdinand Jodl, the brother of Alfred Jodl, who would become a top commander in World War II and was convicted and hanged as a war criminal at Nuremberg. The lesser-known brother was "outstanding as a teacher," Wedemeyer recalled, and overall he found the lectures at the German War College to be "thought-provoking" and comprehensive.

It was the practical training that left a particularly strong impression. "One of the map problems given while I was a student in Berlin involved a hypothetical attack against Czechoslovakia," he wrote. "Later, it developed that the problem was not so hypothetical." In his 1938 report, Wedemeyer included a broad array of details on everything from German weaponry to courier pigeons, but he didn't spell out the obvious key conclusion. In his memoir, he made up for that omission. Pointing out that he could not have predicted the mistakes that would lead Hitler to disaster, he declared: "But assuredly I recognized that the Nazi leaders were preparing for war."

During his studies in Berlin, Wedemeyer was careful not to discuss politics with his German counterparts. But he did write later that they sometimes "subtly revealed" their disapproval of their rulers. "There would be veiled statements, sometimes hints which would indicate shame, disgust, or displeasure with the Nazis." He met General Ludwig Beck, who was ousted as the army's chief of staff in 1938 and would later be executed for his role in the July 20, 1944, plot against Hitler. And among Wedemeyer's classmates was Captain Claus von Stauffenberg, who carried the briefcase with the bomb that failed to kill the German leader; he was promptly executed as well. During his time at the German War College, Wedemeyer recalled, Stauffenberg recited poetry at parties and was "not always discreet in expressing his contempt for the Nazis or for Hitler." But he was hugely popular, and he was never denounced for his views. Nonetheless, Wedemeyer felt that such anti-Nazi sentiment wasn't all that widespread within the military in that period.

Wedemeyer also had the opportunity to observe Nazi bigwigs up close. Invited to a party where several of them were present, he wrote off Hess as "stolid, not overly intelligent," but Goebbels was "a dynamo with a brain" and Goering "gave the impression of being jovial and an ebullient extrovert."

As such descriptions imply, Wedemeyer genuinely enjoyed his two years in Berlin. He found both his classmates and instructors, whatever their views, to be "at all times friendly." And soon he felt comfortable enough to engage in a bit of humor. When he first started arriving for classes, he didn't know what to say when the cleaning women working on their hands and knees in the hallway would shoot out their right arms and greet him with "Heil Hitler." Then, he started replying with "Heil Roosevelt." By his second year, those exchanges had become legendary in the school, and the charwomen would greet him with the Nazi salute but say "Heil Roosevelt." He then replied, "Heil Hitler."

Later, when Wedemeyer was suspected of pro-German sympathies, he explained how easily such banter could be misinterpreted. But there was little doubt that, even after World War II, he felt far more sympathetic to Germany than most of his countrymen. "... however greatly one was revolted by Hitler's treatment of the Jews and his arrogant bullying of small neighboring nations, one was compelled by knowledge of the record and the facts of Germany's situation to understand the dynamic of self-preservation which underlay the Nazi revolution," he wrote. Germans felt that Hitler had raised them from the abyss, he added. "It did not require any prolonged study of history to learn how false was the popular image of Germany as the most aggressive of nations and recurrent disturber of the peace."

At the German War College, Wedemeyer pointed out that he was exposed to constant lectures about the Bolshevik menace. "Beneath the propaganda I discerned a great deal of truth about Communist aims, practices, methods unknown or ignored in America until recently," he wrote. In other words, he came to believe that the Roosevelt Administration was wrong to consider Germany to be the main danger in Europe. "I was convinced that the German search for *Lebensraum* did not menace the Western World to anything like the same degree as the world-wide Communist conspiracy centered in Moscow."

Like Lindbergh, Wedemeyer gained remarkable insights into the German military buildup but came away convinced that the United States should stay out of the looming conflict in Europe. According to Kay Smith, however, Wedemeyer and her husband also had a significant talk in 1938. "It was Al with whom Truman first discussed plans for an assault of Germany if needed," she wrote in her unpublished memoir. "That discussion took place in our apartment."

The two men regularly compared notes on their experiences, and Smith shared his knowledge about Germany's rapid military buildup, which he was conveying in his regular reports to Washington. "I like to think that some of Truman Smith's shrewdness and knowledge rubbed off on me during my German War College period," Wedemeyer wrote. Once he returned to the United States, Wedemeyer had little patience for those who were curious about the political situation in Germany. "I had been disillusioned by the superficiality and nonmilitary type of questions put to me," he observed. "I had been asked all sorts of questions about Hitler's peculiarities, the Nazi persecution of Jews, and about Goebbels and Goering's love life, but almost nothing pertaining to strategy, or German capabilities, military training, and organization."

But there was one man who asked about exactly those subjects based on Wedemeyer's lengthy report: General George Marshall, who was chief of war plans. "When I reported to him, he had a copy on his desk, and had made many notes, indicating that he had read the report carefully," Wedemeyer recalled. Marshall asked, "What is the most important lesson you brought back from the German experience?" The young officer replied that the Germans would never fight a war again the way they did the last time. Instead of trench warfare, they would use new equipment and tactics based on "high mobility." As Wedemeyer noted in a memorandum decades later, "I don't want to sound like I am bragging, however I can assure you that these discussions, especially concerning our strategy and our tactics as the war advanced, were almost daily occurrences in General Marshall's office—just the two of us."

Wedemeyer was boasting, of course, but justifiably so. Marshall chose him in the spring of 1941 to help draft the "Victory Program" outlining how the United States needed to mobilize its manpower and resources to prepare for war. By then a major, Wedemeyer worked diligently to prepare this ambitious plan, despite his sympathies for the America First movement that was fervently campaigning against the country's entry into World War II. And in making those preparations for war, Wedemeyer drew extensively on his firsthand knowledge of Germany, the product of his two years at the German War College. The irony was that while Wedemeyer, like Lindbergh, opposed the Roosevelt Administration's drift toward direct involvement in World War II, both men provided intelligence that would prove invaluable when their country joined the conflict.

In a 1937 updated edition of his famous book *Germany Puts the Clock Back*, Edgar Mowrer, the *Chicago Daily News* correspondent who had been forced to leave Germany in 1933, chronicled Hitler's increasingly aggressive behavior, including moving troops into the demilitarized Rhineland, his repudiation of the Versailles Treaty and all its restrictions on a new military buildup, and Germany and Italy's direct aid for the fascist forces in the Spanish Civil War. "A brief calendar of the first four years of Hitler reads like a hymn of victory from a Prussian historian or war poet," he wrote.

By the end of 1938 and early 1939, the calendar was much fuller and the hymn soaring to new heights, extolling triumph after triumph. Austria had been annexed and Czechoslovakia carved up. To support the Nationalists against the Republicans in Spain's civil war, Hitler had dispatched troops and his newest fighter planes to that country, using the conflict there as a testing ground for his latest weaponry and offsetting Stalin's support for the Republican side. In March 1939, Hitler had demanded the Baltic port of Memel—or, as it is called today, Klaipeda—from Lithuania, and that tiny country quickly capitulated. Nothing, it seemed, stood in the way of more German victories. When the Spanish Civil War ended with the Nationalists triumphant, Beam watched from the windows of the U.S. Embassy the April victory parade of the German troops returning from there. He admitted it was "an awesome sight."

While Roosevelt still insisted he wanted to do everything to ensure the peace, by early 1939 he was beginning to make preparations for an alternative scenario. In his State of the Union address on January 4, he stressed that there were "many methods short of war, but stronger and more effective than mere words, of bringing home to aggressor governments the aggregate sentiments of our own people." Specifically, that meant upping military expenditures, which he promptly did by submitting a budget request with a 30 percent overall increase to $1.3 billion, not including an additional $500 million for acquiring new military aircraft.

For a while, the administration had considered sending Wilson back to his post in Berlin, but that idea was scuttled when Hitler took over what was left of Czechoslovakia in March. In the internal discussions in the State Department, Messersmith—the former consul general in Berlin—"his eyes aglow, favored any move directed against the Nazis," Moffat recorded in his diary. The two men were friends, but they frequently engaged in verbal jousts. "George, I wonder if you know what you are doing," Moffat told him on one occasion. "You are helping us into this war which is coming on." Messersmith replied by insisting that it was impossible for Hitler and the Western democracies to coexist.

Many of his colleagues were more cautious, and Roosevelt was still inclined to offer what he hoped would be seen as an olive branch. On April 14, he sent an appeal to Hitler and Mussolini that they pledge not to attack thirty-one countries in Europe and the Middle East—including the most likely next target, Poland—for at least ten years.

The president wasn't optimistic about the chances for success, but he was still stung by the mocking response from Berlin. On April 28, Hitler addressed the Reichstag, but he was focused on his audience abroad. Representing the U.S. Embassy, Beam witnessed his delivery, which the German leader had prepared for by first asking several of the thirty-one states whether they feared a German attack. "The great majority had replied in the negative which enabled Hitler to read out their names slowly, with an air of false drama," the young diplomat recalled. "It was a beautifully-acted farce which provoked loud laughter."

Beam didn't overlook the "particularly chilling nature" of the speech, despite that bit of theater. Poland wasn't one of the countries that Hitler had asked for its opinion, and he proceeded to denounce that country's refusal to accede to his demands for Danzig. He also castigated the British for taking Poland's side in this dispute. He renounced both the 1934 German-Polish nonaggression pact, which was supposed to ensure peace between those neighbors for ten years, and the 1935 Naval Agreement with Britain, which limited the German Navy to 35 percent of the tonnage of the British fleet. As Beam put it, Hitler was performing "as the world's then most powerful head of state"—and he clearly meant for everyone to understand that.

Despite Hitler's increasingly belligerent tone, there were still plenty of Americans who wanted to believe he was no threat to them. It was hardly surprising that those who desperately wanted to keep their country out of another global conflagration should feel that way, and some American envoys could be counted among them. Shortly after the Munich Pact, Joseph Kennedy, the American ambassador in London, had floated the idea that democracies and dictatorships "could advantageously bend their energies toward solving common problems by an attempt to re-establish good relations on a world basis." But it was surprising when Wiegand, Hearst's veteran correspondent who had covered Germany since World War I, produced a major two-part article that encouraged exactly those kinds of illusions.

Writing in the April and May 1939 editions of *Cosmopolitan*, Wiegand offered a lengthy profile of Hitler, examining his personality and politics. The magazine claimed the author was "the undisputed dean of American foreign correspondents and one of the greatest reporters of our time," citing as evidence Wiegand's early contacts with Hitler, dating back to 1921. In particular, it explained how the correspondent was "more than a little psychic himself" to recognize so early that Hitler had to be taken seriously. "It takes genius to know genius," it declared, with no trace of irony. "And a genius indeed is Karl von Wiegand."

Wiegand's first installment in the April issue described how Hitler had become "a veritable human meteor streaking the dark political skies of Europe—an ill omen to millions, a sign to other millions." Like a meteor, Hitler "is being consumed by fires of his own being," including "his unbelievably deep hatred for the Jews" and "his insatiable greed for ruthless power." But Wiegand was also clearly in awe of what this strange figure he had first met in Munich had achieved. "Measuring his personal achievements, future historians may record Adolf Hitler as the political genius of this era, perhaps of this century," he wrote. Nonetheless, he indicated that Hitler was acutely conscious that a climax was coming soon and his own life could be cut short. As a result, his actions were marked by "a fever of impatience, haste, hurry, drive," which is "a state of mind in which any man may stumble."

In his second installment in the May issue, however, Wiegand delivered an oddly reassuring message to his American readers: "Adolf Hitler is no physical menace to the United States except (1) in an agreement or alliance with Great Britain; (2) in the event that England should turn Fascist, or (3) if Nazi Germany should conquer England. The probability of any of these eventualities is remote."

Hitler had demonstrated his own near psychic qualities by predicting that neither Britain nor France would fight to save Czechoslovakia, he added. When it came to what the German leader would do next, Wiegand declared that he was no prophet—but that didn't prevent him from making a sweeping prediction. "Hitler has achieved without war what no other man has accomplished for centuries," he wrote. "As I know Der Führer, he will not in his senses stake those achievements and his unique place in history on the uncertain gamble of a deliberately planned aggressive war."

Suddenly, just as war was looming, Wiegand was sounding less like a seasoned correspondent and more like one of those naïve American visitors to Germany that Howard K. Smith had written about—stuck in stage-one or stage-two thinking about what Hitler and his movement truly represented.

## 10

*"On Our Island"*

On April 20, 1939, AP bureau chief Lochner dutifully set out to observe the lavish celebration of Hitler's fiftieth birthday. "I sat for four hours in the reviewing stand watching the biggest military display in German history," he wrote his daughter and son back in Chicago on April 26. "You can imagine how a pacifist like myself falls for that stuff!" Among the troops on parade was Wolfgang Wosseng, who had worked as an "office boy" for Lochner and was then called up as a Potsdam grenadier. While everyone else was wildly cheering, Lochner couldn't help thinking that Wosseng could be forced to shoot at similar young men in different uniforms very soon. "If that parade is a sample, I tell you the next war will be more terrible than anything the world has known," he continued in his letter. "The war of 1914 will have been child's play compared to this."

Unlike Wiegand, Lochner was far from convinced that Hitler would stop with the easy conquests, avoiding the fatal step that would trigger a new conflagration. "I fear the Germans make one big mistake: they completely underestimate the potential forces arrayed against them," he explained to his children. Warning that it is always dangerous to underestimate one's opponents, he added: "Queer that the top leaders in Germany should repeat that mistake of 1914–1918! Remember how they used to scoff at the possibility that America could ship troops across the ocean? Now they drill into the German people that England is decrepit and won't fight; that France is torn with domestic strife; that the U.S.A. is a big bag of wind, etc., etc. A great pity!"

But Hitler and his entourage weren't the only ones to indulge in wishful thinking. The reports by Truman Smith and others in the U.S. Embassy in Berlin about the rapidly growing strength of the German military were often greeted with skepticism in Washington, and the authors viewed as alarmists. Still, there was a realization that war was a growing possibility. By early summer, Moffat, the State Department's Chief of the Division of European Affairs, put the chances of a new conflict at 50-50.

For American correspondents and officials, the key question was how well prepared were the countries Germany was most likely to attack—first of all, Poland. Knickerbocker, the former Berlin correspondent who was still traveling around Europe, recalled that everyone wanted to know whether the Poles could hold out long enough for the French to mobilize an offensive and come to their rescue. "Optimistic Poles said they could hold out for three years; pessimistic Poles said one year," he wrote. "The French thought the Poles could hold out for six months."

On August 18, Moffat noted in his diary: "The Polish ambassador called. He had little to offer other than to reiterate the belief of his Government that German strength was overrated . . . He said that the German army was not the army of 1914. The officers had insufficient training and had not been allowed to remain long enough with the same units of troops. The best generals had been liquidated, and the remaining generals were merely 'Party hacks.' !! The German people did not want to fight, and it would be suicidal to start a war when conditions were already so bad that people were being rationed as to foodstuffs."

Moffat concluded, "The whole conversation represented a point of view of unreasonable optimism and still more unreasoning underrating of one's opponent, that, if typical of Polish mentality in general, causes me to feel considerable foreboding."

As he continued to cover the unfolding drama in Europe for CBS, Shirer was beyond foreboding. He was deeply pessimistic. Even his good friend John Gunther, the former *Chicago Daily News* reporter who had launched what would prove to be a highly successful career as an author with his 1936 bestseller *Inside Europe*, was more reserved in his judgments after the sellout of Czechoslovakia. In the introduction to the new edition of the book that was published near the end of 1938, he noted "the death of the Czechoslovak nation in its present form," but declared, "There is a chance—just a chance but a chance—that the Munich Agreement may bring a European settlement." As late as July 28, 1939, when Shirer met Gunther in Geneva, the CBS man wrote in his diary, "John fairly optimistic about peace."

Returning to Berlin in early August, Shirer found his darkening mood turning into open anger. On the train from Basel, he observed that the passengers "looked clean and decent, the kind that made us like Germans, as people, before the Nazis." In a discussion with someone he identified as Captain D—"a World War officer of proved patriotism"—Shirer recorded that the German, who had earlier professed to be against a new war, "became violent today at the very mention of the Poles and the British," taking his cue from Hitler's attacks on both. His diary entry on August 9 chronicles their heated exchange:

> He thundered: "Why do the English butt in on Danzig and threaten war over the return of a German city? Why do the Poles [sic] provoke us? Haven't we the right to a German city like Danzig?"
>
> "Have you the right to a Czech city like Prague?" I asked. Silence. No answer. That vacant stare you get on Germans.
>
> "Why didn't the Poles accept the generous offer of the Führer?" he began again.
>
> "Because they feared another Sudetenland, Captain."
>
> "You mean they don't trust the Führer?"
>
> "Not much since March 15," I said, looking carefully around before I spoke such blasphemy to see I was not being overheard. Again the vacant German stare.

March 15, 1939, was the date when German troops had marched into Prague and Hitler declared, "Czechoslovakia has ceased to exist!"

Shirer could see that the same fate awaited Poland. The next day, he marveled: "How completely isolated a world the German people live in." German newspapers were trumpeting headlines like "Poland? Look Out!" and "Warsaw Threatens Bombardment of Danzig—Unbelievable Agitation of the Polish Archmadness."

"For perverse perversion of truth, this is good," Shirer noted. "You ask: But the German people can't possibly believe these lies? Then you talk to them. So many do."

Convinced that Hitler and the Germans were about to plunge the continent into a new war, he used his diary as a way to release his frustration, not sparing anyone. "Struck by the ugliness of German women on the streets and cafés," he wrote. "As a race they are certainly the least attractive in Europe. They have no ankles. They walk badly. They dress worse than English women used to."

From Berlin, Shirer went to Danzig, finding the city "completely Nazified," but he quickly concluded the real issue was not the status of that purportedly "Free City." In a broadcast from the neighboring Polish port city of Gdynia on August 13, he talked about the relative calm in Danzig, despite all the speculation that "this powder-keg of Europe" was about to ignite a new war. He concluded that Hitler might not be pushing for a confrontation over the status of that city as quickly as generally believed. But Danzig, he warned, "is only a symbol—for both sides. The issue, of course, for the Poles, is the future of Poland as an independent nation with a secure outlet to the sea. For the Germans it's the future of East Prussia cut off from the motherland, the future of the whole German stake in the East. And for most of the rest of Europe the issue is that of German domination on the continent."

Taking the train from Gdynia to Warsaw right after making that broadcast, Shirer chatted with two Polish radio engineers who expressed confidence about their country's ability to resist Hitler. "We're ready. We will fight," they told him. "We were born under German rule in this neighborhood and we'd rather be dead than go through it again." In the Polish capital, he was further impressed by how "calm and confident" the inhabitants seemed, despite the relentless propaganda onslaughts from Berlin. His worry, though, was that the Poles were "too romantic, too confident" and they were ignoring the signals that the Soviet Union might also have designs on them.

By the time he left Warsaw to return to Berlin a week later, Shirer had formed a judgment about how the Poles would react to any attempted takeover of their country. "I think the Poles will fight," he concluded. "I know I said that, wrongly, about the Czechs a year ago. But I say it again about the Poles."

On August 23, 1939, German Foreign Minister Joachim von Ribbentrop and his counterpart Vyacheslav Molotov signed the Nazi-Soviet Pact in a Kremlin ceremony, with Stalin looking on. Two days earlier, Anthony Biddle, the American ambassador to Poland, had asked for permission from Washington to begin evacuating the families of his staffers. The news of Ribbentrop's imminent mission to Moscow was already out, and, as Moffat wrote in his diary that day, it came as a "bombshell." The senior State Department official concluded: "There is no doubt that Germany has pulled off one of the greatest diplomatic coups for many years ... It looks to me as though Germany had promised Russia no objection to the latter taking over Estonia and Latvia and, in effect, agreeing to some form of new partition of Poland." In his own mind, Moffat had already upped the odds of war breaking out to 60–40 in midsummer, and now he raised them further to 75–25.

In Berlin, many of the American correspondents were as usual keeping late hours at their favorite restaurant, Die Taverne, on the night of August 23–24, when they heard the official news about the pact. "It goes much further than anyone dreamed," Shirer wrote in his diary. "It's a virtual alliance and Stalin, the supposed arch-enemy of Nazism and aggression, by its terms invites Germany to go in and clean up Poland."

Several German editors who had been writing virulently anti-Soviet articles up till then came into the restaurant and ordered champagne, Shirer observed, and they were suddenly presenting themselves "as old friends of the Soviets!" The seemingly hardened American reporter was stunned by the enormity of the agreement between the two totalitarian systems. While Shirer knew what it meant, he clearly didn't understand the Soviet leader as well as he did Hitler. "That Stalin would play such crude power politics and also play into the hands of the Nazis overwhelms the rest of us," he wrote.

Shirer and an American colleague he only identified as Joe sat down with the German editors and promptly got into a heated argument. "They are gloating, boasting, sputtering that Britain won't dare to fight now, denying everything that they have been told to say these last six years by their Nazi lords [about the Soviet Union]," Shirer recorded. The two Americans pushed back, reminding them of how they had written about the Bolsheviks until then. "The argument gets nasty," Shirer concluded. "Joe is nervous, depressed. So am I. Pretty soon we get nauseated. Something will happen if we don't get out." The Americans made their excuses and left, walking through the Tiergarten to cool off in the night air.

As news of the Nazi-Soviet Pact sank in, Britain and France reaffirmed their commitments to Poland. In the wake of the takeover of Czechoslovakia in March, both countries had pledged to defend Poland, and on August 25, British and Polish officials formally signed the Anglo-Polish military alliance in London. But Hitler was still counting on outmaneuvering Britain, as he continued to exchange messages with Prime Minister Chamberlain's government in London and meet with its ambassador in Berlin, Sir Nevile Henderson. Shirer was convinced that war was coming, but he pointed out: "The people in the streets are still confident Hitler will pull it off again without war."

The State Department urged Americans not to travel to Europe unless absolutely necessary. American diplomats in Berlin could monitor the war preparations firsthand, making them even less likely to see a chance for avoiding a conflict than their bosses back in Washington. Jacob Beam recalled: "From about the middle of August, searchlights pierced the Berlin skies, pin-pointing planes at what seemed to be very great heights. Troop convoys crossed the city escorted by roaring motorcycle brigades manned by goggled riders looking like men from Mars." On August 26, he added, the government issued a new long list of items to be rationed, including food, shoes and soap. Those who owned automobiles were instructed to turn in any backup batteries they had.

As Hitler and his entourage saw it, Germany was now fully prepared to strike.

*          *          *

Recalling the final days of August 1939 seventy years later, Angus Thuermer still felt somewhat sheepish about how he handled his assignment at the time. Lochner, his bureau chief, had instructed the junior AP reporter to travel to Gleiwitz, along the Polish border, since he knew "something was going to happen." That proved to be quite an understatement.

One evening, Thuermer took a taxi outside of town and promptly found himself in the midst of a Wehrmacht regiment marching along the border. Realizing that he had better leave before he got into trouble, Thuermer ordered the taxi to take him back to Gleiwitz. A couple of evenings later—August 31, to be exact—he was awakened by sounds outside his hotel. He looked out of his seventh-floor window and saw German troops in a field car followed by countless others marching. Then a band suddenly appeared. That convinced him it was only an exercise. "You don't take a band to go to war," he said, recalling his thinking at the time. So he went back to sleep. The next morning, September 1, he looked out the window again and saw trucks bringing back wounded German soldiers from Poland. The German invasion of Poland was under way.

Alarmed that he had slept through the first night of the conflagration that would become World War II, Thuermer rushed to find the press officer of a German Army unit that had moved into his hotel. Introducing himself, he explained that he was eager to accompany German troops into Poland, since it was normal practice for AP reporters to do so. They had been allowed to accompany German troops into Austria and the Sudetenland, he pointed out. "Yes, Herr Thuermer, but this time it is different," the German press officer replied. "You go back to Berlin and to the Propaganda Ministry and they will tell you what is happening."

The German officer was right, of course: This time was different. This was really war.

Back in Berlin, some American diplomats had received almost as clear signals on the eve of the German invasion. Walking to work on August 31, William Russell, a twenty-four-year-old clerk in the embassy's consular section, had already seen the morning headlines in the German papers: "Last Warnings" and "Unendurable Outrages" and "Murderous Poles." He jumped as a siren shrieked nearby, evidently a test of the air raid warning system, and he observed the traffic jam in Potsdamer Platz caused by army trucks full of soldiers, along with motorcycles and cannon transporters. He could also see aircraft circling above Berlin. "The excitement of a city preparing for war pounded in my veins," he recalled.

Just as Russell was approaching the embassy, a small man with a shaved head, holding a gray hat in his trembling hand, touched his arm. "I must talk to you," he said in a whisper.

The man quickly confirmed that Russell, whom he had seen in the immigration section, indeed worked there. Hans Neuman was a Jew who hadn't been able to push his way through the crowd to the door of the embassy that morning, and he was frantic. Russell instructed him to keep walking as he explained more. Neuman said he had been released a week earlier from Dachau, and now he was desperate for an American visa. "The Gestapo ordered me out of the country ten days ago," he pleaded. "I've got to get out today, or never."

Russell asked him if he was telling the truth, since a lot of applicants were willing to say anything that would get them a visa. "My God, look at my head if you don't believe me," Neuman replied. The American noted the red gashes under the bit of hair that had grown back since his head was recently shaved—the telltale sign of a prisoner.

And Neuman offered a concrete reason why he had to get out that day. "War is going to start tonight. I have friends who know," he told Russell. "If I don't get across the border, I'll lose my last chance to escape. God knows what they'll . . ."

Although the young American had heard many similar pleas, he believed Neuman and promised to help him. Entering the embassy, Russell was confronted by "a madhouse" overflowing with others clamoring for a prized American visa to get out. He found Neuman's paperwork and appealed to Vice-Consul Paul Coates to let him jump the long queue, but Coates chastised him for allowing his personal sympathy for Neuman to sway him. "It's not fair to all the others," he said.

Russell wouldn't give up. "I know it's not fair," he replied. "Nothing's fair, if you want to be strictly truthful. It's not fair of the German police to order this man to get out of his homeland when he has violated no law and has no place to go to. It isn't fair to push a man around until he's half crazy. I'm not concerned about fairness."

Russell overheard a woman nearby imploring another colleague to do something for her husband, who was imprisoned in Dachau. "I'm sorry," the American told her. "There are thousands of applicants registered before your husband. He has at least eight years to wait."

"But you will just have to do something," the woman pleaded. "He will die there. If war comes, they will never let him out of that place."

The consular official shook his head, signaling an end to their conversation. As she gathered her paperwork and left, the woman broke into tears. American quota laws hadn't changed to accommodate the mostly Jewish applicants who, according to Russell, "were to be found in every nook and cranny" of every American consulate in Germany.

Still, Russell worked all day to get Neuman his visa. Seeing his determination, another consular officer finally relented near closing time, finding him a quota number to assign to Neuman. He even suggested that Russell drive him to the airport to make sure he was allowed to get on a plane to Rotterdam, since it was too late at that point for him to get a Dutch visa. At Tempelhof Airport, two storm troopers, dressed in black uniforms, and two other officials examined Neuman's passport. They also asked Russell what he was doing there. The American explained that he was from the embassy and wanted to make sure that Neuman got on the plane to Rotterdam, since he had an American visa and was due to sail from the Dutch port to the United States.

"Herr Neuman has a visa to the United States," one of the storm troopers said sarcastically, pointing out that he didn't have a Dutch visa. "Well, isn't that nice?"

But then one of the other officials intervened. "Let him go," he said. "We'd have one Jew less. Let the Dutch worry about what to do with him."

A customs officer took a final look at Neuman's passport and stamped it. "See that you don't come back to Germany," he told him. "If you do, you'll be sent back to a certain place."

Neuman's story would prove to be one of the few with a happy ending on that last day before the war broke out. Later, he sent Russell a postcard confirming that he had sailed from Rotterdam.

Another story with a happy ending involved Józef Lipski, the Polish ambassador to Germany. His British counterpart, Sir Nevile Henderson, had called Lipski to inform him about his stormy meeting with Foreign Minister von Ribbentrop, which had left little doubt that the Germans were about to attack Poland. That conversation had taken place at 2 A.M. on August 31. Around noon the same day, Jacob Beam spotted Lipski sitting in his car at a Shell station, waiting for his tank to be filled. After the war, Beam met Lipski and told him he had seen him then. Lipski explained that he had stayed with his car, fearing that the Germans might seize it. Early that evening, only a few hours before the Germans invaded, Lipski escaped back to his homeland.

If many American diplomats and journalists in Berlin had a better sense of the enormity of the storm that Hitler was unleashing than others looking from afar, most of them still hadn't recognized how quickly Hitler's forces would be able to overwhelm Poland and later most of continental Europe.

In his address to the Reichstag on September 1, Hitler wore an army jacket. "I have once more put on that coat which was most sacred and dear to me," he declared. "I will not take it off again until victory is secured, or I shall not survive the outcome." Hitler claimed he had made "endless attempts" to keep the peace, but that Polish troops had attacked German territory, leaving him no choice but to act. Beam, who was in the Reichstag to hear him, found the speech impressive, aimed at convincing Britain and France not to enter the fray. He called his language "less belligerent and intimidating" than in earlier speeches.

Shirer, who listened to the speech from the radio studio since he had to immediately transmit its contents, had a different impression. He detected "a curious strain, as though Hitler himself were dazed at the fix he had gotten himself into and felt a little desperate about it." Hitler explained that Goering would be his successor if anything happened to him, and that Hess would be next in line. Shirer agreed with a colleague that the speech sounded like the dictator's swan song.

At 7 P.M. while Shirer was still at the radio station, the air raid sirens sounded and the German employees took their gas masks down to the bomb shelter. The American didn't have a mask and no one offered him one, but he was instructed to follow. He did, but then in the darkness slipped away, returning to a studio where a candle was burning so he could jot down his notes. "No planes came over," he recorded later that night in his diary. Expecting Britain and France to make good on their promises to defend Poland right away, he added: "But with the English and French in, it may be different tomorrow. I shall then be in the by no means pleasant predicament of hoping they bomb the hell out of this town without getting me." In fact, the British and French didn't declare war on Germany until September 3.

That first evening of the war Shirer found it "curious" that the restaurants, cafés and beer halls were still full of people. And writing in his diary at two-thirty in the morning, he added: "Curious that not a single Polish bomber got through tonight. But will it be the same with the British and the French?" The next day, he noted further: "No air-raid tonight. Where are the Poles?"

In his radio broadcast on September 2, Shirer reported that Berliners, who were nervous during the first night of the blackout, were beginning to sense that life didn't have to change much. "After, say, about 1 A.M. this morning, when it became fairly evident that if the Poles were going to send over any planes they would have come by that time, most people went to sleep. Taxis, creeping along with little slits of light to identify them, did a big business all through the night."

After Hitler's declaration of war, Russell, the young embassy clerk, recalled in a similar vein: "One expected something terrific to happen immediately. Nothing did." But like Shirer and other Americans in Berlin, Russell noticed that the mood was quite different from the jubilation that had accompanied the outbreak of the previous war. "The people I have met seem calm and sad and resigned. They stand around in little groups in front of our Embassy building, staring at us through the windows. I think this is nothing like the beginning of the World

War in 1914." Russell added: "Today, I think they have been led into
something which may turn out to be too big for them."

How correct he would prove to be, but only much later. The string
of initial German victories in Poland, the Americans in Berlin reported,
produced increasing confidence among the German people and the military in the wisdom of Hitler's actions. On September 6, Shirer noted in
his diary, "It begins to look like a rout for the Poles." In the following days,
he added that the U.S. military attachés were stunned by the speed of the
German advance, and many correspondents were depressed. Britain and
France were formally at war, but "not a shot yet—so the Germans say—
on the western front!" On September 13, Russell despaired in his diary:
"The war is raging in Poland. What can England and France be thinking
of? we ask each other. Why don't they attack Germany now, so she will
have to fight on two fronts?"

When the Soviet Union attacked Poland from the east on September 17, the Americans in Berlin knew that country's fate was sealed. For
the correspondents, another sign was the sudden willingness of the German authorities to allow them to go to the front. Arriving in Sopot on
the Baltic coast, Shirer wrote in his diary on September 18: "Drove all
day long from Berlin through Pomerania and the Corridor to here. The
roads full of motorized columns of German troops *returning* from Poland. In the woods in the Corridor the sickening sweet smell of dead
horses and the sweeter smell of dead men. Here, the Germans say, a
whole division of Polish cavalry charged against hundreds of German
tanks and was annihilated."

Reaching Gdynia the next day, Shirer witnessed the Germans merci-
lessly bombarding one of the last Polish units still resisting them in that
area—from the sea, and from three sides on land. The German battle-
ship *Schleswig-Holstein* was anchored in Danzig's harbor, firing shells at
the Polish position, while the artillery was opening up from positions
surrounding it. Tanks and airplanes were also attacking the Poles, who
desperately fought back with nothing more than rifles, machine guns and
two antiaircraft guns. "It was a hopeless position for the Poles. And yet
they fought on," Shirer wrote in his diary. "The German officers with us
kept praising their courage."

Joseph Grigg, a Berlin correspondent for United Press, was among the first group of foreign newsmen to reach Warsaw, arriving on October 5. They were brought there to see Hitler come to the Polish capital for his victory parade. Grigg was struck by the sight of the heavily bombed city after holding out for one month against the German onslaught. "Such devastation would be difficult to imagine. The whole center of the city had been laid in ruins," he recalled. "The Polish population looked bewildered and stunned." He concluded that the Poles never had a chance against the German invaders, who had knocked out most of the Polish Air Force on the first day of the invasion. "The advance of the German mechanized forces across the flat plains of Poland was unleashed with a precision and swing never before seen in history."

Later, Grigg met General Alexander Loehr, the former chief of the Austrian Federal Air Force who had become the commander of Hitler's Air Fleet Southeast, which was responsible for the air campaign against Poland. The correspondent asked him how he could justify this "blitzkrieg without warning." Loehr calmly explained that this was really a more humane type of warfare. "It is our new philosophy of war," he declared. "It is the most merciful type of warfare. It surprises your enemy, paralyzes him at one blow and shortens a war by weeks, maybe months. In the long run it saves casualties on both sides."

The AP's Lochner had witnessed what this "humane" type of warfare had consisted of. He was permitted to cross the border from Gleiwitz during the fighting in Poland, and in the small town of Graszyn saw that all the buildings along the main road had been razed—not simply hit by bombs and shells as in other places. The army colonel who was his guide explained that this was done in retaliation for sniping by Polish civilians.

Lochner also heard a story from an informant in the German Army who described how his detachment had occupied another small Polish town, bringing along their wounded. The local pharmacist and his wife, who were Jews, "worked like Trojans to help us dress the wounds," the informant told Lochner. "We all respected the couple." The grateful soldiers assured the couple they would be protected by the German Army. Then the detachment was ordered to move on. "Even before we had time to depart, the SS were there," he added. "A few minutes later the Jewish couple was found by one of our men with their throats slashed. The SS had killed them."

The message Hitler delivered to the foreign correspondents who were brought to Warsaw on October 5 was one of pure menace. His face pallid but acting like "a triumphant conqueror," Grigg reported, Hitler briefly met the reporters at Warsaw's airport before boarding his flight back to Berlin. "Gentlemen, you have seen the ruins of Warsaw," he told them. "Let that be a warning to those statesmen in London and Paris who still think of continuing this war."

By this point, according to Russell in Berlin, many Germans had become convinced by the lack of a military response from Britain and France "that Germany is invincible." But the young American also met Germans who had come to the opposite conclusion. "I hope they [the British and the French] hurry up and break through the Westwall," one of them told him, referring to Germany's defensive line built opposite France's Maginot Line. "When our army is defeated, that will be the end of Hitler. If we lose we will not be free; but then we are not free now."

Although Russell claimed that this was far from an isolated voice, Hitler's latest victory—combined with Nazi terror and propaganda— ensured that most Germans, as the *Chicago Tribune's* Sigrid Schultz put it, were increasingly willing to obey their leader's demand to "follow me blindly." The veteran Berlin correspondent added, "And the masses did believe." She cited the example of her maid, who appeared one morning shortly after the invasion of Poland, her eyes red from crying. Her husband had been assigned as a stretcher-bearer at a hospital near Berlin, and he had described to her in vivid detail how the Poles had supposedly burned off the skin of Germans on their side of the border right before Hitler's armies attacked, turning their limbs into charred stumps.

Schultz asked her if her husband had seen any such cases, and the maid acted offended that she would doubt her. But later she admitted that her husband had only viewed slides presented by Nazi propagandists. Still, the maid's conviction grew that her American employer wasn't properly sympathetic to Nazi Germany. "It wasn't long before my maid was one more servant in the Gestapo system keeping tabs on the activities of the correspondents," Schultz reported. "Our mail, our telephone conversations, our visitors, were all regularly reported to the police."

The Propaganda Ministry had invited Schultz and other correspondents to a preview of the first newsreels of the war. As scenes of German troops rounding up anguished Polish prisoners flashed on the screen, Schultz recalled, there were "squeals and shouts of delight from leading German officials." Once the newsreels were in the theaters, Schultz went to see how the public reacted. Images of Polish Jews in caftans or rags who were visibly terrified by their captors triggered "loud guffaws and shrieks of laughter," she wrote.

After the first reports of mass murders in Poland filtered back to Germany, Schultz was at a reception full of Nazi officials. "I don't see why you Anglo-Saxons get so excited about what happens to a few Poles," a high-ranking SS officer told her. "Your reaction shows you and your countrymen do not have the scientific approach to the problem."

Schultz asked what the scientific approach was. Three men, including Roland Freisler, the Justice Ministry official who would later become the notorious president of the People's Court, offered an impromptu lecture on racial theory. The Slavs were only white on "an inferior level," they explained, and they outnumbered the pure white Germans; their birth rate was much higher as well, which would mean a doubling of their populations by 1960. "We indulge in no sentimentality," Freisler continued. "We shall not allow any of our neighbors to have a higher birth rate than ours, and we shall take measures to prevent it." Slavs and Jews would only be permitted to survive "if they work for us," he added. "If they don't they can starve."

Schultz observed that if one of her "leg men" had brought her such a story, she probably would have been disbelieving. But she heard this in person, and Freisler clearly "didn't realize, or care, how horrifying his remarks appeared to an American."

Joseph Harsch, a reporter for the *Christian Science Monitor*, was in Rome in October 1939 when he received a terse cable from his foreign editor in Boston: "Now go to Berlin." It was still remarkably easy to do so. Harsch went to the German Embassy to apply for a visa and received it three days later, and the concierge at his hotel picked up a ticket for the sleeper to Berlin. He boarded the train in the evening and arrived there the next morning. He had reached the capital of the country that had plunged the continent into a new war, but the only "abnormality," as Harsch sardonically recalled, was that when he got off the train at the Friedrichstrasse Bahnhof there were no porters to help him with his luggage. He got around that problem by leaving his belongings at the station, then checking into the nearby Continental Hotel and sending a hotel porter back to pick them up.

Joining Shirer and other American colleagues, he soon switched over to the more elegant Adlon Hotel, getting a room in the back wing overlooking the garden of Joseph Goebbels, whose Propaganda Ministry was a block away. Harsch often saw his children playing there. Everything about Harsch's arrival seemed deceptively easy. The spying that Schultz and other veterans noticed wasn't all that apparent to a newcomer like him, but he was quick to see that the Germans were intent on making him feel comfortable. He was issued a ration card of a "heavy worker," and he was free to import extra food—eggs, bacon, butter, cheese—from Denmark. "As an American correspondent at a time when German policy was keyed to keeping the United States out of the war as long as possible, I settled into a privileged life," he wrote.

Harsch wore a small American flag pin on his lapel, which he felt avoided any misunderstandings about who he was when he talked with Germans. He was pleased to see that most people still spoke freely to American reporters, and he could travel almost anywhere he wanted and file stories. Official Germans didn't seem particularly secretive either, even when it came to subjects like concentration camps for political prisoners and Jews. Looking back at that period in the autobiography he wrote near the end of his life, Harsch observed: "The label *concentration camp* had not then acquired the sinister connotation it has today . . . There was nothing sufficiently unusual about the internment camps in Germany to attract the special attention of American correspondents in Berlin in 1939 and 1940."

Harsch encountered difficulties with the authorities only when he began doing occasional radio broadcasts for CBS, subbing for Shirer when he was out of town. The rules for broadcasters were far tougher than anything print journalists faced. As Harsch noted, all scripts had to be approved by a group of censors, with one representative each from the Foreign Ministry, the Propaganda Ministry and the Military High Command. A censor also carefully monitored the reading of the approved scripts on air and could cut the correspondent off instantly if he deviated from it.

Oddly, there was often less of a sense of danger than when other American correspondents, like Edgar Mowrer, had reported on the Nazis coming to power. Richard Hottelet, a recent Brooklyn College graduate who was an aggressive United Press reporter in Berlin, didn't hesitate to board a train full of Polish Jews who were being expelled from Germany. While he found the conditions in the third-class cars "pretty awful, pretty depressing," they were still mild compared to the cattle car deportations that would soon follow. And Hottelet wasn't worried about his personal safety as he pursued such stories. "I was an American, I was working for an American organization, I didn't feel threatened," he declared. "I knew the situation was odd but not menacing." In fact, Hottelet would later experience the inside of a German prison, but he still vividly recalled that sense of invulnerability during an interview seventy years later.

The conflict Hitler had unleashed quickly lapsed into its "phony war" stage, with the Germans biding their time for their spring 1940 new offensives and the French sitting quietly behind their Maginot Line. On October 10, 1939, Shirer traveled to Geneva, and as his train ran along the Rhine, he could see French and German soldiers building up fortifications on their respective sides. "The troops seemed to be observing an armistice," he wrote in his diary. "They went about their business in full sight and range of each other . . . Queer kind of war."

The Royal Air Force attacked German naval targets, only to suffer serious losses and inflict little damage. On October 2, the RAF made its first night raid on Berlin, dropping only propaganda leaflets "in the vain hope that people reading them would be incited to revolt," consular clerk Russell scoffed. "They might as well have saved their gasoline." During this early stage of the conflict, there was no air war to speak of, and the blackout in Berlin felt more like a precaution than a necessity. Britain and France rejected Hitler's "peace proposals" after his victory over Poland, and the British naval blockade meant that rationing was tightened further. But many Germans still held out "the hope of an early victory and peace," as Otto Tolischus, the Berlin correspondent of the *New York Times*, wrote. Whatever sacrifices they had to make were justified, he added, by the regime's slogan: "It is better to live safely than to live well."

In the immediate aftermath of the Polish campaign, Americans in Berlin could see one indication of the early cost of the war: the death notices that appeared in local newspapers. "One Breslau daily, especially, is just filled every day with casualty notices—old, established names where the young man, the hope of the family, fell," the AP's Lochner wrote to his children in Chicago on October 8. "Right among our own friends and in one case even relatives . . ." He added that social life was disappearing "because everyone lives on bread cards, meat cards, fat cards, etc., hence has no accumulated reserves with which to entertain guests."

Lochner noted that people were reluctant to go to unfamiliar places in the evening because of the blackout, and accidents were frequent. As the nights grew longer, the young diplomat Russell observed that this was at least to one group's advantage. "In the darkness, certain girls made easy pickups," he pointed out. While prostitution was technically illegal in Nazi Germany, the blackouts made it a lot easier. "Even the old girls, the wrinkled ones, stood on corners with their ugly features safely hidden in the darkness and shone their flashlights on their legs in invitation."

George Kennan, a Russian specialist who had volunteered to go to Berlin to help chargé d'affaires Alexander Kirk with his administrative duties, arrived in the German capital shortly after the war began. One of his strongest memories of that period was of returning home after work in the evenings: "the groping in pitch blackness from column to column of the Brandenburg gate, feeling my way by hand after this fashion to the bus stop . . . the wonder as to how the driver ever found his way over the vast expanse of unmarked, often snow-covered asphalt . . . the eerie walk home at the other end, again with much groping and feeling for curbstones."

Despite all those daily inconveniences, it was still relatively easy to overlook the fact that the war was on since the fighting was taking place elsewhere. On a visit to Hamburg about a month into the war, Kennan was making his way back to his lodgings one evening when a woman emerged from a street corner and said cheerfully: "Shan't we go somewhere?" Kennan indicated he wasn't interested in her services but he'd buy her a drink—and pay her what she normally charged for more than that. At her favorite bar, she told him her story: that she had a daytime job packing parcels, where the pay was bad but it was her way of avoiding the roundups of street girls who were sent to labor camps; that she was engaged to an army flyer who was on duty in Poland, "a complete egoist" who treated her badly; and that she made her real money on the streets at night—of course, unbeknownst to him.

There was nothing all that extraordinary in her story, and nothing all that unusual that Kennan would find it intriguing to talk to a fairly sophisticated streetwalker. He may have been destined for a distinguished career as a diplomat and scholar, but he was still a young man at the time. The most memorable part of his encounter, though, was what was left unsaid. "It was only after I got home it occurred to me that neither of us had mentioned the war," he wrote.

Among top Nazi leaders, the mood was one of growing confidence that events were moving their way. At the Soviet Embassy's November 7 reception to celebrate the anniversary of the Bolshevik Revolution, a group of American correspondents chatted with Goering as he stood at the buffet drinking a beer and smoking a cigar. Shirer, who was part of this group, had thought the Luftwaffe commander might be upset with America's increasingly open support for Britain and growing talk of supplying that country with large numbers of airplanes.

But Goering was in an expansive, jovial mood. "If we could only make planes at your rate of production we should be very weak," he declared. "I mean that seriously. Your planes are good, but you don't make enough of them fast enough." He added that "one day you'll see who has been building the best and the most planes."

When the Americans asked why German planes had only attacked British warships, he replied that they were important targets and "give us good practice."

"Are you going to begin bombing enemy ports?" the Americans persisted.

"We're humane," Goering responded. Shirer and the others couldn't help laughing. "You shouldn't laugh," he admonished them. "I'm serious. I *am* humane."

In less official settings, Americans in Berlin were surprised to discover occasional flashes of genuine wartime humor. Harsch, the newcomer from the *Christian Science Monitor*, heard one story that was making the rounds of a working-class neighborhood. According to the joke, a disguised Hitler goes to a beer hall and asks the proprietor what people really think of *Der Führer*. The proprietor leans forward and whispers to him: "I couldn't afford to have any of my customers hear me say it, but I, personally, don't think he's so bad."

As the American reporters and diplomats learned, many Germans were also listening to foreign radio stations, despite the fact that this was strictly forbidden. Russell estimated that 60 to 70 percent did so in secret, and he noticed that the stores sold out all their old-fashioned radio headphones during the first week of the war. While his estimate was probably high, he encountered enough Germans who signaled their reservations about Hitler and the war, however obliquely, that he was hesitant to make sweeping judgments about the national mood.

"If the United States goes into this war, there is one thing I do not want to forget," he wrote. "There are millions of people in Germany who do not agree with the policies of their leaders. And there are other millions, simple people, who believe exactly what their leaders tell them— especially when they tell them the same thing day after day. I do not want to go blind with hatred and forget that." Kennan echoed those sentiments. "It was hard to associate oneself with much of the American press and of Washington officialdom in picturing the German people as a mass of inhuman monsters, solidly behind Hitler and consumed with a demonic enthusiasm for the ruin and enslavement of the rest of Europe," he wrote in his memoirs.

Even Shirer, who was far less forgiving, was encouraged by the occasional encounter with a German who represented the kind of free thinking that had until recently flourished in that country. In January 1940, he met with a woman in Berlin to give her some provisions he had brought for her from her relatives abroad. He described her as "the most intelligent German female I have met in ages." She bemoaned her countrymen's slavish obedience to authority, and their willingness to follow its Nazi leaders, who represented the barbarian impulses that always lurked below the surface. She saw those rulers as intent on destroying Western civilization and its values, despite the contribution of so many Germans to the development of that civilization.

It was a recipe for self-destruction, she explained to Shirer, the result of an unwillingness or inability of her countrymen to think and act for themselves. "A German will think he has died a good German if he waits at a curb at a red light, and then crosses on a green one though he knows perfectly well that a truck, against the law though it may be, is bearing down upon him to crush him to death."

The American diplomats and correspondents continued to live, as the consular clerk Russell put it, "isolated on our island in the middle of Berlin." He attributed the gas rationing for embassy employees less to wartime shortages than to the desire of the Nazis to limit the mobility of the Americans in their midst. The authorities also tapped their phones and didn't mind that the Americans realized it, since this was meant to make them cautious in contacts with Germans.

Rationing for the general population kept getting stricter, with everything from toilet paper to shoelaces disappearing, and stores began putting up small signs proclaiming GOODS DISPLAYED IN THE WINDOWS ARE NOT FOR SALE. But most Americans lived in a parallel universe. On Thanksgiving Day 1939, when the war was into its third month, Kirk, the embassy's senior diplomat, invited a contingent of his countrymen in Berlin for the customary afternoon meal. "A hundred or so hungry Americans charged into several turkeys assembled on the buffet table," Shirer noted in his diary.

The CBS correspondent then went on to a dinner at the home of Dorothy and Fred Oechsner, the United Press manager in Berlin, where Shirer tucked into another turkey. He was so thrilled by the whipped cream on the pumpkin pie that he talked Dorothy into going to the broadcast studio at midnight to explain to listeners back home how she had used "a new-fangled machine" to extract the cream from butter.

Despite their unique circumstances, the Americans did get around, and the diplomats in particular were constantly contacted by those seeking their help. As Christmas approached, Russell reported, "embarrassingly large baskets of food, wine, champagne and delicacies of all sorts in Berlin were delivered to our residences." Those who still had the means to put together those kinds of packages never included a card identifying themselves, but usually in a short time they would send a letter to the recipient asking for help. At the end of the letter, the supplicant would inquire whether the Christmas present had arrived safely—and then would sign with his or her full name and address. Other visa applicants offered bribes of money to the Americans right in the consulate, although trying to do so secretly and using "veiled language."

In January 1940, as a bitter cold winter set in, the Americans flooded the tennis court in the back of the embassy, turning it into an ice-skating rink. But for all their amenities, including shipments of warm winter clothes from Denmark, they were in close enough contact with life around them to dismiss reports back home about the desperate conditions of most Germans and the possibility that this could bring down the Nazi regime.

To be sure, the privations of the war were making themselves felt, and Kennan was struck by the "unmistakable inner detachment of the people from the pretentious purposes of the regime." But he also remarked on "the way life went on, as best it could, under the growing difficulties of wartime discipline." Russell reported a similar lack of enthusiasm for the war, adding: "But here Germany was, right before my eyes, working and living and going strong." In other words, the speculation back in the United States that the Germans were prepared to rise up in revolt was nothing more than wishful thinking.

As the embassy staffers arranged the paperwork for numerous Americans who had surfaced to make arrangements to return home in those first months of the war, their island felt lonelier than before. And they weren't completely immune to the deteriorating living conditions. By January, hot water was usually no longer available in their apartments, prompting the embassy to put in two tin bathtubs on the building's upper floor, one for women and one for men.

Late in January, Russell was invited to lunch at the apartment of Consul Richard Stratton, where he met Jane Dyer, whose brother was also working at the embassy. She was up for a visit from Rome, where she was studying music, but her real home was Alabama. "I never expected to be so far away from home in my life," she proclaimed in a husky voice with a thick southern accent that instantly charmed Russell, who had grown up in neighboring Mississippi. After lunch, they played records, and Russell danced with her. All of which made for a lovely afternoon. Toward the end of it, Dyer asked: "Is Germany really at war? I mean, I haven't seen anything to remind me of war. Everything is the same as it always was."

It was Stratton who replied. "You don't feel anything yet. Just like those children playing out in the street. They don't feel the war either— yet. But the time will come when war will come home to all of us—to Americans, Russians, Africans, children and unborn babies. I think so, anyway."

The party was over, and Dyer and Russell pondered his words in silence.

## 11

◆———◆———◆

# Feeding the Squirrels

William Russell had announced his plans to leave Berlin during that first winter of the war. His supervisors in the consular section offered to try to get him a raise and a new title, but he knew that he was at a disadvantage because he had been hired directly by the embassy after he had studied German at the University of Berlin. The foreign service liked to reward those who rose through the normal channels, starting in Washington and then going to their first assignments abroad. Besides, he wanted to try his luck as a writer, and he already had penned much of the manuscript of the book that he would publish in 1941 with the title *Berlin Embassy*. It was a vivid account of his experiences there, providing Americans with the kind of personal insights that were often missing from news reports.

On April 10, 1940, three days before his scheduled departure, Russell was sitting in his parked car in the back of the embassy with a German girlfriend. "We had not gone there to spoon, but to listen to the automobile radio," the young clerk recalled somewhat defensively. The morning newspapers had been filled with what he called the "sickening news" that German troops had moved into Denmark and Norway. On the radio, Goebbels was reading the ultimatums that were delivered to the Nazis' next victims, claiming that Germany had "no territorial ambitions" against them and that "neither of these two countries will be used as a base for operations against the enemy."

Russell started to make a sarcastic comment, but then he saw that his girlfriend had tears in her eyes. "That hateful damn liar!" she exclaimed. "That hateful damn liar!"

For Russell, this was one of the final reminders that not all Germans were marching in lockstep behind Hitler. Before driving off three days later, he said good-bye to a long list of acquaintances from his three-year sojourn in Berlin—"Americans, Germans, Nazis, anti-Nazis, rich, poor, intellectuals, bums," as he put it. Reaching Innsbruck, he was summoned to Gestapo headquarters ostensibly for questioning about his car's papers. They also searched his car, leaving his manuscript strewn about—but still intact.

He drove on to Italy. At the border, a fat customs official couldn't have been friendlier as he stamped his passport. "Now, why do you want to leave Germany, young man? You liked our country, didn't you?" When Russell reflexively assented, he added: "You come back when we have peace, eh?"

Germany had been exciting, even pleasant at times, for the young man from Mississippi, but Russell found it hard to imagine a peaceful continent anytime soon. When he was sitting in his car with his girlfriend in Berlin, he had concluded that Hitler "had embarked on a course from which there could be no turning back." Looking back at the steep hills behind him as he crossed into Italy, he was stripped of all illusions. "Not a gun to be seen, not a building, not a soldier," he wrote. "Yet I knew those woods were teeming with soldiers, bristling with guns."

Many American officials had come to much the same conclusion even before the Germans occupied Denmark and Norway. But there was still often far too much wishful thinking about Germany in the United States, particularly when it came to imagining that internal discontent spurred by shortages might topple Hitler's regime and limit its military reach. Jacob Beam visited Washington during that first winter of the war and indicated that he had been treated like a social pariah for warning about how powerful Germany had become. "The last thing Washington upper circles wanted to be told was the truth, that Hitler controlled the world's most efficient war machine," his friend Joseph Harsch concluded.

The young diplomat told Harsch and other American reporters that they hadn't succeeded in conveying to their readers the extent of Germany's frightening might. "Jake Beam found himself being accused of being pro-Nazi when he tried to tell people in Washington that the German tanks were not immobilized from lack of oil and grease," Harsch added. Like Truman Smith, the military attaché who had concluded his final tour in Berlin in April 1939 after providing a steady stream of incisive intelligence reports about Germany's rapid militarization, Beam learned that bad news was often greeted with suspicion about the motives of the person who delivered it.

Smith, of course, had been the first American diplomat to meet Hitler, back in 1922. At the beginning of March 1940, Undersecretary of State Sumner Welles was the last one to do so. He went to Europe on what he described as a fact-finding mission, without the power to negotiate—or, more important, to threaten the use of force if Hitler didn't back down. "Only one thing could have deflected Hitler from his purpose: the sure knowledge that the power of the United States would be directed against him if he attempted to carry out his intention of conquering the world by force," Welles wrote in his memoir. Facing strong pressure from isolationists to stay out of the war in Europe, the Roosevelt Administration wasn't about to let its envoy suggest anything like that.

Welles knew Berlin from an earlier era. Arriving on the morning of March 1, he got an immediate introduction to the new Berlin as he was driven from the Friedrichstrasse Bahnhof to the Adlon Hotel. Along Unter den Linden, the city's premier boulevard, armed guards stood watch as Polish prisoners shoveled snow from the streets. On the same day, he met with Foreign Minister von Ribbentrop, accompanied by Alexander Kirk. The chargé d'affaires had been cut off from direct contacts at that level because of the Nazi regime's irritation that Roosevelt had ordered Ambassador Wilson back to Washington after Kristallnacht, so Kirk was pleased to get in the door. But the meeting was a complete disappointment.

Welles suffered through three hours of "pomposity and absurdity" and "an amazing conglomeration of misinformation and deliberate lies," he recalled. The foreign minister, he wrote, had "a very stupid mind." Because he didn't want to do anything that might jeopardize his appointment with Hitler the next day, the envoy from Washington offered only the most cautious responses to Ribbentrop's propagandistic monologue.

At eleven the next morning, Welles was escorted into Hitler's new Chancellery, which he considered "a monstrous edifice" with the feel of a modern factory. Hitler was cordial but formal as he met him, and he struck Welles as taller than he expected. "He had in real life none of the ludicrous features so often shown in his photographs," Welles noted. "He seemed in excellent physical condition and in good training . . . He was dignified, both in speech and in movement."

But if Welles may have been unduly impressed by the contrast between Hitler in real life and the numerous caricatures of him in the West—certainly "excellent physical condition" wasn't a term even his aides employed—the American diplomat was coolly analytical about his message. The German leader claimed to want peace with England and to have spread German rule only where it was absolutely necessary. "I did not want this war," he insisted. "It has been forced upon me against my will. It is a waste of my time. My life should have been spent in constructing and not in destroying."

Predictably, those protestations were accompanied by new threats. Hitler warned against trying to make a distinction between the Nazis and the German people, insisting that he had "the support of every German." Then he added: "I can see no hope for the establishment of any lasting peace until the will of England and France to destroy Germany is itself destroyed. I feel that there is no way by which the will to destroy Germany can itself be destroyed except through a complete German victory."

Winding up, Hitler once again claimed that he only wanted "lasting peace." But if anything, his entire performance had the opposite effect upon his guest. "I remember thinking to myself as I got into the car that it was only too tragically plain that all decisions had already been made," Welles recalled. "The best that could be hoped for was delay, for what little that might be worth."

Some Americans still refused to accept that verdict. In particular, James D. Mooney, the president of the General Motors Overseas Corporation, had hopes that a wider war could be averted. In October 1939, Otto Dietrich, Hitler's press chief, asked AP bureau chief Lochner to help set up a meeting with Mooney, who oversaw GM's plants in Germany and all around the globe. The purpose, he said, was to see if the United States could help defuse the conflict between Germany and England and France. Clearly, the other aim was to keep the Americans out of the war. Lochner, who had been a peace activist during World War I, agreed to do so—although he expressed surprise that Dietrich had turned to him since he was familiar with "my uncompromising anti-Nazi views."

On October 19, Mooney met with Goering, who dangled the vision of an accord between his country and the United States, Britain and France. In Paris, Mooney reported his conversation to American Ambassador William Bullitt, who was dismissive of the whole idea that Mooney should be involved in any search for a negotiated solution. Roosevelt met Mooney in the White House on December 22 and the businessman took his willingness to hear him out as a signal that he could continue his quest on an unofficial basis.

On March 4, 1940, two days after Hitler met Welles, Mooney was ushered into the Chancellery for his own face-to-face meeting with Hitler. Evidently, the Nazis still believed that he might play the mediation role they had suggested to him. Treating him with the utmost seriousness, Hitler told Mooney that Germany was willing to respect England's world power status so long as Germany was respected in a similar way. He claimed that this could be the basis for a peace agreement with Roosevelt, which could then lead to arms reductions and new international trade. After more meetings with German officials, Mooney sent five messages to Roosevelt about his talks. In a letter dated April 2, the president thanked him for them, writing that they had been of "real value" to him.

But Mooney failed to get in to see Roosevelt personally to follow up. He was convinced that presidential aide Harry Hopkins and others, who saw him as trying to push a policy of appeasement, blocked him at every turn. Recognizing that he wasn't going to influence the course of events,

Mooney wrote Roosevelt a letter tinged with frustration, expressing his regret that he hadn't had "the opportunity to present to you some of the arguments for getting back on the course that you and I believed in last winter." He added, "I still hope before general hostilities break out again against England—and it is beginning to look as though this may happen very soon . . . that I may be able to interest you in taking a position for peace."

Interestingly, Lochner, who had tried to help Mooney at every turn, apparently had hoped the same thing. The AP bureau chief was indeed anti-Nazi, but he remained a peace activist at heart—even after the invasion of Poland.

Welles had been exactly right: the decisions were already made. Hitler's armies attacked Denmark and Norway in April and then invaded Holland, Belgium and France in May, rolling up victories at a pace that startled even the American correspondents and diplomats in Berlin who had been the most prescient about Germany's intentions. After listening to Foreign Minister von Ribbentrop proclaim on April 9 that it was Britain that was guilty of "the most flagrant violation of a neutral country" and Germany's forces were merely protecting their latest victims, Shirer confessed: "I was stunned. I shouldn't have been—after so many years in Hitlerland—but I was."

Denmark surrendered on the same day as the German troops appeared. Harsch flew to Copenhagen in a German transport plane and reported at the end of the day: "I never dreamed that I should ever see such heartache in a people." He found the Danes "crushed, physically and mentally." Broadcasting from Berlin, Shirer reported that the Germans had expected the Norwegians to fold just as quickly—but they were wrong on that count. The Norwegians fought back on land and sea, aided by Britain's Royal Navy and troops from both Britain and France. On April 14, Shirer wrote a thought in his diary that he could never get past the censor for his broadcast: "Hitler is sowing something in Europe that one day will destroy not only him but his nation."

After Hitler launched the invasion of the Low Countries on May 10, not waiting for an end to the fighting in Norway, "the German steam-roller," as Shirer called it, looked to be unstoppable. And the German authorities were confident enough to permit American correspondents to join German troops on the march in Belgium on May 20. "It's been dream of every newsman in Berlin ever since 5/10 when Reich's gigantic offensive via Holland, Belgium began to see Hitler's amazing, awe inspiring armed forces in action," Lochner, one of the first three correspondents to do so, reported to New York that day.

Excited by his access, Lochner marveled how German air power had "revolutionized" the way wars were fought. Luftwaffe scouter planes first assessed the strength of enemy forces, he explained to his readers, then unleashed their "terrorizing" Stukas and bombers, which "dash madly down upon enemy." Once the planes had done their damage, the infantry followed up with "death disdaining courage," leaving the enemy in complete confusion.

As for the human toll, Lochner was inclined to take much of what he saw at face value. While he informed his readers that he saw "human drama of misery, terrifying first glimpse of horrors wrought by modernist warfare, and strange contrasts of German kindness and German inexorability," he emphasized the former. There were "dejected civilians" on the road, he reported, but German soldiers "seemed anxiousest [sic] to be nice to children, to deal courteously with grownups." The average German soldier, he continued, "is bitter, unyielding, determined even terrible fighter but he also has [a] vast sentimental strain in him."

If Lochner appeared to be unduly credulous about what he was seeing in the presence of his German minders, Shirer—who entered Belgium at the same time—was more cautious. In his radio broadcast, he reported that Belgians he encountered in Brussels, the capital that emerged unscathed, said that "the behavior of German troops had been correct." But he stressed that the Belgians he saw on the roads looked "dazed and bitter and sad." And the housing blocks in the university city of Louvain, where British troops had set up a headquarters, were "a terrible sight to behold" after the battles there. As he waded through the debris in the streets of Saint-Trond, another Belgian town, he jotted quick notes: "houses smashed . . . shambles . . . bitter Belgium civilians . . . women sobbing . . .

their menfolk? . . . where? . . . here houses destroyed at random . . . Stukas careless? . . . on purpose?"

In his diary, Shirer also noted that he and his colleagues had expected the inhabitants of Louvain to tell them about German responsibility for the destruction. "But eyeing the German officers with us, they grow sly, act shy, and tell us nothing," he wrote. A German nun recounted how she huddled with fifty-six children in the cellar of a convent after the bombs started falling without warning on May 10. She emphasized that Belgium had not been at war and not done anything to provoke such an attack. Then, she noticed the German officers watching her speak to the Americans.

"You're German, aren't you?" one of them asked her.

She confirmed her nationality and hastened to add in a frightened voice: "Of course, as a German, I was glad when it was all over and the German troops arrived."

Lochner never alluded to the intimidating effect of the German officers who served as their escorts and how this may have colored what he heard. He and two other reporters—Guido Enderis of the *New York Times* and Pierre Huss of the International News Service—were given special treatment by Karl Boehmer, a German army officer assigned to the Propaganda Ministry. During their tours of newly conquered territory, Boehmer often took them in his own car, which was inevitably first to arrive in most places, while other American reporters followed in cars that were ordered to observe an official speed limit of about 25 miles per hour. The latter reporters complained that the privileged threesome was too chummy with Boehmer and the Nazis in general, although the three responded that they were simply doing their jobs. "Some of the correspondents accused Lochner and Huss of being pro-Nazi because they gained more privileges in trips and tips than some of the other men," wrote Henry Flannery of CBS, who arrived in Berlin that fall to prepare to succeed Shirer, "but I had no reason to feel that this was true."

When it came to describing Hitler's aims, Lochner didn't hesitate to be blunt. After driving through Muenster, the town where the Treaty of Westphalia was signed in 1648, he reported that the German leader planned, "when he has forced England, France on knees," to make their representatives submit to his dictates there. "In other words, Hitler isn't content now with wiping out last vestiges Versailles Treaty," he transmitted to New York. "His mind goes back to 1648 when Holy Roman Empire of German nation was broken up into principalities and powerless miniature states." His intent was "to rectify that mistake."

General Walther von Reichenau, the commander of the 6th Army, which had rapidly subdued Belgium and would continue to another victory in France, exuded confidence when he met with Lochner and the other correspondents following his forces. "Every German soldier knows why he is fighting," he declared. "It's to be or not to be for Germany. I have talked to many French, English prisoners in their own language. They don't know what it is all about. Our men have supreme confidence in our military leadership. Others don't in theirs. There can be no doubt about the outcome."

Since the U.S. Embassy in Berlin had taken over the interests of France and Britain once the war broke out, its diplomats were able, under the terms of the Hague Convention, to inspect camps with prisoners from those countries. Some British flyers had been shot down even before the German military machine turned west, and the Germans had also seized some early French prisoners in raids across the border. Of course, the number of prisoners grew rapidly as soon as the fighting started in earnest. All of which meant that Americans from the Berlin embassy were able to take their own measure of the morale of the captured pilots and soldiers.

"A most discouraging difference between the French and the British became manifest," Jacob Beam wrote. "The French officers for instance cared very little for their men, and a spirit of defeatism was universal . . . Among the British on the other hand, discipline and high morale prevailed."

By June 14, the German Army had entered Paris, and, on June 22, a French delegation signed the armistice in the same railway carriage in Compiègne that had been used for the signing of the armistice of 1918. The spirit of defeatism was such that, as Shirer recorded in his diary after returning from newly occupied Paris, with few exceptions "France did not fight. If she did, there is little evidence of it." Although Hitler had decided to hold the ceremony in Compiègne, not Muenster as Lochner had predicted, the AP reporter had been right that he was intent on demonstrating that Germany was settling its historical scores.

As other Americans living in Germany could attest from personal observation, no vision was too grandiose for Hitler at that moment of his successive military victories. Pierre Huss was one of a small group of Berlin correspondents who were invited to Les Invalides in Paris when Hitler paid a visit to Napoleon's tomb soon after the French surrender. As the reporters watched, the Nazi leader was lost in his thoughts. "He folded his arms and murmured something we could not hear; his lips moved, as if he were talking to himself, and once or twice he shook his head," Huss recalled.

Hitler snapped back into focus as he leaned forward on the balustrade to stare down at Napoleon's tomb. "Napoleon, *mein lieber*, they have made a bad mistake," he said in a suddenly audible voice. Huss confessed, "It startled me, standing there across from a live war lord and above a dead emperor." The correspondent also couldn't figure out what Hitler meant.

The German ruler pointed down and repeated that this was "a big mistake," explaining to everyone around him: "They have put him down into a hole. People must look down at a coffin far below them . . . They should look up at Napoleon, feeling small by the very size of the monument or sarcophagus above their heads." Then, exhibiting the kind of understanding of basic psychology that had helped him orchestrate his rallies for maximum impact, he added: "You do not impress people if you walk in a street and they are on top of a building. They must look at something above them; you must be the stage and the center of attraction above the level of all eyes."

If his listeners had any doubts about who he was really talking about, he quickly dispelled them. "I shall never make such a mistake," he declared. "I know how to keep my hold on people after I have passed on. I shall be the *Führer* they look up at and go home to talk of and remember. My life shall not end in the mere form of death. It will, on the contrary, begin then."

\*     \*     \*

Standing at the rostrum of the Reichstag on July 19, Hitler was practically preening—not just for his Nazi followers but also for the diplomatic corps and foreign press in attendance. "It was Hitler triumphant, at the peak of his career, savoring to the full his victories," Harsch wrote, calling it a scene that "no one present could ever forget." The Nazi leader dispensed promotions and decorations for his generals, and theatrically picked up a small box he had placed on the corner of the Speaker's desk occupied by Goering as the president of the Reichstag. Opening it to display a diamond-studded Grand Cross of the Order of the Iron Cross, he awarded it to his loyal follower, whom he also elevated to the rank of Reich marshal, a special rank above all field marshals.

Hitler then directed his words across the English Channel. He denounced Winston Churchill, who had replaced Chamberlain as prime minister at the same time as the Germans launched their invasion of the Low Countries, as a warmonger. But he also claimed that a peace deal was still possible. "I consider myself in a position to make this appeal since I am not the vanquished begging favors, but the victor speaking in the name of reason," he declared. "I see no reason why this war must go on."

The Reichstag erupted with applause. Harsch was standing beside Alexander Kirk, who, the reporter noted, displayed "a languid air." A German Foreign Ministry official rushed up to the American chargé d'affaires. "Oh, Mr. Ambassador, isn't it wonderful, now we can have peace," he proclaimed. Kirk had no intention of falling into a diplomatic trap. He ostentatiously stifled a yawn with his hand, offering a nonreply. "I am hungry," he said. "Where might I find food?"

By most accounts of the Americans in Berlin, ordinary Germans weren't nearly as exultant as their leaders might have expected. On the day Paris fell, loudspeakers on Wilhelmplatz, flanked by Hitler's Chancellery, the Propaganda Ministry and, close by, Goering's Air Ministry, blared party songs. Harsch, who watched the scene, counted no more than a hundred or so people on the big square. An excited announcer declared that German troops were marching on the Place de la Concorde, followed by the playing of "Deutschland über Alles." "The little groups of people put up their right arms in perfunctory Nazi salutes," Harsch recalled. "The loud-speakers went silent. And everyone walked away. Not a sound of cheering. Not an exclamation of pleasure."

But Harsch understood that the lack of jubilation didn't signal the kind of breakdown in morale that many in the West had hoped for. "The loot of war of every description which poured into Germany from mid-summer 1940 through the autumn months seemed a convincing argument to many Germans that war can be profitable and that a final victory would burden their bare tables and empty cupboards with the good things of the earth," he wrote. This made the Nazis' case better than the official propaganda. "Dr. Goebbels let Dutch cheese, Belgian laces and Parisian silks do his talking for him."

To be sure, the sudden appearance of women in stockings in Berlin without multiple runs, along with the infusion of new supplies of food and clothing, didn't last long. Rationing remained in place, and so did a stricter work regimen. Still, Harsch, Shirer and others pointed out that most ordinary Germans wanted peace—but, in the sense that their leaders did, which meant on Hitler's terms. They wanted to avoid more fighting if possible, but they wanted victory in any case. Many Germans were elevated to much more senior positions in the occupied lands than they could have ever aspired to hold at home—and quickly became accustomed to their new status. "These Germans have not only acquired the actual means to wealth beyond their wildest dreams but have established themselves as privileged permanent residents in every sense," Harsch explained.

Then, too, the successive German victories turned even some early skeptics into true believers. Schultz, the *Chicago Tribune* correspondent, told the story of the wife of a professor she knew who had been "a violent anti-Nazi." After her son became a member of the Hitlerjugend, the Gestapo arrested him for homosexuality. The parents frantically appealed to Schultz for help, and the American suggested they get a good Nazi lawyer and prepare to offer big donations to the party. Schultz also arranged for one of her Nazi contacts to take a high party official to a lavish dinner to soften him up. Eventually, "by dint of perjury and bribes," Schultz wrote, the boy was released, avoiding what the high party official described as the "inferno" of a concentration camp. The father also had to join the party to demonstrate his loyalty.

Nonetheless, when Germany invaded Norway, the mother came to Schultz all excited. "Maybe it was meant for us to go through Nazism— it has made us strong," she told the American, who was startled by her transformation. "It has brought us great military victories, and it will bring us more." Based on such experiences, Schultz concluded, "The lust for conquest is there, deep in the heart of the German woman." In her 1944 book *Germany Will Try It Again*, she predicted that, once Germany lost the war, many of those women would be disillusioned "but not with Nazism—only with its failure."

As one of the few women correspondents in Berlin, Schultz was particularly interested in Nazi policies about women and the family. While Nazis were undermining the security of the country and its people, she pointed out, they shrewdly won many women over by appealing to their emotions and insecurities.

From its early days, the Nazi Party made a show of raw virility. "I have seen the sex instinct deliberately aroused in many ways," Schultz wrote. "At mass meetings, speeches dwelling on the copulative prowess of the Nazi male would send the Storm Troopers marching out of the hall all set for a demonstration. They never had to wait long for a partner. German women would wait outside the meeting places." With Hitler intent on boosting the birth rate, newsstands displayed "books and magazines filled with nude men and women," as the CBS newcomer Flannery observed. "It was plain that Nazi Germany planned all this to but one end."

With more and more men serving far from home and, especially after Germany invaded the Soviet Union in June 1941, dying there, the authorities stepped up their campaign for more births, whatever a woman's marital status. "The word *illegitimate* must be blotted out of the German language," Minister of Labor Robert Ley declared. Flannery reported that women who felt they needed more social respectability could legally take the name of a soldier who had died in battle. While Nazi propagandists claimed that unwed mothers were giving birth to children of "young German heroes," Schultz pointed out that the real fathers were often "the married bosses of little secretaries, filing clerks and saleswomen." This created a class of women "who clung to Nazism because the Nazi Party would protect their illegitimate children," she added.

The American reporters began to notice a parallel trend: the disappearance of those who were deemed physically or mentally unfit. In a broadcast on December 11, 1940, Flannery mentioned a German claim that British bombers had hit a nursing home in southwestern Germany. When Hitler added in a speech that the British were targeting German hospitals, he concluded that all of this was a cover-up for "their murder of the insane, crippled, hopelessly ill, even aged."

Flannery learned of a young man in Leipzig who had become suspicious of a proliferation of death notices that contained the phrase "After weeks of uncertainty we received the unbelievable news of his death and cremation." The young man called on some of the families, discovering that in each case the dead person had been confined to an institution. Flannery inquired about all those death notices with identical wording, but Nazi officials denied that any murders were taking place. Indirect confirmation came in another form: subsequent death notices avoided such telltale phrases.

When Flannery was first assigned to Berlin in October 1940, he was hardly a fervent anti-Nazi. "I was one of those people who were known as 'open-minded,' who did not believe that Nazi Germany was necessarily a threat to the United States, who believed it was at least possible that we might do business with Hitler," he recalled. After his first couple of months in Hitlerland, he was becoming far less "open-minded."


While Flannery and many of his colleagues found it increasingly difficult to hide their growing abhorrence of Nazi practices, a few Americans lived in Berlin apart from their fellow countrymen for the opposite reason: they had signed up to work for German radio's English-language broadcasts. They served as the Nazis' American propagandists.

In some cases, they appeared to be motivated by little more than opportunism. Edward Delaney was a failed actor who had bounced around various stage- and film-related jobs in Australia and South Africa, and also done a public relations stint for MGM based in Chicago. Casting about for something new, he went to Berlin in the summer of 1939 and met with Hans Schirmer of the Foreign Ministry. According to Delaney, Schirmer explained he was looking for someone who could broadcast "human interest" material about Germany "to counteract much adverse criticism by those who, for the most part, knew little or nothing about conditions in that part of Europe."

Delaney claimed that he was assured his job would not be connected to Goebbels's Propaganda Ministry, but it was a flimsy distinction. The American left little doubt why he jumped at the opportunity. "The remuneration he [Schirmer] mentioned was acceptable," he recalled. Soon he was denouncing the British for "wanton, premeditated murder" and Roosevelt for pushing the United States toward war. Later, he would justify his actions on the grounds that he was a de facto spokesman for America's isolationist movement and a pioneer in warning about the dangers of Communism as opposed to Nazism. Shirer delivered his verdict on Delaney in his diary on September 26, 1940: "He has a diseased hatred for Jews, but otherwise is a mild fellow and broadcasts the cruder type of Nazi propaganda without questioning."

In his brief remarks about the American propagandists, Shirer called Frederick Kaltenbach "probably the best of the lot, actually believing in National Socialism with a sincere fanaticism and continually fighting the Nazi Party hacks when they don't agree with him." (Kaltenbach should not be confused with Hans V. Kaltenborn, the famous American radio broadcaster who had often visited Germany and interviewed Hitler.) In part, Shirer's postwar novel *The Traitor* is based on Kaltenbach's story, although his main character also shares the traits of some of the other American propagandists. The novel is much less compelling than Shirer's nonfiction, particularly *The Rise and Fall of the Third Reich*, but it provides intriguing testimony to his grim fascination with those Americans who had gone to the other side.

Born in Dubuque, Iowa, in 1895, Kaltenbach was the son of a German butcher who had immigrated to the United States. As a teenager, he felt the pull of his father's country of origin—and, along with his brother Adolph, he traveled around Germany just as World War I broke out in 1914. Although the German police arrested them on suspicion of spying on more than one occasion, Kaltenbach titled his diary chronicling their adventures *Through the Fatherland on Bycycles*. He would tell his Nazi employers later that this trip made him feel "swept by a powerful emotion" that led him to love both Germany and America, prompting him to want to promote good relations between the two.

Back in Iowa, he became a teacher at Dubuque High School, but he was fired in 1933 after he set up a "hiking club" that was almost a straight copy of the Hitlerjugend, complete with brown shirts for uniforms. Following that episode, Kaltenbach returned to Germany, where he immediately became entranced by the country's new rulers. On June 25, 1933, he sent a postcard to his family back home showing Hitler in uniform, his swastika armband prominently displayed, looking into the distance in what is meant to be a commanding pose. The caption read: "Reichskanzler ADOLF HITLER." Kaltenbach's handwriting was scrunched to squeeze into the small space, but his terse phrases conveyed his growing infatuation.

*Dear Folks:*
*Here I am in the midst of things—Hot stuff, see all, hear all. About to view the Changing of the Guard. You should see the uniformed Nazi soldiers. Enjoying the night life too. Hotel costs me 65 cents per. Can get meals for 1 Mark. Sandwiches and drinks at automat for 2.5 cents. Shall see palaces, museums-zoo-movies-attend Nazi celebrations Spreewald-Potsdam-May go to Danzig-*

*Love, Fritz*

Kaltenbach was one of the first Americans to work for German radio during the Third Reich. In his broadcasts addressed to "Dear Harry," which stood for his supposed friends in Iowa, he urged his countrymen to open their eyes to the virtues of Hitler's Germany.

By contrast, Douglas Chandler was a latecomer among the Americans working for German radio, starting his broadcasts as "Paul Revere" in the spring of 1941. But he more than made up for that with his vitriol. "Roosevelt, himself an off-spring of Spanish Jews, is a mere tool of the Jewish conspiracy against all Nordic Aryans," he declared. As a freelance journalist who had bounced around the continent with his wife, Laura, and two daughters, he had met up with Hanfstaengl and other Nazi propagandists in the early days of the new regime. In Berlin, he also visited U.S. military attaché Truman Smith and his wife, Kay, since they had known each other in New York in the mid-1920s. Kay claimed that Chandler had suffered a "nervous breakdown" after his initial career in finance collapsed along with the stock market in 1929.

Kätchen, the Smiths' daughter, still remembers a lunchtime visit of the Chandlers. She was struck by the appearances of their two young girls with "ponytails and dirndls, looking more German than the Germans." Chandler told Kay he was thinking of getting German citizenship for himself and his family since he felt the United States was turning socialist. "I told him he was a great fool," Kay recalled. It was a tense encounter, and later, when the Smiths were back in Washington, she heard "Paul Revere" on the radio and instantly recognized the voice of Douglas Chandler.

Delaney, Kaltenbach and Chandler were three of the six Americans indicted *in absentia* for treason by a Washington, D.C., grand jury on July 26, 1943. A few months earlier, Delaney had left Berlin and his propaganda work behind, and moved to Slovakia, then Prague. At the end of the war, he was detained by the U.S. Army Counter-Intelligence Corps, released, detained and then released again. When he finally returned to the United States, he was arrested again but his indictment was dismissed, and for the rest of his life he claimed he had been persecuted because of his anti-Communist views. Kaltenbach wasn't so lucky. Captured by the Red Army on July 14, 1945, he died in a Soviet camp in eastern Germany in October.

Chandler's wife, Laura, died in Berlin in 1942, and Douglas was captured by the Americans in Bavaria in May 1945. Sent back to the United States the following year, he was tried, convicted and sentenced to life imprisonment. His daughter later wrote to Truman Smith asking him if he would testify on his behalf. "Truman wrote her he was sorry for her but that he could not testify on behalf of anyone who had betrayed his country," Kay Smith recalled. But the loyal daughter kept lobbying for her father, appealing to President Kennedy in July 1963. On August 5, Kennedy commuted Chandler's sentence. After his release, Chandler spent the final period of his life on Tenerife in the Canary Islands, leaving the country he had betrayed behind.

It wasn't just the American propagandists who were choosing sides in the rapidly escalating war. Mildred Harnack, who had grown up in Wisconsin and then met and married the German exchange student Arvid Harnack, had remained one of the closest American friends of Martha Dodd during her time in Berlin. Like Martha, she had become fascinated by the Soviet Union, seeing it as an alternative to the Nazi dictatorship she lived in. Even the Nazi-Soviet Pact didn't seem to undermine her faith that Stalin's system was a genuine alternative to Hitler's. By the late 1930s, she and her husband were part of a loose network of resisters intent on doing what they could to undermine the Nazi regime. Later, the Gestapo would dub this network the Rote Kapelle, the Red Orchestra.

Understandably, the growing dangers for anyone pursuing such a course may have prompted Mildred to submit applications in October 1939 to both the Rockefeller and Guggenheim fellowship programs. If she had been accepted by either, she presumably would have returned to the United States to work on a book about American literature, her field of study. But the Guggenheim committee considered her "a beginner," and she failed to get either fellowship.

One of Mildred's jobs before the war was to hunt up English-language books for a German publisher, which allowed her to travel around Europe. During those trips, she may have helped Jews and others to escape from Germany, although the evidence is patchy. Her husband Arvid worked in the Economics Ministry, which also allowed him to travel and contact foreigners. He became particularly friendly with Donald Heath, a first secretary at the U.S. Embassy, and Mildred tutored his son. Heath began sending reports to Washington about how the Germans assessed their economic capabilities based on someone he identified as a "confidential" or "well-placed" source. After the war, Heath told his family that Arvid was that source.

Shareen Blair Brysac, Mildred Harnack's biographer, points to Arvid's ties with Heath as evidence that he thought of himself as "a German patriot" who was willing to work with the United States as well as the

Soviet Union—in other words, anyone who would help topple Hitler's regime. "Harnack never regarded himself as an agent of a foreign power, nor did he follow Soviet orders," she wrote.

But Brysac documented how a Soviet agent, Alexander Korotkov, visited the Harnacks on September 17, 1940. He thus reestablished a Moscow connection that had been broken when the Harnacks had decided it was too dangerous to maintain their earlier Soviet ties in Berlin. Korotkov wrote to Moscow that Arvid had agreed to send reports, not because he considered himself an agent but because the Soviet Union was "a country with whose ideals he feels connected and from which he awaits support." On September 26, 1940, as Germany's fighters and bombers were fighting and losing the Battle of Britain, Harnack sent his first intelligence report, warning Moscow that by the beginning of the following year Hitler was planning to launch an attack on the Soviet Union.

It was a warning that Harnack and other members of the Red Orchestra, which included Luftwaffe intelligence officer Harro Schulze-Boysen, repeated on several occasions—and Stalin refused to believe. The resisters kept taking huge risks in gathering and sending more information as the Gestapo closed in on them. They also weren't helped by their Soviet handlers, who were guilty of major security lapses in their own radio transmissions. In late August and early September 1942, the German authorities rounded up the Red Orchestra members and anyone suspected of ties to them, arresting an estimated 139 people, including the Harnacks.

All the chief participants in the group were tried for treason. Arvid was among those immediately sentenced to death. Mildred was initially treated with more sympathy by the judges, who chose to view her as a woman who had been led astray by her German husband. She was sentenced to six years in prison and six years' "loss of honor." The first round of executions took place on December 22, 1942, with hanging as the chosen instrument of death for Arvid, Schulze-Boysen and two others. Afterward, the guillotine was used on four more members of the group.

In the end, Mildred wasn't spared either. She was put on trial again. The new charge was that she had seduced an Abwehr lieutenant to steal state secrets, which offered a lurid justification for the death sentence that promptly followed. The only American woman executed by the Gestapo, Mildred Harnack uttered these final words before she was guillotined in Berlin's Plötzensee Prison on February 16, 1943: "And I have loved Germany so much."

Most Americans who still remained in Germany in 1940 and 1941, of course, were neither traitors nor resistance fighters. But the diplomats and journalists, like the Roosevelt Administration back home, were increasingly open in choosing sides as well. The success of the Royal Air Force in winning the Battle of Britain, which forced Hitler to abandon Operation Sealion, the planned invasion of England, had cheered the Americans in Berlin who had watched Hitler's military machine score one victory after another up till then. Although the diplomats and journalists had different roles to play, they often acted on the implicit assumption that they supported a common cause. Colonel John Lovell, a military attaché at the Berlin embassy, easily enlisted some of the American correspondents to monitor the numbers on the collars and shoulders of soldiers they saw coming through Berlin. "When a new number showed up we would report it to John," recalled Harsch of the *Christian Science Monitor*.

Since Lovell knew which units had been deployed on the Western Front, he assumed that when their soldiers began appearing in Berlin this was a signal that these units were moving east. Harsch had moved from the Adlon Hotel to a house known as the Cercle Français, which had been taken over by the American Embassy and where Lovell and several other staffers were living. One evening in December, the colonel invited Harsch to a dinner for the military attachés of Germany's eastern and southeastern neighbors. After a French dinner that included a rare endive salad, Lovell asked his guests to come to the library, where he spread out a map of Eastern Europe. He then offered his estimates on where German troops were deployed and their battle readiness, and invited his guests to do the same. He added that these forces could move either east or south, but he believed they were more likely to move east—against the Soviet Union.

The attachés from Hungary, Romania, Yugoslavia, Bulgaria and

Greece offered minor modifications in some cases, but largely agreed with Lovell's assessment. They also agreed that it looked like the German forces were getting ready to move east. The Soviet attaché then went to the map and acknowledged that his estimates on deployments were almost exactly the same. But he claimed that the German military machine would probably turn south next. Still, he warned that if they did turn against his country "it will not be a Sunday promenade."

In fact, Hitler's decision to abandon the invasion of England had prompted the Nazi leader to pursue his other dream: a swift victory over the Soviet Union. This was supposed to isolate Britain further and convince it that, in the end, a German victory was inevitable. The *Chicago Tribune*'s Schultz recalled a conversation with Karl Boehmer of the Propaganda Ministry about this time. He didn't mention a possible invasion of Russia but suggested the Germans would engineer a takeover from within. "Just imagine what we can do with Russia's resources," he declared. "She squanders them as badly as America does hers." Schultz claimed she then asked if his country planned to control America's resources as well, and that he replied, "Why, yes."

That may have been a bit of showboating on Boehmer's part. In reality, Hitler hadn't yet abandoned hope of keeping the United States out of the war, despite Roosevelt's growing support for Britain. On December 7, 1940, the president declared that "the best immediate defense of the United States is the success of Great Britain." In a fireside chat on December 29, he denounced Nazi plans "to dominate the rest of the world" and famously pledged that his country would be "the great arsenal of democracy." All of which set the stage for the Lend-Lease Act that was signed into law on March 11, 1941, allowing for the shipment of massive amounts of military equipment and other supplies to Britain. But Hitler still clung to the belief that his planned invasion of the Soviet Union would convince the Americans that they had to abandon Europe, including their British friends, to German might.

On June 22, 1941, Hitler's armies launched Operation Barbarossa, the attack on Stalin's Soviet Union. The Soviet dictator had refused to believe all the warnings not just from his spies but also from Britain and the United States. As a result, German forces initially scored easy victories against the unprepared Red Army troops and pushed deep into Soviet territory, making it look like Hitler's calculations would be proven right again. In the August 4, 1941, issue of *Life* magazine, Hanson W. Baldwin, America's most authoritative military writer, argued that the outcome of the war depended on what would happen on the Eastern Front. A successful German campaign would result in the completion of "the conquest of Europe," he declared, dooming Britain as well. He discussed the possibility that Hitler's armies could be defeated or at least worn down by a long, costly campaign. "But on the basis of all past experience—on our limited knowledge of the Red Army, on the operations of the first month—the world can anticipate in Russia another quick and decisive German victory," he concluded.

For the Americans who lived and worked in Germany, however, Hitler's optimistic predictions looked more and more unrealistic. The further his armies marched, the more strains they noticed on the home front. Life was changing in Hitlerland—for the Americans, but also for the Germans. And it wasn't for the better.


During the Battle of Britain in August and September 1940, RAF bombers rarely made it to Berlin, but their initial forays were enough to shake the confidence of the inhabitants of the German capital who had been assured that it was invulnerable. On September 10, Berlin endured what Shirer described as "the severest bombing yet," as firebombs hit the Ministry of Munitions right between the Adlon Hotel and the U.S. Embassy. Although the incendiaries were put out before they did much damage, they were scattered in various places, including the yard of the Adlon and the garden of the embassy. That evening after he had completed his broadcast, Shirer was rushing back to the Adlon in the dark when his car hit some debris, skidded and came to a stop about 20 feet from a fresh bomb crater. "I almost met a quick end last night," he wrote in his diary the next day.

Shirer recorded that Donald Heath had an even closer call at the embassy. A splinter from the same bomb that made the crater had flown through Heath's office double window 200 yards away, passing directly over his desk and embedding itself in the wall on the opposite side. Heath had been scheduled for night duty, but chargé d'affaires Kirk had relieved him.

The German press trumpeted headlines vowing revenge for such bombings, which it claimed were targeting children, hospitals and other civilian targets. While London was living under the genuine terror of the Blitz, Berliners could be excused for believing that their country was suffering almost as much. "Night Crime of British Against 21 German Children—This Bloody Crime Cries Out for Revenge," one newspaper proclaimed. Another warned, "'Assassins' Murder Is No Longer War, Herr Winston Churchill!—The British Island of Murderers Will Have to Take the Consequences of Its Malicious Bombings."

For some time after the Battle of Britain, the Americans in Berlin felt almost eerily detached from the actual fighting. "Except for the outbursts from the Nazi orators . . . and except for the reports of feverish diplomatic activity and rumours of troop movements, we in Berlin hardly knew a war was on during the early part of 1941," Flannery recalled. In that period, Americans still noticed relatively few wounded soldiers on the streets of Berlin. "But after the Russian campaign began, I saw them in every block along the principal streets—young men with their arms in slings, with an arm gone, walking with crutches or canes, or without one of their legs," Flannery added.

When the CBS reporter approached a newsstand one day, he overheard the newsdealer ask a woman if she was all right. In a hollow voice, she replied: "No, I just had bad news, and must phone my husband at work. You know we lost a son in Poland, and another in France. Now I have word that Johann is gone, too, our last son. He has been killed in Russia."

Even during Germany's early victories in the Soviet Union, the newspapers left no doubt that the cost was high. Flannery estimated that almost half of German families had suffered a loss—and he saw that people were increasingly depressed. As the RAF bombings intensified, this, too, contributed to the drop in morale. Flannery, who was doing full-time duty in Berlin since Shirer's departure in November 1940, was leaving his dentist one day when the woman elevator operator began complaining about the war's hardships. "*Mein Gott, mein Gott,*" she told him, "*warum?* Why? It's all caused by a mere handful of men."

Flannery found himself within a block of falling bombs on more than one occasion. On a night when Colonel Lovell was watching a raid from the roof of an embassy house near the zoo, the bombs hit so close that the attaché threw himself flat. "I thought I was gone," he said.

Sigrid Schultz observed another more subtle side of the war that was taking its toll as well. On the train from Berlin to Basel, she shared a compartment with a Luftwaffe colonel who freely discussed how the war was changing family relationships. "I love my wife and my children," he said, "but when we soldiers get home, all our families can talk about is how many potatoes they get and what kinds of sandwiches other people have in their air-raid shelters." The implicit message: Germany's fighting men were impatient with what they often saw as the petty concerns of their families back home.

Earlier, Schultz had talked with a woman who appeared to have none of the material worries of so many of the other civilians; she exuded self-confidence. "I do war work. I am a plastic surgeon," she said. "I ought to be prosperous; I'm working hard enough beautifying bustlines."

When Schultz asked her what this had to do with the war, she replied: "Why, when the German men come home from France and the Balkans, they criticize the figures of their wives. All the Nazis have money, you know, so I operate."

For most Germans who were losing hope of a quick victory, there were far more serious worries—keeping themselves adequately fed and clothed, especially during the winter. And for Jews, there was genuine terror, which had begun long before the war and the bombings, as the remaining Americans knew well.

Angus Thuermer, the young AP correspondent, had first rented a room in a fourth-floor Berlin apartment; one floor below, there was a Jewish family. He recalled that a woman had come out of the third-floor apartment one day and tried to throw herself down the stairwell, but she was stopped from committing suicide. A day later, Thuermer saw that the apartment's door had its lock removed and a Gestapo seal placed over the empty hole. But another day or so later, he found the door open. Walking in, he saw an "Aryan" family looking around. On the dresser, they spotted several cans of food. "Oh, look at that: see what fancy food they were eating," one of the Germans said.

Some of the Americans still lived with a lingering sense of guilt decades later about how they failed to respond to appeals for help from Jews. Thuermer recalled a knock on his door very late one night. When the American opened it, he saw a thin man wearing a coat with a yellow star on it; around his neck, he wore the Medal of Honor from the previous war. "I wonder if I could pay you marks here in Germany and you pay me in an account in dollars," he said. Thuermer tried to explain that, although he was working for the AP and no longer a student, he was still getting a preferential exchange rate provided to foreign students in violation of the rules. This meant he was "a little crooked" already and felt he couldn't take another risk. His visitor left disappointed.

One night in October 1941, Howard K. Smith, who had just quit the United Press and jumped to CBS to replace Flannery, received a similar knock on the door at around 2 A.M. His visitor was Fritz Heppler, a Jew of about the same age as the young American reporter; they had met during an air raid about a year earlier. Heppler told him that the Gestapo was conducting raids of Jewish apartments all over town, ostensibly looking for hoarded foodstuffs. They had raided his apartment, too, but not finding anything, they released him. Heppler had been defiant the previous time he met Smith, but now his fear was palpable. "It's come," he said, alluding to the roundups of Jews, who were then deported to the east. "I knew it would come, as soon as they started losing." He pleaded for Smith to help him get out of the country. The reporter offered him a cigarette and said he would see if he could help him get an American visa, but claimed that he was exaggerating the danger. Then he shoved him out the door.

"My callousness on this occasion can hardly be justified," Smith wrote later, recalling that he forgot about Heppler the next day and didn't even attempt to bring his case to the embassy's attention. "Not that it would have helped him; but it would have helped soothe my own conscience," he added. Smith never saw Heppler again.

At the American Embassy, Kennan and other diplomats often felt overworked and besieged. Since the German government had ordered the closure of ten U.S. consulates in other cities in 1940, everyone came to the Berlin embassy for help. "The increasingly desperate situation of the German Jews, and Jews from the German-occupied areas, and the heavy attendant pressures brought to bear upon us to effect their release and removal to the United States, added to the burden," he wrote. He bitterly noted that he and his colleagues had been put in an impossible position. "These pressures tended often to be generated in powerful congressional circles at home and to be passed on, unmitigated, to us by the Department of State anxious to get itself out of the firing line and too timid to point out to the Congressmen what could and could not (sometimes in light of the laws they themselves had created) be done to aid such people."

When Alexander Kirk left Berlin in October 1940, Kennan's personal workload increased further. Leland Morris replaced Kirk as chargé d'affaires, but was a far weaker figure. As a result, Kennan was often the de facto man in charge. Jacob Beam, by then the longest-serving embassy staffer despite his young age, would write later: "Time proved him [Kennan] to be a better historian than executive." Still, Kennan and the rest of the embassy staff deserved credit for continuing to keep their country's outpost in Berlin functioning as best they could. Aside from taking on the interests of Britain and France, the embassy assumed responsibility for successive countries that came under Nazi rule. This meant more and more work; it also meant that the American diplomats were feeling more and more alone.


The American journalists felt lonelier as well. Some of the best known of their colleagues had already pulled out. Shirer departed in December 1940, and Harsch and Schultz left in January 1941. Unlike many of their countrymen back home who still were hoping the United States could stay out of the war, those correspondents were convinced that it would prove impossible to stay on the sidelines. Harsch was planning on writing a book in the hopes of enlightening his countrymen, and, to do so, he needed to return. "I felt that perhaps the time had come to get home and write down all the things I had not felt free to say when writing from Berlin itself," he recalled.

The print journalists didn't labor under the same heavy censorship as their radio colleagues, but there were always unspoken rules. Foremost among them, as Pierre Huss put it, was that "you must never, either by act or word of mouth or in a dispatch, say or suggest anything which might be a slur or a reflection on the office and the person of the Fuehrer." Although the International News Service correspondent also pointed out that he and his American colleagues were "the hottest game of the Nazis" right up till mid-1941, since the Germans still hoped to keep the United States out of the war, he complained that afterward the de facto censorship meant that reporters were expected to rely mainly on official information—and disinformation. "Everything else was taboo," he wrote.

Harsch traced the more hostile attitude toward the American correspondents further back—in particular to Roosevelt's victory in the November 1940 elections over Wendell Willkie. Although Willkie was a liberal Republican who would later support Roosevelt and do battle with the isolationists, he sent mixed signals during the campaign on what course he would steer if he were elected. His sister Charlotte was married to Commander Paul Pihl, the U.S. naval attaché for air in Berlin, and they would hold frequent Sunday salons attended by officials from the Foreign Ministry and the Luftwaffe. "Many times I heard her say that if her brother were to win the 1940 election he would keep the United States out of the war," Harsch wrote.

As American support for the British war effort was ramped up in early 1941, the pressures on the foreign correspondents increased as well. Ostensibly, they were given special treatment. Two press clubs were set up to attend to their needs, with plenty of wining and dining included, but the clubs' primary purpose was to disseminate propaganda and keep tabs on what the reporters were doing. The Gestapo "knew everything about each of us," Howard K. Smith wrote. "They maintained agents in the two press clubs, vile little fellows who tried to appear chummy." They also kept agents at other popular hangouts, such as the Adlon Hotel and Die Taverne.

All of which made Smith and others completely disbelieve the official reason why seven Gestapo agents showed up at Richard Hottelet's door at 7 A.M. on Saturday, March 15, 1941. Taken to the Alexanderplatz Prison, Hottelet, Smith's colleague in the United Press's Berlin bureau, was told he had been arrested "on suspicion of espionage." As Smith curtly put it, "Had he been a spy, the Gestapo would have known it."

Beam, who was transferred back to the State Department by this time, believed that Hottelet was picked up in retaliation for the arrest of a German journalist in Washington on spying charges. But Smith was convinced that the real reason was both more personal and more general. He pointed out that Hottelet had been bursting with anger at the Nazis—a result of the fact that he had lived in Berlin "too long for his own safety." Hottelet could "no longer hide his nausea and bob his head stupidly at the inane dinner-table propaganda essays of the little Propaganda Ministry bureaucrats in the Press Club restaurants," Smith wrote. "To use Dick's own expressive language: he hated their goddam guts." Since the Nazis were looking for someone to arrest so that they could intimidate the other American reporters in Berlin, he continued, Hottelet was the obvious target.

Hottelet found himself in a solitary cell with a stool, a cot and a toilet in the corner. From six-thirty in the morning till four-thirty in the afternoon, he wasn't allowed to sit or lie on the cot. He wasn't allowed any reading matter initially either, and his glasses were taken away "to prevent suicide." That meant he spent long hours sitting on the stool and reading what other prisoners had written on the wall. It appeared to be a cell used often for foreigners. Someone had written in English HOME, SWEET HOME, DEAR MOTHER WHERE ARE YOU? Another inscription was VIVE L'INTERNATIONALE. There was writing in Russian, too, but Hottelet couldn't read it.

His diet consisted mostly of dry black bread, ersatz coffee and bean, noodle or barley soup. He realized that the prison was very international: the inmates were Russian, Polish, Czech, Japanese and Italian. They also included several Catholic priests.

At first, the Gestapo interrogated him often, sometimes twice a day. When he denied the accusation that he was a spy, his interrogators tried to scare him. "You won't feel quite so confident when you are sweating under the lights and we throw questions at you," they told him. Or: "You will sit until you confess. You will soften up. You'll be soft as butter. We've got plenty of time."

But Hottelet's treatment was radically different than that accorded most prisoners. His nationality and profession still offered him a degree of protection. An official from the American consulate was allowed to visit him, bringing fresh clothes—although the prisoner was denied the soap, toothbrush and toothpaste he also brought. On May 3, Hottelet was transferred to the Moabit Prison in another part of the city, where the food was better. When word got around that he was American, trusties began slipping him extra potatoes, which helped him fend off hunger. Soon he was allowed to receive a daily newspaper and two books a week from the prison library. The most interesting book he found was *De Profundis*, Oscar Wilde's meditative essay that he wrote during his imprisonment in England.

On July 8, to his complete surprise, Hottelet was released and delivered to a representative from the U.S. Embassy. He had lost fifteen pounds during his incarceration, but this, again, was nothing compared to what routinely happened to other prisoners. Still, Smith and other colleagues understood the message from the Nazis: American reporters were no longer untouchable—and they had better be extra careful. On July 17, Hottelet quietly left Berlin. Describing his sense of freedom as he saw the New York skyline later that month, he wrote, "Now I know doors which I can open myself are something to be thankful for and not to be taken for granted."

The German press minders abandoned any pretense of friendliness in dealing with the remaining, shrinking contingent of American reporters in Berlin. "Your situation is anomalous," a Propaganda Ministry official told Smith after he switched to CBS in October 1941. "We do not want you here and you do not want to stay. Why don't you leave?" For the radio broadcasters, overt censorship was increasingly heavy-handed, disallowing mentioning, as Smith recalled, anti-Jewish measures or the executions of "Czech patriots or of French 'communists' and hostages." His texts were "utterly vapid," Smith despaired. Like other American reporters, he began methodically destroying all his notes as soon as he had used them, leaving his desk almost empty, except for pencils, pens and ink. The assumption was that anything could prove to be incriminating for the reporters and their sources.

Two of the correspondents who had returned to the United States a few months earlier were already getting their books rushed into print. In June 1941, Shirer's *Berlin Diary: The Journal of a Foreign Correspondent, 1934–1941* hit the bookstores. In one of his final diary entries from Berlin, he conceded that his observations were hardly dispassionate. "We who have been so close to the German scene, who have seen with our own eyes the tramping Nazi boots over Europe and heard with our own ears Hitler's hysterical tirades of hate, have found it difficult to keep a sense of historical perspective," he wrote. And like almost all the reporters who had lived in Berlin in that era, he found himself constantly returning to the question of "the strange contradictory character of the German people"—and how Hitler had managed to take such complete control of them.

Shirer rejected the notion, which he ascribed to many American liberals, "that Nazism is a form of rule and life unnatural to the German people and forced upon them against their wish by a few fanatic derelicts of the last war." He conceded that the Nazis had never won a majority of the votes in a free election, only a plurality. "But for the last three or four years the Nazi regime has expressed something very deep in the German nature and in that respect it has been representative of the people it rules." Unlike other nationalities, the Germans lacked "balance," he maintained, and their inner contradictions and frustrations made them lurch from one extreme to another. The Weimar era was an extreme form of liberal democracy, he argued, "and now they have turned to the extremes of tyranny" because in the chaos of the twentieth century it was too difficult for them "to think and make decisions as free men."

This led Shirer to his theory about the "two characters" of Germans. "As an individual he will give his rationed bread to feed the squirrels in the Tiergarten on a Sunday morning. He can be a kind and considerate person. But, as a unit in the Germanic mass he can persecute Jews, torture and murder his fellow men in a concentration camp, massacre women and children by bombing and bombardment, overrun without the slightest justification the lands of other peoples, cut them down if they protest, and enslave them."

Then, Shirer addressed the burning question of the moment in his country: was Hitler contemplating war with the United States? "I am firmly convinced that he does contemplate it and that if he wins in Europe and Africa he will in the end launch it unless we are prepared to give up our way of life and adapt ourselves to a subservient place in his totalitarian scheme of things." The contest between tyranny and democracy, he added, "is as inevitable as that of two planets hurtling inexorably through the heavens towards each other." Addressing the America First movement and other isolationists, he concluded: "The Lindberghs and their friends laugh at the idea of Germany ever being able to attack the United States. The Germans welcome their laughter and hope more Americans will laugh . . ."

Upon his return to the United States, Harsch had written a twelve-part series for the *Christian Science Monitor* that he turned into a book, delivering his completed manuscript to the printer on June 22, 1941, the day Hitler's armies invaded Russia. Called *Pattern of Conquest*, it echoed many of Shirer's themes—and specifically its immediate message. "The question before the American people is a clear one," he wrote. In a world where a titanic struggle for dominance was taking place, "America can either belong to that dominant force or submit to it." If the United States permitted Germany to win "by default," it would soon become a satellite of Hitlerland. "The alternative for America is to take its stand with Britain," he concluded. "The two together can unquestionably defeat Germany."

Huss stayed in Berlin for the International News Service until November 1941, and he, too, wrote a book about his experiences when he returned home. Entitled *The Foe We Face*, it was published in 1942 when the United States was already in the war. Shortly before his departure from Berlin—only a month before the Japanese attack on Pearl Harbor that would prompt Hitler to declare war on the United States—Huss interviewed Hitler for the last time.

Their meeting took place at Wolf's Lair, the headquarters for the Eastern Front. As Huss followed Hitler's erratic steps on a path in the woods, the Nazi leader eerily enacted the scene that Shirer had conjured up earlier in his characterization of the German people. Spotting a squirrel, Hitler pulled out a bag of hazelnuts from his coat pocket. "Quietly, and with a half-smile on his pinkish face," Huss wrote, he approached it, holding out some nuts. Unafraid, the squirrel jumped up into his hand— to Hitler's delight. Once it had gathered the nuts and scampered off, he said: "*Ja*, if the world would only mind its own business like this little squirrel."

While Hitler boasted to Huss that he would outlast "your President Roosevelt" and "this crazy man Churchill," and that Stalin's Red Army was already "practically smashed," Huss detected more than contempt in Hitler's repeated mentions of "Herr Roosevelt—and his Jews." He complained bitterly that the American president "wants to run the world and rob us all of a place in the sun . . . Every time I reached forth my hand he slapped it down." He blamed Roosevelt for conspiring to keep Britain in the war and, as he became more incensed about his alleged misdeeds, Huss felt "that just for that second an icy chill had crept between us."

It was then that Huss claimed he understood what triggered Hitler's denunciations. "Mighty Hitler of the Nazi Reich and the New Order Europe basically and by instinct *fears* President Franklin D. Roosevelt of the United States of America," he wrote. Which was why, Huss added, "like a tiger at bay, he wants to spring and land the knockout blow to paralyze the power of the man and the land he fears more than anything else in the world."

While Huss's account may have been colored by his desire to bolster the morale of his countrymen at this early stage of their involvement in the war, he was correct in his analysis about Hitler's primary motive. As he did when he invaded the Soviet Union, Hitler was gambling that another escalation was the only path left to victory.

## 12

## The Last Act

During the late months of 1941, George Kennan monitored the progress of Hitler's armies in the Soviet Union on a large map of that country in his office, comparing what was happening then to Napoleon's Russian campaign in 1812. "The similarities in timing and geography were often striking," he observed. Despite the signs that the German drive to take Moscow was faltering, he wasn't yet sure about the outcome. But he noted the parallel steady deterioration of relations between Germany and the United States, and his sense "that things were now out of control—not only out of *our* control (we, after all, in our poor overworked embassy, had never at any time had any influence on the course of events) but out of everyone's control."

Kennan and other Westerners did not know yet that the battle for Moscow would result in the first defeat of Hitler's army. It was a titanic struggle, the biggest battle of World War II and of all time, involving 7 million troops. The combined losses of both sides—those killed, taken prisoner or severely wounded—were 2.5 million, of which nearly 2 million were on the Soviet side. German troops had reached the outskirts of Moscow, a direct result of Stalin's grievous miscalculations, starting with his refusal to believe that Germany would invade his country.

But the Soviet capital was ultimately saved because Hitler committed even bigger mistakes, refusing to listen to his generals who wanted him to push directly to the Soviet capital. He ordered a diversion south to take Kiev, insisting that it was vital to seize control of the agricultural riches and raw materials of the Ukraine first. By the time his troops resumed their drive on Moscow, they were caught in heavy autumn rains that turned Russian dirt roads into swamps, and then by swiftly plummeting temperatures. Since Hitler had firmly believed that Moscow would be quickly overrun, most of the German troops had not even been issued winter uniforms. All of which meant that, as the Soviet writer Vasily Grossman wrote, "General Mud and General Cold" dramatically slowed and weakened the invaders.

Taking full advantage of his good fortune, Stalin rushed in troop reinforcements from the Soviet Far East. On December 6, the day before Pearl Harbor, his forces launched their first major counteroffensive, pushing back those German troops who had made it closest to the capital.

Like other foreigners, American diplomats and journalists based in Moscow had been evacuated to the Volga city of Kuibyshev back in October when it looked like the city would fall to the Germans. Without direct reporting from those observers, most of the world was slow to recognize that the Soviet counteroffensive was the beginning of a huge turnabout on the Eastern Front. But Hitler—who had only recently been confidently expounding on his vision of how the conquered Soviet territories would make Germany an economic powerhouse—had come to recognize that his troops would not be able to take the Soviet capital that winter. Still, he continued to hope that they would do so later, and his propagandists insisted that this change of plans only reflected a temporary setback.

On Sunday evening, December 7, Kennan picked up a weak but audible shortwave news broadcast from the United States about the Japanese attack on Pearl Harbor. He called Leland Morris, the chargé d'affaires, who was already asleep, and several other embassy officers, and arranged to meet them for a late night meeting at the embassy. While Pearl Harbor did not automatically trigger a state of war with the United States, and Hitler would in fact wait until he addressed the Reichstag four days later to issue his declaration of war, the American diplomats in Berlin had to assume their mission was coming to an end.

There was no evidence that Hitler remembered Putzi Hanfstaengl's warnings that it would be fatal to end up on the opposing side of the Americans in another global conflict. Instead, the Nazi leader immediately convinced himself that Japan's attack was the best news possible since it would mean that the United States would be completely preoccupied by the war in the Pacific, with little energy or resources left to aid Britain and the Soviet Union. The day after Pearl Harbor, he declared: "We can't lose the war at all. We now have an ally which has never been conquered in 3,000 years."

The leader who was most genuinely pleased by the consequences of Pearl Harbor was Churchill. In a transatlantic phone call on that fateful day, Roosevelt uttered the words that the British prime minister had wanted to hear: "We are all in the same boat now." As Churchill would tell Congress on December 26, "To me the best tidings of all is that the United States, united as never before, have drawn the sword for freedom and cast away the scabbard."

Kennan noted that during the four days of "excruciating uncertainty" as he and his colleagues waited for Hitler to address the Reichstag, the embassy was methodically cut off from the outside world. The telegraph office no longer accepted its telegrams, and, by Tuesday, the embassy's phones stopped functioning. "We were now on our own," he pointed out. Figuring they had to prepare for the worst, the diplomats began burning their codes and classified correspondence on Tuesday night. The sudden rash of small fires, which spewed ashes over nearby buildings, prompted a German building inspector to warn the embassy that it was endangering the neighborhood.

Of course, the neighborhood—in both the narrow and broader sense—was endangered by much more than swirling ashes. Kennan clearly understood that much better than Hitler did.

The remaining American journalists in Berlin—only fifteen, less than a third of their earlier number—realized that their assignments were likely to be ending as well. On the night that the diplomats were burning their documents, word spread among the correspondents that the FBI had arrested German newsmen in the United States. They knew no details of those arrests, which were carried out as part of a sweep against "enemy aliens," but they had little doubt what would happen next. Louis Lochner of the AP met with a German Foreign Ministry official early on Wednesday, December 10, who assured him any reprisals "will be done in the noblest manner." If any confirmation was needed, this was it: the reprisals were coming.

Along with his young reporter Angus Thuermer, Lochner went next to the daily news conference, conducted by Paul Schmidt, the chief of the Foreign Ministry's press department. By then, most of the press corps knew what was happening. "Many a European correspondent with whom I had worked shoulder to shoulder for years, came to say goodbye and to express the hope that America would bring freedom to a sorely tried European continent," Lochner recalled. Schmidt arrived and announced the arrest of the German newsmen in the United States. "I must therefore ask the American correspondents here present to leave the conference and proceed forthwith to their homes," he added.

Everyone knew this meant house arrest until the next orders, and the Americans began walking out. As they did so, the others—"from Switzerland, Sweden, Spain, Argentina, even Japan, and from virtually all the subjugated countries of Europe," as Lochner wrote—lined up to shake their hands. Schmidt stood at the door and shook each correspondent's hand as well.

As they exited, Lochner turned to Thuermer and told him to drive quickly back to the office so that he could file a final story and say goodbye to the German staffers, defying the order to return straight to their homes. Lochner sent a brief dispatch about their impending house arrest, and Thuermer was at the telex machine when he received an informal query from the Berne bureau about what was really happening. BYE-BYE. WE JUGWARDING NOW, he replied in what he thought was lighthearted cable shorthand. Over breakfast in Chicago the next morning, his father read the AP story quoting his son as saying that he and the other Americans were heading to jail.

Returning to their homes, the American reporters packed up their belongings, fully expecting a knock on the door from the Gestapo. But the afternoon and evening dragged on and no one came. Friends kept dropping by to visit Lochner and his German wife, Hilde, and they fielded constant phone calls as well. Finally, when the last visitor was gone, the couple decided to prepare for bed since nothing more appeared to be happening. But just before 1 A.M., the doorbell rang. Hilde opened the door, and two men stepped in asking for Lochner.

"Here I am," Lochner called out from the corridor, which was dimly lit because of blackout regulations. The men pointed their flashlights at him and showed their Gestapo badges, ordering him to come with them. Lochner picked up his packed bag. "But how did you know that we were coming?" one of the men asked. Lochner shot back: "Why do you think I'm a newsman?"

Thuermer was even more determined to show he wasn't surprised when the same two officers knocked sharply on his door and announced: "*Geheime Staatspolizei!* Come with us." Already in his pajamas, the young American responded: "Where have you been?" When that made the two visitors pause, he added: "I got so fed up I got undressed, got in these pajamas, and was about to go to bed." Thuermer pulled out a pack of Chesterfields, offering it to the grateful officers, who abruptly abandoned their air of brisk efficiency and sat down to smoke them as he changed into regular clothes. Everyone was taking their time. But then one of the officers casually mentioned that they had someone waiting in the car downstairs and it was very cold outside. "It was my chief," Thuermer recalled, half-amused and still half-alarmed by the memory of keeping Lochner in that uncomfortable position. "I was freezing his buns off."

Lochner and Thuermer were taken to the third floor of the Alexanderplatz police station, which was the Gestapo's section. After they entered through a door with steel bars and a huge lock, they were put into a large room that was adorned with stern portraits of Hitler and SS chief Heinrich Himmler. They then waited as more American reporters were brought in, until they numbered fifteen in all. Ed Shanke, another AP correspondent, arrived feeling particularly stiff after his long wait in a small car. Carefully spreading out a newspaper on a table, he stretched out his legs and put them on it. A guard immediately jumped up. "We still have *Kultur* in Germany," he snapped. "Take down your feet. You can do that when you get to America, but such manners aren't tolerated in a civilized country like ours. Here we are still human."

The guards didn't seem to know what to do with their captives. In fact, the journalists learned later that the Gestapo hadn't received the instructions from the Foreign Ministry to wait until the following day—Thursday, December 11—to round them up. "The Gestapo had decided to grab us in the middle of the night, as they were wont to grab Jews, republicans, and nonconformist clergymen," Lochner wrote later. "So here we were, fifteen marooned and forgotten newsmen." But any doubts that the Americans were in a very different situation than the Nazis' other prisoners were erased the next day when they started complaining they were hungry. The Gestapo hadn't made any arrangements to feed them, but a guard offered to get them food if they would pay for it. The result was a meal of meatballs and boiled potatoes, along with a salami "wurst." As Lochner noted, the total cost for everyone was 60 cents.

At the embassy that Thursday, the diplomats watched the preparations for Hitler's Reichstag speech, which included the arrival of sound trucks and large groups of people right outside the embassy building. The diplomats nervously closed the metal blinds, but, as Kennan recorded, no action was taken against them. Instead, while Hitler was announcing his declaration of war on the United States, denouncing Roosevelt and the "entire satanic insidiousness" of the Jews who were backing him, the phone suddenly rang in the embassy for the first time since service had been cut off. It was a summons for Morris to the Foreign Ministry. There, Foreign Minister von Ribbentrop kept him standing as he read out the declaration of war and screamed, "Your President has wanted this war; now he has it."

At about the same time, the American correspondents were transferred to an unheated summer hotel annex in Gruenau, a Berlin suburb. But they soon received cheering news: the State Department had declared it would consider the arrested German newsmen to have diplomatic standing, which meant that would be the case for the arrested American journalists as well. The next day, a surprise visitor showed up.

An anonymous caller had tipped off Hilde Lochner about where her husband and the others were taken, and she had managed to talk her way past the guards to deliver apples, cigarettes, canned food and American magazines. The spirits of the journalists soared.

Hitler had ordered that the Americans had to be out of Berlin by the end of the week. On Saturday, Kennan was the one who was summoned to the Foreign Ministry, where he was instructed that all the American staffers had to vacate their apartments and report to the embassy with their luggage the following morning. That same day the American journalists were released with the same orders. Returning to their homes to gather up their belongings, several journalists discovered that intruders had already helped themselves to their possessions during their time in detention—everything from canned meat and cigarettes to clothing and silverware.

When everyone dutifully showed up on Sunday morning, they found the embassy surrounded by troops and occupied by the Gestapo. The Americans were then bussed to the Potsdamer train station, where they boarded a special train. Their destination: Bad Nauheim, a spa town near Frankfurt. They were told they would be held there until an exchange could be arranged for the German diplomats and journalists who were being held in the United States. So began the last act for the Americans in Germany, which, in keeping with many of their earlier experiences, demonstrated that they still maintained a privileged status.

The detained Germans in the United States fared very well. They did their time, as it were, at the Greenbrier, the plush spa hotel in White Sulphur Springs, West Virginia, which had no problem accommodating them. By contrast, Jeschke's Grand Hotel in Bad Nauheim, which eventually accommodated a total of 132 Americans after a few more were added from occupied Europe, was hardly prepared for the sudden influx of boarders. It had been closed at the start of the war in September 1939, and basic services like heat, water and electricity had been cut off. In the interim, heating pipes had burst during the winter months. In January and February 1942, as temperatures dropped, the Americans would keep

their overcoats on when they went to the dining room and then rush back
to their beds to keep warm. Of course, these were hardly hardships compared to what was happening elsewhere in occupied Europe. Nonetheless, the Americans had been promised special treatment, and they were
quick to complain whenever they felt it came up short.

The most constant complaints were about food. German officials
maintained that the detainees were receiving 150 percent of the normal
German civilian rations, and the Americans didn't doubt it. But even that
preferential diet was a far cry from what most of the detainees had been
used to in Berlin. "This showed us how tightly the Germans had pulled
in their belts," Lochner wrote in an AP dispatch after he returned home.
He added that, during the five months they ended up spending in Bad
Nauheim, American men on average lost 10 pounds and women 6.7
pounds; in extreme cases, he added, there were losses of 35 pounds. All
of which hardly constituted evidence of genuine hardship.

After they returned home, many of the Americans were reluctant to
talk too much about their complaints at the time, recognizing how petty
they sounded—particularly as they learned more about how Germans
were treating most of their captives. SS Captain Valentin Patzak, who
was in charge from the German side, worked closely with Kennan, who
became the real leader of the Americans on a day-to-day basis, while
Morris took a more passive role. To deal with the constant problems in
the accommodations, the Germans simply went out and arrested who-
ever they needed—an electrician or plumber—assigning them to make
repairs at the hotel before releasing them. Occasionally, food supplies
from the abandoned U.S. Embassy in Berlin were delivered to the hotel.

Patzak also allowed the Americans to write letters, although they were
subject to censorship. The detainees could not send telegrams, but they
could receive them. Kennan and Morris were allowed to call the Swiss
officials who represented U.S. interests in Berlin, which was the only permitted use of the phone. Much of the day-to-day handling of the Americans and their complaints was left to the two senior Americans, which
minimized direct interactions between the Germans and most of their
detainees. Kennan promptly organized a secretariat, which issued a variety of regulations. Morris insisted, for instance, that men had to wear coats

and ties in the public rooms of the hotel, and that everyone had to assume responsibility for keeping their rooms clean. Another order read: "It is in the general interest not to listen to or pass on rumors."

Rumors flew all the time, of course, especially about how long the detention would drag on. As weeks turned into months, the real challenge was in dealing with what Lochner called "a rather unique American experience in the art of fighting boredom." But the detainees did pretty well in that department. The AP's Ed Shanke had smuggled in a small RCA battery-operated shortwave radio, and he invited his friends to "choir practice" in his room at nine in the evenings to listen to the BBC news from London.

Alvin Steinkopf, another AP reporter, was a source of entertainment one day when he received a surprise visit from Otty Wendell, a waitress at Die Taverne, the journalists' popular Berlin hangout. She had arranged for her family in Frankfurt to send her a telegram asking her to visit because someone was ill, and she went from there to Bad Nauheim, where she joined the Americans as they were taking a walk around the grounds. She brought liquor that Steinkopf shared with his colleagues, and then spent the night with him. The next morning as she tried to leave, the Gestapo arrested her. But, incredibly, Steinkopf managed to convince them to let her go and to cover up the incident, since the ease with which she had slipped into the hotel would reflect badly upon their guard duties.

But what really kept morale up was an expanding program of activities that the Americans organized. Two of the military attachés started a gymnastics class, and soon this was followed by the founding of "Badheim University," with the motto "Education of the ignorant, for the ignorant, by the ignorant, shall not perish from the face of the earth." For all the self-mockery, many of the classes were quite serious. Kennan taught a Russian history course that attracted a record 60 students, while other detainees taught classes in foreign languages, civics, philosophy and "Plains Indian Dancing." A chorus attracted 24 members, and the internees also staged occasionally raucous skits, including some in drag.

The journalists put out several issues of the *Bad Nauheim Pudding*, which qualified as the only American newspaper left in occupied Europe. But they promptly got into arguments with Kennan about what could or couldn't be published. The diplomat was intent on not doing anything to offend the German authorities, and he viewed the reporters as the rowdiest and least controllable members of the group.

The Americans were always looking for new physical activities as well. As the weather improved, they were allowed to take walks along a stream called the Usa—whose name provided fodder for endless jokes. But the real breakthrough came when Kennan won permission for the group to use a municipal athletic field for baseball games. One of the military attachés had brought some basic equipment, but most of the gear was homemade.

Wrapping champagne corks or golf balls with socks, cotton and other makeshift fillers, the medical staffers used adhesive tape and stitched together balls. Thuermer picked up a bough during one of the walks along the Usa, bringing it back to the hotel. There, United Press correspondent Glen Stadler used his sharp Finnish knife to carve it into a 33-inch bat, complete with a grip. Thuermer insisted on penciling in a "trademark" as well. (After leaving the bat for many years in his garage in Middleburg, Virginia, after the war, Thuermer donated it to the Baseball Hall of Fame in Cooperstown.) Otherwise useless diplomatic pouches served as bases.

The games became very popular. About 50 men played on four teams—two for the diplomats, one for the military attachés and one for the journalists—and some of the women came to watch and cheer. Kennan, who played catcher for the Embassy Reds, was especially pleased that this activity provided a distraction from the daily carping about conditions in Bad Nauheim. The diplomat wrote later that he had responsibility "for disciplinary control of this motley group of hungry, cold, and worried prisoners" and "their cares, their quarrels, their jealousies, their complaints filled every moment of my waking day."

One reason for those complaints may have been that the war often seemed to be a distant abstraction, despite the sightings of British bombers targeting nearby Frankfurt or Stuttgart. In Berlin, the war and Nazi terror had been a daily reality; in Bad Nauheim, the Americans were largely cut off from the outside world and left to focus only on themselves.

By the time the arrangements were made for the release of the Germans at the Greenbrier and the Americans in Bad Nauheim, Kennan's irritation with the countrymen under his charge had reached its peak. The Americans were taken to Frankfurt, and from there boarded two special trains for Lisbon. As they chugged through Spain, Kennan noted that they had to lock the compartments "to keep the more exuberant members of our party (primarily the journalists) from disappearing into the crowded, chaotic stations in search of liquor and then getting left behind."

When they reached a small Portuguese border station, Kennan got off the train to meet Ted Rousseau, the assistant naval attaché from the U.S. Embassy in Lisbon, leaving everyone else locked up in the train. Upon hearing that breakfast was available at the station, he exacted payback for the months of complaints he had endured about the food in Bad Nauheim. At the breakfast buffet, he ate alone, stuffing himself with eggs. As he confessed in his memoir, this was especially satisfying because he was "leaving the rest of them to nurse their empty bellies over the remaining six or seven hours of rail journey."

Kennan had another reason to be bitter. The State Department had informed the Americans who had spent five months in Bad Nauheim that they would not be paid for that period. "We had not, you see, been working," as Kennan acidly observed. Then there was the initial news that many of the Americans would not be boarding the ship from Lisbon since those spaces would be given to Jewish refugees. Kennan blamed congressmen who were anxious to please their constituents by bringing over the refugees, considering the fates of these noncitizens "more important than what happened to us." In this respect, he, too, appeared to have little concern for the broader context of the times—especially for the plight of European Jews.

Kennan and Morris managed to get the State Department to reconsider both of those directives. But their anger only grew when, upon arriving in Lisbon, a new telegram ordered several of the diplomats to report for duty the very next day in Portugal instead of going home. "The department obviously had not the faintest idea of the condition, nervous and physical, in which these people found themselves, and had not bothered to use its imagination," Kennan wrote. At that moment, he found himself defending the same people who had tested his patience in Bad Nauheim.

Whether the Americans who reached Lisbon stayed on for new assignments in Europe or, as most did on May 22, boarded the *Drottning-holm*, a white Swedish ship that had the word DIPLOMAT painted in large dark letters on both of its sides to assure safe passage to New York, they knew that fortune had smiled upon them. As they reemerged into the larger world—a world at war because of the course of events in Nazi Germany, the country they had called their temporary home—they began to put their personal experiences in perspective again. "Yes, for us there was an end to the pall of the *Geheime Staatspolizei* [Gestapo]," Thuermer recalled. "We were lucky. We happened to be foreigners, American foreigners."

That is a fitting epithet for most of the Americans who lived in Germany during this period. They were lucky to be able to observe firsthand the unfolding of a terrifying chapter of the modern era; they were even luckier to be Americans, which meant they could do so from a protected vantage point. They were truly privileged eyewitnesses to history.

# Afterword

Early in his political career, long before he became the all-powerful ruler of the Third Reich who was the target of assassination plots, Adolf Hitler narrowly escaped death. On November 9, 1923, when he and General Ludendorff led their followers in the final act of the Munich Beer Hall Putsch, they were met by a hail of machine-gun fire from the police. One of the bullets struck down Max Erwin von Scheubner-Richter, a close confidant of the Nazi leader; the two men had been marching arm-in-arm, and a slight difference in the trajectory of that bullet would have changed the course of history.

That was pure chance, but what happened the next day was something else. It is impossible to know whether Hitler was really about to shoot himself when he picked up his revolver in Helen Hanfstaengl's house as the police were arriving to arrest him. But by grabbing the gun away from him and berating him for even thinking of such a thing, the American wife of Hitler's propagandist Putzi Hanfstaengl may have played as pivotal a role as chance had the day before. If so, this was a clear case of the wrong person appearing at the wrong time.

All of which raises the biggest "what if" question of history: without Hitler, what would have happened to Germany after World War I? The

Americans who lived through the collapse of the Weimar Republic, Hitler's rise to power and the Nazi era did not explicitly address that question, which can never have a definitive answer. But the common thread that runs through so many of the Americans' accounts is their fascination with Hitler. Their experiences and observations strongly suggest that, without Hitler, the Nazis never would have succeeded in their drive for absolute power. The country still might have embarked on an authoritarian course, possibly a military dictatorship. But whatever might have emerged would not have been on the terrifying scale of the Third Reich, with all its terrifying consequences.

Even those Americans who initially dismissed the Nazi leader as a clownish figure came to recognize that he possessed an uncanny ability to mesmerize his followers and attract new ones. He knew how to tap into his countrymen's worst instincts by playing on their fears, resentments and prejudices more masterfully than anyone else. He possessed a combination of peculiar personal qualities and oratorical skills that fueled his movement's rise. No other leading Nazi was as effective a mobilizing force as he was. Not Goering, not Goebbels, not his early rival Gregor Strasser. They, too, would have tried to exploit their countrymen's anger and confusion following their defeat in World War I and the successive economic crises, but without the same results.

As the less than noble ending to their saga makes clear, the Americans in Hitler's Germany were prone to all the normal human failings, including a certain amount of self-centered pettiness during a time of epic tragedy. Many were superficial in their observations, some were deliberately blind, and a few became Nazi apologists. But most of the Americans came to understand what was happening around them, even if they often found it hard to grasp the full implications. This was hardly surprising. After all, they came from a country that was democratic and pragmatic and were plunged into a society undergoing a horrific transformation in the name of a demented ideology.

Among the journalists, William Shirer stood out in terms of his ability to discern the meaning of events as they happened, avoiding the trap of wishful thinking. Little wonder that his *Berlin Diary*, published in 1941, propelled him to initial fame, and that he cemented his reputation as a distinguished author with *The Rise and Fall of the Third Reich*. First published in 1960, this masterful account was an immediate bestseller and continues to be essential reading for anyone trying to understand Hitler's Germany.

Shirer was far from alone, however. Edgar Mowrer and Sigrid Schultz also were journalists who were rarely fooled. Consul General George Messersmith stood out among the American diplomats for the same reason, and for his passion and courage. Truman Smith, the first American official to meet Hitler, proved to be both an astute political observer and a remarkably able military attaché, taking the measure of Germany's rapidly growing military might. Many others served in the Berlin embassy with distinction, including young staffers like William Russell and Jacob Beam.

Several of the Americans would reach the apogee of their careers long after they left Hitler's Germany. Beam became a top-level diplomat, serving as U.S. ambassador to Poland, Czechoslovakia and the Soviet Union. George Kennan would not only become famous as the architect of containment and then ambassador to the Soviet Union, but also as a historian and frequent critic of American foreign policy during the later decades of the Cold War. Richard Helms rose to the top of the Central Intelligence Agency, and Howard K. Smith became the coanchor of *ABC Evening News* when network television reigned supreme.

All of the Americans—whether journalists, diplomats, academics or simply family members—were profoundly affected by their time there, and some far more than others.

After her return to the United States and marriage to the wealthy financier Alfred Stern in 1938, Martha Dodd continued as a Soviet agent, following the path that she had first embarked on in Berlin with her lover Boris Vinogradov, the Soviet diplomat. In 1953, when she heard that she was about to be summoned to testify before the House Un-American Activities Committee, she and Alfred fled to Mexico. They moved to Prague in 1957, the year they were indicted for espionage back home. The indictment was dismissed upon review in 1979 for lack of sufficient evidence, but the couple never returned to the United States. Long after his tenure as CIA director, Helms concluded from Soviet intelligence cables that came to light in the 1990s that they both were indeed part of a Soviet spy ring. "She continued to serve as a spy throughout her life," he wrote, pointing out that her work in Berlin "was probably the peak of her spy career." Alfred died in Prague in 1986, and Martha died there in 1990.

Putzi Hanfstaengl was among the Germans living in Britain who were rounded up as potential security threats at the beginning of World War II. Transferred to an internment camp in Canada, he managed to get a letter smuggled out that reached the desk "of my Harvard Club friend, Franklin Delano Roosevelt," as he grandiosely put it. In the summer of 1942, he was transferred to American custody. Arriving in Washington, he was met by his son Egon, who had been studying at Harvard but then dropped out to join the U.S. Army. Now a sergeant, he greeted his father in uniform.

Putzi provided information on Hitler and other Nazi leaders along with analysis of German radio broadcasts for American intelligence. In 1944, the Americans transferred him back to Britain. After the war ended, he was sent to an internment camp in Germany and finally released on September 3, 1946. He spent the rest of his life in Munich. While Putzi proclaimed his disillusionment with Hitler, he left the impression that the years in his company were the high point of his life. His grandson Eric, who was born in New York in 1954 but grew up in Germany, recalls that Putzi was endlessly telling people about the old days, effectively boasting about how close he was to Hitler. While he could be jovial and entertaining, Eric said, "most of the time he was on the Hitler trip—it was terrible." In an interview with an American scholar in 1971, four years before his death at the age of eighty-eight, Putzi declared that Hitler was "still in his bones."

Helen, who had moved back to the United States in 1938 after their divorce, returned to Munich in the mid-1950s and died there in 1973. She, too, never completely lost her sense of wonderment about Hitler, or about the fact that she had once been so close to the Nazi leader and an object of his awkward affection.

To be sure, most Americans had far less personal involvement with Hitler—and played a far more positive role. Their overall record, not just of the final group that made it to Lisbon but also of many of their predecessors, was impressive. They served as America's eyes and ears in Germany, and they helped produce the proverbial first draft of history. Like all first drafts, it isn't always on the mark, but it offers highly unusual, very personal perspectives on Hitler's rise and Germany's march to the abyss.

By and large, these Americans helped their countrymen begin to understand the nature of Nazi Germany: how it ruthlessly eliminated its political opponents; how it instilled hatred of Jews and anyone else deemed a member of an inferior race; and how it was preparing its military and its people for a war for global domination. The best of them, listening closely to this drumbeat of German militarism, recognized the looming danger. By so doing, the Americans in Germany gradually eroded isolationist sentiments and prepared their countrymen psychologically for the years of bloodshed and struggle ahead. This was the real contribution of the Americans in Hitler's Germany.

# Acknowledgments

Sometimes a book idea seems so obvious after the fact that it's hard to recall where it originated. But I have no such problem in the case of *Hitlerland*. Christina, or Krysia as family and friends call her, and I were driving back to New York after visiting my parents in Washington when we began discussing what I might write about next. I mentioned that when I had worked on *The Greatest Battle*, I had particularly enjoyed exploring the activities and perceptions of the foreign community in Moscow as the German forces mounted their drive that nearly reached the Soviet capital. Krysia then asked the question: "Has anyone written about Americans in Germany in the 1920s and 1930s?" She pointed out that so much was written about Americans in Paris and London, but she hadn't seen a book that recounted the experiences of their counterparts in Germany.

We had lived in Berlin and Bonn when I was reporting for *Newsweek*, and I thought I was reasonably familiar with the major books depicting the 1920s and 1930s, but I had never thought about that question. I knew of a few individual memoirs and histories written by Americans in Germany but couldn't think of a book that examined their lives and perceptions in a comprehensive way. I was intrigued and soon confirmed that no such book existed. The next question was whether there would be enough sources of information to tell their story; in fact, I quickly ascertained that there were far more published and unpublished accounts, correspondence and other documents providing firsthand impressions and recollections of Americans than I had imagined.

When I started this project, there were a few people still alive who now figure in these pages, sometimes discovered almost by accident. Ina Navazelskis, a former journalistic colleague who now works at the Holocaust Museum in Washington, alerted me to the letters of Phillips Talbot, an Asian scholar who, as a young man, visited Germany in 1938. I reached Talbot by phone, and he agreed to send me copies, and we talked about his experience. He also urged me to get in touch with his old friend Angus Thuermer, who had been a young AP reporter in Berlin in the late 1930s. With the help of his daughter Kitty Thuermer, I was able to visit him and his wife, Alice, in their home in Middleburg, Virginia, interviewing him at length, obtaining a copy of his unpublished memoirs and going through his remarkable photo albums that include the photos from Bad Nauheim that appear here. Sadly, neither Talbot nor Thuermer lived to see the publication of this book.

There were also the personal acquaintances I hadn't realized had anything to do with the subject of my book until I started running across their names in my preliminary research. Richard Hottelet, the retired television correspondent who was one of the original "Murrow boys," was someone I had known for quite some time. But I only discovered when I began my research that he had served in Berlin for United Press in the early period of World War II and ended up imprisoned by the Gestapo; although he was dealing with some health problems, he immediately agreed to be interviewed. Similarly, I hadn't known that the late Jacob Beam, the father of my friend and journalistic colleague Alex Beam, had served in the U.S. Embassy in Berlin in the 1930s. Alex was able to provide me with his unpublished manuscript.

Some of the children and grandchildren of the protagonists in this book offered valuable insights and materials about those who are no longer with us. In Middletown, Connecticut, Katharine (Kätchen) Truman Smith Coley freely shared her memories of her parents, Truman and Katharine Smith, and vivid recollections of her time in Berlin in the mid-1930s as a young girl. She also allowed me to use the remarkable photo from that period showing her uneasily holding Goering's lion; the photo had been hanging on her refrigerator. In Munich, Eric Hanfstaengl talked about his grandparents Ernst ("Putzi") and Helen, and allowed me to use the photo of his grandmother dressed up as the Statue of Liberty and holding the American flag on the steps of Hoboken's City Hall. Two granddaughters of Louis Lochner—Anita Lochner, who lives in Berlin, and Barbara Roth, who lives in Geneva—extended their assistance, too. To everyone with those kinds of personal connections, I'm especially grateful.

Given the passage of time, though, I had to rely mostly on the written testimonies left behind by the American eyewitnesses. Many were published at the time, although now largely forgotten. But others had never appeared in print. To track down the latter, I received help from numerous archivists and librarians at a broad array of institutions that contain the papers and other records of many of these Americans.

As in the past, I found an amazing assortment of original documents in the archives of the Hoover Institution. Thanks to the hospitality of Dave Brady and Mandy MacCalla of the Media Fellows Program, I was able to make several trips there. On my visits, archivists Carol Leadenham, Brad Bauer, Irena Czernichowska, and Zbigniew Stanczyk provided me with invaluable assistance that allowed me to keep discovering new materials. And even from afar, Brad, who is a remarkable German specialist, helped me connect the dots and fill in missing pieces. He also first put me in touch with Anita Lochner and Kätchen Coley.

I want to thank another former journalistic colleague, John Daniszewski of the Associated Press, for connecting me with Valerie Komor, who runs that organization's archives. Valerie immediately offered her help, and so did her colleague Sam Markham. It was a particular pleasure to find Sam there; he was a young boy when his family and ours were friends and neighbors in Bonn in the mid-1980s. I want to thank Carol Kahn Strauss at the Leo Baeck Institute for putting me in touch with Frank Mecklenburg, the chief archivist, who immediately tipped me off to a fascinating travel diary. I also received help from many others in places like the Library of Congress and Columbia University's Rare Book and Manuscript Library; I apologize for not listing everyone here.

As I would tell others about what I was doing, I would often get valuable leads from unexpected sources. In the Hoover archives, I was changing places at the copying machine with John McLaughlin, who, it turned out, had written his Ph.D. dissertation on Albert Wedemeyer—and promptly helped me locate Wedemeyer's records from his time at the German War College. David Marwell, the director of the Museum of Jewish Heritage in New York, shared his dissertation on Ernst ("Putzi") Hanfstaengl. Richard Wilson, who teaches architectural history at the University of Virginia, tipped me off to Philip Johnson's experiences in Germany in the 1920s, and Bill Ury led me to explore the early days of the Experiment in International Living in Germany. John Birkelund urged me to check out the warnings of Ferdinand Eberstadt on the German debt deals as the Depression hit.

Several close friends, like David Moore and Arlene Getz, helped me locate other sources. I owe thanks to many others—Steve and Ardith Hodes, Francine Shane, Robert Morea, Victor and Monika Markowicz, Jeff Bartholet, Fred Guterl, Sandra and Bob Goldman, Eva and Bart Kaminski, Alexandra and Anthony Juliano, to name just a few—for their encouragement and moral support. As usual, David Satter, who has been such a good friend since we first met in Moscow in the early 1980s, was always ready to read my chapters as I produced them, offering spot-on critiques and suggestions.

At the EastWest Institute where I now work, I'm grateful for the support of my colleagues and all the board members who keep us on track. I want to thank, in particular, John Mroz; Francis Finlay; Ross Perot, Jr.; Mark Maletz; Leo Schenker; Stephen Heintz; and Maria Cattaui. I also want to thank my talented, highly dedicated team of Abby Rabinowitz, Dragan Stojanovski and Tracy Larsen, and earlier Sarosh Syed.

Then there are the people who were directly involved in this project from the very beginning and really made it happen. My agent, Robert Gottlieb, enthusiastically encouraged me to pursue this idea, and Alice Mayhew at Simon & Schuster nursed it to fruition, providing the kind of subtle guidance each step of the way that any writer can only hope for.

Every superlative in the world has been used to describe Alice's skills as an editor; they all are accurate. Her colleague Roger Labrie, as always, provided tremendous help as well. I also want to thank many other members of the Simon & Schuster team, including Rachel Bergmann, Julia Prosser, Rachelle Andujar, Michael Accordino, Gypsy da Silva, and copy editor Fred Wiemer. At the Trident Media Group, Gottlieb's agency, I am grateful for the enthusiastic support of Erica Silverman, Claire Roberts, and Adrienne Lombardo.

Finally, of course, there is my family. My parents, Zygmunt and Marie, have always read everything I've produced, and they were eager to receive each chapter as soon as I wrote it. When my father was hospitalized in the summer of 2010, the first thing he told me was that he was sorry he had to stop reading the chapter he was on three pages before the ending. Although he lived for nearly another year, he wasn't able to read again. But he kept asking me about my progress as long as he could. There's no way to express fully my debt to him and to my mother. I also want to thank my sisters, Maria and Terry, and their spouses, Roberto and Diane.

My four grown children—Eva, Sonia, Adam, and Alex—know how much I rely on their love and encouragement, along with all their practical help whenever I need it (which is often). I want to offer special thanks to Eva and Taylor, who were always ready to be first readers and first responders on this project. Like Sonia and Eran and Adam and Sara, they have families of their own now. The names of all their wonderful offspring appear in the dedication to this book. A promising young writer, Alex was my in-house sounding board for many ideas. I also want to make special mention of the generosity of spirit of my brother-in-law, Waldek Kowalski, and his wife, Ewa.

That brings me back to Krysia, who sparked this project in the first place. The best thing that ever happened in my life was meeting and marrying her during a whirlwind semester as an exchange student at the Jagiellonian University in Krakow. Because of me, she never finished her studies. But she has been educating me ever since and continues to be my muse, editor, and so much more.

# Photo Credits

# Notes

**INTRODUCTION**

PAGE

1   *Born in Chicago* and other biographical background: Sigrid Schultz, *Germany Will Try It Again*, viii–ix, 123; and Nancy Caldwell Sorel, *The Women Who Wrote the War*, 3–4.

1   *"Few foreign painters"*: Schultz, 123.

1   *"enemy aliens"*: Ibid., viii.

2   *"a sour, disagreeable little man"* and other quotes about Raeder: Ibid., 11.

4   *"Nobody had read"*: Otto Strasser, *Hitler and I*, 58.

4   *"most Americans"*: Edgar Ansel Mowrer, *Triumph and Turmoil*, 164.

5   *"the American colony"* and other Lochner quotes: Louis Lochner, *Always the Unexpected: A Book of Reminiscences*, 151, 123.

6   *reaching a peak*: Howard K. Smith, *Last Train from Berlin*, 344.

6   *Mowrer, for instance*: Mowrer, 166.

6   *"One thing one forgets"*: Conquest interviewed by author (2009).


**CHAPTER ONE: "NERVOUS BREAKDOWN"**

PAGE

10   *a loaf of bread*: Peter Gay, *Weimar Culture*, 154.

10   *"Orchestra stalls"*: Anton Gill, *A Dance Between Flames*, 75.

10   *Carl Zuckmayer attended* and *"could be freely handled"* and other quotes about the party: Ibid., 85.

10   *"People have forgotten"*: Michael Danzi, *American Musician in Germany, 1924–1939*, 45–46.

11  *"The contrast"*: Kurt G. W. Ludecke, *I Knew Hitler*, 10.

11  *"political zanies"*: Ben Hecht, *A Child of the Century*, 252.

11  *"all was politics"* and *"Germany is having"*: Ibid., 264–265.

12  *"a few years of"* and *"to be in"* and *"call into play"*: Hugh R. Wilson, *Diplomat Between Wars*, 3–5.

12  *"Rioting seemed to be"* and *"I myself have seen"* and *"vituperative"*: Wilson, 94–95.

13  *"The shabbiness"*: Ibid., 94.

13  *"traces of"*: Ibid., 103.

13  *"the interior was"* and rest of Katharine Smith's quotes and descriptions of early days in Berlin in this chapter: Katharine Alling Hollister Smith autobiographical writings and correspondence, Truman Smith Papers, box 14, Hoover Institution Archives.

14  *He was a 1915 Yale graduate* and other biographical details: Robert Hessen, ed., *Berlin Alert: The Memoirs and Reports of Truman Smith*, xiii–xiv; and Katharine (Kätchen) Truman Smith Coley interviewed by author (2010).

15  *"With the end of the war"*: Wilson, 103.

15  *"The Germans, then"*: Ibid., 98.

17  *"A flame of resentment"*: Ibid., 100.

17  *Major General Henry T. Allen* and quotes from his report: "Finds Negro Troops Orderly on Rhine," *New York Times*, Feb. 20, 1921.

18  *"I am afraid"*: Schultz, 101.

18  *"Your French friends"*: Karl H. von Wiegand Papers, box 6, Hoover Institution Archives.

18  *"a fair way"* and *"A cruel thing to do"* and early bio of Wiegand: Ibid., box 47 (notes for outline of an autobiography he never wrote).

18  *finding work at the Associated Press* and subsequent move to United Press: Ibid., box 30.

19  *"Food Shortage Alarms All Germany"*: Ibid., box 25 (not marked from which Hearst paper).

19  *In one letter from 1921*: Ibid., box 6.

19  *"I am looking"* and Wiegand reply: Ibid., box 7.

20  *"Houghton Girls Make Berlin Debut"*: Ibid., box 25.

21  *"Hitler Styled"*: Ibid., box 25.

22  *"Something is brewing"* and account of Houghton's concerns: Jeffrey J. Matthews, *Alanson B. Houghton: Ambassador of the New Era*, 68.

22  *"being without"* and *"seems to have had"* and *"try to make"*: Hessen, ed., 43.

23  *a clear-cut set* and orders as quoted: Ibid., 44.

23  *four hundred visas* and *"It seemed to us"*: Robert Murphy, *Diplomat Among Warriors*, 31.

23  *"It was a welcome"*: Ibid., 32.

23  *Murphy told Smith* and Smith's quotes summarizing Murphy's views: Hessen, ed., 48–50.

24  *"healthy drift away"* and rest of General von Kressenstein's views: Ibid., 53.

24   *Friedrich Trefz and his views* as quoted by Smith: Ibid., 56.

25   *Scheubner-Richter and rest of visit* to Nazi headquarters: Ibid., 56–57.

25   *General Ludendorff and his remarks:* Ibid., 58–59.

26   *New York tenement house:* Ibid., 46.

26   *"A marvelous demagogue":* Ibid., 60.

26   *"Parliament and":* Ibid., 61.

26   *The question whether:* Ibid., 65.

26   *"The diary I kept":* Ibid., 18.

27   *"some arrangement" and "disquieting":* Matthews, 68.

27   *"The most active":* Ibid., 69.

27   *"How does this" and rest of exchanges* with Drey: Murphy, 38.

28   *"Interview with Adolf Hitler" and all quotes from it:* State Department (RG 59) microfilm publication #M336: *Records of the Department of State Relating to Internal Affairs of Germany, 1910–1929,* file: 862.00/1228 on roll 18, National Archives. Also in Murphy, 40–41.

29   *In a letter to Murphy:* Robert D. Murphy Papers, box 43, Hoover Institution Archives (hereafter, Hoover).

29   *"No, this is":* Murphy, *Diplomat Among Warriors,* 39.

29   *"Look after him" and Fate Fakirs:* Ernst Hanfstaengl, *Hitler: The Missing Years,* 31.

29   *"I was the leading:"* Ernst Hanfstaengl, taped interview by John Toland, Library of Congress.

30   *"The Hanfstaengls were":* Hanfstaengl, *Hitler,* 24.

30   *Putzi's grandfather* and family background: Peter Conradi, *Hitler's Piano Player,* 12; and Hanfstaengl, 23–24.

30   *Harvard days* and details of time there: Conradi, 19–20; and Hanfstaengl, 26–27.

30   *"I hate to say":* Hanfstaengl, taped interview by Toland, Library of Congress.

30   *"Some fool" and rest of canoeing incident:* Hanfstaengl, 26; and Conradi, 19.

31   *"a fellow extrovert,"* quotes about FDR and former President Teddy Roosevelt, and early World War I avoiding of internment: Hanfstaengl, 27–28.

31   *A Department of Justice report* and Nicholas Roosevelt quotes: Conradi, 31–32.

32   *"riven by faction" and "It became evident":* Hanfstaengl, 29–30.

32   *"a very pleasant":* Ibid., 31.

32   *"A lovely way":* Katharine Smith, Truman Smith Papers, box 14, Hoover.

32   *"worked like" and "I met the most remarkable"* and rest of Smith-Hanfstaengl conversation: Hanfstaengl, 32.

33   *"All that is":* Hanfstaengl, taped interview by Toland, Library of Congress.

**CHAPTER TWO: UP IN THE AIR**
PAGE

34   *Kindlkeller description* and *"In his heavy boots":* Hanfstaengl, 33.

34   *police agents:* Hanfstaengl interviewed by Toland, Library of Congress.

34   *"electric" and "In his early years":* Hanfstaengl, 33.

35    *"a charge which"* and rest of Hitler speech: Ibid., 35.

35    *"especially the ladies":* Hanfstaengl interviewed by Toland, Library of Congress.

35    *"Transfixed"* and quotes on how Hanfstaengl was impressed and wanted to explain America's importance: Hanfstaengl, 35–36.

35    *"Ah, you are"* and rest of exchange with Hitler: Hanfstaengl interviewed by Toland, Library of Congress; and Hanfstaengl, 36–37.

36    *"a sallow, untidy":* Hanfstaengl, 32.

36    *"The first followers":* Ibid., 37.

36    *"the earnest, magnetic"* and rest of Helen's account and quotes: Helene Niemeyer "Notes," FDR Library; and Helene Niemeyer, taped interview by John Toland, Library of Congress. Ernst Hanfstaengl's comments in this section are from Hanfstaengl, 38–39.

38    *family photos:* courtesy of Eric Hanfstaengl, the grandson of Helen and Ernst Hanfstaengl.

38    *"He had been so struck"* and Kay's account of visit by Putzi and Helen: Katharine Smith, box 14, Hoover.

39    *"What wonder":* Niemeyer "Notes."

40    *"a definite public character"* and Knickerbocker biographical details: H. R. Knickerbocker, *Is Tomorrow Hitler's? 200 Questions on the Battle of Mankind,* foreword by John Gunther, xii–xiii.

40    *"The first impression"* and *"the expression of his face":* Ibid., 1–2.

40    *"He is softly fat":* Ibid., 3.

40    *"He knew the thing":* Hanfstaengl, 49.

41    *"hysterical enthusiasm"* and Hanfstaengl's introduction of Harvard marching songs and Hitler's reactions: Ibid., 51.

41    *he put up $1,000:* Ibid., 53.

41    *"If there is"* and Hitler's views of the U.S., Henry Ford and Ku Klux Klan: Ibid., 40–41.

42    *the price for the three beers:* Ibid., 96.

42    *"Quiet!"* and most of Beer Hall Putsch account: John Toland, *Adolf Hitler,* Vol. I, 163–165.

42    *"Gentlemen, not one of us":* Otto Strasser, *Hitler and I,* 41.

42    *press conference:* Hanfstaengl, 99.

42    *"REBELS IN COUP":* Wiegand Papers, box 26, Hoover.

43    *Fourteen Nazis died* and other putsch details: Ian Kershaw, *Hitler, 1889–1936: Hubris,* 210–11. (Other accounts put the number of Nazis shot and killed as sixteen, not fourteen. Hitler would regularly honor sixteen "martyrs" of the Beer Hall Putsch once he took power.)

43    *"I can testify":* Murphy, 39–40.

43    *Ludendorff surrendered:* Kershaw, 211.

43    *"My God"* and Hanfstaengl's actions and *"The last place":* Hanfstaengl, 105–106.

44    *"one of his theoretical passions":* Ibid., 50–51.

44    *"a neuter":* Niemeyer interviewed by Toland.

44    "*To my utter amazement*" and rest of account of Hitler's arrival through doctor's explanation of how they got to the Hanfstaengl house: Niemeyer "Notes."

45    *The next morning* and events then in Hanfstaengl's house: Toland, 183–184.

45    "*Now all is lost*" and rest of Helen's account of Hitler when facing arrest, along with scene with gun: Niemeyer "Notes" and Niemeyer interviewed by Toland.

46    "*What are the bad*": Niemeyer "Notes."

47    "*a cultural riot*" and "*the leaders of*" and other Mowrer descriptions: Edgar Ansel Mowrer, *Triumph and Turmoil*, 194–197.

47    "*In Berlin ice*" and other Lilian quotes about initial impressions: Lilian Mowrer, *Journalist's Wife*, 180–183.

47    "*but something in*" and other comments on appeal: Ibid., 190.

48    "*the most vital*": Ibid., 201.

48    "*Nowhere in the world*": Ibid., 205–206.

48    "*They were so wonderfully*": Ibid., 190–191.

48    "*a full-fledged*" and Lilian's other comments about women: Ibid., 192.

48    "*It was the greatest*" and other film observations: Ibid., 213–214.

49    "*Quit bothering*": Edgar Ansel Mowrer, 199.

49    "*I was becoming*": Lilian Mowrer, 191.

49    "*All in all*": Matthews, *Alanson B. Houghton, Ambassador of the New Era*, 75–76.

49    "*to save what is*": Ibid., 77.

49    "*I feel as if*": Ibid., 87.

50    "*just claims*": Manfred Jonas, *The United States and Germany: A Diplomatic History*, 172.

50    "*The United States is*": Ibid., 181.

50    "*The Americanization*": Wiegand Papers, box 27, Hoover.

51    "*By the early twenties*" and "*that complex of factors*": Edgar Ansel Mowrer, 187, 189.

51    "*It's madness*" and "*an intensity*" and details of Baker's stay, including gifts: Jean-Claude Baker and Chris Chase, *Josephine: The Hungry Heart*, 124–129.

52    "*The period immediately*": Edgar Ansel Mowrer, *Germany Puts the Clock Back*, 153.

52    "*sexual perversions*": Ibid., 155.

52    "*These were elegant*": Hecht, 256.

52    "*The air we breathed*": Franz Schulze, *Philip Johnson: Life and Work*, 412.

52    "*I think if it*" and "*The Americans*": Ibid., 53–54.

53    "*Treason to the Republic*": Lilian Mowrer, 186.

53    "*had the same goal*": William Shirer, *The Rise and Fall of the Third Reich: A History of Nazi Germany*, 115.

53    "*You may pronounce*": Ibid., 118.

54    "*He spoke with*" and rest of Mowrer report: Lilian Mowrer, 186.

54    "*While the putsch*" and "*vanished into oblivion*": Murphy, *Diplomat Among Warriors*, 40.

55    "*even as a side issue*" and "*as far as*": Hamilton Fish Armstrong, *Peace and Counterpeace: From Wilson to Hitler*, 309–310.

55    "*Hemingway by the way*": Hubert Renfro Knickerbocker Papers, Columbia University Rare Book and Manuscript Library.

55   *Knickerbocker, who would:* Richard Lingeman, *Sinclair Lewis: Rebel from Main Street,* 313.

55   *some accounts claim:* Peter Kurth, *American Cassandra: The Life of Dorothy Thompson,* 487.

56   *"Do come on up"* and rest of Lilian Mowrer's account: Lilian Mowrer, 221.

56   *"International relations":* Victoria de Grazia, *Irresistible Empire: America's Advance Through Twentieth-Century Europe,* 75.

56   *"These were the brilliant":* Kurth, 93.

57   *"an authentic record"* and *"The Graf Zeppelin is more than":* Wiegand Papers, box 30, Hoover.

57   *"You have indeed cared"* and other correspondence: Wiegand Papers, box 8, Hoover.

57   *"brilliant British woman"* and *"internationally-known": New York American,* Sept. 1, 1929; and Wiegand Papers, box 30, Hoover.

58   *"full of promise":* Kurth, 92.

58   *"Though externals":* Lilian Mowrer, 247.

58   *"Where but":* Edgar Ansel Mowrer, *Triumph and Turmoil,* 160.

58   *"They all had"* and *"These Germans":* Lilian Mowrer, 254.

58   *"loose emotional fervor"* and subsequent Lilian Mowrer quotes: Ibid., 255.

59   *"If one wants":* Kurth, 93.

59   *"like a death's head"* and *"If only I could":* Lilian Mowrer, 225.

59   *"Do you think":* Ibid., 224.

59   *"The strange bit of history":* Hecht, 296–297.

60   *"In him all morality":* Ibid., 298.

60   *"I know who caused":* Max Wallace, *The American Axis: Henry Ford, Charles Lindbergh, and the Rise of the Third Reich,* 20.

60   *"I regard Henry Ford"* and description of Annetta Antona interview with Hitler: Ibid., 1–2.

60   *"Mr. Ford's genius":* Prince Louis Ferdinand, *The Rebel Prince: Memoirs of Prince Louis Ferdinand of Prussia,* 241.

61   *"a prosperous, energetic":* Wiegand Papers, box 8, Hoover.

61   *"a high proportion of"* and *"One could sense":* Wilson, *A Diplomat Between Wars,* 115.

61   *"Look out"* and Bouton's account of encounter with Sinclair Lewis: S. Miles Bouton Papers, box 4, Hoover.

62   *In 1925, Jacob Gould Schurman* and his building fund for Heidelberg University: Maynard Moser, *Jacob Gould Schurman: Scholar, Political Activist, and Ambassador of Good Will, 1892–1942,* 156–158.

62   *"the will to war":* Ibid., 169.

62   *"The Republic":* Ibid., 170.

63   *"itch to pour":* Ibid., 191.

63   *"You see we"* and rest of Mowrer-Friday exchange: Lilian Mowrer, 236.

63   *"an orgy of spending"* and *"the stunning new"* and *"the entire rolling stock":* Ibid., 239.

63   *Schurman received a warning:* Moser, 204.

63  *"Hey, this thing's a fake"*: Robert C. Perez and Edward F. Willett, *The Will to Win: A Biography of Ferdinand Eberstadt*, 44.

64  *$300 million in new American loans*: Moser, 206.

## CHAPTER THREE: WHALE OR MINNOW?

PAGE

65  *"I'm going to have to start"*: Bella Fromm, *Blood and Banquets: A Berlin Social Diary*, 18; Fromm biographical details, ibid., 3–6.

65  *"Let's have"*: Ibid., 19.

66  *diary entry of July 16 and all quotes*: Ibid., 20.

66  *"a gentle-looking man"* and *"an attractive woman"*: Ibid., 24.

66  *"Even the international"* and *"I like Berlin"*: Ibid., 28.

67  *"Fortunately for us"* and other Knickerbocker quotes: "Covering Berlin," *Public Ledger*, April 21, 1930, Knickerbocker Papers, Columbia.

67  *the party boasted 108,000*: Frederick L. Schuman, *The Nazi Dictatorship: A Study in Social Pathology and the Politics of Fascism*, 72.

68  *"Now he is again"* and all other quotes from Wiegand's session with Hitler: Wiegand Papers, box 30, Hoover.

69  *"The German people"*: Mowrer, *Germany Puts the Clock Back*, 198.

70  *"So had a majority"* and *"flocked to the Nazis"*: Charles W. Thayer, *The Unquiet Germans*, 12–13.

70  *"The most remarkable"*: Mowrer, *Germany Puts the Clock Back*, 22.

70  *"with the raucous voice"* and rest of incident on train: Lilian Mowrer, 234.

71  *"The seats swarmed"* and rest of Enid Keyes's account from her letter: *American Girl, German Wife: The Letters of Enid Keyes Mehnert, 1931–1935*, Enid Keyes Mehnert Papers, Vol. 1, Hoover.

72  *"Dad, what do you think"* and rest of exchange between Arthur and his father, along with *"chariot bumping"*: Mowrer, *Germany Puts the Clock Back*, 120–121.

73  *"I never saw"* and rest of quotes from December 27, 1931, letter: Knickerbocker Papers, Columbia.

73  *"We are for"* and rest of exchange with streetwalkers: Mowrer, *Triumph and Turmoil*, 210–211.

73  *"too hot to publish"*: Ibid., 211.

73  *"I can't ever walk"* and other Mehnert quotes: Mehnert Papers, Hoover.

74  *"You see defiance"* and *"This country has"*: Morrison letter, Knickerbocker Papers, Columbia.

75  *"Hitler is a homo-sexual"* and rest of letter to Winner: Knickerbocker Papers, Columbia.

77  *Abraham Plotkin was* and other information about his background and trip: Plotkin, *An American in Hitler's Berlin: Abraham Plotkin's Diary, 1932–33*, Introduction, xii–xl.

77  *"hide their poverty very well"* and *"from their appearances"*: Ibid., 6.

77    *"You Americans"*: Ibid., 62.

78    *one family's diet*: Ibid., 58.

78    *The head of a district health department*: Ibid., 75.

78    *"fascinated by"* and rest of exchange with streetwalkers: Ibid., 12–16.

78    *"Do you have a fascist party"* and rest of exchange with German Jews: Ibid., 38–39.

79    *"Hitlerism is rapidly going"*: Ibid., 29.

79    *"One felt as if"*: Ibid., 67.

79    *"showmanship"* and *"So this was"*: Ibid., 68, 70.

80    *"like a faithful dog"* and rest of Corwin's visit to Heidelberg: R. LeRoy Bannerman, *On a Note of Triumph: Norman Corwin and the Golden Years of Radio*, 22.

80    *"We are beyond"*: Ibid., 22–23.

80    *On Saturday, December 5, 1931*, and quotes from Hitler and Sackett at and about their meeting: Bernard V. Burke, *Ambassador Frederic Sackett and the Collapse of the Weimar Republic, 1930–1933*, 8–9, 185–186.

81    *"If only I"* and rest of scene between Hitler and Helen: Niemeyer interviewed by Toland, Library of Congress.

82    *"I felt Hitler"*: Hanfstaengl, 123.

82    *"Why don't you find"*: Niemeyer interviewed by Toland.

82    *"an empty-headed"*: Hanfstaengl, 162.

82    *"I always had the feeling"*: Niemeyer interviewed by Toland.

82    *Otto Strasser* and his claims about Geli and Hitler: Ronald Hayman, *Hitler + Geli*, 145.

83    *"The whole affair"*: Hanfstaengl, 165.

83    *"of an American woman"* and *"a German propagandist"*: Dorothy Thompson, *"I Saw Hitler!,"* 3–4.

83    *"lofty and remote"*: Ibid., 5.

83    *"Fussy. Amusing"*: Ibid., 13.

83    *"an immense, high-strung"*: Peter Kurth, *American Cassandra: The Life of Dorothy Thompson*, 160.

83    *John Farrar*: Marion K. Sanders, *Dorothy Thompson: A Legend in Her Time*, 166.

84    *"The times in which"*: Thompson, vi.

84    *"Gone 'legal'"*: Ibid., 4.

84    *"terrorizes the streets"*: Ibid., 12.

84    *"When finally I walked"*: Ibid., 13.

85    *"He is formless"*: Ibid., 13–14.

85    *"an insignificant"* and contrast with Hindenburg and Brüning: Ibid., 14–15.

85    *"The Jews are"*: Ibid., 34.

85    *"Hitler's tragedy"*: Ibid., 35.

85    *"If Hitler comes into"*: Ibid., 36.

86    *"Mrs. Lewis, the wife"* and rest of Ludecke-Hitler exchange: Ludecke, *I Knew Hitler*, 531.

86    *One of Putzi's classmates* and rest of Harvard connections with Kaltenborn: H. V. Kaltenborn, *Fifty Fabulous Years, 1900–1950*, 51.

86 *"felt that any"* and details of interview procedures: Hans V. Kaltenborn, "An Interview with Hitler," *Wisconsin Magazine of History*, Summer 1967.

87 *"Why does your"* and Hitler's response: Kaltenborn, *Fifty Fabulous Years*, 186–187.

87 *"he has no capacity"*: Kaltenborn, "An Interview with Hitler."

88 *"A dictatorship is"*: Kaltenborn, *Fifty Fabulous Years*, 188.

88 *"I could understand"*: Kaltenborn, "An Interview with Hitler."

88 *"After meeting Hitler"*: Kaltenborn, *Fifty Fabulous Years*, 186.

88 *"Most people"*: Ibid., 185.

## CHAPTER FOUR: "I WILL SHOW THEM"
PAGE

89 *"I'll give the Hitlerites"* and other quotes from Lochner: Louis Lochner, *Always the Unexpected*, 209–210.

90 *"it was obviously"*: Burke, *Ambassador Frederic Sackett*, 262.

90 *"rule alone"* and descriptions of Hitler and Goebbels: Ibid., 247.

91 *"I am told that"* and *"The Nazi meetings"*: Plotkin, 102–103.

91 *"the bloody Jews"* and *"run out of his control"* and *"like a bunch of schoolboys"*: Ibid., 108.

91 *"a banker named Arnholt"* and *"Merely wondering"* along with the rest of Mowrer account: Mowrer, *Triumph and Turmoil*, 212.

92 *"I am going to Munich"* and rest of Schacht-Mowrer exchange: Ibid., 213.

92 *"whenever a political melodrama"* and rest of Fromm-Wiegand exchange: Fromm, 62–63.

93 *While Ambassador Sackett*: Burke, 274.

93 *"The German government"* and *"I do not think"*: Fromm, 67.

93 *At an "intimate" dinner* and rest of Schleicher-Fromm exchange: Ibid., 68–69.

94 *"dancing between four masters"* and rest of Plettl-Plotkin exchange: Plotkin, 122–123.

95 *"in no way alarmed"* and *"rapidly increasing"*: Burke, 277.

95 *"sudden and unexpected"*: Ibid., 281.

95 *"We have hired Hitler"* and *"in the driver's seat"*: Lochner, *Always the Unexpected*, 210–211.

95 *He had arrived in Germany*: Bouton, "My Years in Germany" (Reprinted from the Proceedings of the Institute of Public Affairs, Ninth Annual Session, University of Georgia, Athens, Georgia, January 23–25, 1935), S. Miles Bouton Papers, box 4, Hoover.

96 *"It requires no great skill"*: "Bouton, Home from Europe, Tells of Germany in 1925," *Baltimore Sun*, box 1, Hoover.

96 *"Read that treaty"*: Bouton Collection, box 4, Hoover.

96 *"It was several minutes"*: "A Veteran Journalist Reports," c. 1962, Bouton Papers, box 6, Hoover.

96  *"does not come into consideration"*: Untitled copy of dispatch dated August 9, 1930, Bouton Papers, box 1, Hoover.

96  *"For the last five years"*: Bouton, "My Years in Germany," box 4, Hoover.

97  *"represents a remarkable"* and rest of quotes from original manuscript of March 1932 article "Hitler's Shadow Across Germany": Bouton Papers, box 1, Hoover.

98  *"That they put me down"* and rest of Lochner's letter: "Round Robins from Berlin: Louis P. Lochner's Letters to His Children, 1932–1941," *Wisconsin Magazine of History*, Summer 1967.

99  *"foreigners and Jews"* and rest of Lilian Mowrer's account, including description of Edgar Mowrer's conversations with Nazis over beers: Lilian Mowrer, 266–268.

100  *"But I have only heard"* and rest of Lilian's conversation with her daughter: Ibid., 275.

100  *"sick of everything"* and other quotes from book: Mowrer, *Germany Puts the Clock Back*, 196–198.

100  *"Did he believe"*: Ibid., 194.

101  *"I could see the man's face"*: Sigrid Schultz, *Germany Will Try It Again*, 87–88.

101  *"While others slept"*: Mowrer, *Germany Puts the Clock Back*, 207.

101  *"singularly unmoved"* and *"Certainly it was"*: Hanfstaengl, 196.

102  *"I sent for"* and *"was, needless to"*: Ibid., 199.

102  *"In strode"* and rest of dinner description: Lochner, *Always the Unexpected*, 186–187.

103  *"a court jester"* and account of Messersmith-Hanfstaengl encounter: Jesse H. Stiller, *George S. Messersmith: Diplomat of Democracy*, 40.

103  *"I knew he was crazy"*: Lilian Mowrer, 299.

104  *"secret" Jew*: Mowrer, *Triumph and Turmoil*, 219.

104  *"Of course, he is"*: Richard Breitman, Barbara McDonald Stewart and Severin Hochberg, eds., *Advocate for the Doomed: The Diaries and Papers of James G. McDonald, 1932–1935*, 28.

104  *"Edgar a Jew?"*: Mowrer, *Triumph and Turmoil*, 219.

104  *According to Putzi*: Hanfstaengl, 175.

104  *"the greatest torchlight procession"* and *"Hitler stationed himself"*: Manuscript of article for *Public Ledger*, May 15, 1933, H. R. Knickerbocker Papers, Columbia.

104  *"The Nazis will make"*: Burke, 282.

104  *"the purely political"* and Sackett's views of Papen and Hugenberg: Ibid., 283–284.

105  *Marinus van der Lubbe*: Kershaw, 456–457.

105  *"a dupe of the Nazis"*: Shirer, *The Rise and Fall of the Third Reich*, 269.

105  *"For the Protection"*: Kershaw, *Hitler, 1889–1936: Hubris*, 459.

105  *"deeply displeased"*: Fromm, 79.

106  *"might deviate from"*: Shirer, *The Rise and Fall of the Third Reich*, 276.

106  *"The nation turned"*: Manuscript of article for *Public Ledger*, May 15, 1933, H. R. Knickerbocker Papers, Columbia.

106  *"It is really as bad"* and other quotes from letter to Lewis: Sanders, *Dorothy Thompson*, 185.

106  *"perfectly mad"* and rest of letter to Cohen: Kurth, 187.

107  *"the auto da fé"*: Manuscript of article for *Public Ledger*, May 15, 1933, H. R. Knickerbocker Papers, Columbia.

107  *"These flames do not only"* and authors of burned books: Philip Metcalfe, *1933*, 123.

107  *"that the truth"*: Undated manuscript titled "Education Is Not Enough" in S. Miles Bouton Papers, box 1, Hoover.

107  *"change his style of reporting"*: Deborah E. Lipstadt, *Beyond Belief: The American Press and the Coming of the Holocaust, 1933–1945*, 22.

108  *"Our orders from our bosses"*: Lochner, *Always the Unexpected*, 252.

108  *"The Nazis have turned loose"*: Plotkin, 194.

108  *"real radicals"* and rest of Messersmith analysis: Stiller, 35–36.

109  *"I am a Jew"*: Metcalfe, 93.

109  *Edward Dahlberg* and *"Four suits"*: Ibid., 93–94.

109  *On March 31, the SA snatched* and Messersmith handling of journalists and subsequent report: Stiller, 36.

109  *He told Messersmith*: Ibid., 43.

109  *"in the hope that"*: Kaltenborn, *Fifty Fabulous Years*, 189.

110  *"a terrifying account"* and *"The Jews are"* and Tiergarten account: Breitman, Stewart and Hochberg, *Advocate for the Doomed*, 28–29.

110  *"highly overwrought"*: Ibid., 30.

110  *"To him the leaders"*: Ibid., 45.

110  *Separately, Knickerbocker*: Ibid., 32.

110  *During the Jewish boycott*: Ibid., 33.

111  *"In each case"*: Ibid., 40.

111  *"No, there is"* and rest of McDonald-Goldman exchange along with account of Hitler meeting the same day: Ibid., 47–48.

**CHAPTER FIVE: "GET OUT, AND FAST"**

PAGE

113  *Armstrong saw groups*: Hamilton Fish Armstrong, *Peace and Counterpeace*, 527.

113  *British and American correspondents* and *"He could hardly"*: Ibid., 530.

114  *"were holding on to"* and *"a flash in the pan"* and rest of Armstrong encounters with Foreign Ministry officials: Ibid., 530–531.

114  *"They had disappeared"* and *"It was staggering"*: Ibid., 531.

114  *he went to meet Hjalmar Schacht* and rest of description of meeting with Schacht: Ibid., 532–533.

115  *Armstrong was startled* and *"Why, Putzi"* exchange: Ibid., 534.

115  *"His general appearance"* and rest of observations and quotes from Armstrong's interview with Hitler: Ibid., 534–540.

117  *A people has disappeared* and other quotes from opening of book: Hamilton Fish Armstrong, *Hitler's Reich: The First Phase*, 1–3.

118  *"Either he is"*: Ibid., 24.

118  *"having given the German spirit"*: Ibid., 65.

118 *"The first phase of"*: Ibid., 66.

119 *"I regard Berlin"* and other efforts to name a new ambassador to Germany: Robert Dallek, *Democrat and Diplomat: The Life of William E. Dodd*, 187–188.

119 *"Peace Speech"*: Shirer, *The Rise and Fall of the Third Reich*, 291–292.

119 *"The speech was"* and rest of Lochner letter to Betty: "Round Robins from Berlin: Louis P. Lochner's Letters to His Children, 1932–1941," *Wisconsin Magazine of History*, Summer 1967.

120 *"a democrat in the"* and *"separation of"*: William E. Dodd, Jr., and Martha Dodd, eds., *Ambassador Dodd's Diary*, xii and x.

120 *"I want to know"*: Ibid., 3.

120 *"an almost sentimental"*: Martha Dodd, *Through Embassy Eyes*, 12.

121 *"The German authorities"*: Dodd and Dodd, eds., *Ambassador Dodd's Diary*, 5.

121 *"exert all possible"*: Ibid., 9.

121 *"Let Hitler"*: Ibid., 11.

122 *"My wife, son and I"*: Ibid., 11.

122 *On the voyage over*: Martha Dodd, *Through Embassy Eyes*, 18.

122 *The Familienblatt* and first meetings with journalists: Dodd and Dodd, eds., *Ambassador Dodd's Diary*, 12–13; and Fromm, 120–121.

122 *"No group of"*: Lilian Mowrer, 286.

122 *Sitting on wooden benches*: Philip Gibbs, *European Journey*, 237.

122 *"his back beaten to pulp"*: Edgar Mowrer, *Triumph and Turmoil*, 218.

123 *"pushed past these bullies"* and Edgar's visit to Jewish doctor: Lilian Mowrer, 289.

123 *A senior press official* and Mowrer's appeals: Ibid., 296–297.

123 *"to allow social and personal"*: Ibid., 298.

123 *"favors"* and visit to concentration camp: Edgar Mowrer, *Triumph and Turmoil*, 221–222.

124 *"were indeed badly beaten"*: "Round Robins from Berlin: Louis P. Lochner's Letters to His Children, 1932–1941," *Wisconsin Magazine of History*, Summer 1967.

124 *"You know, Herr Mowrer"* and rest of Mowrer-Nazi officer exchange: Lilian Mowrer, 300–301.

125 *"If such intelligent"*: Edgar Mowrer, *Triumph and Turmoil*, 225.

125 *One of Mowrer's sources*: Ibid., 218.

126 *"In this country where"*: Ibid., 221.

126 *In July, Colonel Frank Knox*: Ibid., 224.

127 *"I felt at the end"*: Dodd and Dodd, eds., *Ambassador Dodd's Diary*, 24.

127 *"a blow to freedom"*: Edgar Mowrer, *Triumph and Turmoil*, 224.

127 *In the Mowrer household* and *"At this point"*: Lilian Mowrer, 302.

127 *"Oh, Mr. Mowrer"* and other quotes and details from Goldmann incident and aftermath: Lilian Mowrer, 303–305; additional information and *"people's righteous indignation"* from Edgar Mowrer, *Triumph and Turmoil*, 225–226.

129 *"If you were not"* and *"gallant fighter"*: Lilian Mowrer, 308.

129 *"And when are you"* and rest of exchange with young German official: Edgar Mowrer, *Triumph and Turmoil*, 226.

**CHAPTER SIX: "LIKE FOOTBALL AND CRICKET"**

PAGE

130   *"I do not remember"* and other Dodd quotes and descriptions of her Chicago life and about marriage: Martha Dodd, *Through Embassy Eyes*, 5–41.

132   *"a perfect example"*: Fromm, 121.

132   *"pretty, vivacious"*: William L. Shirer, *Berlin Diary: The Journal of a Foreign Correspondent, 1934–1941*, 42.

132   *"Martha had an apartment"*: Katharine Smith, unpublished manuscript of "My Life: Berlin August 1935–April 1939," Truman Smith Papers, box 4, Hoover.

132   *"We liked Germany"*: Martha Dodd, *Through Embassy Eyes*, 23–24.

132   *"The Germans seemed"*: Ibid., 25.

133   *"saloon German"*: Quentin Reynolds, *By Quentin Reynolds*, 104.

133   *"No American"*: Ibid., 105.

133   *"I regret to say"*: Ibid., 107.

133   *"such legendary figures"* and description of Hanfstaengl: Martha Dodd, 25–26.

133   *"You've been here"*: Reynolds, 109.

134   *"we didn't"*: Martha Dodd, 27.

134   *"The excitement of"*: Ibid., 28.

134   *"It will be"* and *"I could not at first tell"*: Reynolds, 118–119.

135   *"tragic and tortured"*: Martha Dodd, 28.

135   *Martha still tried*: Ibid., 28–29.

135   *Hudson Hawley* and *"Writing the story"*: Reynolds, 119–120.

135   *"There isn't one"* and *Norman Ebbutt*: Ibid., 121.

136   *they dispatched officials*: Martha Dodd, 32.

136   *"Putzi serenaded"*: Reynolds, 124.

136   *"Never come"*: Ibid., 125.

137   *"Roosevelt must have"*: "Round Robins from Berlin: Louis P. Lochner's Letters to His Children, 1932–1941," *Wisconsin Magazine of History*, Summer 1967.

137   *"most agreeable"*: Dodd and Dodd, eds., *Ambassador Dodd's Diary*, 13.

137   *"He showed no"*: Ibid., 14.

137   *"well-known internationalist"* and *"So far"*: Ibid., 16.

137   *"the saddest story"*: Ibid., 17.

138   *"are so uncontrollable"*: Ibid., 44.

138   *In a Columbus Day speech*: Ibid., 46.

138   *"It would be no sin"*: Dallek, *Democrat and Diplomat*, 211.

138   *"extraordinary applause"*: Dodd and Dodd, eds., *Ambassador Dodd's Diary*, 46.

138   *"It is evident"*: Ibid., 48.

138   *"He looks somewhat better"* and *"The Chancellor assured me"*: Ibid., 49.

139   *"ranted"* and rest of meeting with Hitler: Ibid., 50.

139   *"Fundamentally, I believe"*: Gordon A. Craig and Felix Gilbert, eds., *The Diplomats: 1919–1939*, 450.

139   *"I walked into the park"*: Dodd and Dodd, eds., *Ambassador Dodd's Diary*, 53.

140 *"just as I would have done"* and *"It was clear to me"*: Ibid., 56.

140 *In early December, Sir Eric Phipps*: Ibid., 63.

140 *On January 1, 1934*: Ibid., 67–68.

141 *"I was afraid"*: Ibid., 68.

141 "Der gute *Dodd*": Hanfstaengl, 204.

141 *"hopelessly weak"*: Dallek, *Democrat and Diplomat*, 227.

141 *"He was a modest"*: Hanfstaengl, 203.

142 *"Any possible concern"* and rest of account and quotes from Eddy visit: Fromm, 123–124.

143 *"On the bridge"* and rest of Morris account: Wright Morris, *Solo: An American Dreamer in Europe: 1933–1934*, 161–163.

144 *"to create a"*: Donald B. Watt, *Intelligence Is Not Enough: The Story of My First Forty Years and of the Early Years of the Experiment in International Living*, 85.

144 *"making friends"*: Ibid., 159.

144 *"From its war-like"*: Ibid., 11.

144 *"The suggestion of"*: Ibid., 115.

144 *"excess of order"* and remainder of Watt quotes: Ibid., 115–117.

145 *"I journeyed toward"* and rest of Schuman quotes: Frederick L. Schuman, *The Nazi Dictatorship: A Study in Social Pathology and the Politics of Fascism*, viii–x.

146 *"pathological hatreds"* and *"Fascism itself"*: Ibid., 505.

146 *"Germany wants to become"* and other Abel quotes: Abel notebooks, Theodore Abel Papers, box 13, Hoover.

147 *"For the Best Personal"*: Theodore Abel, *Why Hitler Came into Power*, 3.

147 *"Heroism had become"*: Ibid., 27.

148 *Eighteen percent*: Ibid., 44.

148 *"the spirit of Jewish materialism"*: Ibid., 45.

148 *"From that time"*: Ibid., 70.

148 *"Schuman concludes"*: Ibid., 189.

148 *He is male*: Ibid., 6.

149 *"frankly state their"*: Ibid., 8.

149 *"In presenting these facts"*: Ibid., 9.

149 *several American publishers rejected*: Theodore Abel Papers, box 14, Hoover.

149 *"Adolf Hitler has become"*: Manuscript of "Nazi Racialism" dated July 9, 1933, H. R. Knickerbocker Papers, Columbia.

149 *"Bloody Jews"*: Manuscript of "Jews" dated July 26, 1933, Knickerbocker Papers, Columbia.

150 *"the supreme boss"*: Manuscript of "Nazi Senate" dated July 9, 1933, Knickerbocker Papers, Columbia.

150 *"The latest Soviet method"*: Manuscript of "Nazi Soviet" dated July 19, 1934, Knickerbocker Papers, Columbia.

150 *"German nudists"*: Manuscript of "Nude Culture" dated May 22, 1933, Knickerbocker Papers, Columbia.

150 *"Europe is in uniform"*: H. R. Knickerbocker, *The Boiling Point: Will War Come in Europe?*, ix.

151  *"the most talked about"*: "U najgłośniejszego reportera świata," *Express Poranny,* November 12, 1932, Knickerbocker Papers, Columbia.

151  *They pressured*: Metcalfe, *1933,* 126.

151  *DANZIG . . . Ten million lives*: Knickerbocker, *The Boiling Point,* 1.

151  *"a tornado of"*: Ibid., 4.

151  *"The Poles were"*: Ibid., 5.

152  *"Its lesson"*: Ibid., 7.

152  *"The odds are"*: Ibid., 240.

152  *"It is the peace"*: Ibid., 267.

153  *"It was impossible"*: Sir Philip Gibbs, *European Journey,* 229–230.

153  *"He was the mesmerist"*: Ibid., 232.

153  *"Most people in"* and rest of exchange with American woman: Ibid., 235–236.

## CHAPTER SEVEN: DANCING WITH NAZIS
PAGE

155  *"a young secretary"* and rest of account of Martha Dodd's June 30 experience: Martha Dodd, *Through Embassy Eyes,* 141–146.

156  *On that morning of June 30* and accounts of Schleicher and Strasser killings: Shirer, *The Rise and Fall of the Third Reich,* 309.

156  *Henry Mann*: Dodd and Dodd, eds., *Ambassador Dodd's Diary,* 131.

157  *The primary targets* and background on Hitler-Röhm tensions: Ian Kershaw, *Hitler, 1889–1936: Hubris,* 500–517.

157  *"The SA and the SS"*: Ibid., 502.

157  *"Only fools"*: Ibid., 504.

157  *The opulent living*: Ibid., 503.

157  *Breaking into Röhm's room* and rest of account of Bad Wiessee raid and announcement: Ibid., 512–517.

158  *"The former Chief of Staff"*: Ibid., 516.

158  *"in full regalia"* and rest of scene with Goering: Sigrid Schultz, ed., *Overseas Press Club Cookbook,* 149.

158  *The body of Gustav von Kahr*: Shirer, *The Rise and Fall of the Third Reich,* 310.

159  *"There was general regret"*: Fromm, 172.

159  *"I hope we may"* and *"black with"*: Martha Dodd, *Through Embassy Eyes,* 155.

159  *At the Fourth of July party* and *"Lebst du noch?"*: Ibid., 157–158.

160  *"that the Germans"*: Ibid., 162.

160  *That same week* and *"Poor Germany"*: Dodd and Dodd, eds., *Ambassador Dodd's Diary,* 119.

160  *In his diary entry of July 8* and *"I can think of"* and *"My task here"*: Ibid., 122–123.

161  *Back in 1925* and rest of early Shirer bio: http://www.traces.org/williamshirer.html, and from William L. Shirer, *Berlin Diary,* 3.

161  *"the worst job I've ever had"*: Shirer, *Berlin Diary,* 10.

161  *"The Paris that"*: Ibid., 4.

161   *"And what a story!"* and rest of June 30 diary entry: Ibid., 11.

161   *"One had almost"*: Ibid., 12.

162   *"another young American"*: William Shirer, *The Traitor*, 58–60.

162   *"Who can be"*: Shirer, *Berlin Diary*, 13.

162   *"unconditional obedience to"*: Shirer, *The Rise and Fall of the Third Reich*, 314.

162   *"The man is"*: Shirer, *Berlin Diary*, 13.

163   *"Nobody believes that"*: Fromm, 174.

163   *"what would have been"*: "Hitler Averted Massacre, Won Army's Fealty" (name of newspaper missing from clipping), Aug. 4, 1934, Karl H. von Wiegand Collection, box 30, Hoover.

163   *"Hitler has attained"*: "Hitler Challenges Foes to Plebiscite Call; Hopes to Show Masses Back Him," *New York American*, Aug. 4, 1934, Wiegand Collection, box 30, Hoover.

163   *"Must brush up"*: Shirer, *Berlin Diary*, 13.

163   *"Herr So-and-So"* and rest of August 25 diary entry: Ibid., 14.

164   *"for Röhm"* and *"in Germany,"* and account of Thompson's trip from Austria to Germany, including stay in Berlin: Dorothy Thompson, "Good-by to Germany," *Harper's*, Dec. 1934.

167   *"In view of"*: Sanders, *Dorothy Thompson*, 392.

167   *"The general feeling"*: Kurth, *American Cassandra*, 202–203.

167   *"a little tearful"*: Sanders, 198.

167   *"blasphemy"* and *"My offense"*: Kurth, 203.

168   *"Germany has gone"*: Ibid., 204.

168   *"I miss"*: Shirer, *Berlin Diary*, 15.

168   *Back in the United States*: Richard Lingeman, *Sinclair Lewis: Rebel from Main Street*, 407.

168   *"My one ambition"*: Sinclair Lewis, *It Can't Happen Here*, 68.

169   *"There is no excuse"*: Lingeman, 409.

169   *"slick, debonair"*: Shirer, *Berlin Diary*, 41.

169   *"Hitlerland"* and *"Naziland"*: Pierre J. Huss, *The Foe We Face*, vii and 6.

169   *"You had to work"*: Ibid., ix.

169   *"alight"* and rest of Huss account of meeting with Hitler in Obersalzberg: Ibid., 1–6.

171   *"Reporting from Germany"*: Lochner, *Always the Unexpected*, 223.

171   *In a letter to William Randolph Hearst*: Karl H. von Wiegand Papers, box 14, Hoover.

171   *On more than one occasion, Sigrid Schultz* and rest of her account: David Brown and W. Richard Bruner, eds., *How I Got That Story*, 75–81.

172   *"Like a Roman Emperor"* and rest of Nuremberg diary entries: Shirer, *Berlin Diary*, 16–23.

174   *"His followers"* and rest of Lochner's account: "Round Robins from Berlin," *Wisconsin Magazine of History*, Summer 1967.

175   *There was, I must admit*: Richard Helms, *A Look over My Shoulder: A Life in the Central Intelligence Agency*, 23.

175 *"the city, the surroundings"*: Ben Procter, *William Randolph Hearst: Final Edition, 1911–1951,* 185.

176 *"a unanimous expression"*: "Hearst Is Quoted as Hailing Nazi Vote," *New York Times,* Aug. 23, 1934.

176 *"Why am I"* and rest of Hearst-Hitler encounter: Procter, 186–187.

177 *"bragging about"*: Fromm, 184.

177 *"Hitler is certainly"*: Procter, 187.

177 *"Hitler needs a woman"* and rest of Martha Dodd's account of her meeting with Hitler: Martha Dodd, 63–65.

178 *"I ostentatiously kept"*: Robert H. Lochner, *Ein Berliner unter dem Sternenbanner: Erinnerungen eines amerikanischen Zeitzeugen,* 12.

179 *"Ever afterwards"*: From "What to Do if Your Moustache Falls Off," unpublished manuscript of Angus Thuermer (courtesy of the author).

179 *"Once you look"* and description of Goebbels reception: Louis Lochner, *What About Germany?,* 120–121.

179 *"extremely pleasant, handsome"*: Martha Dodd, 49.

179 *"blond Aryan"*: Ibid., 50.

179 *"most violent"* and *"the tall boy"*: Ibid., 42.

180 *"She just liked sleeping"*: Katrina Vanden Heuvel, "Grand Illusions," *Vanity Fair,* Sept. 1991.

180 *"at least twelve"* and rest of Martha's early account of Diels: Martha Dodd, 51–56, 134–139.

180 *"I was intrigued"*: Ibid., 53.

180 *"a pathetic"*: Ibid., 134.

180 *"Martha, you are"* and *"I was extremely"*: Ibid., 136.

180 He wanted: Dodd and Dodd, eds., 65; and Martha Dodd, 138.

181 *"a nervous state"*: Martha Dodd, 54.

181 *"a frightened rabbit"*: Ibid., 135.

181 He was a tall, blond and Vinogradov at Die Taverne: Shareen Blair Brysac, *Resisting Hitler: Mildred Harnack and the Red Orchestra,* 155–156.

182 *"they had no future"* along with Mildred Harnack biographical details: Ibid., 99.

182 *"It is said by"*: Ibid., 113.

182 *"hopefulness and achievement"*: Ibid., 119.

182 *"the scene of"*: Ibid., 99.

182 *"amazed at"*: Martha Dodd, 99.

182 On May 27, 1934: Brysac, 149.

183 *"He was isolated"*: Martha Dodd, 84.

183 *"He is not happy"*: Brysac, 150.

183 *"I had had enough"* and rest of Martha Dodd's account and quotes about Russia: Martha Dodd, 169–208.

184 *"for the last two weeks"* and Wolfe's arrival in Berlin: A. Scott Berg, *Max Perkins: Editor of Genius,* 270.

184 *"Tom, a huge man"* and rest of Dodd's account of Wolfe: Martha Dodd, 90–95.

184   *"I feel myself"*: Berg, 271.

184   *"Part of Tom's"*: Martha Dodd, 91.

185   *"like a butterfly"*: Brysac, 179.

185   *"disturbing things"*: Berg, 270.

185   *"If there were"*: Aldo P. Magi and Richard Walser, eds., *Thomas Wolfe Interviewed, 1929–1938*, 67.

185   *"a much soberer person"*: Martha Dodd, 94.

185   I Have a Thing to Tell You *excerpts*: C. Hugh Holman, ed., *The Short Novels of Thomas Wolfe*.

187   *"I came away"*: Magi and Walser, eds., 88.


**CHAPTER EIGHT: "A MAD HATTER'S LUNCHEON PARTY"**

PAGE

188   *"the season of"* and other quotes: Thomas Wolfe, *You Can't Go Home Again*, 484–486.

188   *"Jews, Frenchmen"*: David Clay Large, *Nazi Games: The Olympics of 1936*, 43.

188   *"plot of Freemasons and Jews"*: Ibid., 49.

189   *"a disgrace and"*: Ibid., 58.

189   *"For us National Socialists"*: Ibid., 61.

189   Theodor Lewald background: Susan D. Bachrach, *The Nazi Olympics: Berlin 1936*, 13.

189   *"enormous propaganda"* and rest of Lewald pitch: Large, 63.

189   *"My personal"*: Bachrach, 45–47.

189   *"competitors of all"*: Large, 71.

190   *"no discrimination"* and other details of Brundage visit: Ibid., 79.

190   *"the token Negro"* and rest of Sherrill account: Ibid., 84–85.

190   *"flagrant discrimination"* and rest of Dodd's account: Ibid., 97.

191   *"this will be"* and rest of Messersmith, Geist accounts: Ibid., 94–96.

191   *"A consummate"*: Ibid., 98.

191   The daily spectacle: Wolfe, 485.

192   *"At last he came"*: Ibid., 486.

192   *"Berlin is now"*: Large, 187.

192   *"Everything was free"*: Rudi Josten interviewed by Peter Gehrig, Dec. 4, 2004, and Mar. 23, 2005, Oral History Collection, Associated Press Corporate Archives.

192   The Nazis even allowed: Large, 186.

192   *"A glittering swirl"*: Fromm, 226.

192   *"I'm afraid the Nazis"*: Shirer, *Berlin Diary*, 65.

192   Carla de Vries: Large, 225.

192   Swimmer Eleanor Holm Jarrett: Ibid., 180.

193   *"an orgasmic"* and *"It was unfair"*: Fromm, 225.

193   *"a war whoop"* and *"Hitler twisted"*: Martha Dodd, 212.

193   *"Negroes should not"*: Bachrach, 96.

193   *Cheers went up* and invitations to black athletes: Ibid., 95.

193   *"Jesse Owens ran"*: Oliver Lubrich, ed., *Travels in the Reich, 1933–1945: Foreign Authors Report from Germany*, 138.

194   *"Owens was a quiet"*: Helms, *A Look over My Shoulder*, 26.

194   *"I have been treated"* and rest of DuBois account: Lubrich, ed., 142–143.

195   *"Wearing gray flannel"*: Fromm, 225–226.

195   *"When Huber presented"* and rest of Morris story: Leni Riefenstahl, *Leni Riefenstahl: A Memoir*, 196–198.

196   *"his sad fate"*: Ibid., 200.

196   *At an official function* and Hitler-Smith exchange: Robert Hessen, ed., *Berlin Alert*, 47.

196   *"Berlin was so familiar"* and other Katharine Smith quotes throughout: Katharine Alling Hollister Smith, "My Life: Berlin August 1935–April 1939," Truman Smith Papers, boxes 4 and 16, Hoover.

197   *"Your past relationship"*: Hessen, ed., 27.

199   *Kätchen, who was*: Kätchen Coley interviewed by author (2010).

199   *"of air corps"*: Hessen, ed., 78.

199   *"their wits alone"*: Ibid., 83.

199   *"How fast can you"*: Katharine Smith's unpublished memoir.

200   *Two months later* and origins of proposal to Lindbergh: Hessen, ed., 87–88.

200   *"I need hardly tell you"*: Ibid., 89.

200   *"extremely interested"*: Ibid., 91.

201   *"Colonel Smith is"* and other diary quotes: Anne Morrow Lindbergh, *The Flower and the Nettle: Diaries and Letters of Anne Morrow Lindbergh, 1936–1939*, 72–76.

202   *"We, who are in aviation"*: Hessen, ed., 95.

202   *"But no more speeches"*: Katharine Smith's unpublished memoir.

202   *"Goering showed many facets"*: Hessen, ed., 101.

202   *"blazoned in"*: Anne Morrow Lindbergh, 85.

203   *"I find that to laugh"* and description of lion encounter: Katharine Smith's unpublished manuscript, except where Anne is quoted.

203   *"I see and say nothing"*: Anne Morrow Lindbergh, 86.

203   *When Goering's lion*: Kätchen Coley interviewed by author (2010).

204   *"Smith, there are"*: Hessen, ed., 102.

204   *At Rostock*: Ibid., 96–97.

204   *"we have nothing"* and *"a spirit"*: A. Scott Berg, *Lindbergh*, 357.

204   *"obtain technical parity"*: Truman Smith, "An American Estimate of the German Air Force" (Nov. 1, 1937), *Airpower Historian*, April 1963, in Truman Smith Papers, box 9, Hoover.

205   *"German aviation"* and *"the best promotion"*: Fromm, 224.

205   *"How well and how"*: Albert C. Wedemeyer Papers, box 61, folder 19, Hoover.

205   *"I have had"* and rest of August 5 letter: Anne Morrow Lindbergh, 87.

206   *"While I still have"*: Berg, 361.

206   *"he is undoubtedly"*: Ibid.

206 *The event that would cement* and Truman Smith's description, along with Wilson's letter to Lindbergh: Hessen, ed., 132–133.

207 *"a victory by"*: Berg, 382.

207 *"Hitler's realistic"* and misjudgments about military disaffection: Truman Smith, "Party and Army: Germany–November 1937," Truman Smith Papers, box 2, Hoover.

207 *"I was astonished"*: Original manuscript of Smith's *The Facts of Life*, 104, Truman Smith Papers, box 2, Hoover.

208 *"I could feel"*: Hanfstaengl, *Hitler*, 129.

208 *"No!"* and other quotes from Hanfstaengl: interviewed by Toland, Library of Congress.

208 *"It would be reasonable"*: Hanfstaengl, 170.

208 *"one of my most bitter"*: Wiegand memo, Karl von Wiegand Papers, box 30, Hoover.

209 *"probably likes to"*: Ibid., box 14, Hoover.

209 *"an immense, high-strung"*: Shirer, *Berlin Diary*, 17.

209 *"I wonder why"* and rest of Hanfstaengl-Fromm exchange: Fromm, 163.

210 *"no discourtesy of any kind"* and rest of this description of Hanfstaengl arrival controversy: "Reunion: Hanfstaengl's Arrival Greeted by 3,000 Students," *Newsweek*, June 23, 1934.

210 *Benjamin Halpern* letter and *Crimson* editorial: Conradi, *Hitler's Piano Player*, 145.

210 *"There you are"*: Hanfstaengl, 223.

211 *"I see America"*: Ibid., 222.

211 *"It was really like"*: Ibid., 250.

211 *"the demon"*: Ibid., 213.

211 *"Putz hastily"*: Katharine Smith's unpublished memoir.

212 *"to play that"*: Hanfstaengl, 265.

212 *"Yes, he was extraordinary"* and rest of Helen's account: Niemeyer tape, Toland Collection, Library of Congress.

213 *Putzi began smuggling* and claims about helping others: Hanfstaengl, 274.

213 *According to Putzi's* and subsequent events of purported plot against him: Ibid., 276–284.

214 *"a harmless joke"*: Conradi, 209.

214 *"an elaborate hoax"*: David George Marwell, "Unwonted Exile: A Biography of Ernst 'Putzi' Hanfstaengl," Ph.D. dissertation, 13; and Marwell interviewed by author (2011).

214 *Back in Berlin* and rest of Lochner's account of tracking down Hanfstaengl: Lochner, *Always the Unexpected*, 184–186.

215 *"I certainly would not"*: Dodd and Dodd, eds., *Ambassador Dodd's Diary*, 119.

215 *"What in the world is the use"*: Dallek, *Democrat and Diplomat*, 271.

216 *"telegram deficiency"*: Ibid., 272–273.

216 *"a historian of"* and other Smith quotes: Hessen, ed., 79.

216 *"I have seldom"*: Katharine Smith's unpublished memoir.

217 *"four years' service"*: Dallek, 295.

217   *"In Berlin once more"*: Dodd and Dodd, eds., *Ambassador Dodd's Diary*, 430.

217   *"There were and are still"*: Ibid., 445.

217   *"Hitler intends to"*: Dallek, 332.

217   *"The Russians of"*: Martha Dodd, 343.

218   *"Martha argues that"*: Allen Weinstein and Alexander Vassiliev, *The Haunted Wood: Soviet Espionage in America—the Stalin Era*, 52.

218   *"frankly expressed"*: Ibid., 53.

218   *"we have agreed"* and subsequent encounter with Slutsky, and Martha's statement: Ibid., 55–56.

219   *"Boris, dear!"*: Ibid., 61.

## CHAPTER NINE: "UNIFORMS AND GUNS"
PAGE

220   *"whether it was"* and other quotes from Smith: Howard K. Smith, *Last Train from Berlin*, 4–16.

222   *Like many wealthy undergraduates* and quotes from JFK's diary: Lubrich, ed., *Travels in the Reich*, 159–161.

223   *"The trip up the Rhine"* and rest of diary entries along with letter from German engineer to Randolph: Rebecca McBride, "Europe 1938: Travel Diary of John F. Randolph Annotated by His Daughter," Leo Baeck Institute Archives.

224   *"I simply draped"*: Howard K. Smith, 26–27.

225   *"Murrow, Columbia Broadcasting"* and Shirer about Murrow: Shirer, *Berlin Diary*, 79–80.

226   *"Personally, they have not"* and other reflections on Berlin experiences: Ibid., 83–87.

226   *"The worst has happened"*: Ibid., 95.

227   *"plays nicely"*: Ibid., 90.

227   *"a shouting, hysterical"*: Ibid., 97.

227   *"What's that"*: Ibid., 100.

227   *"Well, meine Damen"* and rest of café scene: Ibid., 101.

227   *"Where did"* and flights: Ibid., 103.

228   *"This morning when"*: William L. Shirer, *"This Is Berlin": Radio Broadcasts from Nazi Germany*, 14.

228   *"entanglements"* and Hoover visit to Germany: Gary Dean Best, *Herbert Hoover: The Postpresidential Years, 1933–1964*, Vol. I, *1933–1945*, 103.

228   *"that Hitler was"* and other Arentz quotes: Oral history interview of Samuel S. Arentz by Raymond Henle, Oct. 5, 1966, Herbert Hoover Oral History Program, box 2, Hoover. Additional details on Hoover-Hitler meeting, from Richard Norton Smith, *An Uncommon Man: The Triumph of Herbert Hoover*, 253–256.

229   *Greeted by*: Richard Norton Smith, 255–256.

229   *"Yes, that's"* and discussion of Russia: Arentz interviewed by Henle.

229   *"many menaces"*: Best, 103.

229 *"have all the hideous"*: Ibid., 104.

230 *"a longer period"* and other Jacob Beam quotes: Jacob Beam's unpublished manuscript with no title page (courtesy of Alex Beam).

231 *The daughter of* and rest of background of Muriel White: "American Countess Menaced with Bomb," *New York Times,* Jan. 16, 1911.

231 *"Foreign women"* and American Women's Club: Sigrid Schultz, *Germany Will Try It Again,* 137.

231 *"commanded a hysterical"*: Ibid., 135–136.

232 *"the great improvement"* and other Dilling quotes about Nazi Germany: Glen Jeansonne, *Women of the Far Right: The Mothers' Movement and World War II,* 13.

232 *Schultz recalled seeing Dilling* and exchange with young American woman and Hoffmann quote: Schultz, 136.

236 *"the principal impression"* and other quotes from March 3, 1938, letter: Hugh R. Wilson, Jr., *A Career Diplomat, The Third Chapter: The Third Reich,* 18–21.

236 *"in the sense of"*: Ibid., 21–22.

236 *"One may judge"*: Ibid., 63.

237 *"the smoke and dust"* and rest of letter to Hull: Ibid., 22–26.

237 *"confess that their hearts"*: Ibid., 26.

237 *"of bringing our people"* and Wilson's response: Ibid., 28.

237 *"an attempt to work out"*: Ibid., 37.

237 *And he worried*: Ibid., 38.

237 *"Twenty years ago"*: Ibid., 39.

238 *Among Beam's acquaintances*: Beam's unpublished manuscript; and John V. H. Dippel, *Two Against Hitler: Stealing the Nazis' Best-Kept Secrets,* which offers an extensive account of Respondek's role. Information about Beam's encounter with Respondek and Muckermann, along with their background information, is drawn from both of these accounts.

240 *"We had watched"*: Erich von Manstein, *Lost Victories,* 23–24.

240 *"the spontaneous outburst"*: Wilson, *A Career Diplomat,* 51.

240 *"stout piece of work"*: Beam, unpublished manuscript.

240 *"I do think"*: Nancy Harvison Hooker, ed., *The Moffat Papers: Selections from the Diplomatic Journals of Jay Pierrepont Moffat, 1919–1943,* 217.

240 *"completely different"* and rest of Beam's observations: Beam, unpublished manuscript.

241 *"He's still got"*: Shirer, *Berlin Diary,* 142.

241 *"For if they do"*: Ibid., 135.

241 *"a curious commentary"* and rest of September 30 entries: Ibid., 144–145.

241 *Angus Thuermer*: quotes and information from Thuermer interviewed by author (2009) and Thuermer's unpublished manuscript "What to Do if Your Moustache Falls Off."

244 *Charles Thayer* and his account: Charles W. Thayer, *The Unquiet Germans,* 161–163.

245 *Phillips Talbot* and his account: Phillips Talbot letter of Dec. 27, 1938 (courtesy of Talbot and the Holocaust Museum); and Talbot interviewed by author (2009).

245   *In a letter to:* Wilson, *A Career Diplomat*, 60.

246   *"It was suggested":* Albert C. Wedemeyer, *Wedemeyer Reports!*, 50.

247   *"tall and handsome":* Katharine Smith's unpublished memoir, Truman Smith Papers, boxes 4 and 6, Hoover.

247   *Kätchen Smith:* Kätchen interviewed by author (2010).

247   *"out-going, hard-working"* and *"I hope she is not":* Katharine Smith memoir, Truman Smith Papers, boxes 4 and 6, Hoover.

247   *147-page report* and all quotations from report: Albert C. Wedemeyer Papers, box 6, folder 35, Hoover.

248   *"German methods":* Wedemeyer, *Wedemeyer Reports!*, 50.

248   *"outstanding as":* Ibid., 52.

248   *"One of the":* Ibid., 53.

249   *"But assuredly":* Ibid., 60.

249   *"subtly revealed"* and *"There would be"* and *"not always discreet":* Ibid., 56–57.

249   *"stolid, not overly"* to *"at all times friendly":* Ibid., 54.

249   *"Heil Hitler":* Ibid., 37.

250   *" . . . however greatly":* Ibid., 11.

250   *"Beneath the propaganda":* Ibid., 10.

250   *"It was Al":* Katharine Smith memoir, Truman Smith Papers, boxes 4 and 6, Hoover.

250   *"I like to think":* Wedemeyer, 60.

250   *"I had been disillusioned":* Ibid., 61.

251   *"When I reported"* to *"I don't want to sound like":* Memorandum to Colonel Eiler, Albert C. Wedemeyer Papers, box 6, folder 35, Hoover.

252   *"A brief calendar":* Mowrer, *Germany Puts the Clock Back*, 250.

252   *"an awesome sight":* Beam, unpublished manuscript.

252   *"many methods"* and budget request: Manfred Jonas, *The United States and Germany: A Diplomatic History*, 233.

252   *"his eyes aglow":* Hooker, ed., 232.

252   *"George, I wonder"* and rest of Messersmith-Moffat exchange: Jesse H. Stiller, *George S. Messersmith: Diplomat of Democracy*, 135.

253   *On April 14:* Jonas, 234.

253   *"could advantageously bend":* Hooker, ed., 220.

254   *"the undisputed dean"* and other quotes from *Cosmopolitan*, April and May 1939 issues: Wiegand Papers, box 31, Hoover.

**CHAPTER TEN: "ON OUR ISLAND"**

PAGE

256   *"I sat for four hours"* and other Lochner quotes from letters: "Round Robins from Berlin," *Wisconsin Magazine of History*, Summer 1967.

257   *The reports by Truman Smith:* Joseph C. Harsch, *Pattern of Conquest*, 41.

257   *By early summer:* Hooker, ed., *The Moffat Papers*, 251.

257 *"Optimistic Poles"*: H. R. Knickerbocker, *Is Tomorrow Hitler's? 200 Questions on the Battle of Mankind*, 29.

257 *"The Polish ambassador"*: Hooker, ed., 249.

258 *"the death of"*: John Gunther, *Inside Europe*, xxviii.

258 *"There is a chance"*: Ibid., xxii.

258 *"John fairly optimistic"*: Shirer, *Berlin Diary*, 170.

258 *"looked clean"* and exchange with Captain D: Ibid., 171.

259 *"How completely isolated,"* German headlines, *"For perverse"* and *"Struck by"*: Ibid., 172–173.

259 *"completely Nazified"*: Ibid., 174.

259 *"this powder-keg"* and rest of Gdynia broadcast: Shirer, *"This Is Berlin,"* 53.

259 *"We're ready"* and Warsaw visit entries: Shirer, *Berlin Diary*, 176–178.

260 *"bombshell"* and *"There is no doubt"* and odds of war: Hooker, ed., 250–251.

260 *"It goes much further"* and scene in Die Taverne: Shirer, *Berlin Diary*, 180–181.

261 *"The people in the streets"*: Ibid., 183.

261 *"From about the middle"* and other Beam recollections: Beam, unpublished manuscript.

262 *"something was going to"* and rest of Thuermer account: Thuermer interviewed by author (2009).

263 *"The excitement of"* and rest of William Russell's account of August 31: William Russell, *Berlin Embassy*, 5–29.

265 *Józef Lipski* and his story: Beam, unpublished memoir.

265 *"I have once more"*: Ibid.

265 *"a curious strain"* and rest of Shirer's account of Sept. 1–2: Shirer, *Berlin Diary*, 197–199.

266 *"After, say, about 1 A.M."*: Shirer, *"This Is Berlin,"* 71.

266 *"One expected"*: Russell, 31.

266 *"The people I have met"*: Ibid., 33–34.

267 *"It begins to"* and rest of Shirer's initial war diary entries: Shirer, *Berlin Diary*, 204–207.

267 *"The war is raging"*: Russell, 38.

267 *"Drove all day"* and rest of Shirer account of Baltic coast fighting: Shirer, *Berlin Diary*, 212–214.

268 *Joseph Grigg* and his account, including Hitler at Warsaw airport: Frederick Oechsner, *This Is the Enemy*, 143–151.

268 *The AP's Lochner* and stories from Poland: Louis Lochner, *What About Germany?*, 124–125.

269 *"that Germany is invincible"* and *"I hope"*: Russell, 51.

269 *"follow me blindly"* and exchange with maid: Schultz, *Germany Will Try It Again*, 186–187.

270 *"squeals and shouts"* and rest of reactions to newsreels and massacres: Ibid., 187–189.

270 *"Now go to Berlin,"* getting to Berlin and early days there: Joseph C. Harsch, *At the Hinge of History, A Reporter's Story*, 38–43.

272   *"pretty awful"* and *"I was an American"*: Hottelet interviewed by author (2009).

272   *"The troops seemed"*: Shirer, *Berlin Diary*, 234.

272   *"in the vain hope"*: Russell, 128.

273   *"the hope of"* and *"It is better"*: Otto D. Tolischus, *They Wanted War*, 199.

273   *"One Breslau daily"* and rest of Oct. 8 letter: Louis Lochner, "Round Robins from Berlin," *Wisconsin Magazine of History*, Summer 1967.

273   *"In the darkness"*: Russell, 53.

273   *"the groping"*: George F. Kennan, *Memoirs: 1925–1950*, 107.

274   *"Shan't we go"* and rest of encounter with streetwalker: Ibid., 109–112.

274   At the Soviet Embassy's and exchange between American correspondents and Goering: Shirer, *Berlin Diary*, 245–246.

275   *According to the joke*: Harsch, *Pattern of Conquest*, 59.

275   *Russell estimated*: Russell, 75.

275   *"If the United States"*: Ibid., 90–91.

275   *"It was hard"*: Kennan, 112.

276   *"the most intelligent"*: Shirer, *Berlin Diary*, 284.

276   *"isolated on our island"*: Russell, 84.

276   GOODS DISPLAYED: Ibid., 101.

276   *"A hundred or so"* and Oechsner dinner: Shirer, *Berlin Diary*, 252.

277   *"embarrassingly large"* and follow-up: Russell, 49–50.

277   *In January 1940*: Ibid., 128.

277   *"unmistakable inner detachment"*: Kennan, 108–109.

277   *"But here Germany was"*: Russell, 129.

278   *two tin bathtubs*: Ibid., 131–132.

278   *"I never expected"* and rest of Jane Dyer episode: Ibid., 142.

## CHAPTER ELEVEN: FEEDING THE SQUIRRELS

PAGE

279   *"We had not"* and rest of Russell departure from Germany: Russell, 203–208.

280   *"The last thing"*: Harsch, *At the Hinge of History*, 47.

281   *"Only one thing"*: Sumner Welles, *The Time for Decision*, 77.

281   *Arriving on the morning* and rest of Welles visit: Ibid., 90–109.

283   *"my uncompromising"* and account of Mooney mission: Lochner, *Always the Unexpected*, 262–272.

284   *"I was stunned"*: Shirer, *Berlin Diary*, 312.

284   *"I never dreamed"*: Harsch, *At the Hinge of History*, 48.

284   *Broadcasting from Berlin*: Shirer, "This Is Berlin," 246–247.

284   *"Hitler is sowing"*: Shirer, *Berlin Diary*, 317.

285   *"the German steamroller"*: Ibid., 335.

285   *"It's been dream"* and other Lochner quotes from Belgium: Lochner, "The Blitzkrieg in Belgium: A Newsman's Eyewitness Account," *Wisconsin Magazine of History*, Summer 1967.

285   *"the behavior of"*: Shirer, *"This Is Berlin,"* 289.

285   *"houses smashed"*: Shirer, *Berlin Diary*, 353–354.

286   *"But eyeing"* and exchange with German nun: Ibid., 360.

286   *He and two other reporters* and account of tensions among American correspondents: Harsch, *At the Hinge of History*, 45.

286   *"Some of the correspondents"*: Henry W. Flannery, *Assignment to Berlin*, 41.

287   *"when he has forced"* and *"Every German soldier"*: Lochner, *"The Blitzkrieg in Belgium."*

287   *"A most discouraging"*: Beam, unpublished manuscript.

287   *"France did not fight"*: Shirer, *Berlin Diary*, 434.

288   *"He folded his arms"* and rest of Hitler at Napoleon's tomb: Pierre J. Huss, *The Foe We Face*, 210–212.

289   *"It was Hitler triumphant"* and rest of July 19 event, including Kirk's reaction: Harsch, *At the Hinge of History*, 49–50.

289   *"The little groups"*: Harsch, *Pattern of Conquest*, 53–54.

290   *"The loot of"*: Ibid., 45–46.

290   *"These Germans"*: Ibid., 46–47.

290   *a violent anti-Nazi* and rest of Schultz's observations on German women: Schultz, *Germany Will Try It Again*, 143–146.

291   *"books and magazines"*: Flannery, 115.

291   *"The word illegitimate"*: Ibid., 114.

292   *"their murder of"* and *"After weeks of"*: Ibid., 110–111.

292   *"I was one of"*: Ibid., 13.

293   *"human interest"* and other Delaney quotes: Edward L. Delaney, *Five Decades Before Dawn*, 58.

293   *"wanton, premeditated"*: Ibid., 85.

293   *"He has a diseased"* and other Shirer remarks about Americans working for German radio: Shirer, *Berlin Diary*, 528–529.

294   *"swept by"* and *"hiking club"* episode: John Carver Edwards, *Berlin Calling: American Broadcasters in Service to the Third Reich*, 8–9.

294   *On June 25, 1933*: Postcard from and clippings about Frederick Kaltenbach, Frederick W. Kaltenbach Papers, box 1, Hoover.

294   *"Dear Harry"*: Edwards, 11.

294   *"Roosevelt, himself an off-spring"*: Horst J. P. Bergmeier and Rainer E. Lotz, *Hitler's Airwaves: The Inside Story of Nazi Radio Broadcasting and Propaganda Swing*, 61.

295   *"nervous breakdown"* and other Katharine Smith quotes about Chandler: Katharine Smith's memoir in Truman Smith Papers, boxes 4 and 16, Hoover.

295   *"ponytails and dirndls"*: Kätchen Coley interviewed by author.

295   *Delaney, Kaltenbach and Chandler* along with details of their fates: Bergmeier and Lotz, 45–64.

296   *"a beginner"* and details of Mildred's applications: Brysac, *Resisting Hitler*, 258.

296   *One of Mildred's jobs* and Mildred's reported role in escapes: Ibid., 245. Also Anne Nelson, *Red Orchestra: The Story of the Berlin Underground and the Circle of Friends Who Resisted Hitler*, 163–164.

296    *Her husband Arvid* and relationship with Heath: Ibid., 224–227.

296    *"a German patriot"*: Ibid., 266. A similar argument is made by Anne Nelson in *Red Orchestra*.

297    *"Harnack never"*: Ibid., 264.

297    *But Brysac documented* and rest of Korotkov-Harnack story, including Korotkov quote and Harnack's first intelligence report: Ibid., 261–267.

297    *They also weren't helped*: Ibid., 307.

297    *In late August* and estimate of arrests: Ibid., 329.

297    *"loss of honor"* and other verdicts: Ibid., 359; rest of Mildred's story, 359–379.

298    *"And I have loved"*: Ibid., 379.

298    *"When a new number"* and account of Lovell's activities, including dinner with military attachés: Harsch, *At the Hinge of History*, 54–55.

299    *"Just imagine"* and rest of Schultz-Boehmer exchange: Schultz, 162–163.

299    *"the best immediate defense"* and fireside chat: Jonas, 248.

300    *"the severest bombing yet"* and rest of Shirer's account of bombing on September 10: Shirer, *Berlin Diary*, 503–504.

301    *"Night Crime"* and other headline: Ibid., 509.

301    *"Except for"*: Flannery, 151.

301    *"But after the Russian campaign"* and *"No, I just had bad news"* and depression: Ibid., 378–380.

302    *"Mein Gott"* and *"I thought I was gone"*: Ibid., 384–385.

302    *"I love my wife"* and exchange with woman plastic surgeon: Schultz, 138–139.

302    *Angus Thuermer* and story of third floor apartment and Jewish visitor: Angus Thuermer interviewed by author.

303    *Howard K. Smith* and Heppler episode: Howard K. Smith, 184–187.

304    *"The increasingly desperate"*: Kennan, 106.

304    *"Time proved him"*: Beam, unpublished manuscript.

304    *Aside from taking on*: Kennan, 106. (Kennan estimated that the U.S. represented the interests of eleven countries by the time of Pearl Harbor.)

304    *"I felt that"*: Harsch, *At the Hinge of History*, 56.

305    *"you must never"*: Huss, 214.

305    *"the hottest game"* and *"Everything else"*: Ibid., ix–x.

305    *"Many times I heard her say"*: Harsch, *At the Hinge of History*, 55.

305    *"knew everything"*: Howard K. Smith, 226.

306    *"on suspicion of espionage"* and rest of Hottelet's account: Richard C. Hottelet, "Guest of Gestapo," *San Francisco Chronicle*, Aug. 3, 1941; Hottelet interviewed by author.

306    *"Had he been"* and other Smith comments about Hottelet: Howard K. Smith, 226–227.

306    *Beam, who*: Beam, unpublished manuscript.

307    *"Your situation is"*: Howard K. Smith, 346.

307    *"Czech patriots"*: Ibid., 348.

307    *"utterly vapid"*: Ibid., 349.

307   *Like other American reporters:* Ibid., 344.

308   *"We who have been"* and on German character: Shirer, *Berlin Diary*, 584–585.

309   *"I am firmly convinced":* Ibid., 591–592.

309   *"The question before"* and *"The alternative":* Harsch, *Pattern of Conquest*, 303–304.

309   *Huss interviewed Hitler* with quotes and description: Huss, 279–300.


## CHAPTER TWELVE: THE LAST ACT

PAGE

311   *"The similarities"* and rest of descriptions and quotes on December 7 and immediate aftermath: Kennan, *Memoirs*, 134–135.

311   *It was a titanic struggle* and statistics on battle for Moscow: Andrew Nagorski, *The Greatest Battle: Stalin, Hitler, and the Desperate Struggle for Moscow That Changed the Course of World War II*, 2.

312   *"General Mud and General Cold":* Antony Beevor and Luba Vinogradova, eds., *A Writer at War: Vasily Grossman with the Red Army, 1941–1945*, 223.

312   *Germany an economic powerhouse:* Kershaw, *Hitler, 1936–1945: Nemesis*, 434.

313   *"We can't lose":* Ibid., 442.

313   *"We are all":* Winston S. Churchill, *The Grand Alliance*, 605.

313   *"To me the best tidings":* Richard M. Langworth, ed., *Churchill by Himself: The Definitive Collection of Quotations*, 132.

313   *The sudden rash of:* Charles B. Burdick, *An American Island in Hitler's Reich: The Bad Nauheim Internment*, 9.

313   *only fifteen, less than a third:* See Howard K. Smith, 344, for original number of about fifty.

314   *"enemy aliens":* For a description of one of these cases, see HistoryLink.org Essay 8654.

314   *"will be done"* and rest of Lochner account of press conference, including Schmidt quote: Lochner, *What About Germany?*, 360–361.

314   BYE-BYE and rest of Thuermer account: Thuermer, unpublished manuscript, and interview with author.

315   *Friends kept dropping by* and account of Lochner's arrest: Lochner, *What About Germany?*, 363–364.

316   *"We still have"* and *"The Gestapo"* and breakfast: Ibid., 364–366.

316   *At the embassy* and scene with von Ribbentrop: Kennan, 135–136.

316   *"entire satanic insidiousness":* Kershaw, 446.

316   *cheering news:* Lochner, *What About Germany?*, 366–367.

317   *Hitler had ordered:* Kennan, 136.

317   *Returning to their homes:* Burdick, 28.

317   *132 Americans:* Louis Lochner, "Americans Fed Better Than Germans, But Still Lose Weight," AP dispatch published in the *Frederick Post*, May 20, 1942, Associated Press Corporate Archives.

317   *It had been closed:* Burdick, 37.

317   *In January and February:* Lochner, *What About Germany?*, 369.

318   *"This showed us":* Lochner, AP dispatch, May 20, 1942.

318   *To deal with the constant problems* and *Patzak also allowed:* Burdick, 47.

319   *"It is in the general interest":* Ibid., 46.

319   *"a rather unique":* Lochner, *What About Germany?*, 369.

319   *The AP's Ed Shanke:* Ibid., 370–371; and Burdick, 48.

319   *Alvin Steinkopf:* Burdick, 51, 57.

319   *"Badheim University"* and *"Education of the ignorant":* Burdick, 62–63. Other details about activities from Thuermer, unpublished manuscript, and Thuermer interviewed by author.

320   *Kennan won permission* and other baseball details: Burdick, 85; also Thuermer, unpublished manuscript, and interview.

320   *"for disciplinary control":* Kennan, 136.

320   *British bombers:* Burdick, 96.

321   *"to keep the more"* and breakfast story at the border: Kennan, 137–138.

321   *"We had not":* Ibid., 139.

321   *"The department":* Ibid., 139–140.

322   Drottningholm: Burdick, 106.


**AFTERWORD**

PAGE

326   *"She continued to serve":* Helms, 20.

326   *"of my Harvard Club friend":* Hanfstaengl, 293.

326   *Arriving in Washington:* Ibid., 294.

326   *"most of the time":* Eric Hanfstaengl interviewed by author (2009).

326   *"still in his bones":* Marwell, 517.

# Bibliography

**ARCHIVAL SOURCES**

Associated Press Corporate Archives, New York, NY

Franklin D. Roosevelt Library, Hyde Park, NY

Hoover Institution Archives, Stanford, CA

Leo Baeck Institute Archives, New York, NY

Library of Congress, Washington, DC

National Archives, College Park, MD

Rare Book and Manuscript Library, Columbia University Libraries Archival Collections, New York, NY


**UNPUBLISHED MANUSCRIPTS FROM PRIVATE COLLECTIONS**

Jacob Beam, unpublished manuscript (with no title page), courtesy of Alex Beam.

David Marwell, "Unwonted Exile: A Biography of Ernst 'Putzi' Hanfstaengl," Ph.D. dissertation, State University of New York at Binghamton, 1988.

John J. McLaughlin, "General Albert Coady Wedemeyer, 1897–1989: Soldier, Scholar, Statesman," Ph.D. dissertation, Drew University, 2008.

Angus Maclean Thuermer, "What to Do if Your Moustache Falls Off (Fairly True Reports from a CIA Man)," courtesy of the author and his family.

(Unpublished manuscripts from archives are included in the Notes.)


**BOOKS**

Abel, Theodore. *Why Hitler Came into Power.* Cambridge and London: Harvard University Press, 1986.

Armstrong, Hamilton Fish. *Hitler's Reich: The First Phase*. New York: Macmillan Co., 1933.

———. *Peace and Counterpeace: From Wilson to Hitler*. New York: Harper & Row, 1971.

Bachrach, Susan D., United States Holocaust Memorial Museum. *The Nazi Olympics: Berlin 1936*. Boston: Little, Brown & Co., 2000.

Baker, Jean-Claude, and Chris Chase. *Josephine: The Hungry Heart*. Holbrook, MA: Adams Publishing, 1995.

Bannerman, R. LeRoy. *On a Note of Triumph: Norman Corwin and the Golden Years of Radio*. New York: Carol Publishing Group, 1986.

Beevor, Antony, and Luba Vinogradova, eds. *A Writer at War: Vasily Grossman with the Red Army, 1941–1945*. New York: Pantheon Books, 2005.

Berg, A. Scott. *Lindbergh*. New York: G. P. Putnam's Sons, 1998.

———. *Max Perkins: Editor of Genius*. New York: E. P. Dutton & Co., 1978.

Bergmeier, Horst J. P., and Rainer E. Lotz. *Hitler's Airwaves: The Inside Story of Nazi Radio Broadcasting and Propaganda Swing*. New Haven and London: Yale University Press, 1997.

Best, Gary Dean. *Herbert Hoover: The Postpresidential Years, 1933–1964*. Vol. I, *1933–1945*. Stanford, CA: Hoover Institution Press, 1983.

Bouton, S. Miles. *And the Kaiser Abdicates*. New Haven: Yale University Press, 1920.

Breitman, Richard, Barbara McDonald Stewart and Severin Hochberg, eds. *Advocate for the Doomed: The Diaries and Papers of James G. McDonald, 1932–1935*. Bloomington and Indianapolis: Indiana University Press, 2007.

Brown, David, and W. Richard Bruner, eds. *How I Got That Story: By Members of the Overseas Press Club*. New York: E. P. Dutton & Co., 1967.

Brysac, Shareen Blair. *Resisting Hitler: Mildred Harnack and the Red Orchestra*. New York: Oxford University Press, 2000.

Burdick, Charles B. *An American Island in Hitler's Reich: The Bad Nauheim Internment*. Menlo Park, CA: Markgraf Publications Group, 1987.

Burke, Bernard V. *Ambassador Frederic Sackett and the Collapse of the Weimar Republic, 1930–1933: The United States and Hitler's Rise to Power*. Cambridge: Cambridge University Press, 1994.

Churchill, Winston S. *The Grand Alliance*. Boston: Houghton Mifflin Co., 1950.

Cloud, Stanley, and Lynne Olson. *The Murrow Boys: Pioneers on the Front Lines of Broadcast Journalism*. Boston and New York: Houghton Mifflin Company, 1996.

Conradi, Peter. *Hitler's Piano Player: The Rise and Fall of Ernst Hanfstaengl, Confidant of Hitler, Ally of FDR*. New York: Carroll & Graf Publishers, 2004.

Costello, John, and Oleg Tsarev. *Deadly Illusions*. New York: Crown Publishers, 1993.

Craig, Gordon A., and Felix Gilbert, eds. *The Diplomats: 1919–1939*. Vol. II, *The Thirties*. New York: Atheneum Books, 1968.

Cuthbertson, Ken. *Inside: The Biography of John Gunther*. Chicago: Bonus Books, 1992.

Dallek, Robert. *Democrat and Diplomat: The Life of William E. Dodd*. New York: Oxford University Press, 1968.

———. *Franklin D. Roosevelt and American Foreign Policy, 1932–1945*. New York: Oxford University Press, 1979.

Danzi, Michael. *American Musician in Germany, 1924–1939.* Schmitten, West Germany: Norbert Ruecker, 1986.

De Grazia, Victoria. *Irresistible Empire: America's Advance Through Twentieth-Century Europe.* Cambridge: Harvard University Press, 2005.

Delaney, Edward L. *Five Decades Before Dawn.* Pasadena, CA: Deljon Publishers, 1969.

Deuel, Wallace R. *People Under Hitler.* New York: Harcourt, Brace & Co., 1942.

Dippel, John V. H. *Two Against Hitler: Stealing the Nazis' Best-Kept Secrets.* New York: Praeger Publishers, 1992.

Dodd, Martha. *Sowing the Wind.* New York: Harcourt, Brace & Co., 1945.

———. *Through Embassy Eyes.* New York: Harcourt, Brace & Co., 1939.

Dodd, William E., and Martha Dodd, eds. *Ambassador Dodd's Diary, 1933–1938.* New York: Harcourt, Brace & Co., 1941.

Edwards, John Carver. *Berlin Calling: American Broadcasters in Service to the Third Reich.* New York: Praeger Publishers, 1991.

Fallada, Hans. *Every Man Dies Alone.* New York: Melville House, 2009.

———. *Little Man, What Now?* New York: Melville House, 2009.

Ferdinand, Prince Louis. *The Rebel Prince: Memoirs of Prince Louis Ferdinand of Prussia.* Chicago: Henry Regnery Co., 1952.

Flannery, Harry W. *Assignment to Berlin.* New York: Alfred A. Knopf, 1942.

Ford, Henry. *The International Jew.* Filiquarian Publishing, 2007.

Friedrich, Otto. *Before the Deluge: A Portrait of Berlin in the 1920s.* New York: Harper Perennial, 1995.

Fromm, Bella. *Blood and Banquets: A Berlin Social Diary.* New York: Carol Publishing Group, 1990.

Gay, Peter. *Weimar Culture: The Outsider as Insider.* New York: Harper Torchbooks, 1970.

Gibbs, Philip. *European Journey.* New York: Literary Guild, 1934.

Gill, Anton. *A Dance Between Flames: Berlin Between the Wars.* London: Abacus, 1995.

Gunther, John. *Inside Europe.* New York and London: Harper & Brothers, 1938.

Hanfstaengl, Ernst. *Hitler: The Missing Years.* New York: Arcade Publishing, 1994.

Harsch, Joseph C. *At the Hinge of History: A Reporter's Story.* Athens and London: University of Georgia Press, 1993.

———. *Pattern of Conquest.* New York: Doubleday, Doran & Co., 1941.

Hayman, Ronald. *Hitler + Geli.* London: Bloomsbury Publishing, 1997.

Hecht, Ben. *A Child of the Century.* New York: Ballantine Books, 1970.

Helms, Richard, with William Hood. *A Look over My Shoulder: A Life in the Central Intelligence Agency.* New York: Random House, 2003.

Hertog, Susan. *Anne Morrow Lindbergh: Her Life.* New York: Doubleday & Co., 1999.

Hessen, Robert, ed. *Berlin Alert: The Memoirs and Reports of Truman Smith.* Stanford, CA: Hoover Institution Press, 1984.

Hitler, Adolf. *Mein Kampf.* Boston: Houghton Mifflin Co., 1971.

Holman, C. Hugh, ed. *The Short Novels of Thomas Wolfe.* New York: Charles Scribner's Sons, 1961.

Hooker, Nancy Harvison, ed. *The Moffat Papers: Selections from the Diplomatic Journals of Jay Pierrepont Moffat, 1919–1943.* Cambridge: Harvard University Press, 1956.

Hull, Cordell. *The Memoirs of Cordell Hull*, Vol. I. New York: Macmillan Co., 1948.

Huss, Pierre J. *The Foe We Face*. New York: Doubleday, Doran & Co., 1942.

Jeansonne, Glen. *Women of the Far Right: The Mothers' Movement and World War II*. Chicago and London: University of Chicago Press, 1996.

Jonas, Manfred. *The United States and Germany: A Diplomatic History*. Ithaca and London: Cornell University Press, 1984.

Kaltenborn, H. V. *Fifty Fabulous Years, 1900–1950: A Personal Review*. New York: G. P. Putnam's Sons, 1950.

Kennan, George F. *Memoirs: 1925–1950*. Boston: Little, Brown & Co., 1967.

Kershaw, Ian. *Hitler, 1889–1936: Hubris*. London: Penguin Press, 1998.

———. *Hitler, 1936–1945: Nemesis*. New York: W. W. Norton & Co., 2000.

Knickerbocker, H. R. *The Boiling Point: Will War Come in Europe?* New York: Farrar & Rinehart, 1934.

———. *Is Tomorrow Hitler's? 200 Questions on the Battle of Mankind*. New York: Reynal & Hitchcock, 1941.

Kurth, Peter. *American Cassandra: The Life of Dorothy Thompson*. Boston: Little, Brown & Co., 1990.

Langworth, Richard, ed. *Churchill by Himself: The Definitive Collection of Quotations*. New York: Public Affairs, 2008.

Large, David Clay. *Nazi Games: The Olympics of 1936*. New York and London: W. W. Norton & Co., 2007.

Lewis, Sinclair. *It Can't Happen Here*. New York: New American Library, 2005.

Lindbergh, Anne Morrow. *The Flower and the Nettle: Diaries and Letters of Anne Morrow Lindbergh, 1936–1939*. New York and London: Harcourt Brace Jovanovich, 1976.

Lingeman, Richard. *Sinclair Lewis: Rebel from Main Street*. New York: Random House, 2002.

Lipstadt, Deborah E. *Beyond Belief: The American Press and the Coming of the Holocaust, 1933–1945*. New York: Free Press, 1986.

Lochner, Louis P. *Always the Unexpected: A Book of Reminiscences*. New York: Macmillan Co., 1956.

———. *What About Germany?* New York: Dodd, Mead & Co., 1943.

Lochner, Robert H. *Ein Berliner unter dem Sternenbanner: Erinnerungen eines amerikanischen Zeitzeugen*. Berlin: Edition Goldbeck-Löwe, 2003.

Lubrich, Oliver, ed. *Travels in the Reich, 1933–1945: Foreign Authors Report from Germany*. Chicago and London: University of Chicago Press, 2010.

Ludecke, Kurt G. W. *I Knew Hitler: The Story of a Nazi Who Escaped the Blood Purge*. New York: Charles Scribner's Sons, 1938.

Magi, Aldo P., and Richard Walser, eds. *Thomas Wolfe Interviewed, 1929–1938*. Baton Rouge & London: Louisiana State University Press, 1985.

Mahoney, Barbara S. *Dispatches and Dictators: Ralph Barnes for the Herald Tribune*. Corvallis: Oregon State University Press, 2002.

Manstein, Erich von. *Lost Victories*. Chicago: Henry Regnery Co., 1958.

Matthews, Jeffrey J. *Alanson B. Houghton: Ambassador of the New Era*. Lanham, MD: SR Books, Rowman & Littlefield Publishing Group, 2004.

Metcalfe, Philip. *1933*. Sag Harbor, NY: Permanent Press, 1988.

Morris, Wright. *Solo: An American Dreamer in Europe: 1933–1934*. New York: Penguin Books, 1984.

Moser, Maynard. *Jacob Gould Schurman: Scholar, Political Activist, and Ambassador of Good Will, 1892–1942*. New York: Arno Press, 1982.

Mowrer, Edgar Ansel. *Germany Puts the Clock Back*. Paulton and London: Penguin Books, 1938.

———. *Triumph and Turmoil: A Personal History of Our Times*. New York: Weybright & Talley, 1968.

Mowrer, Lilian T. *Journalist's Wife*. New York: William Morrow & Co., 1937.

Murphy, Robert. *Diplomat Among Warriors*. London: Collins, 1964.

Nagorski, Andrew. *The Greatest Battle: Stalin, Hitler, and the Desperate Struggle for Moscow That Changed the Course of World War II*. New York: Simon & Schuster, 2007.

Nelson, Anne. *Red Orchestra: The Story of the Berlin Underground and the Circle of Friends Who Resisted Hitler*. New York: Random House, 2009.

Norwood, Stephen H. *The Third Reich in the Ivory Tower: Complicity and Conflict on American Campuses*. Cambridge: Cambridge University Press, 2009.

Nowell, Elizabeth. *Thomas Wolfe: A Biography*. New York: Doubleday & Co., 1960.

Oechsner, Frederick. *This Is the Enemy*. Boston: Little, Brown & Co., 1942.

Perez, Robert C., and Edward F. Willett. *The Will to Win: A Biography of Ferdinand Eberstadt*. Westport, CT: Greenwood Press, 1989.

Plotkin, Abraham. *An American in Hitler's Berlin: Abraham Plotkin's Diary, 1932–33*. Urbana and Chicago: University of Illinois Press, 2009.

Powers, Thomas. *The Man Who Kept the Secrets: Richard Helms and the CIA*. New York: Pocket Books, 1981.

Procter, Ben. *William Randolph Hearst: Final Edition, 1911–1951*. New York: Oxford University Press, 2007.

Reynolds, Quentin. *By Quentin Reynolds*. New York: McGraw-Hill Book Co., 1963.

Riefenstahl, Leni. *Leni Riefenstahl: A Memoir*. New York: St. Martin's Press, 1993.

Russell, William. *Berlin Embassy*. New York: MacFadden Books, 1962.

Sanders, Marion K. *Dorothy Thompson: A Legend in Her Time*. Boston: Houghton Mifflin Co., 1973.

Schultz, Sigrid. *Germany Will Try It Again*. New York: Reynal & Hitchcock, 1944.

———, ed. *Overseas Press Club Cookbook*. New York: Doubleday & Co., 1962.

Schulze, Franz. *Philip Johnson: Life and Work*. New York: Alfred A. Knopf, 1994.

Schuman, Frederick L. *The Nazi Dictatorship: A Study in Social Pathology and the Politics of Fascism*. New York: Alfred A. Knopf, 1936.

Sherwood, Robert. *Roosevelt and Hopkins: An Intimate History*. New York: Harper & Brothers, 1948.

Shirer, William L. *Berlin Diary: The Journal of a Foreign Correspondent, 1934–1941*. New York: Galahad Books, 1995.

———. *The Rise and Fall of the Third Reich: A History of Nazi Germany*. Greenwich, CT: Fawcett Publications, 1965.

———. *"This Is Berlin": Radio Broadcasts from Nazi Germany.* Woodstock, NY: Overlook Press, 1999.

———. *The Traitor.* Toronto: Popular Library, 1961.

Smith, Howard K. *Last Train from Berlin.* New York: Alfred A. Knopf, 1942.

Smith, Richard Norton. *An Uncommon Man: The Triumph of Herbert Hoover.* Worland, WY: High Plains Publishing Co., 1984.

Sorel, Nancy Caldwell. *The Women Who Wrote the War.* New York: Harper Perennial, 2000.

Stiller, Jesse H. *George S. Messersmith: Diplomat of Democracy.* Chapel Hill and London: University of North Carolina Press, 1987.

Strasser, Otto. *Hitler and I.* Boston: Houghton Mifflin Co., 1940.

Thayer, Charles W. *The Unquiet Germans.* New York: Harper & Brothers, 1957.

Thompson, Dorothy. *"I Saw Hitler!"* New York: Farrar & Rinehart, 1932.

Toland, John. *Adolf Hitler.* 2 vols. New York: Doubleday & Co., 1976.

———. *Captured by History: One Man's Vision of Our Tumultuous Century.* New York: St. Martin's Press, 1997.

Tolischus, Otto D. *They Wanted War.* New York: Reynal & Hitchcock, 1940.

Wallace, Max. *The American Axis: Henry Ford, Charles Lindbergh, and the Rise of the Third Reich.* New York: St. Martin's Press, 2003.

Watt, Donald B. *Intelligence Is Not Enough: The Story of My First Forty Years and of the Early Years of the Experiment in International Living.* Putney, VT: Experiment Press, 1967.

Wedemeyer, Albert C. *Wedemeyer Reports!* New York: Henry Holt & Co., 1958.

Weinstein, Allen, and Alexander Vassiliev. *The Haunted Wood: Soviet Espionage in America—the Stalin Era.* New York: Random House, 1999.

Welles, Benjamin. *Sumner Welles: FDR's Global Strategist.* New York: St. Martin's Press, 1997.

Welles, Sumner. *The Time for Decision.* New York and London: Harper & Bros., 1944.

Wilson, Hugh R., Jr. *A Career Diplomat, The Third Chapter: The Third Reich.* New York: Vantage Press, 1960.

———. *Diplomat Between Wars.* New York and Toronto: Longmans, Green & Co., 1941.

Wolfe, Thomas. *You Can't Go Home Again.* New York: Perennial Library, Harper & Row, 1973.

**INTERVIEWS**

Katharine (Kätchen) Truman Smith Coley (2010)

Robert Conquest (2009)

Eric Hanfstaengl (2009)

Richard Hottelet (2009)

Anita Lochner (2010)

David Marwell (2011)

Phillips Talbot (2009)

Angus Thuermer (2009)

# INDEX

# About the Author

Award-winning journalist Andrew Nagorski is vice president and director of public policy at the EastWest Institute, a New York–based international affairs think tank. During a long career at *Newsweek*, he served as the magazine's bureau chief in Hong Kong, Moscow, Rome, Bonn, Warsaw, and Berlin. He is the author of four previous books and has written for countless publications. He lives in Pelham Manor, New York.